CW01183397

Encountering *Disgrace*

Encountering *Disgrace*

Reading and Teaching Coetzee's Novel

Edited by
Bill McDonald

CAMDEN HOUSE
Rochester, New York

Copyright © 2009 by the Editors and Contributors

All Rights Reserved. Except as permitted under current legislation,
no part of this work may be photocopied, stored in a retrieval system,
published, performed in public, adapted, broadcast, transmitted,
recorded, or reproduced in any form or by any means,
without the prior permission of the copyright owner.

First published 2009
by Camden House

Camden House is an imprint of Boydell & Brewer Inc.
668 Mt. Hope Avenue, Rochester, NY 14620, USA
www.camden-house.com
and of Boydell & Brewer Limited
PO Box 9, Woodbridge, Suffolk IP12 3DF, UK
www.boydellandbrewer.com

ISBN-13: 978–1–57113–403–5
ISBN-10: 1–57113–403–4

Library of Congress Cataloging-in-Publication Data

Encountering Disgrace : reading and teaching Coetzee's novel / edited by Bill McDonald.
 p. cm.
 Essays developed over three years studying the novel Disgrace, with ideas from students on a half dozen campuses, especially the University of Redlands' Johnston Center students participating in the fall 2006 "Coetzee" seminar, who influenced interpretations in at least five of the essays included.
Includes bibliographical references and index.
ISBN-13: 978–1–57113–403–5 (alk. paper)
ISBN-10: 1–57113–403–4 (alk. paper)
 1. Coetzee, J. M., 1940– Disgrace. 2. Coetzee, J. M., 1940– —Study and teaching. 3. South Africa—In literature. 4. Rape in literature.
5. Race in literature. 6. Animals in literature. 7. Fathers and daughters in literature. 8. Self-knowledge in literature. 9. Ethics in literature.
10. Postcolonialism in literature. I. McDonald, William E., 1940–
II. Title.

PR9369.3.C58.D534 2009
823'.914—dc22

2008048737

A catalogue record for this title is available from the British Library.

This publication is printed on acid-free paper.
Printed in the United States of America.

Cover photograph – Abandoned Farmhouse near Molteno, Eastern Cape,
25 February 2006, Copyright by David Goldblatt.

Contents

Acknowledgments	vii
Introduction Bill McDonald	1

I. Reading *Disgrace*

1:	"We are not asked to condemn": Sympathy, Subjectivity, and the Narration of *Disgrace* Michael G. McDunnah	15
2:	Beyond Sympathy: A Bakhtinian Reading of *Disgrace* James Boobar	48
3:	"Is it too late to educate the eye?": David Lurie, Richard of St. Victor, and "vision as eros" in *Disgrace* Bill McDonald	64
4:	*Disgrace* and the Neighbor: An Interchange with Bill McDonald Kenneth Reinhard	93
5:	To Live as Dogs or Pigs Live Under Us: Accepting What's on Offer in *Disgrace* Pat Harrigan	106
6:	Tenuous Arrangements: The Ethics of Rape in *Disgrace* Kim Middleton and Julie Townsend	116
7:	Dis(g)race, or White Man Writing Sandra D. Shattuck	138
8:	Clerk in a Post-Religious Age: Reading Lurie's Remnant Romantic Temperament in *Disgrace* Gary Hawkins	148
9:	Saying it Right in *Disgrace*: David Lurie, *Faust*, and the Romantic Conception of Language Patricia Casey Sutcliffe	173

10: The Dispossession of David Lurie 202
    Kevin O'Neill

II. Reading *Disgrace* with Others

11: Community Reading: Teaching *Disgrace* in an
    Alternative College Classroom 233
    Matthew Gray

12: Out of the Father's House into a Community of Readers 248
    Kathy Ogren

13: Sympathy for the Devil: On the Perversity of
    Teaching *Disgrace* 264
    Daniel Kiefer

14: Teaching *Disgrace* in the Large Lecture Classroom 276
    Nancy Best

15: Discussing *Disgrace* in a Critical Theory Class 288
    Bradley Butterfield

16: *Disgrace* in the Classroom: A Tale of Two
    Teaching Strategies 297
    Raymond Obstfeld

17: The Bodies of Others: A Meditation on the
    Environs of Reading J. M. Coetzee's *Disgrace* and
    Caryl Phillips's *The Nature of Blood* 313
    Jane Creighton

18: *Disgrace* as a Teacher 330
    Rabbi Patricia Karlin-Neumann

Works Cited 341

Notes on the Contributors 353

Index 357

Acknowledgments

Our project has been a group effort at every stage. A stranger to our story could easily imagine horrific outcomes of such a tight-knit group of friends and colleagues rigorously critiquing each other's drafts again and again. But no such outcomes came close to happening. Without exception — and without exaggeration — every participant accepted criticism without defensiveness, and cheerfully undertook the many rewrites that multiple readings produced. Many volunteered for special tasks, and all stuck with the project in the face of their many other responsibilities. I won't catalog the specific contributions of each person, since everyone made important contributions beyond the drafting of their own pieces: revising others' essays, helping with proofreading and bibliographic tasks, and discovering ways past dilemmas that I couldn't solve. But Michael McDunnah stands first among these equals, especially during the final year of the project. During that time he not only proposed detailed and decisive revisions of four of our essays, but as our leading critic of Coetzee's work wrote the third section of the introduction. He was the main person I turned to when difficulties arose, and he never failed to find inventive solutions or to offer candid advice. My work would have been much harder, and our book distinctly poorer, without his dedication.

Beyond our group, we are grateful to the students who read *Disgrace* with us on a half dozen campuses and contributed their ideas and judgments to our thinking. This applies especially to the Johnston Center students who read the novel twice in the fall of 2006 "Coetzee" seminar, and who worked with us on interpretations that bore fruit in at least five of our essays. Next, the project simply would not have happened without the generosity of Kathryn Green (JC 1976); everything we achieved follows from her gift and her loyalty to the Johnston Center and our project. Kathryn's funding created what she terms "ripple effects," such as the formation of academic and personal bonds between participants who had not met prior to the project, or the ways that collective thinking and writing have enriched our individual teaching practices. The University of Redlands' helped to defer other costs; our gratitude to Dean Barbara Morris for supporting our work in this way. Redlands librarian Sandra Richey, queen of interlibrary loan services, quickly located hard-to-find sources. We thank Camden House's two outside readers, who markedly improved our book with their commentaries. We owe more, however, to our editor,

Jim Walker, for his patience, sharp eye, forthrightness, and strong support throughout the process. We happily name him an honorary Johnstonian with all the rights and privileges appertaining thereto. Finally, our gratitude to all our spouses and families, who generously supported us throughout our three-year immersion in this great novel.

B. McD.
September 2008

Introduction

Bill McDonald

SINCE IT FIRST APPEARED IN 1999, Nobel Laureate J. M. Coetzee's novel *Disgrace* has provoked wide readership, political controversy, and strong critical performances. Set in post-apartheid South Africa, the novel follows Prof. David Lurie as he encounters disgrace, first through his sexual exploitation of one of his students, and then through the gang-rape of his only daughter. Lurie's refusal to negotiate his public confession of guilt over his abusive affair leads to his dismissal, and his daughter's refusal to pursue her black rapists' capture baffles and angers him. These parallel events force him to radically re-evaluate his life, with harrowing results. The novel's stark portrayal of the "new" South Africa outraged many in that country, who found the book regressive, even racist. It also challenged audiences worldwide to look past easy personal and political solutions to the dilemmas of race and gender. It earned Coetzee a second Booker Prize, and has already provoked a great deal of critical attention in the academy, and well beyond. This is the first full-length book devoted to interpreting *and* teaching this important and disturbing novel.

In many ways our book closely resembles other academic essay collections on individual texts. We are eager to contribute to the critical conversation burgeoning around Coetzee's great novel, and to enrich its teaching in college classrooms. But in other ways our book is significantly different from its companions in this genre, and in ways that will shape, we hope, how readers approach it. To make these differences clear and useful, we need first to say a few things about how our project began, and about its participants. Then we'll provide an overview of the essays themselves: their goals and organization. Finally, we'll briefly locate *Disgrace* within Coetzee's body of work, and our work within the body of Coetzee criticism.

I

In May of 2005, with the generous support of writer and philanthropist Kathryn Green, five professors and some twenty alumni of the University of Redlands' Johnston Center for Integrative Studies gathered in Southern California to launch a special book project. We ranged in age from 21 to 65, and represented graduating classes from 1972 to 2005 and faculty appointments from 1969 to 2004. About half the alumni participants are now literature or humanities professors in their own right, while others include a national ACORN administrator, a non-profit grant writer, a rabbi, a community educator, a new-media book editor, a climate-change activist — community-oriented careers typical of Johnston Center graduates. We termed ourselves "Unsolitary Readers," a gathering of literature enthusiasts across time and space, to evoke the communal ground of our individual ways of reading. After choosing *Disgrace* as our subject, we spent many hours in conversation about it, developed the essay topics you see below, discussed drafts online, often at several stages, and then gathered again in the summer of 2007 for an intensive period of rereading and critiquing each other's work. We shared the line editing, research, and Web site development, tasks that usually fall to a single person.

It is important here to give a quick overview of the Johnston Center's methods and philosophies. The Center houses about 200 undergraduates on the University of Redlands' campus of 2,500. Johnston students negotiate course content with their instructors, drawing up "contracts" specifying their goals and the means for achieving them. In lieu of grades, faculty members write narrative evaluations of each student's work based on the terms of these contracts. A parallel process creates individualized BA or BS requirements: students in their second year each draft a "graduation contract" in lengthy consultation with their faculty advisor, and then negotiate the terms of that contract with a faculty–student committee. This contracting draws its authority from the Johnston community of students, faculty, and administrators who together practice consensus politics, and who live and work together in ways that celebrate both individual distinction and group solidarity. (For more information on the Center, visit our Web site: information posted below.) Because of this shared experience in an academic community, our writers easily found common ground despite their age differences. We had read great books together through different iterations of the same courses; my four Johnston faculty colleagues and I had also co-taught courses with nearly half of the alumni participants, and with each other. We certainly don't read "as one," as the various essay titles alone make clear, but we do read from a strong sense of solidarity and shared experience that values literature and encourages a variety of literary engagements.

Plainly, then, this is *not* a book written by established Coetzee scholars revisiting his most controversial novel. While we very much admire such collections, we believe that valuable new angles on the novel—critical and pedagogical — can be achieved by a more democratic design. Neither Festschrift nor conference report, our group project is a rare experiment in Anglo-American humanities scholarship and pedagogy: a group of well-trained, thoughtful, enthusiastic readers with a common educational history working together.

The result is a book that we believe honors *Disgrace*, and which will inaugurate many conversations about its vision. We also believe we've produced a useful text for several groups: Coetzee scholars, of course, but also humanities professors with other expertises; graduate students but also motivated undergraduates; book club leaders but also other unsolitary readers outside the academy. We're particularly interested in developing conversations about the reading and teaching of the novel, and have, with our publisher's generous permission, established a link on the Johnston Center Web site where these conversations can continue. As a final goal, we want to elaborate, directly and indirectly, Johnston Center learning and pedagogy for our fellow teachers around the country.

II

We've organized our book into two main sections: the critical essays and the teaching essays. Their content and the connections between them need a few words of explanation.

Because we hope that readers will think through each essay with its writer, we offer here a short field guide to our major themes rather than a summary that reduces the essay to an information packet. Taking our cue from the novel itself, we chose as our first main subject "narrative ethics," broadly conceived to include the ethical dilemmas facing the characters and their culture, the ethical shaping achieved by *Disgrace's* narrative, and the ethical challenges it presents for teaching. More specifically, nearly all of the interpretive essays and several of the teaching essays take up the relationship between empathy and ethics, but in quite diverse ways. Michael McDunnah opens our book with a synoptic account of this subject in *Disgrace*. His views are supported by several pieces, including Kevin O'Neill's and my own, while James Boobar, Pat Harrigan, and Ken Reinhard explore the limitations of an ethic grounded in identification and empathy. A second leading subject, central to several essays — Gary Hawkins, Casey Sutcliffe, Daniel Kiefer — and implicit in several others, arises directly from David Lurie's own scholarly work on Wordsworth, Byron, and Berlioz: Romanticism and its vicissitudes. These essays take up the ethical implications of Romanticism, providing continuity, but aren't confined to that theme. Third, our collection features a number of intertextual readings, placing *Disgrace* in relationship to a wide variety of texts, from the medieval mystic Richard of St. Victor to Wallace Stegner and Caryl Phillips. Virtually every essay, both critical and pedagogical, undertakes at least one such comparison, often comparisons with ethical import. Narrative ethics, Romanticism, intertextuality: these are subjects that subtly interconnect in *Disgrace's* web, and should make our critical essays stimulating to readers and teachers with very different interests.

In addition to these overarching themes, a group of essays present strong readings of the novel's rape scenes (Kim Middleton and Julie

Townsend, McDunnah, and Hawkins), and Kevin O'Neill's piece anchors our exploration of animal–human relationships. And while several essays connect the novel to South African history and political life, we have no essay devoted specifically to those subjects because a number of fine articles and chapters already in print by scholars of South African literature do justice to them (see section IV of this introduction). In lieu of a formal review of Coetzee criticism, we highlight several themes from that large body of work in this introduction, and then engage a number of them in our critical essays, especially those by Hawkins, McDunnah, Middleton and Townsend, O'Neill, and myself. Finally, for the broader audience we hope to reach, a group of essays — Patricia Karlin-Neumann, Jane Creighton, O'Neill, and Kiefer — offer the reader personal meditations on the novel as the means of their analyses and pedagogies. This group also includes two essays addressed to those readers — and there have been a goodly number — who have found *Disgrace* racist or sexist, or cold and distancing. Pat Harrigan's and Sandra Shattuck's essays begin with those reservations and write forward from them.

As both complement and contrast to our critical contributions, this volume also approaches *Disgrace* as an occasion for pedagogy. For these teaching essays we reasoned that the diversity of models and pedagogies represented by our many different campuses and teaching situations would be most useful to readers working in similarly diverse environments. We begin with Matt Gray's and Kathy Ogren's essays on seminars and "unsolitary reading" practices, using the Johnston Center as examples, then move to five quite different teaching situations with correspondingly different teaching methods and reflections. We decided quickly against highly unifying models, for example having all the teaching essays focus solely on the themes of the critical essays. That would have been too confining, preventing our teachers from honoring the course-specific questions raised by their students, and forcing their general reflections about teaching *Disgrace* in their respective settings into a single mold. In short, we opted for coverage and variety over tight formal connections between our two major sections. Further, in both sections we've deliberately kept the untidy edges and overlapping analyses, offering readers multiple, dialogic views of the novel's major scenes and themes. Having said that, nearly all the teaching essays *do* take up the novel's ethical questions and continue conversations begun in the critical pieces. But they don't systematically elaborate the ideas presented in the book's first section.

Academic readers usually encounter essays on teaching a particular text in anthologies such as those published by the MLA. These typically offer advice on specific teaching strategies for the text in question, and we do a good deal of that ourselves. But we also wanted our essays to stimulate larger reflections that arise from teaching Coetzee's novel and that affect the teaching of many other fictions. So, for example, Daniel Kiefer explores the difficult problem of student resistance to, even disapproval of, faculty members who find themselves defending dislikable protagonists. In making a case for teaching *Disgrace*, or any fiction, in a large lecture class, Nancy Best challenges the assumption that small seminar classes with active students always promote better reading, and also shows how some seminar-teaching techniques can carry over to large-group instruction. Raymond Obstfeld turns to a different audience and a different set of pedagogies: creative-writing students in a community college who read *Disgrace* as part of their development as novelists. He also speaks for those readers impatient with the language of academic criticism. Veteran professor Kathy Ogren becomes a student again in a Coetzee seminar, and analyses the effects that unfamiliar position has on her understanding of her teaching and her scholarship. She also quotes from student writing on *Disgrace*, a subject not usually examined in essays on teaching a specific book, and then proposes a way to use our volume as a teaching tool. Like *Disgrace* itself, we hope that the teaching essays carry the reader beyond useful classroom strategies to the larger questions and self-reflections that every professor must wrestle with, and that ultimately may produce valuable insights for teaching literature.

Ultimately, each of the critical essays has direct implications for teaching, and each of the teaching essays explores at least one of the novel's ethical issues. This mutuality is grounded not only in thematic inquiries, however, but also in a discovery we made, or perhaps re-made, as we worked together: unsolitary reading and teaching are close companions, and sometimes indistinguishable. Seminar exchanges can be seen as a type of mutual instruction, and collaboration in reviewing drafts weds reading and persuasion. Reading and teaching are multiple and discursive, dialogic in virtually every way. Altogether, we believe that the hybridity of our book to be one of its principal strengths, in part because it has something to offer several different audiences but also because it preserves the energy and dynamism of the "differences within unity" that have powered our project from its beginning. We also hope that the teaching essays will involve the lay reader as well as the engaged teacher, since they are themselves full of ideas about the novel. We hope to get more conversations going, not have the last word.

III

For those readers and teachers with limited familiarity with Coetzee's writing before and after *Disgrace*, a few words may help to situate the novel in the author's complex and controversial body of work.

Disgrace's international reception confirmed Coetzee's place as a major novelist even as it inflamed the ongoing debate about his position in the culture and climate of his native South Africa. Though highly praised and prized, *Disgrace*'s implicit critique of the Truth and Reconciliation Commission, and its depiction of black assailants raping a white woman, drew heavy condemnation. Critics, including several prominent South African writers, accused Coetzee of deliberately arousing old racist fears and racial tensions just as the new, post-apartheid society was coming into being.

Indeed, Coetzee's place as a "South African author" has long been a matter of controversy. Famously reluctant to assume any role as a public figure, and openly suspicious of political discourse, Coetzee strongly resists the notion of art as a political obligation. *Age of Iron* (1990) and *Disgrace* are his only novels set in contemporary South Africa. Yet Coetzee has grappled extensively with the issues of the writer in South Africa in his nonfiction, most notably in *White Writing* and *Giving Offense,* and writes with full awareness of the forces that shape and necessarily preoccupy his own writing and the literature of his country. "It is exactly the kind of literature you would expect people to write from a prison," he has said, "unnaturally preoccupied with power and the torsions of power" (*Doubling the Point*, 98). There are many readers who find covert representations of apartheid in nearly everything Coetzee writes; certainly each of his novels is preoccupied with relationships of power and oppression. But Coetzee always locates this inequity in individuals, in the intrinsic impossibilities of reciprocity, of sympathy, of shared language and community.

So the tensions between aesthetics, ethics, and politics do not merely fuel the critical and cultural debate around Coetzee; as we see in *Disgrace,* they themselves constitute a primary subject of the novels. This is evident from his first novel *Dusklands* (1974), comprised of two linked narratives juxtaposing the American insurgence in Vietnam with the white domination of the Hottentots in eighteenth-century South Africa. The associative relationships between the two narratives introduce both Coetzee's thematic preoccupations and his approach to them: two historic atrocities of colonization are linked in Eugene Dawn and Jacobus Coetzee (an ancestor of the author), individuals who adhere to the subjugation of others not just as a means to assert the self but also — linguistically and existentially — to create and define it.

Coetzee explores this theme of definition of self through subjugation of the other again in *Waiting for the Barbarians* (1980), which draws its title from the Cavafy poem of the same name. ("What's going to happen to us without barbarians? / They were, those people, a kind of solution.") While the novel deals with an "empire" on the brink of revolution, Coetzee deliberately uncouples the novel from specific location in history or geography. Like much of Coetzee's work it has allegorical elements: not in the simplistic sense of encoding one thing to stand for another, but as a way to strip away the distractions of specificity to confront essential, universal themes, explored through and illuminating the individual enmeshed in the world.

Coetzee has said of South Africa that "everyone born with a white skin is born into the caste . . . you cannot resign from the caste. You can imagine resigning, you can perform a symbolic resignation, but short of shaking the dust of the country off your feet there is no way of actually doing it" (*Doubling the Point*, 96). Coetzee has rarely written from a perspective outside his "caste," an authorial choice based on his recognition of the limits of narrative engagement with, and co-optation of, "the other." *Life & Times of Michael K* (1983) is the main exception to this rule, and yet even its title character — a poor, harelipped farmer wandering through the political revolution exploding around him — remains largely unknowable, less subject than an object of flawed interpretation for both the reader and the other characters in the novel.

Many of Coetzee's protagonists, like Coetzee himself, are born into a relative position of power and privilege. Yet, also like the Coetzee of the third-person memoirs *Boyhood* (1997) and *Youth* (2002), these protagonists are themselves marginalized, isolated, and incomplete. In Coetzee's work, the dynamics of inequity alienate and isolate the privileged and the powerless alike: "In a society of masters and slaves, no one is free" (*Doubling the Point*, 96). Yet in virtually every fiction the decisive events are almost always brought about by encounter with "the other": of another race, gender, and/or culture. These figures typically remain largely, or totally, silent — though not necessarily powerless — and ultimately unknowable. More and more in the later novels — including *Disgrace* and *Elizabeth Costello* — a similar role is also occupied by animals.

Still, even the failed effort to truly engage with the other has a deconstructive effect on the worldview of the protagonists, who, like David Lurie in *Disgrace*, often undergo a stripping away of their authority, preconceptions, and identity — usually traumatic, often violent, and, if redemptive, only obscurely so. This frequently involves a "symbolic resignation" from the caste, which is sometimes involuntary (Jacobus Coetzee), sometimes tentative (Lucy in *Disgrace*, Mrs. Curren in *Age of Iron*), and sometimes transformative (the Magistrate in *Waiting for the Barbarians*, and arguably David Lurie in *Disgrace*).

In observing what Coetzee's protagonists share in common, however, it is important to note that they cannot be reduced to thematic representations or allegorical embodiments. Coetzee is too subtle an artist to write simple morality plays, and too sharp an observer of human nature to people his fictions with types. *Waiting for the Barbarians*, for example, may have an allegorical locale, but its protagonist and narrator, the Magistrate, is one of Coetzee's most recognizably human creations: self-satisfied and self-loathing, sympathetic and lecherous, flawed and extremely aware of his flaws. And, as we see most clearly in *Disgrace*, if Coetzee's character arcs tend slightly toward redemption, it is always of a tentative and imperfect kind, marked by regression and relapse, by impure and imperfect motives, by empty gestures and uneasy transformations.

These characters — and Coetzee's novels — resist easy interpretation, and reward rereading. They require the reader to engage ethically and actively with the text, to repeatedly assess and reassess subtly shifting facets of meaning. It is an effect achieved not only through the complexity of Coetzee's narrators, but also through his ongoing experiments with narrative form: non-linear and unreliable narratives, highly subjective first-person narrators, texts-within-texts, and self-referential metafictional play. Coetzee conducts these experiments not for their own sake — "writing-about-writing hasn't much to offer," he says of metafiction (*Doubling the Point*, 204) — but as an exploration of, and an undermining of, linguistic and narrative authority: reality as a creation of language, and the limitations and abuses of this Western concept in a colonial context. Not only does Coetzee consistently dismantle his own narrative authority, but nearly every novel features a writer of some sort demonstrating both the dangers and the limits of subjective authority. Given this, Coetzee's fictions are often compared to those of Beckett and Kafka, and contrasted with those of the committed political realist Nadine Gordimer.

In *In the Heart of the Country* (1977) Magda is a bitterly isolated woman on her father's nineteenth-century South African farm, creating and revising in a chaotic journal narratives of her life that alternately express her desire for personal and communal reciprocity, and her rage at her own marginalized, alienated position. *Foe* (1986), Coetzee's re-imagining of *Robinson Crusoe*, one of the canonical novels of realism and imperialism, brings the ever-present themes of textual authority and marginalization to the surface. The narrator Susan Barton and the author Foe conduct a dance of narrative power that circles around the enigmatic presence of the silent, perhaps tongueless, Friday. *The Master of Petersburg* (1994) again mixes fictional invention with historical and biographical fact to explore the ethics of writing, this time through imagined events in Dostoevsky's life and intertextual echoes of that author's novel *Demons*. Coetzee's novel of contemporary South Africa prior to the fall of apartheid, *Age of Iron*, takes the form of a letter written by Mrs. Curren, an elderly white professor of classics coming to terms simultaneously with the terminal cancer in her body and the racial injustice bringing her country to the brink of revolution.

Coetzee's work since *Disgrace* has seemed to grow more openly opinionated — particularly concerning his strong beliefs in animal rights, a central subject in *Disgrace* — while becoming more provocatively self-referential in a way that both invites and complicates attempts to locate the author and his opinions within his work. Coetzee's authorial stand-in

Elizabeth Costello originally appeared in public "lectures," which Coetzee then expanded upon and presented as fiction in *The Lives of Animals* (1999) and *Elizabeth Costello* (2003). Costello reappears in (and seems to be the metafictional author *of*) *Slow Man* (2005). His most recent novel, *Diary of a Bad Year* (2007), creates a triptych of opinion and fiction centered around a fictionalized South African author living in Australia, who has authored several novels including one called *Waiting for the Barbarians*.

Readers of *Disgrace*, then, will find echoes, variations, and expansions of its preoccupations in virtually any other Coetzee novel they turn to, as well as in his extensive body of non-fiction, particularly *White Writing* (1988), *Doubling the Point* (1992), and *Giving Offense* (1997). For all the evolving differences in form and voice that his works offer, differences that pay tribute to Coetzee's brilliant artistry, his central ethical passions have remained the same.

IV

Critical response to *Disgrace* — from theory-shaped essays to popular reviews — has been prolific, intensely written, and of unusually high quality. Scores of articles and reviews have appeared, and few other contemporary novels have stimulated so much worthy critical attention. Nearly everyone writes of the confluence of *Disgrace's* literary sophistication and its ethical probity. Veteran Coetzee scholars are familiar with all these publications, and the range of essays in our book makes a systematic review of the criticism seem out of place. But since the majority of readers and teachers of the novel are not masters of the critical literature, another short field guide will help them navigate this rich and extensive material. (See our bibliography for complete information on each title.)

While ours is the first book devoted to *Disgrace*, both the South African journal *Scrutiny2*, edited by Leon de Kock, and *Interventions: The International Journal of Postcolonial Studies*, edited by Derek Attridge, have devoted special issues to the novel. Both, particularly the Attridge volume, contain an impressive line-up of essays for the reader familiar with the idioms of contemporary academic criticism. Of the many fine studies of Coetzee published before 1999, we profited most from Jane Poyner's *J. M. Coetzee and the Idea of the Public Intellectual*, Dominic Head's *J. M. Coetzee*, and David Attwell's *South Africa and the Politics of Writing*. If the reader has time only for one earlier essay on the novel, one that takes up nearly all the novel's principal subjects, we recommend Derek Attridge's "Age of Bronze, State of Grace: Music and Dogs in Coetzee's *Disgrace*" in his *J. M. Coetzee and the Ethics of Reading*. And for those who can't quite articulate, or conquer, their continuing resistance to the novel, we suggest James Wood's "Coetzee's *Disgrace*: A Few Skeptical Thoughts" in

The Irresponsible Self: On Laughter and the Novel, or the slightly more acerbic earlier version of the essay in *The New Republic*, May 10, 2001. Wood has plenty of reservations — ". . . its somber tidiness . . . [its] unnatural containment" — but, like nearly every other commentator, praises the book's "vigorous honesty" and its "truthful, spare, compelling, often moving, and thematically legible" prose (Wood, 248).[1]

Generally, critical explorations can be grouped into three major areas. First, many writers take up the book's representation of the dramatic social and cultural shifts in post-apartheid South Africa. These highly complex, interrelated subjects — colonialism and postcolonialism (including intellectual colonization), globalization, land (re)distribution, the upsurge of murder and rape, race and politics, the traditions of the *plaasroman*, the "language question" and the cultural hegemony of English — have been written about with great authority by a number of Coetzee scholars, many of whom have deep roots in the country. From the beginning of his career, critics and fellow writers have argued relentlessly over the level and depth of Coetzee's political commitments as expressed in his fiction. We make only passing contributions to this set of subjects, and have learned the most from the books by Attridge, Rita Barnard, Meg Samuelson, the two books by Mark Sanders, especially *Ambiguities of Witnessing: Law and Literature in the Time of a Truth Commission*, and the articles by Zoë Wicomb, Rita Barnard (2002 and 2003), Timothy Strode, and Gareth Cornwell. On the novel's stormy reception in South Africa, the most stimulating discussions come from Peter McDonald, Sanders (2000 and 2007), and Attridge (2002).

Second, critics have read *Disgrace* as continuing the unsettling accounts of "the other," whether figured in terms of race, gender, species, or the unknowable in any creature, that run through all of Coetzee's writing. Our own writing about the ethical dilemmas raised by alterity stand at the center of our book and continue discussions begun by Attridge, David Atwell (2002), and Farred (*Scrutiny2*) on race, Elleke Boehmer and Lucy Graham (2003) on gender and sexual politics, and Laura Wright and Rosemary Jolly on both gender and animals. For those who think empathy an insufficient ground for ethical understanding we especially admire the work of Mike Marais on empathetic identification vs. "the Levinasian notion of self-substituting responsibility" (*Scrutiny2*) and the essays of Wicomb and Sanders (2007, chapter 6). An important subset of *Disgrace*'s ethical inquiry is the nature of violence, a disruptive feature of virtually every Coetzee novel, and one taken up by Grant Farred (*Interventions*) and Sanders (2007) as part of a wider discussion of the historical in ethical self-understanding.

Third, *Disgrace* ponders the relevance of Western philosophy, language theory, and art for interregnum and postcolonial societies. Byron, Wordsworth, opera, and the Faust legend all play important parts in *Disgrace*, and another dozen figures from Richard of St. Victor to Rilke make significant appearances. *Disgrace* can almost be read as an intertextual opera, with many voices struggling to still be heard, like Byron and Teresa Guiccioli in David Lurie's opera drafts. These imported traditions can seem utterly foreign to post-1994 South Africa; David Lurie's students have no easy way to connect Wordsworth's Mont Blanc to Table Mountain. Mike Marais's excellent *Scrutiny2* article begins with this subject, and Graham Pechey takes up Romanticism's role in colonization. At the same time all of Coetzee's work — fictions, essays, reviews — is thoroughly grounded in Western language, aesthetics, and novel-making. More specifically, there are a host of formal literary issues that each novel of Coetzee raises — *Disgrace's* firm realism, for example, contrasts with the more experimental novels that precede and follow it — and several of our essays concentrate on *Disgrace's* formal side (McDunnah principally, but also Boobar and myself) and on its limit-testing of inherited forms and ideas (Hawkins, Sutcliffe, Reinhard, and especially O'Neill). For those interested in language and language theory, see Wicomb and Sanders (*Interventions* and 2007, chapters 5 and 6). Many critics have written sharp analyses of these subjects, and of specific scenes in the book — we learned, once again, from Attridge, Michael Holland, Marais (2005), Sanders, and Wright — but we try for more synoptic coverage. In general, critics have followed Coetzee's example in integrating literary topics and close readings firmly with the ethical.

Who, then, is our book for? Ideally, it's for every reader of the novel, and especially for those who read it with others: in college classes and graduate seminars, in book clubs, among fans of the upcoming film *Disgrace*, starring John Malkovich. We hope to lessen the gap between academic criticism and the reading group participant or amateur reader who is enthralled by Coetzee's great novel and who would like to think it through with others. In every sense, then, this is a group project grounded in long friendships and a common undergraduate educational experience, and designed both to illuminate *Disgrace* and to celebrate the academic community that shaped us as readers, teacher, scholars, writers, and human beings.

Web site information. On our Web site we have posted two essays written specifically for book club leaders by veteran leaders of those organizations. One offers ideas for organizing such gatherings, and the second an account of how one group of readers encountered *Disgrace*. We also have posted a full description of the Johnston Center, other material on *Disgrace* that we couldn't include in our book, and, with our publisher's generous encouragement, a few excerpts from several of the teaching essays. We hope to stimulate interactive exchanges with teachers around the country who have chosen *Disgrace* for their classes, or who are also interested in larger questions of narrative ethics and its connection to pedagogy and humanities teaching in general. In short, we're looking for more unsolitary readers — and teachers — with whom to continue our conversations. Go to: http://johnstoncenter.org/content/the-disgrace-project.

Note

[1] See also the clever essay by Morgan Meis comparing Wood and Coetzee.

I. Reading *Disgrace*

1: "We are not asked to condemn": Sympathy, Subjectivity, and the Narration of *Disgrace*

Michael G. McDunnah

I

> Sympathy has everything to do with the subject and little to do with the object, the "another" . . . There are people who have the capacity to imagine themselves as someone else, there are people who have no such capacity (when the lack is extreme, we call them psychopaths), and there are people who have the capacity but choose not to exercise it . . . [T]here is no limit to the extent to which we can think ourselves into the being of another. There are no bounds to the sympathetic imagination.
>
> — J. M. Coetzee, *Elizabeth Costello*

THE "SYMPATHETIC IMAGINATION" — the ability to recognize, relate to, and enter the subjective experience of another being — is of the greatest importance in the work of J. M. Coetzee. Long before the term appears in *Elizabeth Costello* we see this capacity — or lack thereof — as a central issue in many of his books, from the demonizing of the nomads in *Waiting for the Barbarians*, through the developing sympathies of Mrs. Curran in *Age of Iron*, and even in Coetzee's own childhood as represented in *Boyhood* and *Youth*.[1] But nowhere, arguably, does he deal with the issue as directly as in *Disgrace*.

The challenge is made explicit early in the novel as David Lurie lectures his students on the characterization of Lucifer in Byron's poem "Lara." Already a self-consciously Byronic and Luciferian character, Lurie delivers this talk during his own fall from grace, at the moment when his private transgressions first flare into public scandal. Describing Lucifer as an "erring spirit" (32) whose actions are made "not on principle but on impulse" (33), Lurie draws our attention to the *narrative* voice of Byron's poem:

> Note that we are not asked to condemn this being with the mad heart, this being with whom there is something constitutionally wrong. On the contrary, we are invited to understand and sympathize. But there is a limit

> to sympathy. For though he lives among us, he is not one of us. He is exactly what he calls himself: a *thing,* that is, a monster. Finally . . . it will not be possible to love him, not in the deeper, more human sense of the word. (33–34)

A thing, a monster, difficult to relate to, perhaps impossible to love. this is our protagonist. As readers our sympathies are challenged from the very beginning: from the first chapter, the peculiar first sentence, even the implied verdict of the novel's title. We are reluctant to associate ourselves too closely with David Lurie, who seems a man entirely lacking in sympathy, unable or unwilling to enter into the being of another.

Coetzee, however, sets us the ethical challenge of understanding and sympathizing with Lurie by charging us to "think ourselves" into his being. Even as we resist association with Lurie we are required to follow his journey exclusively through his own limited perspective, without the comfort of any authorial presence to assist us in making ethical judgments. I will argue that, far from being a solely stylistic choice, the narrative voice of *Disgrace* is fundamentally a mimetic representation of David Lurie's consciousness, and therefore a principal means by which Coetzee creates and illuminates his character.

More importantly, I will argue that this intentional tension — between the technique's compulsion towards identification and the reader's ethical impulse towards disassociation — creates a narrative space in which Coetzee plays out, and perhaps even resolves, the essential themes of the novel. I am proposing that a careful examination of the narration provides an understanding of Lurie's developing sympathetic imagination that the text does not make explicit because Lurie himself is unaware of it.

Reading is an intrinsically sympathetic activity, and whether we read the novel as a dark fable of ethical failure, or hear in it the faint, faltering notes of grace, depends on our willingness to look beyond the apparent limits of sympathy. We are asked to look beyond what the monster may call himself, and we are not asked to condemn.

II

> It would be easier for you, I know, if the story came from someone else, if it were a stranger's voice sounding in your ear . . . So I ask you: attend to the writing, not to me.
> — Coetzee, *Age of Iron*

It is hard to imagine asking more of a first sentence than Coetzee accomplishes in the opening of *Disgrace*: "For a man of his age, fifty-two, divorced, he has, to his mind, solved the problem of sex rather well" (1).

Apart from a surprising amount of exposition delivered with an impressive economy of words, Coetzee establishes a narrative point of view, introduces several themes of the novel, and hints at the problematic nature of the protagonist. We immediately encounter this character who sees sex as a "problem" to be solved, and who rationalizes his solution to that problem in a manner that is simultaneously self-pitying, self-serving, and self-congratulatory. Twenty-one words into the novel this is a great deal of insight about our focal character.

I want to draw particular attention to the phrase "to his mind." It is this phrase that establishes our close point of view, but even in doing so it invites several careful layers of ironic distance: primarily, as readers, our distance from the character (whose mind, we already suspect, may work quite differently than our own), but also the character's self-observation, his subjective (and perhaps tentative) opinion of *himself*. Remove the phrase from the sentence and the narrative perspective would shift outward to an objective (though perhaps ironic) narrator, or else further *within* the character, who would then come to seem less thoughtful and reflective, and more sociopathic. Combined with the qualified "rather well," "to his mind" makes us very aware that this is a subjective point of view and, more importantly, one that understands and embraces its own subjectivity.

Right from this beginning Coetzee compels the reader to walk a fine line in relation to David Lurie. The distancing ploys and metafictional tricks Coetzee employs in other novels are noticeably absent from *Disgrace*. For example, one piece of information *not* provided in the opening pages is the focal character's *name*; in fact, throughout the novel the narrator of *Disgrace* never once refers to Lurie by name: he is only named (often erroneously) in dialogue or newspaper accounts. This is unusual for a third-person novel, and a sign that the narration is localized within a subjective perspective that has no need to name itself. There are only infrequent attributions (such as "he thinks" and "he feels"), and these are almost always indicative of Lurie's self-observation; they are not an external narrator specifying *which* thoughts are Lurie's (which might imply that others are *not* his own).

Further evidence supports this reading, particularly when contrasted with other Coetzee works. Unlike *Life & Times of Michael K*, for example, *Disgrace* presents no gaps between the voice of its narrator and the linguistic capacity of its protagonist, nor are we provided with any information or interpretation that does not come from Lurie himself.[2] *Disgrace*'s narration is not fragmented or unreliable like that in *Dusklands* or *In the Heart of the Country*, nor does Coetzee juxtapose conflicting narrative voices as he does in *Foe*, *Michael K*, and *Diary of a Bad Year*.

Several critics and reviewers have commented that the narration of *Disgrace* is so closely attuned to Lurie's perspective that it approximates a first-person narration. This, however, is an oversimplification that ignores the precise frequencies of Coetzee's narrative tuning.[3] Written in the first person, *Disgrace* would raise the question (as *Waiting for the Barbarians* does): what are we truly reading? A written account? A confession? We would wonder: to whom is Lurie telling this story, and what is his motivation? While it seems self-evident that third-person narration distances the reader from the protagonist, in this case it serves the opposite purpose. A first-person narrator would be suspect and demand questioning — demand, in fact, distancing ourselves from the narration. The unobtrusive narration of *Disgrace*, on the other hand, does not invite the same skepticism or compel such distance. In its free indirect discourse the third-person narrator acts as the guarantor of the truth of Lurie's *subjective* reality: to use Mike Marais' term, the novel refuses to establish an "ironic contract" between the reader and author that bypasses the character. This is not to say that irony is not in play in *Disgrace,* or that Coetzee does not intend the reader to look beyond the narrated text. But Coetzee does not intentionally deconstruct the authority of the narrative voice here as he does in other novels. The ironic moments in *Disgrace* are largely predicated on intrinsic, situational irony rather than tongue-in-cheek narration. In most cases, Lurie himself is aware of the irony, and his self-awareness — even self-effacement — lessens the reader's need to read the voice as unreliable or ironic.

While the subjective reality of the novel is effectively Lurie's, it should be noted that we rarely experience this reality from eye level. There is in fact a curious absence of immediacy, particularly in the opening sections. Compared, for example, to the relatively rich prose of *Life & Times of Michael K* or *Waiting for the Barbarians,* there are few descriptive passages and little physicality; only occasionally are Lurie's actions or experiences described from within. More significantly, we are often denied access to Lurie's thought processes; we do not, for example, "hear" him think through many of the catastrophic decisions he makes in the first six chapters.

While this limited viewpoint would seem to contradict the closeness of the reader–character relationship I have proposed, I would argue that these narrative skimmings and omissions are not departures from Lurie's subjective perspective but demonstrations of it. The narration observes only what Lurie notices, omits what he himself ignores or misses. In this way, *Disgrace* — like other Coetzee novels — can be read as an *overheard* text, a word-representation of Lurie's world- and self-view. Therefore, by noting the expansions and contractions of the narrative lens we can gain insight into the limits of Lurie's perceptions, the parameters of his self-awareness, and the stumbling development of his sympathetic capacity.

III

> Desire seemed to bring with it a pathos of distance and separation which it was futile to deny.
> — Coetzee, *Waiting for the Barbarians*

It is significant that the first situation in which we encounter David Lurie is one of objectification — a relational state diametrically opposed to the sympathetic imagination. From this first chapter — as he puts into practice his "solution" to the "problem of sex" — we see how the narration is both driven by and illustrative of Lurie's character and consciousness. For example, Soraya, unlike our protagonist, is immediately named, and repeatedly referred to by name. In this context the naming signifies not her singularity but her status as an object in Lurie's eyes, her relative position as "other" — all the more so because, as Lurie is aware, "Soraya" is not her real name.

The selective descriptions are also meaningful. After providing a step-by-step account of the weekly protocols of arrival and preparation, the narration describes their actual sexual encounters: "He strokes her honey-brown body, unmarked by the sun; he stretches her out, kisses her breasts; they make love" (1). The only details provided are in a sequence of three transitive verbs, emphasizing Lurie's physical objectification of Soraya: *his* manipulation of, and appreciation of, *her* body. Then, in the final clause, "they make love," the thin illusion of mutual subjectivity made transparent by the hurried, euphemistic, contextually inappropriate phrasing.

The lack of detail is a reflection, certainly, of Lurie's voluntary self-deception, but this absence of narrative interest also suggests that the true value of this experience for Lurie has little to do with sex. (Of their sexual relations we are told only that "Soraya is not effusive" [1], and that "intercourse between Soraya and himself must be, he imagines, rather like the copulation of snakes: lengthy, absorbed, but rather abstract, rather dry, even at its hottest" [2–3].)

The vast majority of the narrative in this chapter is spent not on Lurie's experience in Soraya's flat but on his life outside it, suggesting a connection between these objectified, commodified encounters with Soraya and Lurie's dissatisfaction with his day-to-day life. Though he "believes" he is "happy" (2), the interspersed accounts of his existence suggest bitterness, boredom, and isolation. His scholarly work is "bogged down in tedium" (4). He "makes no impression on his students," whose "indifference galls him more than he will admit" (4). In contrast to his students, Soraya is described as "a ready learner, compliant, pliant" (5). The institution at which Lurie works is, "to his mind, emasculated" (4).

This associative narration suggests that Lurie's real need is to feel less powerless, less generally impotent: to feel and exercise his authority, his subjective narrative power. In that apartment — an unconvincing stage furnished with only the necessary props — Lurie and Soraya play out a script *he* has constructed. Soraya is both actress and audience: Lurie talks with her about his life, presenting an image of himself that is carefully controlled, and edited. (He "speaks to her with a certain freedom," and "trusts her, within limits" [3].) Though he exhibits a cursory curiosity about Soraya's "real" life, he does not really question her, does not care to see her as a full individual. He preserves the storytelling authority of *I* for himself.

"Then one Saturday morning everything changes," as Lurie accidentally encounters Soraya on the street. Lurie stalks her — that word is used, although, characteristically, in Lurie's mind it is "Eros" that "stalks" — but Soraya catches him, and "this glance between himself and Soraya he regrets at once" (6).

We do not really know from the text why, following this meeting, their professional relationship breaks down. It is telling that Soraya does *not* refuse to see him immediately, in fact continues to see him for four more Thursdays. We can hypothesize that, however Lurie may project it onto Soraya, it is the change in *his* behavior that leads to her termination of their agreement.[4] It is tempting to read this resulting awkwardness in their professional relationship as a sign that Lurie is troubled by his sudden awareness of her subjectivity, or her life as an individual; that would be a comforting sign that he possesses, after all, a nascent sympathetic imagination. But his expanded understanding of Soraya is not what troubles him; after all, he has already demonstrated enough imagination to picture a family life for her (3). The moment of crisis is brought on not by what *he* sees, but when "Soraya's eyes meet his" (6). The illusion shattered is not of her objectivity, but of his own subjectivity, as he becomes aware of how she sees him. This is reinforced as the narrative lens shifts suddenly to how Lurie's sexual powers have faded over the years, until "overnight he became a ghost" (7). Following this incident, Lurie sees himself through the eyes of her children (6), and becomes conscious of how "prostitutes speak among themselves about the men who frequent them, the older men in particular" (8). Soon, he knows, "he will be shuddered over" like a cockroach (8), another of many references that imply the objectification of people by comparing them to animals. In their last four meetings, Soraya "transforms *herself* into just another woman and *him* into just another client" (7; my emphasis): Soraya has become subject, and Lurie object.

His attempt to recast the scenario with another, younger "Soraya" is unsatisfying: with prostitutes, apparently, the illusion of subjectivity has been destroyed. The departmental secretary he turns to next points out the generation gap between them, and insists on having her own subjective, erotic experience, "a froth of excitement that in the end only repels him" (9). Neither of these incidents — or characters — is described in detail; the narrative attention they receive is in exact proportion to Lurie's interest in them.

Lurie makes one last attempt to reclaim dominance over Soraya. Significantly, though he now knows her real name, *we* are not allowed to know it: the narration reflects Lurie's adherence to her objectifying "stage" name (9). She rejects him again, but even in defeat we hear him attempt to reshape the narrative: "What should a predator expect when he intrudes into the vixen's nest, into the home of her cubs?" (10). Now objectifying *her* through animal metaphors, he has revised his self-vision; he is no longer pathetic, but has reclaimed dominance and authority.

This episode ends, however, with a surprising emotion that almost subliminally challenges our perception of Lurie and contradicts nearly everything he believes about himself: "a shadow of envy passes over him for the husband he has never seen" (10). It is a passing acknowledgement that his solution to "the problem of sex" — the problem of intimacy, of emotion, of human interaction — is insufficient. It is a sign that — despite his certainty that "his temperament is not going to change" (2) — he is in fact *capable* of change. And it is important to note that Lurie is the *object* of this sentence, passively experiencing this unexpected emotion. It is a hint that any hope of redemption will involve a willingness to surrender his subjective status.

IV

> As for sex between teachers and students, so strong is the tide of disapproval nowadays that uttering even the mildest word in its defence becomes (exactly) like battling that tide . . . What you face when you open your lips to speak is not the silencing stroke of the censor but an edict of exile.
>
> — Coetzee, *Diary of a Bad Year*

Through his experience with Soraya, Lurie has glimpsed both his own objectification and the failure of his cold and logical solution approach to human interaction. Perhaps more importantly, through this experience (and simply by being "a man of his age") he has begun to grapple with his own mortality. Something enters him, or is awakened in him: Lurie calls it Eros, by which he primarily means desire. We, however, also hear the Freudian meanings of the word as not merely sexual drive but also creativity and self-preservation: the "life instinct" that exists in opposition to *thanatos*, the "death instinct." In the weeks following Soraya's absence from his life Lurie briefly turns these erotic — which is to say creative — energies onto the opera he is composing, but they are quickly redirected towards Melanie Isaacs, one of his "indifferent" students.

Since we have already made the association between Lurie's sexual decline and his professional "emasculation," it is not surprising that he would attempt to reclaim his authority by seducing one of his students. The narrative offers no particular explanation, however, for why he should choose Melanie Isaacs. She is described as a so-so student, her conversation is unremarkable, and she and Lurie share little in common. (He finds her beautiful, but Cape Town is "a city prodigal of beauty, of beauties" [12].) As the relationship plays out, we come to suspect that Melanie's attraction lies only in her availability and vulnerability.

I would suggest that, through this affair, Lurie is working out both the dark side of his relationship with Soraya and the flash of revelation he experienced at its end. He is both attempting to reclaim his dominant position as "predator" *and* responding to an as-yet unrealized need for an emotional connection with another human being. While the affair is another, more destructive expression of his need to sustain himself through the creation and control of objectifying narratives, it is also a misdirected eruption of his repressed humanity, and thus a strange, complicated step on his crooked path towards grace. As Lurie himself realizes later, "in the whole wretched business there was something generous that was doing its best to flower" (89).

The narration reflects Lurie's dual and conflicting desires. On the positive side, Lurie's narrative focus expands, becoming — slightly, but measurably — less egocentric and solipsistic. Unlike the earlier scenes with the two Sorayas and Dawn, we are provided with real-time details of his interactions with Melanie. The long scene of their first "date" (11–17), for example, has a realistic integrity — and an absence of narrative ellipses — that makes it virtually unique in the novel. There are more frequent descriptions, and conversations are reported at length rather than being condensed in Lurie-centric narration. This intensification of realism signifies a shift in Lurie's consciousness, a more genuine engagement: unlike Soraya's carefully compartmentalized place in his life, Melanie is "a presence in his life, a breathing presence" (23).

It would be a mistake to overstate this change, however, for Lurie's engagement is less with Melanie as an individual than with the situation. Their conversations lack real exchange, let alone connection: his lines are stilted, rehearsed, and no doubt recycled — "Smooth words, as old as seduction itself" (16) — while her dialogue is uninspired and largely perfunctory. Nothing she says or does seems to charm Lurie, or repel him, or move him. Her obvious lack of interest in his interests does not concern him; her lack of enthusiasm for his attentions does not dissuade him; her emotions evoke no sympathy in response. All he feels for her is desire, the excitement of seduction, and this feeling does not grow *from* their interactions so much as it is superimposed on them.

And while the narration reflects Lurie's partial recognition of Melanie's individuality by allowing her speech and a real-time presence, it — which is to say, Lurie — denies her any psychic, subjective life. As readers we may find the characterization of Melanie insufficient and frustrating, particularly when we seek to understand some of the more ethically complicated moves she makes. That Melanie's motives and feelings remain unclear, however, is less a function of intentional ambiguity on Coetzee's part, and more a reflection of *Lurie's* almost complete disinterest in her interior life. (He is surprised to hear that Melanie "takes things to heart" [37]; he has simply never given her that much thought.) Melanie has the flatness of a narrative foil because that is precisely what she is for Lurie: a character to play out his own drama against, a means for him to reassert his exclusive subjectivity. We are forced to recognize the absent presence of a "real" Melanie, glimpsed through Lurie's subjective observations and half-hearted speculations.

Once again, we are walking a fine line, accompanying a narrator who is limited but not wholly unreliable. It is tempting, for example, to read ironically some of Lurie's observations: when Melanie's smile is described as "sly rather than shy" (11), as "evasive and perhaps even coquettish" (12), it is hard not to suspect that these are Lurie's lecherous, hopeful misreadings. Yet there is also a candor in the narration that suggests Lurie is capable of seeing her misgivings honestly. When he phones her for their second meeting, for example, he recognizes that she is simply "too confused" to "wriggle out" (18). To the extent that he considers her, he seems to see clearly her lack of enthusiasm, her hesitation, her shame. Lurie may get caught up in the drama of his own Byronic longings, but he neither romanticizes her nor their "relationship," and this narrative candor makes it possible to trust that the presentation of Melanie is limited but not overly biased.

One could argue, in fact, that, if the narrative is biased it may at times err on the side of *blaming* Lurie, who exaggerates his own powers to reinforce his subjective authority. Far from glossing over his own responsibility, Lurie goes out of his way to *claim* it, denying Melanie's agency even when it would be in his best interest to acknowledge it. Recognizing that she has begun to manipulate him, for example, he would rather assert his crimes than admit her power: "if she is behaving badly, he has behaved worse . . . he is the one who leads, she the one who follows" (28). When she files charges against him, Lurie decides she must have "crumpled" under pressure from her parents and boyfriend: "She is too innocent for that, too ignorant of her power" (39). When he imagines her filing the complaint, the language becomes, for an entire paragraph, synechdochal, a literal denial of subjectivity: "A hand takes up the pen . . . The hand slows, settles, makes its X . . . Finally, at the foot of the page, the date and her signature"

(39–40). When the committee suggests he reads Melanie's statement, he refuses, denying her — as he did Soraya — the narrative authority of *I*.

At the heart of the account of Lurie's affair with Melanie lies one of the most ambiguous and controversial scenes in the novel, when Lurie arrives at Melanie's apartment and forces himself upon her. It is certainly the most potentially alienating passage for readers of *Disgrace,* and the most problematic in terms of constructing an ethical response to Lurie and the narrative voice. It is here that most readers feel the absence of an authorial presence — of a higher authority — most keenly: without an objective verdict on Lurie's actions, and denied Melanie's interpretation of the event, we are left, as always, with Lurie's highly limited — but not wholly dishonest — perspective. Once again Lurie's candor and self-awareness compel a strange trust precisely *because* they are repellent: there are enough honestly ugly admissions to complicate even darker readings. As readers our sympathetic connection threatens to snap — and yet never quite does. (Compare, for example, the multiple interpretations of a similarly ambiguous scene in *In the Heart of the Country,* where the realistic integrity is not just frustrated but fractured, and therefore throws the reader into conflict with the narration.) Here, by stretching the connection and sustaining the tension, Coetzee forces us to recognize the authenticity of Lurie's subjective experience, and to engage in an active, ethically responsible dialogue with its narrative.

We are not provided any explanation of Lurie's intentions in going to Melanie's apartment: "At four o'clock the next afternoon he is *at* her flat" (24, my emphasis). This simple syntactical choice suggests that Lurie is acting on an unexamined impulse, and that, as he later says of Lucifer, the "source of his impulse is dark to him" (33). In narrative time, however, the encounter abruptly follows a scene from the previous day in which Lurie stalks her at the theater. He is just self-aware enough to realize that the two scenes are related — "Something to do with the apparition on the stage" (25) — and so our attention is drawn back to the theater:

> An unseemly business, sitting in the dark spying on a girl (unbidden the word *letching* comes to him). Yet the old men whose company he seems to be on the point of joining . . . Can they be blamed for clinging to the last to their place at the sweet banquet of the senses? (24)

Once again Lurie has encountered a vision of himself as a lecherous old man, someone to be "shuddered over." Once again, his instinct is to reject this self-image, invoke the life-force *eros,* and reclaim authority through an objectifying narrative. It is appropriate that his assault on Melanie follows seeing her on stage, for a character in a play — his play — is exactly how he relates to her.

The moment Melanie opens the door, however, Lurie's script is thwarted, his narrative authority challenged. The "apparition on stage" is nowhere to be seen: now a more childish (and more authentic) Melanie appears in T-shirt, shorts, and "slippers in the shape of comic-book gophers which he finds silly, tasteless" (24). (Note the objectifying animal association, the first of three in this scene: she will also "burrow like a mole" and "go slack . . . like a rabbit" [24–25].) Needing to assert his narrative in spite of her rejection, the language upon his entrance is brutal: he is an "intruder who thrusts himself upon her"; "her limbs crumple"; "words heavy as clubs thud into the delicate whorl of her ear." "'No, not now!' she says, struggling," but "nothing will stop him" (24–25).

Once he overcomes her resistance, however, the brutality is gone. The narration reflects that he has — momentarily — reestablished his preferred self-image as desired seducer. The language becomes softer, even tender, and (once more using three transitive verbs) echoes the illusion of "making love" with Soraya: "He carries her to the bedroom, brushes off the absurd slippers, kisses her feet" (25). He has successfully — if temporarily — recast her as the seduced: he interprets her lack of resistance as complicity, even cooperation, and so for a paragraph Melanie becomes a (curiously passive) active subject:

> She does not resist. All she does is avert herself: avert her lips, avert her eyes. She lets him lay her out on the bed and undress her: she even helps him, raising her arms and then her hips. Little shivers of cold run through her; as soon as she is bare, she slips under the quilted counterpane like a mole burrowing, and turns her back on him. (25)

Again there is an echo of "compliant" Soraya, who learned to please him by being "quiet and docile" (1). But Soraya was a conscious and compensated actress in Lurie's fantasy narrative. Melanie is not, and here the narrative integrity of the script he superimposes on her begins to betray itself. "She does not resist" — but resistance is not supposed to be part of the script at all; the word would not have come up with Soraya. The fact that it is used here implies Lurie's growing awareness of her reluctance, and of his own transgression. Melanie "averts herself," "turns her back," withdrawing from the consensual role.

This increasing awareness of her reluctance ultimately becomes impossible to ignore, and in the next paragraph, in the act itself, the illusion cannot be sustained:

> Not rape, not quite that, but undesired nevertheless, undesired to the core. As though she had decided to go slack, die within herself for the duration, like a rabbit when the jaws of the fox close on its neck. So that everything done to her might be done, as it were, far away. (25)

The scene began with Lurie asserting himself in the active role, moved to his failed projection of Melanie's complicity, and now, with the failure of his seduction narrative, culminates in this paragraph of subjectless sentences. Once again, the need to deny the word "rape" merely emphasizes the cracks in Lurie's narration. He suddenly has no illusions about Melanie's complicity — and yet neither does he fully implicate himself, and so the syntax here denies both their subjectivities. This can obviously be read as his refusal to accept responsibility, a reluctance to look too closely at his ugliest moment. And yet I would argue that this failure of narrative authority also reflects a strange turning point for David Lurie, a sudden shattering of his exclusive subjectivity. In committing this horrendous act he is no longer able to deny the experience of the very real, fully human Melanie. The sympathetic walls come down, and Lurie — however briefly, however reluctantly — actually sees into Melanie's experience in a way he has not before. (One wonders, for example, how "desired" their first sexual encounter was, during which Melanie was "passive throughout," and after which she was "lying beneath him, her eyes closed, her hands slack above her head, a slight frown on her face" [19]. The only difference between the two scenes may be Lurie's level of self-awareness.) It is noteworthy that, upon leaving Melanie's apartment, Lurie immediately seems to recognize his culpability, and in the process experiences the first authentic, sympathetic emotion we have seen him exhibit in the novel:

> He obeys, but then, when he reaches his car, is overtaken with such dejection, such dullness, that he sits slumped at the wheel, unable to move.
> A mistake, a huge mistake. At this moment, he has no doubt, she, Melanie, is trying to cleanse herself of it, of him. He sees her running a bath, stepping into the water, eyes closed like a sleepwalker's. He would like to slide into a bath of his own. (25)

I do not mean to imply that Lurie experiences a fully-conscious revelation, but this profound failure of his exclusive subjectivity constitutes a catalytic crisis in the novel. As Elizabeth Costello repeatedly asserts, the sympathetic imagination is an *emotional* capacity, not a rational, intellectual one, and the development of Lurie's has only just begun.

V

> Realism has never been comfortable with ideas . . . So when it needs to debate ideas, as here, realism is driven to invent situations . . . in which characters give voice to contending ideas and thereby in a certain sense embody them . . . In such debates ideas do not and indeed cannot float free: they are tied to the speakers by whom they are enounced . . .
>
> — Coetzee, *Elizabeth Costello*

John Lanchester has called the opening of *Disgrace* a "masterpiece of misdirection" (Lanchester, 2005), and indeed Coetzee thwarts reader expectations several times throughout the novel. The first of these abrupt shifts occurs after the sixth chapter, as Lurie, in disgrace, leaves the city and the university and the book we thought we were reading behind.

Before proceeding it is helpful to consider the function of this narrative "misdirection." The David Lurie we will encounter in the remainder (and bulk) of the novel is, both personally and circumstantially, a much more sympathetic character. A slightly lost man in his declining years, he is the victim of violence and the worried father of a horribly traumatized daughter. Taken by itself, the story of Lurie's time in Salem would almost automatically evoke compassion in the reader, and the thematic concerns of the novel would seem more outwardly focused on race relations and the political future of South Africa. Critics of *Disgrace* have read it this way, some finding in it an almost apocalyptically bleak parable of white guilt or paranoia.[5]

This is not to say that the racial, sexual, and economic politics of post-apartheid South Africa are not important to the novel, or to deny the validity of these more centrifugal analyses. However, the inclusion of the opening chapters suggests that *Disgrace* is primarily a centripetal exploration of universal themes through one individual in specific situations; it is more mimetic than didactic, psychological more than allegorical. The novel's central concern is *not* necessarily violence, rape, animal cruelty, or racial conflict, but a microcosmic examination of the failures of sympathetic imagination that make these things possible. In this sense, the relationship between the Cape Town and Salem sections of *Disgrace* functions in much the same way as the twinned narratives — and narrators — of *Dusklands*, which reflect and illuminate each other's themes of dehuminization in a way that transcends the situational specificity of either.

In his Jerusalem Prize acceptance speech, Coetzee says that "the deformed and stunted relations between human beings that were created under colonialism and exacerbated under what is loosely called apartheid have their psychic representation in a deformed and stunted inner life"; the fundamental problem, he suggests, is "a failure of love" (*Doubling*, 97–98). Tethering us to Lurie's limited viewpoint, Coetzee creates and maintains active tension by repeatedly pulling this sympathetic connection taut: we are forced to read the remainder of the novel over the palimpsest of Lurie's personal, ethical failings — his failure of love. Thus Lurie becomes not merely our guide through, or witness to, the events of the novel, but the embodiment of the core conflict. His consciousness — his stunted inner life — is both what is at fault and what is at stake, and the narration of that consciousness becomes the field on which the issues play out.

VI

> To thinking, cogitation, I oppose fullness, embodiedness, the sensation of being — not a consciousness of yourself as a kind of ghostly reasoning machine thinking thoughts, but on the contrary the sensation — a heavily affective sensation — of being a body with limbs that have extension in space, of being alive to the world.
> — Coetzee, *Elizabeth Costello*

We do not "hear" Lurie make the decision to go to Salem, but we can read the need to reconnect with his daughter as another faltering, semi-conscious move towards a more authentic relationship. Reuniting with Lucy, the narration reveals genuine emotion that is — for Lurie — unusual, and unusually free of irony: "What a nice girl, he thinks, hugging her; what a nice welcome at the end of a long trip!" (59).

From the moment Lurie arrives the narration becomes less myopic and more objective. The prose becomes richer, with more descriptions and more physical immediacy. The point of view is still unquestionably Lurie's, but the lens has turned outward and widened. Without the example of the previous six chapters, we might now characterize the style as more traditional third-person narration, with intermittent free-indirect discourse. I would argue, however, that this broadening of narrative perspective is not a change of style but signifies a further change in the consciousness of our focalizer.

This is also evident in the increased use of attributive phrases, which have been rare up until this point; suddenly, more and more observations are followed with "he thinks," or "he supposes." There are more frequent thoughts and emotions that act *on* him ("Without warning a memory of the girl comes back" [65]), and he is increasingly bewildered by his own reactions ("He is surprised by his outburst" [74].) Lurie experiences an increasing awareness of himself from outside, and the narration now develops a more tentative tone as the cracks in his solipsistic worldview begin to show.

This is most obvious in his relations with Lucy, the first person with whom he demonstrates any authentic connection or honoring of a social contract. Unlike the canned exchanges with Melanie, Lurie's conversations with his daughter exhibit the give-and-take of real interaction, and we now hear in his narration and dialogue the lapses and pauses that indicate a more genuine effort to express himself. ("He tries again, more slowly" [89].) Explaining his stand with the committee, for example, his practiced narrative begins to break down: "through another's ears, his whole tirade sounds melodramatic, excessive" (66). Telling Lucy about Melanie, Lurie doubts himself for the first time: "*I was a servant of Eros:*

that is what he wants to say, but does he have the effrontery? *It was a god who acted through me.* What vanity! Yet not a lie, not entirely" (89). Instead, he describes a dog that had been punished for its desire: "What was ignoble . . . was that the poor dog had begun to hate its own nature . . . It was ready to punish itself" (90). Revising his claim to have been acted upon from without, Lurie has begun to understand that the force that has acted "through him" came from within, from his own suppressed instincts.

During this conversation Lurie remembers the scene in Melanie's apartment, and — though there is no evidence of conscious guilt — we are now presented with a narrative revision of this encounter. Without being aware of it, Lurie rewrites the earlier paragraph in which Melanie was an active, cooperative participant: now both the syntax and the substance find him taking the active role, and Melanie less complicit:

> He sees himself in the girl's flat, in her bedroom, with the rain pouring down outside and the heater in the corner giving off the smell of paraffin, kneeling over her, peeling off her clothes, while her arms flop like the arms of a dead person. (89)

Both the syntactical revision and the previously unmentioned environmental details — the rain, the smell of paraffin — are evidence of a less stubborn solipsism and a more objective view of himself from without. It is an important moment for Lurie, no less so because he is apparently unaware of the change; we read it not as a conscious confession of guilt, but as evidence of a deeper, more fundamental recalibration of his self-perception. Significant, too, is the fact that it comes in Lucy's presence: that Lurie cannot (even in his own mind) sustain his self-justifying illusions demonstrates that a tacit ethical compact exists between them. Lucy is not, for him, a narrative foil like Melanie or Soraya, nor a cardboard antagonist like the members of the disciplinary committee.

Coetzee's placement of this conversation is significant, for it immediately precedes the novel's next and most important turn: the arrival of three assailants, who torture Lurie, kill the dogs, and gang-rape Lucy. The immediately experiential nature of the narration denies us even an extra paragraph-break of foreshadowing, and so the event comes to the reader as it does for Lurie: "Without warning, without fanfare, it is here, and he is in the middle of it" (94). While we once again find ourselves suddenly in a different book from the one we thought we were reading, this juxtapositioning ensures that the opening of the novel — and specifically Lurie's ethical treatment of Melanie — continues to inform and guide our reading of the rest of the novel.

VII

> Fear is, then, a surprising route through which reciprocity is broken off, the other valued at nothing, when we look only at the existential moment, but whereby an even more profound reciprocity returns, through shared fear . . . [T]he aesthetic importance of fear . . . has the unmistakable prominence it does precisely because of the political imagination that locks our own state into play with the state of another — or of many others — and invents in fear an unexpected but crucial kind of civic energy.
>
> — Philip Fisher, *The Vehement Passions*

"So it has come, the day of testing" (94). I have suggested that Lurie underwent a manufactured crisis in Melanie's apartment, a failure of narrative control and a momentary, sympathetic surrendering of subjectivity. Now Lurie has all agency and authority taken from him as he himself is objectified, turned into a thing, a victim. Removed from narrative power, he becomes a supporting character, left to speculate hopelessly on the horrific main event unfolding elsewhere in the house. His attempts to direct or predict the unfolding of the narrative are futile. He hopes, for example, that the men will simply rob them, but set aflame he has a flash of revelation: "So he was wrong! He and his daughter are not being let off lightly after all! He can burn, he can die; and if he can die, then so can Lucy, above all Lucy!" (96).

This moment strikes the reader as a revelation as well. That a father should care more about his daughter than he cares about himself should seem a natural human instinct, but after experiencing the claustrophobic solipsism of Lurie's mind, his expression of concern for Lucy "above all" surprises: it is perhaps his most human and sympathetic moment.[6] It is hard not to read the flames on his head and eyes as purification, a symbolic cleansing of his old life, now "burned, burnt" (71). He has fallen from his intellectual worldview into the physical world, the world of emotion and instinct. Newly born in this "breathing world," "everything is tender" (97).

In the immediate aftermath we hear him fumble to regain control, to subjugate emotion and intellectualize the event: "A risk to own anything . . . That is the theory; hold to the theory and to the comforts of theory" (98). But he is shaken, his authority shattered. Now it is Lucy who exercises authority, and at the hospital she manages him as he once imagined Melanie being managed by her parents. She "fills out the form for him, seats him in the waiting room. She is all strength, all purposefulness, whereas the trembling seems to have spread to his whole body" (101). Lucy refuses his attempts to claim the narrative power, immediately insisting on ownership of her own story: "You tell what happened to you, I tell what happened to me" (99).

In the days following the attack, and indeed throughout the rest of the novel, we see the change within Lurie reflected in the narration. Reluctant to surrender his old, authoritative place in the world, Lurie consciously experiences this change as "despair" (108) and a loss of identity: "Here he is losing himself day by day" (121). Unconsciously acknowledging for the first time the symbolic source of his awakening emotional capacity, he "has a sense that, inside him, a vital organ has been bruised, abused — perhaps even his heart" (107). He begins, reluctantly, to observe himself, and to be aware of these changes:

> Just an after-effect, he tells himself . . . In a while the organism will repair itself, and I, the ghost within it, will be my old self again. But the truth, he knows, is otherwise. His pleasure in living has been snuffed out. (107)

He longs to go back to being a "ghost" within himself — the ghost in the machine, the inviolate subjective consciousness represented in the Cape Town narration — but he knows those days are lost to him, burned, burnt up. However, while he consciously mourns the loss of his "pleasure in living," the truth is that we never saw him exhibit much joy in his intellectual, egocentric life. There are frequent clues in the narration that he may be growing happier as he loses himself in the physical world:

> This is how his days are spent on the farm. He helps Petrus clean up the irrigation system. He keeps the garden from going to ruin. He packs produce for the market. He helps Bev Shaw at the clinic. He sweeps the floors, cooks the meals, does all the things that Lucy no longer does. He is busy from dawn to dusk. (120)

Lurie has, for the moment, put behind the intellect, let go of abstraction. The narration reveals that he not only responds to the immediacy of the physical environment but now starts to view himself as a part of it, and for the first time we hear plural pronouns: "Too close, he thinks: we live too close to Petrus" (127), and "They ought to install bars . . . They ought to turn the farmhouse into a fortress" (113). Though the content of these thoughts reflects a desperate attempt to reclaim power and subjective authority, their expression reflects a move towards an *inclusive* subjectivity — suggesting, in fact, that he has formed a human connection, that the formerly isolated introvert now sees himself as part of a community.

While by "they" and "we" Lurie means only himself and Lucy, the narration reveals that this sense of community — of "civic energy" — increasingly includes others as well. After the attack, the narration finds time to think about Ettinger (100), to speculate at length about Petrus (116–18, for example), and Lurie becomes aware of himself through the eyes of Bill Shaw, who speaks "without irony":

> Bill Shaw believes that, because he and David Lurie once had a cup of tea together, David Lurie is his friend, and the two of them have obligations towards each other. Is Bill Shaw wrong or right? . . . Does the drinking of tea seal a love-bond, in the eyes of Bill Shaw? (102)

The duality in the narration here carefully reflects Lurie's ambiguous acknowledgement of communal ethics: with the slightly mocking tone, and the repetitions of both of their full names, it emphasizes both the snobbish estrangement between them in Lurie's eyes *and* his increasingly objective awareness of himself from without — as a social creature, an individual in the community. Nonetheless, we see that the attack has brought about Lurie's grudging awareness of his interconnectedness, and interdependence: "Yet but for Bill and Bev Shaw, but for old Ettinger, but for bonds of some kind, where would he be now?" (102).

VIII

> In order to be cruel we have to close our hearts to the suffering of the other. It is not inherently easier to close off our sympathies as we wring the neck of the chicken we are going to eat than it is to close off our sympathies to the man we send to the electric chair. . . .
> — J. M. Coetzee, Interview with *Djurens Rätt*

In *Elizabeth Costello* (and elsewhere), Coetzee argues that our failure to identify with animals is the same failure of imagination that leads to crimes against humanity. It is not surprising, then, that Lurie's interactions with animals constitute an essential, parallel narrative in his developing sympathetic imagination.

Arriving in Salem he is at first unmoved by — and even contemptuous of — the efforts of Lucy and Bev to care for animals. But his attention is drawn by Katy, the bulldog, "the abandoned one," and Lucy unintentionally reinforces the association: "No one wants her, and she knows it . . . The irony is, she must have offspring all over the district who would be happy to share their homes with her" (78). A few moments later Lucy tells him not to underestimate Bev — "She is a more interesting person than you think. Even in your own terms" — and David is struck by a welling up not only of inexplicable sympathy and self-doubt, but of something we have not seen him exhibit before: shame:

> His own terms: what are they? That dumpy little women with ugly voices deserve to be ignored? A shadow of grief falls over him: for Katy, alone in her cage, for himself, for everyone. He sighs deeply, not stifling the sigh. "Forgive me, Lucy," he says. (79)

Once again, the ongoing changes in Lurie are evidenced best in the narration. On his first visit with Bev and Bill Shaw, he is "repelled by the odours of cat urine and dog mange," and snobbish about their cluttered house (72). On his first day working with Bev, however, while his conscious thoughts are still mocking, the clinic is described with an intense physicality and breadth of sensory information, this time without snobbery, disgust, or contempt. As the scene progresses David's surface consciousness almost disappears from the scene, as he surrenders himself without comment or complaint to doing what must be done. "Interesting is not the word" (84) — he is fully engaged.

Lurie witnesses Bev's sympathetic imagination at work, and her influence on him is increasingly evident. At times he is startled by the surfacing of his own sympathetic reactions: "To his own surprise, he is trying to comfort her" (83). His sudden admission of "disgrace," and plea to be put to use (85) signal a hesitant recognition that among the animals he might find at least the possibility of redemption.

The sympathetic connection between humans and animals is solidified for Lurie during the attack on the farm, as the narrative literally and symbolically links human and animal responses: humans become animalistic, and animals serve as emotional surrogates for Lucy and Lurie. The dogs provide warnings of the danger, which are ignored. As the attack begins, Lurie's first response is to release the bulldog; then, like a dog himself, "on all fours he creeps into the kitchen" (93). Knocked unconscious, he awakes to find himself caged, with the dogs barking outside; from this vantage point he must watch as they are killed — only his familiar, Katy, will survive. His assailant is unemotional — "placid, without a trace of anger" (94) — while Lurie seems to devolve into an animalistic state, forced down to submission at shoe level. In his rage he moves beyond human language, "hurling out bellows that have no words behind them" (96). Following the attack, Lucy's grief for the dogs — "'My darlings, my darlings!'" (97) — is quickly echoed by Lurie's sympathy for her: "My dearest, dearest" and "My child, my child!" (98–99). Later, as Bev tends to his wounds, "he recalls the goat in the clinic, wonders whether, submitting to her hands, it felt the same peacefulness" (106).

Just as it forces Lurie to grapple with his interdependence of people, the attack has shattered Lurie's previous conviction that "we are a different order of creation from the animals" (74); again we see in the narration his conscious mind struggling to accommodate his newly expanded sense of community. For example, though he attempts to apply to Petrus's sheep the same objectifying logic he has applied to women ("Sheep do not own themselves" [123]), he becomes aware that "a bond seems to have come into existence between himself and the two Persians" (126). Interestingly, the narration begins to reflect his internal conflict in a more conscious way, and here it almost takes the form of an internal debate between his logical mind and his emotional (sympathetic) responses. ("Do I have to change, he thinks? Do I have to become like Bev Shaw?" [126].) Explaining his reaction to Lucy — "I am disturbed. I can't say why" — she jokes, "God moves in mysterious ways, David" (127). As he once invoked Eros to explain his emotional, illogical reactions, so Lucy implies that God — sympathy, love, grace — may be entering him now.

Lurie once thought himself incapable of change. ("The skull, followed by the temperament: the two hardest parts of the body" [2].) Now, with his sympathy awakened, and both his skull and temperament tender, he is forced to reconsider. During his Sunday afternoons euthanizing "superfluous canines," he is once again overcome by sympathy and emotion:

> He had thought he would get used to it. But that is not what happens. The more killings he assists in, the more jittery he gets. One Sunday evening, driving home in Lucy's kombi, he actually has to stop at the roadside to recover himself. Tears flow down his face that he cannot stop; his hands shake.
>
> He does not understand what is happening to him . . . He does not seem to have the gift of hardness. (142–43)

Having feared for his own life and that of his daughter, he is now moved most, it seems, by the way the animals cling to life — the way they sense, and fight against, the "disgrace of dying" (143). He responds, that is, to their *eros*, their drive for survival. He has enough compassion to imagine their last moments and make them as easy as possible:

> Why should a creature with the shadow of death upon it feel him flinch away as if its touch were abhorrent? So he lets them lick him, if they want to, just as Bev Shaw strokes them and kisses them if they will let her. (143)

During his work at the clinic, David's relationship with Bev Shaw also begins to change. Consciously he still thinks of her as a "plain little creature," but as his sympathetic imagination develops he begins, not to *see* her differently, but to *relate* to her differently. She becomes someone to whom he "unburdens" himself (139). One night as they are talking he says something rude, and he has, significantly, become sympathetic enough to fear he has hurt her feelings. In response he makes what is, for him, a surprising and unprecedented effort to see her differently:

> He tries to imagine her twenty years younger, when the upturned face on its short neck must have seemed pert and the freckled skin homely, healthy. On an impulse he reaches out and runs a finger over her lips.
>
> She lowers her eyes but does not flinch. On the contrary, she responds, brushing her lips against his hand — even, it might be said, kissing it — while blushing furiously all the time. (148)

Bev's kissing of his hand echoes the doomed dog, and Lurie's resolve not to "flinch away as if its touch were abhorrent" (143). Even as we recognize the snobbery in Lurie, the lingering Byronic self-image that leads him to take pity on "poor Bev Shaw," we must notice that this encounter with Bev is not about the "problem of sex," and it is not about subjugation or objectification: it is about kindness. He consciously perceives it somewhat contemptuously, but the root of the situation is sympathetic: "So that in the end Bev Shaw can feel pleased with herself" (150). While we would hope for a David Lurie who could consciously love without feeling superior, who could recognize Bev Shaw as (at least) his equal, he is not there yet; nonetheless, his effort to change, driven by sympathy, is encouraging.

It is also important to note that, for the first time in his sexual relations, Lurie is not the aggressor, and he is not the subject. At the door, she rests her head on his chest, and he "lets her do it, as he has let her do everything she has felt a need to do" (150). While his sex with Bev is not "undesired to the core," there is a faint echo of Melanie's passivity "so that everything done to her might be done, as it were, far away" (25). Again, Lurie's passive role can be read as an abdication of responsibility, but also as a sign that he is willing to surrender his control: despite his conscious grasping for superiority, he approaches his relationship with Bev on the footing of equality. By their next encounter things have already grown more equal, and more honest: they do not make love: "they have in effect ceased to pretend that that is what they do together" (162). The syntax here is revealing: now Lurie is not the aggressor, nor does he "allow" Bev Shaw to touch him; instead, they "lie in each other's arms" — for comfort, and companionship, and talk. By their *next* meeting, after David's return from Cape Town, they embrace, and talk, but the sexual element is gone completely. Sex may have been the only way David could make the initial connection — the only way he knew of relating to a strange woman — but we can see that Bev is, in reality, his first female friend.

IX

> Why does her mind go back to this long-past and — really — unimportant episode? The answer: because she has never revealed it to anyone, never made use of it . . . what happened in the rooming house belongs to her and her alone. For half a century the memory has rested inside her like an egg, an egg of stone, one that will never crack open, never give birth. She finds it good, it pleases her, this silence of hers, a silence she hopes to preserve to the grave.
>
> — Coetzee, *Elizabeth Costello*

As I've tried to show, the voice of *Disgrace* is a manifestation of the central issue of the novel; it is itself both the problem and the hope of solution. The book grants Lurie the subjectivity, the exclusive narrative authority, that as readers we hope to see him learn to relinquish, and as a result it continually frustrates the reader with absent intertexts, with deferred or denied narratives that might better explain or expand the tale we are told. We will never know Soraya's real name or hear her story, never understand Melanie's motives or read her statement to the committee. We will never fully understand Bev or Bill Shaw, and we will certainly never see through the eyes of Petrus: "Pressed into the mould of English, Petrus's story would come out arthritic, bygone" (117). We will not share in the "mood of quiet satisfaction" that reigns over the gathering at Petrus's party; whatever the identity of the orator, the "man with the medal," Lurie "has no idea what [he] is saying" (135).

Most important, neither we nor David will ever fully know Lucy's story. As Elizabeth Costello says, "to save our humanity, certain things that we may want to see (*may want to see because we are human!*) must remain off-stage" (*Elizabeth Costello* 168–69). Lucy declines to report the rape, insists on returning to the farm, and she does not feel the need to justify her reasons to David. As much as we are intended to make the association between Lucy and Melanie, Lucy's position also echoes David's earlier stance when he faced the committee. "What happened to me is a purely private matter" (112), Lucy says: "I have . . . the right not to be put on trial like this, not to have to justify myself . . ." (133). Lurie has changed narrative positions from the one he occupied before the committee: there it was he whose actions were impenetrable, he who refused to make his life a "public matter." Now he is the one attempting to interpret, the one seeking public, secular justice.

With "the story Lucy has elected to tell" (108), the issue of narrative authority that has been present throughout *Disgrace* is increasingly foregrounded. Lurie, former professor of literature, is conscious of the importance of language and storytelling, and while he recognizes the limitations — "every word with which one tries to wrap up this day, the day swallows down its black throat" (102) — he still resents both his and Lucy's subjugation in the narrative of others. He sees their story sanitized in the newspaper, where Lucy's name is misspelled and he is objectified as her "elderly father" (115). He imagines the assailants chuckling over Lucy's silence, which to him means conceding a "victory" (110); it is "not her story to spread but theirs: they are its owners" (115). Repeatedly he tries to impose an intellectual narrative on the event, by turns economic ("Too many people, too few things" [98]), feminist ("what women undergo at the hands of men" [111]), or sociological ("it was history acting through them" [156]). While Lucy too recognizes the political context ("what if *that* is the price one has to pay for staying on" [158]), she refuses abstraction and insists on the singularity of her experience, not only for herself but for her rapists: "It was so personal" (156).

Significantly, Lurie tells Lucy, "You did not choose to be the object" (111). To some extent Lucy sees it in the same terms, and describes the intent of the rapists as "Subjection. Subjugation" (159). But from the moment of the attack she resists further subjugation and insists on ownership of her own story. During their first real conversation about the rape, she tells him: "you don't understand what happened to me that day . . . Because you can't" (157). Attempting to prove her wrong, David lays out the facts as he knows them:

> "You were raped. Multiply. By three men."
> "And?"
> You were in fear of your life. You were afraid that after you had been used you would be killed. Disposed of. Because you were nothing to them."
> "And?" Her voice is now a whisper.
> "And I did nothing. I did not save you." (157)

In Lucy's repetition of "And?" we hear how insufficient his version is, how the facts of the event can never be the story of the experience. Trying to provide the emotional truth that surrounds the cold summation, he can only tell his *own* story, the paternal guilt and helplessness that are authentically his.

Similarly, in his genuine and well-intentioned attempt to sympathetically connect with her, he first moves through insufficient narratives — newspaper stories read as a child, the painting of *The Rape of the Sabine Women,* and then, closer to home, his metaphoric self, Byron — but he recognizes that these do not encapsulate Lucy's experience: "From where he stands, from where Lucy stands, Byron looks very old-fashioned indeed" (160). He does not consciously make the association between Lucy and Melanie, between himself and the rapists, between their hatred and his own objectification of women. However, attempting to think himself into her being, he shifts mid-paragraph and finds that he can only "be the men, inhabit them, fill them with the ghost of himself. The question is, does he have it in him to be the woman?" (160).

He does not, and some critics find this failure — this limit of the sympathetic imagination — to be universal in Coetzee's fiction. Pamela Cooper, for example, finds all of Coetzee's women — even the narrators and protagonists — "enigmatic"; their strength and allure stem from unreadability, "an otherness never quite contained within familiar structures of agency or subjectivity." While this observation relates to our earlier discussion of Melanie's function as a narrative device — both in Lurie's self-narrative and in the novel — here Lucy's "unreadability" is an *assertion* of subjectivity, a refusal to be subjugated. As Cooper says:

> Lucy's only recourse is to withhold the narrative of her experience of rape from the men, notably her father, who seek to know and to control its interpretation. By refusing to tell her story she preserves, even as she fills, the gap in the text through which the stories of Coetzee's women seem frustratingly to abscond. (Cooper 2005)

Lucy's decision to bear the child that is the consequence of her rape, and her acceptance of Petrus's proposal, are equally mystifying to David (and therefore, perhaps, to the reader), but she is again unwilling to fully explain or justify her decisions:

> "You behave as if everything I do is part of the story of your life. You are the main character, I am a minor character who doesn't make an appearance until halfway through. Well, contrary to what you think, people are not divided into major and minor. I am not minor. I have a life of my own, just as important to me as yours is to you, and in my life I am the one who makes the decisions." (198)

Lucy's metaphor is of course the novel's reality: *Disgrace* is David's story, not hers, and without her perspective we are left only to speculate on her motives. Her refusal to explain herself to David is an insistence on her subjective right, on a singular consciousness as complex and conflicted as his own. For David, who does not fully understand his *own* life — the decisions he's made and the forces that have shaped him — it should be no surprise that a simple explanation for Lucy's decision is elusive. But even as Coetzee forced us to acknowledge the space where Melanie's story should have been, now he forces us to recognize that Lucy is *not* a narrative foil, insisting that we see her as a fully-formed individual, a "major" character whose true interior life someone else should never expect to fully know. (Throughout the novel Lucy insists on this recognition of subjectivity for others as well as for herself — for Bev, for Petrus, even for her assailants. While David in his rage objectifies Pollux as a "swine" and "jackal," Lucy is able to see "a disturbed child" with an independent existence: "What you think of him is beside the point. He is here . . . he is a fact of life" [206–8].)

David never comes to understand his daughter's decisions, but he comes to accept them; by the end of the novel he has removed himself from Lucy's immediate life and re-established his own separate from hers. It is significant that the last time he sees her in the novel, she is at first not aware that he is there, and he glimpses her in her autonomous life: ". . . here she is, solid in her existence, more solid than he has ever been" (217). David's responsibility is not to completely understand Lucy's life — and certainly not to control it — but to recognize in it a subjective existence, as valid as his own, interconnected but independent: "Visitorship, visitation: a new footing, a new start" (218).

X

> Normally I would say . . . that after a certain age one is too old to learn lessons. One can only be punished and punished. But perhaps that is not true, not always. I wait to see.
>
> — Coetzee, *Disgrace*

I have argued for a gradual but steady progression of Lurie's sympathetic imagination, but I would be oversimplifying the novel to suggest that his path is simple and direct. Coetzee intentionally complicates any redemptive reading of Lurie throughout the book, most obviously in the second Cape Town section: even as the trip itself demonstrates absorption of his lessons, it is also, simultaneously, a return to his old self.

Like his decision to leave Cape Town, David's decision to return goes unnarrated. We are left to infer what his real motives are, and what culmination of changes led to this decision. The move directly follows his conversation about the rape with Lucy, in which Lurie has been forced into a recognition of both his inability to control her story and his own ethical relation to her rapists. We can therefore read in the subsequent return to Cape Town not only a desire to make peace with his past crimes, but an acceptance and exploration of his current role and responsibility: he has removed himself (at least temporarily) from interfering with Lucy's narrative and gone in search of his own. He may not have it in him "to be the woman," but he now has it in himself to be the *father* of a victim; it is important that he does not go to Cape Town to apologize to Melanie, but to her father.

In his conversations with Mr. Isaacs, David demonstrates that he has come to some understanding of the eruption of *eros* that drove his affair with Melanie. While still not taking full responsibility, he has now recognized that it represented a "kindling" of something that lay dormant in him. Possibly in recognition of its potential for destruction as well as its sustaining powers, he has changed his metaphor. "Eros" has now become a "flame-god" [166]. "It could have turned out differently," he says. "But there was something I failed to supply, something . . . lyrical. I lack the lyrical. I manage love too well" (171). Though still incomplete, it is a recognition that his failure was in the attempt to "manage" his humanity, to make no room in his life for the "lyrical" — for deep personal emotions, for true beauty, for flashes of revelation.

Mr. Isaacs' reaction is surprising. Earlier David argued that "redemption belongs to another world, to another universe of discourse" (58), and now Mr. Isaacs says essentially the same thing. "What does God want from you, besides being very sorry?"(172). He points out that since David doesn't pray, he has left himself without a non-secular recourse for redemption, so "God must find his own means of telling you" (172). This echoes Lucy's earlier comment — about David's growing sympathy for animals — that "God moves in mysterious ways." Isaacs is not privy to the ways in which David has already been punished — and moved towards redemption. As readers, however, we are instructed to reread the entire novel in these terms.

As much as returning to Cape Town demonstrates David's progress, however, it is also a return to his old ways, illuminating the flaws of character and ethics that are still deeply ingrained. Though he goes to make peace with the Isaacs family, he ends up fantasizing about Melanie's little sister: "The two of them in the same bed: an experience fit for a king" (164); even in the act of apologizing to Melanie's mother and sister, "the current leaps, the current of desire" (173).

One moment from this scene perfectly encompasses the imperfect and reluctant progress Lurie has made. In conversation over dinner, Lurie presents a simplified narrative of his life on the farm:

> Stitched together in this way, the story unrolls without shadows. Country life, in all its idiot simplicity. How he wishes it could be true! He is tired of shadows, tired of complications, of complicated people. He loves his daughter, but there are times when he wishes she were a simpler being: simpler, neater. The man who raped her, the leader of the gang, was like that. Like a blade cutting the wind. (170)

He longs to be a simpler being, like the man who raped his daughter. It is an extraordinary and terrifying admission of envy, but it is also a recognition of the ways in which he has changed. He used to enjoy the selfish simplicity that comes with the absence of sympathy, the ease of viewing the world without having to consider anyone else's feelings. Now, in the home of the young woman he himself victimized, he both recognizes and laments the fact that he is not the man he was. Significantly, though without a conscious transition, this observation segues into a vision of himself cut open, laid bare, his heart and gall bladder mercilessly examined and discarded. ("The soul, suspended in the dark bitter gall, hiding" [124].)

"[T]here is something unfinished in the business with Melanie" (190), and David goes to see her — although not to talk, and not to apologize. It is an impulse he doesn't fully understand; he wonders if he will get "a flash of feeling, a sign that the affair has not run its course" (190). Instead, seeing her onstage, he realizes that she has, apparently, "grown up, found herself," and understands for the first time that "the trial was a trial for her too . . . perhaps she too has suffered, and come through" (191). While this recognition that their affair was not simply about him is late in arriving, it has finally arrived, in part, through his sympathy for Lucy. (Watching Melanie, he feels "a flush of pride . . . as if she were his daughter" [191].) His vision of Melanie is also an empathetic recognition of Lucy's trial, separate from his own, and a sign of hope that she too will "come through."

He has recognized Melanie's independent existence, acknowledged that while he may have influenced her narrative he never owned it, that it continues without him autonomous and unknowable. This vision of Melanie erupts into a "waking dream," as David is overcome by "images of women that he has known" (192):

> What has happened to them, all those women, all those lives? Are there moments when they, too, or some of them, are plunged without warning into the ocean of memory? The German girl: is it possible that at this very instant she is remembering the man who picked her up on the roadside in Africa and spent the night with her?
> *Enriched:* that was the word the newspapers picked on to jeer at. A stupid word to let slip, under the circumstances, yet now, at this moment, he would stand by it. By Melanie, by the girl in Touws River; by Rosalind, Bev Shaw, Soraya: by each of them he was enriched, and by others too, even the least of them, even the failures. Like a flower blooming in his breast, his heart floods with thankfulness. (192)

It is an epiphany that seems to encompass *eros,* God, and grace through genuine emotion and gratitude. He is now able to see that the women he has known have also known him, that they may be remembering him, seeing him through their own subjective perspectives. It is an understanding of desire, of the "problem of sex," that recognizes interconnection and mutual subjectivity, that allows for "complications, complicated people," for "lives all tangled with his" (192).

But Coetzee refuses to end this section on a note of grace. At this most subjective and sympathetic moment, David is driven from the theater by his first accuser, Ryan: the personification of a public, objective, unsympathetic view of himself. This entire section has confronted him with visions of himself through the incomplete understanding of others, and thus been a prolonged exercise in the surrender of subjectivity. What's more, Lurie is reminded that these women he remembers may not remember *him* as fondly from their own subjective perspectives. "Melanie will spit in your eye if she sees you," Ryan tells him, and, despite his increased awareness, Lurie "had not expected that" (194).

Faced with this verdict he regresses to his old comforting narrative, picking up a young prostitute, "younger even than Melanie." Post-orgasmic, he is "drowsy, contented, also strangely protective" (194). He does in fact have one more revelation — a sudden understanding of himself:

> Not a bad man but not good either. Not cold but not hot, even at his hottest. Not by the measure of Teresa; not even by the measure of Byron.

Lacking in fire. Will that be the verdict on him, the verdict of the universe and its all-seeing eye? (195)

It is his verdict on himself, and at this point it is a fair one; this entire section has tested his nature after the experiences in the country, and still found him lacking: not a bad man, but not a good man either. Fire warms and burns, eros is both enriching and destructive. But the final verdict of the all-seeing eye — whether we take that to mean God or reader — is not yet in on Lurie, and will not even be certain at the novel's close.

XI

> "Then my point would be," says the young man, "that it is the humanities and the humanities alone . . . that will allow us to steer our way through this new multicultural world, and precisely, precisely" — he almost hammers the table, so excited has he grown — "because the humanities are about reading and interpretation."
> — Coetzee, *Elizabeth Costello*

> To whom this writing then? The answer: to you but not to you; to me; to you in me.
> — Coetzee, *Age of Iron*

Finally we come to the most important sympathetic thread interwoven throughout *Disgrace*: the composition of David's opera. During the early scenes with Soraya it is described as a "meditation on love between the sexes" (4). Lurie at this point is clearly unqualified to write such a meditation, and so the seed is planted that this opera will be an expression of his struggle to solve "the problem of sex," another narrative by which we can track his emotional and sympathetic capacity. As opposed to the "tedium" of his scholarship, the opera represents a *creative* project, and as such may be an expression of *eros* in a more productive direction. However, just as he denies his emotional life in the first half of the novel, so does he avoid this interior manifestation; for most of the novel it remains a theoretical project he keeps putting off. (Significantly, he turns to it in moments of boredom or isolation — during his hiatus between affairs [11], and during times of estrangement from Lucy [121, 180–86, 210–15].)

Only as Lurie's sympathetic imagination develops does the project begin to take shape. When it finally does, both the form and content of the opera increasingly reflect the changes within him. He first intends it to focus on Byron during "the last big love-affair of his life" (15); this is how he describes it in attempting to seduce Melanie, reflecting his romantic self-image and his desire to maintain his place "at the sweet banquet of the senses" (24). After his exile and scandal, however, slightly humbled and out of place, Lurie describes the opera with marginally lowered ambitions: instead of grandiose orchestration he now inclines "toward a very meagre accompaniment" (63). Significantly, at this point he plans to write the words — the logical narrative — but to borrow the music from other composers.

Just as he has his narrative authority taken from him in the attack, however, he also loses his textual foundation for the piece: his Byron books are all lost with the stolen car. "But does he need to go on reading?" He should, he thinks, be able now to "invent a Byron who is true to Byron, and a Teresa too" (121). Reflecting his changes, the composition of the opera shifts from an intellectual exercise to a sympathetic one: in creating his characters he now draws on his own emotional reserves. Over the weeks that follow, we hear the tension between his faltering understanding and his stubborn resistance: though he can hear "fragments," his attempt to force onto the piece his pre-conceived narrative stifles him; the "project is not moving" (141). Only after undergoing many of the conscious and unconscious revelations we have already discussed does it become possible for him to forsake his romantic models ("Who have not, he must say, guided him well" [179]), and reconceive his opera.

At first the opera reveals Lurie's association with Byron, the aging seducer. For Byron, "Teresa's soaring arias ignite no spark in him; his own vocal line, dark, convoluted, goes past, through, over her" (180). It is a fair approximation of Lurie's previous relation to the women in his life: his "vocal line," his consciousness as revealed in the narration, has "gone past, through, over" first Soraya, then Melanie, then Lucy, superseding their narratives and denying their experience. Now, however, Byron is moved off-stage, "long dead" (181). Teresa — formerly dismissed and objectified as Byron's "bitch-mate" — takes over the narrative. Lurie is determined to give a voice to this forgotten woman: not the "Teresa that history has bequeathed him" (181) — the one passed down through the narratives of men — but a Teresa he is now capable of discovering within himself. Similarly, it is now the words (for example, *"Che vuol dir . . ."* [213]) he borrows. The music — the emotion — comes from within. "He is inventing the music (or the music is inventing him)" (186).

What is important to note, however, is how the *narration* of this process changes to reveal a David Lurie we have not met before in *Disgrace*. After the austere minimalism of language throughout most of the novel — the solipsistic limitation of Lurie's subjective reality in Cape Town, and the more objective, reactive physicality of the Salem sections — the narration now moves effortlessly back and forth between lush descriptions of his imagined settings, the emotional speculations of his characters, and Lurie's energetic efforts to realize them. Once an "indifferent scholar" and "never passionate," new words appear to capture Lurie's engagement and amazement at what he is creating, at what is happening to him and through him. Melodies "blessedly" reveal themselves, "astonishingly" (183): "He spends whole days in the grip of Byron and Teresa" (185). There is, for the first time, poetry and passion in the narration of Lurie's consciousness; he has learned to supply the lyrical.

There is also, importantly, a culmination of self-awareness, a now conscious acknowledgement of not only the changes he has undergone but also the source and significance of those changes. He knows, for example, that it was "first on Lucy's farm" that the original concept "failed to engage the core of him" (181). In the wake of his experiences, he is now able to recognize that there was "something misconceived about it, something that does not come from the heart" (181). Having previously asked himself whether he has it in him "to be the woman," Lurie now asks of Teresa: "Can he find it in his heart to love this plain, ordinary woman? Can he love her enough to write a music for her? If he cannot, what is left for him?" (182).

The David Lurie who considered his temperament "fixed, set" (2) is now, we see, not only changed but almost desperate for further change. "Will an older Teresa engage his heart as his heart is now?" (181). It is a recognition that in this newborn sympathetic imagination lies his only hope of grace.

The final chapter of the novel opens from a surprising, sustained point of view — Teresa's:

> In her white nightdress Teresa stands at the bedroom window. Her eyes are closed. It is the darkest hour of the night: she breathes deeply, breathing in the rustle of the wind, the belling of the bullfrogs. (213)

We are, as always, inside Lurie's mind, but Lurie is inside Teresa's: he has become, finally, our narrator, the tentative recognizer of someone else's subjectivity. Though it reads like a text within a text, this is of course not his opera, or not any opera that will ever be confined to a page: this is Lurie's sympathetic imagination at work, and we now read him through *his* reading of Teresa:

> Sitting at his table in the dog-yard, he harkens to the sad, swooping curve of Teresa's plea as she confronts the darkness. This is a bad time of the month for Teresa, she is sore, she has not slept a wink, she is haggard with longing. She wants to be rescued — from the pain, from the summer heat, from the Villa Gamba, from her father's bad temper, from everything. (213)

As Lurie imagines himself into the experience of Teresa (with echoes of Lucy), the two narrations almost merge. The banjo in his hands becomes a mandolin in Teresa's; she "sits staring out over the marshes towards the gates of hell," while he "sits at his own desk staring out on the overgrown garden" (184). Our reading of Lurie seems to slip in and out of the opera, sometimes as Teresa, sometimes as Byron, and yet:

> He is in the opera neither as Teresa nor as Byron nor even as some blending of the two: he is held in the music itself, in the flat, tinny slap of the banjo strings, the voice that strains to soar away from the ludicrous. (185)

It is too much to say that he has, finally, found it within himself "to be the woman"; perhaps that is not even, ultimately, a desirable goal. But he has found it within himself to *love* the woman, to put himself for moments in her place, to imagine and support her narrative without controlling it. After trying to shoehorn Teresa into the role history has bequeathed, after creating false and self-serving stage-pieces for Soraya and Melanie, after trying to define and direct Lucy's story, Lurie has arrived at finally at this still-uncertain capacity for sympathetic imagining.

If, as I've suggested, Lurie's narrative embrace of Teresa is an active, semi-conscious move towards redemption, it is also a willing invitation to grace: something that acts upon us, something that may be given to us — gifted to us, deserved or not — if we are only open to it. In Coetzee's extraordinary novel, it is no coincidence that one of the ways in which grace is finally gifted to Lurie is through art. "So this is art, he thinks, and this is how it does its work! How strange! How fascinating" (185). The subject of art is not always easy to explain — "How can he ever explain . . . what Teresa and her lover have done to deserve being brought back to this world?" (212) — and it sometimes — usually — falls short of our ambitious expectations. ("Poor Teresa! Poor aching girl! He has brought her back from the grave, promised her another life, and now he is failing her" [214].)

This "failure" may be a sign of hope for Lurie's future. It is key to our understanding of the novel's end that Lurie does *not* complete his opera, does not even write it down. He is not shaping Teresa's story, he is seeking to understand it, seeking to find it within himself and to find himself within it. ("Why do I write about him?" Mrs. Curran asks of Verceuil in *Age of Iron*. "Because in the look he gives me I see myself in a way that can be written . . . When I write about him I write about myself" [9].) Like David's own story, like Lucy's story, Teresa's story is open ended, resisting conscious determination and easy definition. It will not be romanticized — blown up into "lush arias" (184) — and it will not be unambiguous. The "problem of sex" cannot, and should not, be solved: simplicity, as we've seen, only comes with the denial of emotion, the omission of complexity, the subjugation of viewpoints. Narrative lines are never clean and unambiguous, unless the tale is that of *fall* from grace: falling is always straight.

Just as Coetzee refuses to impose an authorial judgment throughout — insisting on the integrity of Lurie's subjective experience — so, at the end of *Disgrace,* does he resist the artificiality of closure. The end of the novel finds Lurie still uncertain about his own goodness, but even as he protests "it is too late for me," we recognize his acknowledgement that becoming a good person is "not a bad resolution to make, in dark times" (216). Even as he protests that he "lacks the virtues of the old: equanimity, kindliness, patience" (217), we know that Lurie — who is not really, after all, an old man — may yet learn to be a grandfather. We recognize that he is at last able to give "what he no longer has difficulty calling by its proper name: love" (219), even when love means — as it does with Lucy, as it does with Driepoot in the final scene — surrendering control of the narration and selflessly letting go. "Normally I would say . . . that after a certain age one is too old to learn lessons," Lurie says to Mr. Isaacs. "One can only be punished and punished. But perhaps that is not true, not always. I wait to see" (172).

Fire can warm and burn, eros is both enriching and destructive, and God — if there is a God — may find His own way of telling us what we need to know. Grace, like the workings of art, like the experience of emotion, comes to us in ways we can't predict, and sometimes in ways we cannot ourselves perceive:

> As for recognizing it, he will leave that to the scholars of the future, if there are still scholars by then. For he will not hear the note himself, when it comes, if it comes — he knows too much about art and the ways of art to expect that. (214)

As he has done throughout his work, Coetzee resists — even renounces — the "all-seeing eye" of the novelist. The novel's ethical dilemmas remain unresolved, and its characters may not fully connect with one another or reveal themselves to us, but by embodying these limitations the narrative ultimately transcends them. Lurie may not hear the notes of immortal longing, the notes of grace, but Coetzee charges us, the scholars of the future, to strain to hear them through the *plink-plunk* of the narrative banjo, through Lurie's limited understanding of himself. In the always imperfect effort to look beyond the apparent limits of sympathy, it may yet be possible to find grace — in the deeper, more human sense of the word.

Notes

[1] Margaret Lenta makes an interesting observation about Coetzee's memoirs that could just as easily apply to the narrative representation of David Lurie's reality in *Disgrace:* "Few people who have read *Boyhood* and *Youth* can have failed to register that the child and young man at their centre is emotionally stunted, unable to make real contact with others. . . . Access to the mind of the protagonist is essential if

the reader is to understand him. And the sense that the reader receives, of the protagonist's mind being closed to all but himself, is also important."

[2] See Attridge (2004), 32–64, for a discussion of how the narration of *Life & Times of Michael K* distances the reader from the protagonist of that novel.

[3] It is a misstatement that nonetheless persistently clouds Coetzee's work. John Lanchester, for example, describes Lurie as the "narrator" of *Disgrace* in his otherwise excellent review of Coetzee's *Slow Man* in *The New York Review of Books*. And in the American editions of *Boyhood* and *Youth,* even the cover blurbs refer to the protagonist as the "narrator," though the books are written in the third-person. As Coetzee has said, "To rewrite *Boyhood* and *Youth* with *I* substituted for *he* throughout would land you up with two books only remotely related to the originals" (Quoted in Attridge, *Ethics*, 140).

[4] It is even possible that Soraya's disappearance from Discreet Escorts has nothing at all to do with Lurie — but this, of course, would not occur to him.

[5] For example, see Grant Farred, "The Mundanacity of Violence," 352–62.

[6] In *The Vehement Passions*, Philip Fisher explores the moments of clarity that come with strong emotional states — anger, shame, grief, wonder, fear; the intensity of these states, as exceptions to normal experience, have the capacity to map the limits of our subjective power and redefine our moral relationship to the world. Actually using the example of a confrontation with a home invader in his discussion of fear, Fisher says the situation confronts us "with the interpenetration of wills, the modeling of fear in a world where it is no longer possible to act by consulting only your own reading of a situation," and thus becomes "a strange example of sympathy" (Fisher, 128).

2: Beyond Sympathy: A Bakhtinian Reading of *Disgrace*

James Boobar

> We are invited to understand and sympathize. But there is a limit to sympathy.
> — David Lurie to students in his "The Romantics" course in *Disgrace*

> Dostoevsky says "it is simply not good enough to look in your heart and write, that what comes out, when you write is quite as likely to be some self-serving lie as it is to be the ruthless truth about yourself." . . . [M]y sympathy is wholly with Dostoevsky.
> — J. M. Coetzee in an interview with Eleanor Wachtel, *Brick* 67 (2001), 45

I

AT DAVID LURIE'S FEET, the crippled dog Driepoot "sits up, cocks its head, listens" to the sound of the banjo, and in response to Lurie's humming voice "smacks its lips and seems on the point of singing too, or howling" (*Disgrace*, 215). Earlier, Lurie has asked himself: "Why pretend to be a chum when in fact one is a murderer?" (143), and yet at the end of the novel, bearing the crippled dog in his arms, "giving it what he no longer has difficulty in calling by its proper name: love" (219), Lurie escorts Driepoot to annihilation. As Driepoot's "period of grace is almost over; soon it will have to submit to the needle" (215), there seems to be no other choice for Lurie but to relieve Driepoot of the suffering he'll surely endure as a homeless, crippled animal in a township teeming with neglected dogs. But, perhaps, Lurie hastens the end of Driepoot's period of grace, refusing to "save the young dog . . . for another week" (219). In doing so, Lurie annihilates a week of Driepoot's affection streaming against him, of the cocked expression and sensitive eyes trained on him, of play, and the sharpness of an animal alive to each passing moment. Considering Lurie's choice to forego a week, his selfless act of sacrifice for Driepoot seemingly carries within it a shadow of turning away from the possibilities and responsibilities of dialogic engagement, and of turning towards the "proper business of the old: preparing to die" (9). As Coetzee's character Fyodor Dostoevsky concludes in *The Master of Petersburg*: "Death is a metaphor for nothing. Death is death" (118).

Thinking of Lurie's actions at the end of the novel *Disgrace* it may be helpful to consider Coetzee's words about his own essay, "Confession and Double Thoughts":

> In terms brought into prominence in the essay, the debate is between cynicism and grace. Cynicism: the denial of any ultimate basis for values. Grace: a condition in which the truth can be told clearly, without blindness. The debate is staged by Dostoevsky; the interlocutors are called Stavrogin and Tikhon. (*Doubling*, 392)

Coetzee considers this essay "pivotal," as its writing highlighted for him the problem of "how to tell the truth in autobiography" (391–92). Russian literary critic Mikhail Bakhtin's concept of "authoring the self" runs parallel with autobiography, with choices and responses signifying the "words" to the event of writing one's life. As one of Bakhtin's commentators, Michael Holquist writes:

> I am always answerable for the response that is generated from the unique place I occupy in existence . . . Bakhtin conceives existence as the kind of book we call a novel, or more accurately as many novels, for all of us write our own such text, a text that is then called our life. (Holquist, 30)

In considering the acts Lurie undertakes as he authors his life at the conclusion of *Disgrace,* Eleanor Wachtel would seemingly situate his choices within the realm of grace. She writes of Coetzee's work *Elizabeth Costello*:

> His fictional novelist examines animal rights, argues for vegetarianism, and concludes that there is no limit to the extent to which we can think ourselves into the being of another. There are no bounds to the sympathetic imagination. (45)

With this view, Lurie's decision to euthanize Driepoot signals Lurie's movement from selfishness to selflessness and his awakened ability to sympathize with the dreary plight of another without expecting anything in return. The reading of cynicism, on the other hand, finds Lurie's narcissism pitched in a new key, but present all the same, translating the death of another being to provide meaning in Lurie's life even while he escorts Driepoot to his end.

In his further reflection on the difficulties of telling the story about one's self, Coetzee writes: "The only sure truth in autobiography is that one's self-interest will be located at one's blind spot" (*Doubling,* 392). While viewing the novel's conclusion between the polarities of grace and cynicism may risk oversimplification, we may still question: Where is Lurie's blind spot? With Bakhtin, we may question further: Where is the blind spot as Lurie's authors his life?

Wondering if he would dare insert Driepoot into his opera, Lurie asks himself: "Surely, in a work that will never be performed, all things are permitted?" (215). As Coetzee has written extensively on Dostoevsky, including an entire novel narrated from the point of view of Fyodor Dostoevsky, it is hard not to hear Ivan Karamazov from *The Brothers Karamazov* within Lurie's question. Outlining Ivan's belief, Dostoevsky writes that "were mankind's belief in its immortality to be destroyed, not only love but also any living power to continue the life of the world would at once dry up in it. Not only that, but nothing would be immoral any longer, everything would be permitted" (*Brothers Karamazov*, 109). Ivan, the ultimate cynic in Coetzee's formulation of cynicism, stands behind, as it were, Lurie's musings on his opera and Driepoot. Driepoot, of course, doesn't end up in Lurie's opera, but rather, as Bakhtin might say, wanders into Lurie's "own perception of the world that is incarnated in his action and in his discourse" (*Dialogic Imagination*, 335). While Coetzee's novel pushes against any sentimentalizing of the relationship between Lurie and Driepoot, we may still find ourselves wanting to "return the ticket," as Ivan did, and in doing so reject the world Lurie makes, his self-bolstering sympathy gained through euthanasia. But, surely Lurie has grown beyond his narcissism? Then: A question reverberating from Chernyshevsky, through Dostoevsky, and Coetzee arises: "What is to be done?" (*Disgrace*, 129). Nothing?

II

Throughout the novel, Lurie is consistently questioning his world, and any Bakhtinian reading of Lurie's path, which ends with him escorting Driepoot to his death, needs to address the role of questions as illuminated by Bakhtin's notion of dialogism. We can begin by considering an exchange with Petrus, during which Lurie asks himself: "the question is, what is the answer?" (114).

Without the comma, the sentence poses a certain question, but with the comma present the sentence illustrates the interaction of a dialogue: the question — that is, the presentness of the question — poised against the answer which is as yet unknown. The phrase seems to signal Lurie's consciousness as dialogic; or as a consciousness coming into being through collisions that move his consciousness to an as yet unspoken word, what Caryl Emerson calls, "[towards] the possibility of change, of some forward movement" (*The First 100 Years*, 152).

Yet viewing Lurie's question as representative of dialogism quickly becomes problematic because it seems to lack a crucial element: *otherness*. As Holquist writes:

> In dialogism, the very capacity to have consciousness is based on *otherness*. This otherness is not merely a dialectical alienation on its way to a sublimation that will endow it with a unifying identity in higher consciousness. On the contrary: in dialogism consciousness *is* otherness. (Holquist, 18)

In other words, the mere presence of questions doesn't necessarily mark a consciousness as dialogic. In Lurie's case, his question may be a display of solipsistic narcissism. While the question reverberates with two phrases in dialogue, Lurie doesn't seem engaged with *otherness*. Further, engaging otherness and outsidedness carries ethical burdens for Bakhtin because in his view we can only see our selves through dialogic interaction with the world. As Holquist explains:

> Addressivity means rather that I am an event, the event of constantly responding to utterances from the different worlds I pass through . . . at a basic biological level, thirst does not just exist in the natural world, it happens to me and lack of water means nothing without the response of thirst. (Holquist, 48)

As thirst is created by the thirsty, we are created by:

> constant choices, each of which has consequences. Choice is an act in so far as it effects a change between what is said and what was, and thus the act is simultaneous with the difference that defines it. (Holquist, 154)

Because human beings write their lives in dialogue with the world and nothing can happen in isolation, and because choices bear consequences when brought into conflict with the world in dialogue, the life of a human being is an open-ended event. Bakhtin writes: "Nothing conclusive has yet taken place in the world, the ultimate word of the world and about the world has not yet been spoken, the world is open and free, everything is still in the future and will always be in the future" (*Dostoevsky's Poetics*, 166). So Lurie's phrase may indicate his attempt at ultimately avoiding dialogue in the Bakhtinian sense by evading otherness. Similarly, his sympathetic gesture towards Driepoot may be seen as ultimately monologic, dialogue-destroying. But still, Lurie's continual questioning in the novel, and the narrator's relentless questioning of Lurie, combined with his often self-touted status as a reified person incapable of change, certainly warrant consideration as representative of a dialogic consciousness working towards a "new word."

III

Lurie's view of himself and his world is made clear from the opening lines of *Disgrace*: "For a man of his age, fifty-two, he has, to his mind, solved the problem of sex rather well" (1). Lurie sees himself, in Bakhtin's view, as a "finalized" person, and the world as a place where opportunities may be reduced to problems that need solving. The narrator writes, "His sentiments are, he is aware, complacent, even uxorious. Nevertheless he does not cease to hold to them" (2). In perhaps the most glaring example of a consciousness both finalized and finalizing, the narrator writes:

> That is his temperament. His temperament is not going to change, he is too old for that. His temperament is fixed, set. The skull, followed by the temperament: the two hardest parts of the body. Follow your temperament. It is not a philosophy, he would not dignify it with that name. It is a rule, like the Rule of St. Benedict. (2)

As events unfold, Lurie's reified approach to the world is challenged but prevails. For example, in seducing his student Melanie, Lurie spins a well-worn narrative — "barely a term passes when he does not fall for one or other of his charges" (11–12) — of young, sexy beauty that "does not belong to her alone," but rather "is part of the bounty she brings into the world" (16). He champions his sexual liaison when in front of the committee investigating the matter, claiming that he was "a servant of Eros" (52). He pleads guilty, and professing self-awareness claims, "I have not sought counselling nor do I intend to seek it. I am a grown man. I am not receptive to being counselled" (49).

Lurie's reified self-image, however, is challenged dialogically by the narrative's reliance on questions which serve to undermine and complicate a finalizing interpretation of a consciousness that is fixed. From the opening lines, questions highlight Lurie's blind spots, suggesting both the process of the question engaged with some unknown answer and Lurie's inadequate knowledge of himself. In fact, Lurie's questions often immediately complicate his own point of view. Coetzee writes that Lurie "lives within his income, within his temperament, within his emotional means," but the claim is immediately complicated with the question: "Is he happy?" Lurie's reaction is quickly noted: "By most measurements, yes, he believes he is. However, he has not forgotten the last chorus of *Oedipus:* Call no man happy until he is dead" (2). The question calls forth an immediate response, the confidence of which is undermined in the very words used in the response. He believes he is. Believes, but does not know.

Questions often serve as Lurie's attempts to strategize or read the other. Referring to Soraya, Lurie thinks: "Is Soraya's totem the snake, too?" (3). When seducing Melanie, he asks himself, "What, in her heart, is she trying to be?" (27). But even in attempting to "read" Melanie, questions bring the limits of his self-awareness into view. Lurie reassures Melanie of his self-mastery by saying, "I won't let it go too far," but the narrator immediately adds, "Too far. What is far, what is too far, in a matter like this? Is her too far the same as his too far?" (19). After thinking to "rename" her Meláni, Lurie wonders "what else has he not guessed about her?" (37). Lurie's questions often involve discovering, even imposing, erotic narratives on others. Regarding Melanie, he thinks: "What is she offering him? Mistress? Lover?" When meeting Melanie's father, Lurie thinks: "Does the man have adventures?" (165). With Beverly Shaw: "Can he love an ordinary woman?" (182). And thinking of his own experience with the women in his life, Lurie asks himself: "Where do moments like this come from? Hypnagogic, no doubt; but what does that explain? If he is being led, then what god is doing the leading?" (192). Undoubtedly, Lurie's understanding of the erotic other varies from Melanie to Beverly Shaw, especially as he asks himself regarding Bev: "Should he trust Bev Shaw to teach him a lesson?" (210). But the questions find commonality in Lurie's attempts to locate himself in relation to the other. In reexamining his ability to understand Lucy's suffering, Lurie asks himself: "does he have it in him to be the woman?" (160). The question is, what is the answer.

Throughout the narrative, Lurie's questioning expands beyond an encounter with the other and serves to highlight his own ethical or existential engagement with his world. Indeed, questions that display Lurie on the cusp of the "new word" haunt his claim of knowing himself as a finished temperament, as when he asks himself during the ordeal at Lucy's house, "how will they stand up to the testing, he and his heart?" (94). Questions serve to signal Lurie's attempt at understanding the place and position of others in respect to their experiences, and serve to initiate his deepening awareness of others. Regarding Lucy, Lurie thinks: "She is here because she loves the land and the old, *ländliche* way of life. If that way of life is doomed, what is left for her to love?" (113). But, regarding the rape, Coetzee presents Lurie's dialogic consciousness struggling between questions that may produce a new word, while at the same time presenting the limits of the sympathetic imagination. Lurie thinks: "Do they think he has not suffered with his daughter? What more could he have witnessed than he is capable of imagining? Or do they think that, where rape is concerned, no man can be where the woman is. Whatever the answer, he is outraged, outraged at being treated like an outsider" (140–41).

But beyond the illustration of the sympathetic, Coetzee consistently uses questions to represent Lurie questioning his place in the world, especially after the attack: "Why has he taken this job?" (145); "What is on his heart?" (165); "Fallen? Yes, there has been a fall, no doubt about that. But *mighty*? Does *mighty* describe him?" (167). After the dramatic gesture of falling on his knees in front of Melanie's mother and sister, Lurie wonders:

"Is that enough?" (173). Upon returning to his home in Cape Town: "What comes after the end of roaming? . . . The life of a superannuated scholar, without hope, without prospect: is that what he is prepared to settle for?" (175). Having left the Eastern Cape for a while, Lurie thinks that "the dogs released from life within the walls of the clinic will be tossed into the fire unmarked, unmourned" and asks himself: "For that betrayal, will he ever be forgiven?" (178). It's tempting to rephrase Lurie's words: Lurie is, what is the answer?

Perhaps most telling of Lurie's questioning for a new word occurs while he is watching Lucy working among her flowers. He watches the woman who was once "a little tadpole in her mother's body" and who from within will issue "another existence." He refers to himself as a grandfather, and immediately asks himself: "What pretty girl can he expect to be wooed into bed with a grandfather?" Importantly, though, as it underscores the notion that it is not the mere presence of questions that suggests the dialogic but rather the representation of the dialogic through questions engaging, teasing, complicating each other, Lurie asks two lines later: "What will it entail, being a grandfather?" (217). Grandfather. The new word?

While not always indicative of dialogism, Lurie's questions seem to indicate a consciousness amidst dialogic addressivity, and a self struggling to author itself in response to the world. Caryl Emerson writes:

> Bakhtin does not do beginnings and ends. He only does middles. Wholly committed to process and to the dynamics of response, Bakhtin concerns himself very little with how something starts (a personality, a responsibility) or how it might be brought to an effective well-shaped end. (*First 100 Years*, 157)

The question remains: Why does consideration of Lurie's dialogic consciousness, amid the middle of process, rely on the notion of sympathy in the critical closing of the novel?

IV

Indeed, it is difficult to overestimate the importance of Lurie's initiation into a higher ethical awareness of other beings, human and animal, as the novel concludes, especially if we consider Coetzee's words on the suffering body. He writes:

> And again let me again be unambiguous: it is not that one *grants* the authority of the suffering body: the suffering body *takes* this authority: that is its power. To use other words: its power is undeniable.
>
> (Let me add, *entirely* parenthetically, that I, as a person, as a personality, am overwhelmed, that my thinking is thrown into confusion and

helplessness, by the fact of the suffering in the world, and not only human suffering. These fictional constructions of mine are paltry, ludicrous defenses against that being-overwhelmed, and, to me, transparently so.) (*Doubling*, 248)

Whereas Lurie failed to respond to the troubled Melanie, but rather exploited her vulnerability, Lurie responds to the suffering Driepoot. Laura Wright writes:

> The voiceless dog, as representative of absolute alterity — that which evades attempts at imagined identification — in Coetzee's work, becomes a pivot around which altruistic, ethical action is centered. Because we have no access to the interiority of the dog, human response to canine suffering must be based on reasons other than the dog's ability to express gratitude or to ask for help. (Wright, 35)

Enhanced by sympathetic understanding, especially after the torments he and his daughter have suffered, Lurie responds to what he perceives as the inevitable course of Driepoot's life with love and tenderness. Lurie seemingly experiences the heart of Coetzee's ethos. Wright writes:

> Coetzee's writing is filled with dogs, both metaphorical and real, and the dog is what really matters, the primal and essential "other," the locus for all human potential reciprocity, and ultimately as itself, a being deserving of recognition, of care, and perhaps, primarily, of acknowledgement. (Wright, 51)

And one of Bakhtin's most famous translators and commentators provides words that would support a sympathetic reading of Lurie's actions as powerful. Caryl Emerson writes:

> For what matters ultimately to human beings and what generates value in our lives rests on two factors: first, where we turn for help, and then, *the time put in.* (*First 100 Years,* 158)

In his role as *harijan*, Lurie puts in the time to honor the euthanized dogs. With Driepoot, what generates value in Lurie's life is the care and attentiveness with which he'll escort and comfort him in his final moments. And Lurie's time put in, it seems, will continue long after the text concludes.

In addressing Lurie's loving accompaniment to "throw away" dogs, it seems he succeeds where Coetzee's character Fyodor Dostoevsky in *The Master of Petersburg* fails. Dostoevsky comes upon a dog chained to a drain pipe and thinks to himself: "Is this what I will be doing for the rest of my days, he wonders: peering into the eyes of dogs and beggars?" (81). He leaves the dog chained in the cold night, and later in the room he is renting, he ponders the meaning of the encounter, attempting to read the event for signs that generate some meaning in his life. Coetzee's narrator writes: "'Raise up that least thing and cherish it': . . . is the least thing the dog, abandoned in the cold? Is the dog the thing he must release and take with him and feed and cherish, or is it the filthy, drunken beggar in his tattered coat under the bridge?" (81–82). Still unsure of the sign, Dostoevsky returns to the snow-covered street. Coetzee writes:

> He suspects he will not save the dog, not his night nor even the next night, if there is to be a next night. He is waiting for a sign, and he is betting (there is no grander word he dare use) that the dog is not the sign, is not a sign at all, is just a dog among many dogs howling in the night. But he knows too that as long as he tries by cunning to distinguish things that are things from things that are signs he will not be saved . . . he is at wits' end, like a dog on a chain that breaks the teeth that gnaw it. And beware, beware, he reminds himself: the dog on the chain, the second dog, is nothing in itself, is not an illumination, merely an animal likeness! (83)

To Wright, Dostoevsky's reading for signs beyond the obvious present and future suffering of the dog constitutes a failure of the sympathetic imagination and an ethical disgrace. She writes:

> Dostoevsky's belief that the dog tied out in the cold is not the sign that he is seeking enables him to continue to search for esoteric signs instead of reacting to the explicit suffering taking place directly in front of him. (Wright, 22)

Interestingly, Dostoevsky, like Lurie, is seen as relying on questions to engage the world. In Bakhtinian terms, questions become the words in the text of Dostoevsky's self-authoring. It seems especially harsh, however, that Dostoevsky authors himself into the dog's plight via symbolism and analogy. Dostoevsky fails to react to the immediacy of the dog's suffering and instead, through an interpretative exercise, becomes determined to invite a beggar into his warm room. Unlike Lurie, Dostoevsky fails to release the dog: "an opportunity for leaving himself as he is behind and becoming what he might yet be has passed" (82). Summing up Dostoevsky's ethical crime, Wright writes:

> If one is always waiting to see signs, one may miss the opportunity to act in terms of the immediate, and the animal runs the risk of always being viewed as a sign; the dog may continually be viewed as metaphorical in a context that does not recognize as legitimate the interstitial spaces between the binary oppositions of animal and human, a context in which there is no respect for the alterity of the animal. (Wright, 44)

While Dostoevsky reads the dog for its "power as simile or symbol" and not "as a being who suffers unjustly" (Wright, 47), Lurie responds with love and responsibility for Driepoot's plight. Dostoevsky reads the dog as a possible clue to reveal something about the mystery that has become his life, while Lurie, so the argument goes, sees the dog as a particular being

— not a representational sign, as he saw Melanie in the earlier part of the novel. While Dostoevsky continues to act from "*Perversion*: everything and everyone to be turned to another use, to be gripped to him and fall with him" (*Master,* 235), Lurie acts with sympathy. But as we've seen Lurie's consciousness as dialogic in his questioning, we can't help but consider the blind spots of sympathy.

V

Rather than an increased sensitivity, a heightened ethical awareness (Derek Attridge calls it a "grace"), for Bakhtin, sympathy and empathy were incompatible with a world that is fundamentally rife with dialogism. He writes:

> Understanding cannot be understood as emotional empathy, or as the placing of oneself in another's place (the loss of one's own place). This is required only for the peripheral aspects of understanding. Understanding cannot be understood as translation from someone else's language into one's own language. (Cited in *Dostoevsky's Poetics,* xxxiii)

For Bakhtin, the loss of one's place for the merging into another's point of view or the usurpation of another's point of view shatters the "surprisingness" of the future-oriented, unfinished dialogic world in favor of the closed, finished interaction of monological unity in which the other is finalized and the possibility for the interaction of two colliding viewpoints silenced. Bakhtin's famous example of dialogic interaction involves imagining two people standing face to face. Each person needs the other in order to gain a richer understanding of their particular position. Each person is blind to what is behind him, while each person has privileged knowledge of what is behind the other. Should one give up his own point of view for the other's, or usurp the other's point of view, the result would be a unity that diminishes any surplus gained by dialogism. Responding to the often lauded ethical approach of seeing the world from the other's point of view, Bakhtin writes: "What would I have to gain if another were to fuse with me? He would see and know only what I already see and know, he would repeat in himself the inescapable closed circle of my own life; let him rather remain outside of me" (cited in *Bakhtin, Creation of Prosaics,* 54). Only in facing the other and asking him/her what is behind me will I see what is behind me, and vice versa.

The shedding of one ethical or emotional position for another's, even momentarily, is at best mock dialogue and at worst illusory dialogue that results in a mirage, a monological relation to the other, a co-opting or obliteration of the other. It prevents any new word in an unfinished world to emerge from the event of the interaction of two or more points of view. In other words, while often held as the beginning point of high ethical standards, sympathy can be seen as preventing the possibilities for the emergence of the new, becoming only a refraction, a shadow, of the "last word being spoken" on the world. As Holquist concludes:

> For in order to see ourselves, we must appropriate the vision of others. Restated in its crudest version, the Bakhtinian just-so story of subjectivity is the tale of how I get myself from the other: it is only the other's categories that will let me be an object for my own perception. I see myself as I conceive others might see it. In order to forge a self, I must do so from the *outside*. In other words, I *author myself*." (Holquist, 28)

As being is a simultaneous and shared experience, a co-being, sympathy runs the risk of ending the dialogue necessary for the authoring of the self. If we need other, "outside" points of view to author our selves, co-opting another's point of view or giving away our own point of view results in the diminishment of the ability to ultimately author our life. Sympathy, then, according to Bakhtin, obliterates that which is necessary for the authoring of the self: *otherness*. Otherness allows the self to author itself, to gain the "outsidedness" necessary to understand the self. Holquist continues:

> The act of creating a self is not free: we *must*, we *all* must, create ourselves, for the self is not given to any one of us. Or, as Bakhtin puts it, "we have no alibi in existence." (Holquist, 28–29)

As we have no alibi in encountering the closing text of *Disgrace*, and Lurie has no alibi in his final moments with Driepoot, the question is: by reading the ending through the unifying notion of sympathy, are we missing essential dialogic elements that lead to a subtler interpretation of the ending? Is Lurie sacrificing Driepoot in his haste to achieve monologic unity in his role as *harijan*?

VI

Before proceeding to an analysis of the final moments between Lurie and Driepoot, it may be helpful to consider Bakhtin's understanding of the dialogic as present in another context. Fyodor Dostoevsky's *Crime and Punishment* refuses to provide a clear and decisive epiphany after Raskolnikov confesses to the murder of the pawnbroker. During his trial Raskolnikov broods with disgust, and his time in Siberia begins with that same self-disgust. Dostoevsky writes: "He was indeed ashamed even before Sonya, whom he tormented because of it with his contemptuous and rude treatment. But he was ashamed not of a shaved head and chains: his pride was badly wounded" (*Crime and Punishment*, 543). In fact, far from accepting his guilt or sympathizing with his victims, Raskolnikov is still tortured by his intellectual rationalizing: "This alone he recognized as his crime: that he had not endured it, but had gone and confessed" (544). Raskolnikov's fleeing from dialogue, as it were, to the attempted monological unity of rationalizations proves unhelpful. Questions torment Raskolnikov that, as the narrator states, "might herald a future break in his life, his future resurrection, his future new vision of life" (545). Bakhtin would add: the last word on his life is not yet spoken. The space after the question is reserved for the new word. In prison, Raskolnikov is "disliked and avoided by everyone" (546) and "another question remained insoluble for him: why had they [his fellow prisoners] all come to love Sonya so much?" (546). Raskolnikov always took Sonya's hand "as if with loathing, always met her as if with vexation, was sometimes obstinately silent during the whole time of her visit" and "there were occasions when she trembled before him and went away in deep grief" (549). Having followed him to Siberia to see him through his sentence, Raskolnikov knows Sonya's love is deep and unconditional. Finally, during one meeting, life surprises Raskolnikov:

> How it happened he himself did not know, but suddenly it was as if something lifted him and flung him down at her feet. He wept and embraced her knees. For the first moment she was terribly frightened, and her whole face went numb. She jumped up and looked at him, trembling. But all at once, in that same moment, she understood everything. Infinite happiness lit up in her eyes; she understood, and for her there was no longer any doubt that he loved her, loved her infinitely, and that at last the moment had come. (549)

From loathing, through a swirl of questions, Raskolnikov finds himself, along with Sonya, "resurrected by love; the heart of each held infinite sources of life for the heart of the other" (549). The narrator's emphasis on the dialogic interaction is unmistakable as Raskolnikov, through encountering the "outsidedness" of Sonya, sees, in a sense, behind him. His consciousness isn't able to see itself without hers; he can't author himself without her presence. The result of the dialogue is a previously unimagined future world, qualitatively different: "Instead of dialectics, there was life, and something completely different had to work itself out in his consciousness" (550). Raskolnikov embraces the *aporia*, or as Dostoevsky writes in the final paragraph, Raskolnikov gradually makes his "acquaintance with a new, hitherto completely unknown reality" (551).

As *Disgrace* moves toward a conclusion, Lurie, who has been scourged by the novel's events, "has learned by now to concentrate all his attention on the dog they are killing, giving it what he no longer has difficulty in calling by its proper name: Love" (*Disgrace*, 219). Derek Attridge captures the tone of the novel's concluding momentum:

> The novel ends on one of the killing Sundays. All I have said about a dedication to singularity, both in Lurie's new mode of existence and in

> Coetzee's art, is exemplified in these final pages, as Lurie brings in the dog of whom he has grown particularly fond and gives him up to the waiting needle. Coetzee offers no explanation of Lurie's loving dedication to surplus dogs, and certainly doesn't proffer it as a model for the new South Africa, or for any reader's own conduct. If the novel succeeds in conveying something of the operation and importance of what I've been calling "grace" it conveys also that it is not a lesson to be learned or a system to be deployed. (Attridge, 190)

In sympathizing with the brutal fate of these castaway creatures, Lurie seems on the cusp of a new way of interacting with the world. Of Driepoot, Coetzee writes:

> There is only the young dog left, the one who likes music, the one who, given half a chance, would already have lolloped after his comrades into the clinic building, into the theatre with its zinc-topped table where the rich, mixed smells still linger, including one he will not yet have met with in his life: the smell of expiration, the soft, short smell of the released soul. (219)

While Lurie can "save the young dog, if he wishes, for another week," he concludes that "a time must come, it cannot be evaded" (219). Coetzee describes what Lurie will do for the dog when Driepoot's time comes:

> he will have to bring him to Bev Shaw in her operating room (perhaps he will carry him in his arms, perhaps he will do that for him) and caress him and brush back the fur so that the needle can find the vein, and whisper to him and support him in the moment when, bewilderingly, his legs buckle; and then, when the soul is out, fold him up and pack him away in his bag, and the next day wheel the bag into the flames and see that it is burnt, burnt up. He will do all that for him when his time comes. It will be little enough, less than little: nothing. (219–20)

Lurie's imagined actions can be interpreted as his new way of seeing beyond his own concerns, his self-ish awareness. But with dialogism in mind, they may be seen as an obliteration of the other in the service of Lurie's imagination's sympathetic impositions. Instead of writing Driepoot into his opera as a character, Lurie will write Driepoot into his life as a finalized character without the possibility of being. Lurie, then, becomes the monologic author, subordinating simultaneous co-being in the event, to material for Lurie's life that craves a unified meaning: "Servant of Eros" or "Harijan." Attridge writes:

> Lurie's total absorption in the animals' dying is vividly described, but it is his care of the corpses that marks the extreme limit of this theme in the novel. If a dog is an absolute other, what is a dead dog, and what responses does it demand? It would be easy to dump the carcasses in their

black bags at the incinerator on the same day, but he feels he can't simply discard them with all the other garbage. (Attridge, 185–86)

But, rather than stand in the face of dialogue with a particular, simultaneous being whose unconditional love and desire for life can challenge, engage, and tease Lurie's consciousness, a being whose very simultaneous existence is necessary for Lurie's own act of authoring his self, Lurie co-opts Driepoot's existence for his narrative of self-sacrifice.

Lurie's thoughts on Driepoot's final moments interestingly conflate with his vision of Teresa, the heroine of his opera: "Sitting at the table in the dog-yard, he harkens to the sad, swooping curve of Teresa's plea as she confronts the darkness. This is a bad time of the month for Teresa, she is sore, she has not slept a wink . . . She wants to be rescued from the pain, from the summer heat, from the Villa Gamba, from her father's bad temper, from everything" (213). Lurie's casting himself as the sensitive soul who will comfort Driepoot in his last moments seems similar to seeing himself as an "old lag serving out my sentence" (216): an even more tragic sentence, possibly, as we may infer that Lurie imagines his end without such a loving escort accompanying him to his final moment. Lurie "opens the cage" and the dog "wags its crippled rear, sniffs his face, licks his cheeks, his lips, his ears" (220). Lurie does nothing to stop the euthanasia, but rather enacts the language of sacred sacrifice: "bearing him [Driepoot] in his arms like a lamb, he re-enters surgery." He's questioned by Bev: "'I thought you would save him for another week,' says Bev Shaw. 'Are you giving him up?'" He responds: "'Yes, I am giving him up'" (220).

Perhaps, the short statement, the lack of any question in his reaction to Bev's question, the certainty of a pledge to Driepoot that will be carried out in the future, signals the new word emerging? Noting the progressive verb construction, it is tempting to argue that Lurie proclaims to undertake an act that is never to be finished, a constant state of giving up Driepoot, of mourning and honoring, a commitment to continuing dialogic *in memorium*. Maybe. But when considering the foregoing of another week with Driepoot, then, can Lurie's continual mourning be seen as a self-aggrandizing act that not only silences the other, but also finalizes Lurie as he turns away from the "outsidedness" and the possibility of dialogue outside his own imaginings, however beautifully cast?

Lucy refuses to close down dialogic interaction and finalize the other when she explains her feelings for the child in her womb. When asked by Lurie if she loves it, Lucy replies: "The child? No. How could I? But I will. Love will grow — one can trust Mother Nature for that. I am determined to be a good mother, David" (216). Lucy seems to respond to the *aporia* of the question with the realization of the process, or in Bakhtin's terms, in the realization of the future simultaneous co-being with the child: a process that gifts a new word to Lucy through dialogic interaction with an other. Lucy refuses to finalize herself in relation to the process that will unfold, refuses to try to cast a unifying narrative; rather she reacts with "no alibi" and opens herself to future dialogue.

Lurie, on the other hand, seemingly puts his desire to be "giving him up" above the real possibility of interaction for another week. These are his last words spoken on a week that would have necessarily, to Bakhtin, been a week with a last word not yet spoken. Lurie approaches the euthanasia of Driepoot with the certainty of what he will do and how he will react to the events. While earlier in the novel, Lurie's consciousness seemed constantly undermined by questions that highlight his limited self-awareness, here he confidently sees his role regarding Driepoot. The certainty seems to suggest itself in other aspects of Lurie's life in his "new start" with Lucy, and his consideration of the term "grandfather." Similar to the progressive verb tense, it is tempting to view the phrase "I am giving him up" as an unfinalized dialogic relationship with the act itself; one that will continue to generate, inspire, and haunt Lurie in the weeks and years to come. Who knows how Lurie might have been able to see himself with Driepoot's companionship over another week? Lurie chooses to see Driepoot as just like all the other dogs scheduled to be euthanized, rather than honoring the particular animal and the particularities and spirited affection of their shared history.

Undoubtedly, Lurie has become more sensitive in his ability to sympathize with others and genuinely feels for Driepoot in his situation. But, sympathy doesn't seem to be the answer to the question of another week. Driepoot is described as playing, rather than moaning or whining, as a dog that needs to be euthanized immediately would behave.

If we have established the usefulness in Bakhtin's approach in considering Lurie's consciousness as dialogic through the course of the novel, then the dialogic shouldn't be overlooked in favor of a monologic interpretation utilizing sympathy. Considering the "not another week" opens an interpretation involving Lurie's consciousness as continually "middle" without beginning or end, without unity, but continually seeking a "new word." In addition, in moving from a pattern of possession and use to one of recognition of another's suffering, Lurie moves from reification of the self — though, like Raskolnikov, unsuccessfully so — to authoring the self through dialogue. But, how is Lurie viewed as experiencing a new understanding of the dialogic when it seems he silenced at least "another week" of dialogue in his desire to euthanize Driepoot? It is precisely the "not another week" that importantly opens up an interpretation based on dialogism.

The textual focus on the "another week" makes it impossible for Lurie to unify his experience under the experience of sympathy, or, for that matter, according to Attridge's notion of grace. The "not another week" forces the cynical, or self-serving, into dialogue with the possibility of grace. Lurie experiences — and will, in his "giving him up," continue to experience — the dialogic interaction of both possibilities. The question is, why not another week? Readings of Lurie's sacrifice as a kind of continuous, unfinished heroism implicit in reading Lurie's final statement as a vow to constantly give Driepoot up, while touching, finalize the event to one of repetition, suggesting Lurie will know what the future mourning of Driepoot will be. Dialogic considerations where Lurie's sympathy, his tender comforting, is placed in an open-ended interrelationship with his shadowy decision for "not another week" suggest a process towards an unknown new, an as yet unspoken word.

Perhaps that is why David Lurie deserves our sympathy. Or, maybe he deserves more. Coetzee's highlighting of the "not another week" moves the reader from the safe terrain of unifying sympathy to dialogic instability. Coetzee writes:

> Dostoevsky's answer to the question of why the self can no longer desire its own desires is that the promise that comes with the tidings that God is dead, that Man has taken his place, is not fulfilled in experience. (*Doubling*, 131–32)

Immediately after these words, he quotes Dostoevsky:

> Each individual discovers in the solitude of his consciousness that the promise is false but no one is able to universalize his experience. The promise remains true for Others . . . Everyone thinks that he alone is condemned to hell, and that is what makes it hell. (Quoted in *Doubling*, 132)

Unable to annihilate Lurie — Lurie as "the question is" — through emotional identification because of the "not another week" that is both murderous and loving, fearful and heroic, selfish and selfless, the reader, then, becomes the "what is the answer?" The reader and Lurie: his "outsidedness" standing in front of us so we may see the grace and cynicism behind them in a world where, we wonder, are all things permitted?

3: "Is it too late to educate the eye?": David Lurie, Richard of St. Victor, and "vision as eros" in *Disgrace*

Bill McDonald

> In your own Bosom you bear your Heaven
> And earth, & all that you behold, tho' it appears Without, it is Within
> In your Imagination, of which this world of Mortality is but Shadow.
> — Blake, *Jerusalem*

I

DAVID LURIE'S PAST IS LARGELY A BLANK SLATE to readers of *Disgrace*. We know only a few things about his academic career, and even less about his upbringing, marriages, politics, and religion. We do learn, in a fast-moving paragraph, that David was raised "in a family of women. As mother, aunts, sisters fell away, they were replaced in due course by mistresses, wives, a daughter. The company of women made him a lover of women and, to an extent, a womanizer. . . . That was how he lived for years, for decades, that was the backbone of his life" (7). Mothers and sisters, aunts and wives, then a little later "tourists" and "wives of colleagues" (7) appear, then immediately "fall away" from our view, with only Rosalind, wife number two, surviving the sentences that created her. We are left largely with surmises: that he received some musical education, went somewhere to graduate school, has taught for something like a quarter of a century, and thought a photograph of his mother as a young woman worth displaying (15). It's hard to imagine him with sisters.

We also know that David wrote and published three books in earlier phases of his academic career. None of them "caused a stir or even a ripple" (4). Though he is "tired of criticism" now, these books that he wrote about "dead people" once commanded his "heart" (162). It gradually becomes clear that the subjects of these books, though unremarked by David's peers, have remained very much in play in his consciousness and especially his subliminal life, inaugurating, even shaping, aspects of his present experience. Two of them — *Boito and the Faust Legend: The Genesis of* Mefistofele, and *Wordsworth and the Burden of the Past* — do so in immediately apparent ways; the slow evolution of David's own opera on Byron and Teresa Guiccioli runs throughout the story, and his specialization in Romanticism — "Wordsworth has been one of my masters" (13) — yields the two classroom scenes we visit, as well as several other important passages in his narrative. Sandwiched in between, however, is a seemingly anomalous project, *The Vision of Richard of St. Victor.* The writings of an ascetic Scots contemplative in a medieval French monastery seem well removed from David's artistic interests and melancholy secularism; though David may satirize his students' "post-Christian" attitudes (32), he seems to share them (for example, 172). Yet as a young scholar David Lurie thought enough of Richard's work to devote an entire book to him, a task that required considerable time, a mastery of Latin and the complexities of medieval theology, and at least some sympathy with the contemplative life. "Vision as eros" is his book's theme, and while Lurie tells us nothing else directly about his interpretation, Richard's writing, like Boito's opera and Wordsworth's poetry, becomes an intriguing intertext in David's psychic life, giving the reader another, and even more venerable, set of frames for following his journey. Richard's visionary passion also runs under the surface of Coetzee's novel, helping to shape its affirmation of what he elsewhere calls "mystical intuition,"[1] and weaving that visionary experience into the aesthetics and the ethics of *Disgrace.* Coetzee's Latin, "the only language I studied at university," stood him in good stead.[2]

First, a few general things about Richard's accounts of the visionary as they affect *Disgrace.* His descriptions anticipate, and resemble, the accounts of many later visionaries; in addition to Richard, David himself cites Dante, Langland, Byron, Blake, Wordsworth, Yeats, and Rilke. They also resemble the intuited beginnings of fictions that many writers have recounted: the mysterious appearance of a gesture, a voice, a character in motion from "outside" consciousness. In addition, the visionary connects with the ethical choices that David makes at the end of his story; it leads to, but doesn't compel, those decisions. To elaborate just a little, the visionary elements are not in themselves decisive or completing; neither David nor the novel ends with a vision. They enrich David's self-understanding but also highlight some unchanging, and unwelcome, qualities of his character. The novel insists on open-endedness, both because it sees character change as real but always partial, and because the novel itself illuminates, then rejects, any definitive authority. Finality — in vision, in character, in ethical action — is a fiction this fiction stands against.

In what follows I argue that the visionary, the aesthetic, and the ethical are interwoven in the book in ways vital to its meanings.

II, i

Richard (d. 1173), associate of Bernard of Clairvaux and Thomas of Canterbury and successor of the more famous Hugh of St. Victor, holds a significant place in Catholic mystical thinking. He was known as the "Magnus Contemplator," after his treatise "*De Contemplatione*," which Dante mentions in the *Paradiso* as putting forward "all that a mere man can see, and more" (X, 131–32, Ciardi translation). His writings were actively sought out by other monasteries, praised by St. Bonaventure, and included not only contemplative subjects but pedagogic ones as well; like his master Hugh, he wrote specifically to instruct as well as to reveal (St. Victor's teaching program was copied throughout Europe).[3] The narrative of Jacob and his family in *Genesis* provided the scaffold upon which he built a remarkable account of contemplation, while his familiarity with St. Augustine's writings shaped its terminology and modes of argument.

Richard is read today largely for three texts: *Twelve Patriarchs* or *Benjamin Minor: Of the preparation of the soul for contemplation*; *The Mystical Ark* or *Benjamin Major: Of the grace of contemplation*; and for his remarkable work on the Trinity.[4] The first two titles are taken from Psalm 67 (68 in the *KJV* and *RSV*), where Jacob's youngest son Benjamin, "the least of them" (*ibi Beniamin parvulus continens eos*), leads the solemn victory procession of God's faithful into the sanctuary. In the *Benjamin Minor* Richard aligns himself with the tradition of allegorizing not only Benjamin's position as the youngest son, but Jacob's entire family, assigning a stage or "discipline" in spiritual development to his wives Leah and Rachel, their handmaidens, and the birth order of his thirteen children. So, Dan (judgment) and Naphtali (conversion) defend the soul (*Benjamin Minor*, 17–22), Issachar expresses its joy and reward (37–39), Dina its shame (45–59), Joseph its discretion (67–72), and Benjamin the ecstasy of contemplation and interior visions of light (71–75, 82–87). Richard formulates the basic distinction between reason, "by which we distinguish things," and affection, "by which we love," in this way: "These are the two wives of the rational spirit, from which honorable offspring and heirs of the kingdom of heaven are born. Right counsels are born from reason; holy longings from affection" (3). Longing is identified with Leah, who struggles to move past the pleasure of worldly objects, while Rachel, the allegorical embodiment of reason, prepares the way for the trans-rational visions that only her son Benjamin can achieve. Richard works each of these figures in many ways; his allegories are subtle, not reductive or naïve as this quick summary might suggest. Each stage involves a material or historical event, and an accompanying symbolic event in the spirit. These offer a path not only to seminarians, but to any individuals seeking spiritual insight into their own experience; Richard wishes to show the way to a large audience. Self-consciously citing Christ's example, Richard sees himself as a committed teacher as well as thinker ("Learn from me, because I am gentle and lowly in heart").[5] His path repeats a familiar, even archetypal, journey in Western mysticism: from immediate sensuous experience through the complex stages of mental apprehension and meditation — what we would call psychology — to the many layers of contemplation. (These stages align with the many secular accounts given by verbal artists of their creative process.) Self-knowledge is a necessary achievement for the contemplative life, and Richard describes the many difficulties and limitations in the way of that achievement. Finally, it is a path that emphasizes relationships with others and the importance of full community where love may be enacted. That love (charity) may be "violent" (*De Quatuor gradibus violentiae amoris: On the Four Degrees of Violent Charity*), but after its "wounding, binding and languishing" we arrive at the soul reborn (paragraphs 42–47) as it takes on the form of Christ's humility and servanthood, becoming all things to all men . . ." (*DeQuator*, #42–47; Zinn, 9).

II, ii

Among the most telling of Richard's analyses for *Disgrace* comes in chapters 45–49 of *Benjamin Minor*, where he develops a model of shame. Ironically, Richard writes more about Jacob's oft-neglected only daughter Dina (Dinah) than any of her brothers except Joseph and Benjamin, marking shame as a virtue of serious import in his schema.[6] He has a number of things to say about shame and disgrace that resonate with Coetzee's novel.[7] Shame, first, requires the right timing to be powerful, underlining the violence of the process. It requires "hatred" of whatever act led to the person's shame. It has two stages: the lower one of public exposure; and the higher, spiritually more potent one of internal shame of one's act.

These are stages that David clearly moves through. His disgrace comes just at the moment that his belief in any meaningful future collapses (for example, 7, 11, 58). His public disgrace comes well before his interior acceptance of it. While David never "hates" the desire that led to his disgrace, after Lucy's rape he does fully acknowledge the offense he committed against the Isaacs family (163–74, especially 173). Part of the higher shame is an awareness of one's own moral depletion, something that David gradually comes to acknowledge.

One of "virtuous shame's" characteristics is the ability to not feel shame if "you should be compelled to pass before a multitude with a nude body" (47). Richard contrasts this to being "defiled in the mind by an impure thought," a spiritual nudity that, in the right-spirited should produce more shame than public nakedness. Such shame is rare in Richard's accounting, and far up the ladder of inner virtue his students are mounting. Dinah "is that judgment by which everyone is by his own conscience addressed, convicted, condemned and punished with a punishment worthy of the disorder" (48). Shame requires self-consciousness, and is "marvelous" and universal; in spiritual shame the judge and judged, the punisher and punished, become one. Disgrace, then, is a particular kind of virtue, not simply an abasement; it contains within itself, literally and figuratively, a potential of grace.

An important initial step toward this virtuous shame lies in David's superficially surprising reaction to his colleagues' ridicule, the dunce-cap newspaper photograph, and so on. He never seems to suffer the crushing humiliations of public unmasking that many men in his position might feel. He can tell his story with relative ease to his colleagues, and to Rosalind, Bev, even to Lucy. This is because his disgrace grows out of two things: his self-satisfying desire, which in the novel's early pages he prizes above all else; and its near opposite: the despair he feels at having no future — pedagogic, familial, scholarly, artistic, and especially erotic — that unmasking might damage. There is no "public" whose opinion his life's meaning depends upon. And this in turn makes David more open to disgrace's virtue: an internal, spiritual condition in which he resides, and of which he will never entirely be free.

II, iii

> Ethics is the arena in which the claims of otherness — the moral law, the human other, cultural norms, the good-in-itself, etc. — are articulated and negotiated.
> — Geoffrey Harpham, *Shadows of Ethics*

Dinah, of course, is a rape victim in *Genesis*, assaulted by Sichem, son of Emor. Richard allegorizes these two Shechemites as "Love of Vain Glory" and "Love of One's Own Excellence," since they willingly circumcise themselves for Dinah (not God), glorying in their shame. Richard's idealized, "feminine" descriptions of "beautiful" Dinah, however, seem almost an inversion, a predictably pre-feminist inversion, of Lucy. And any allegorical connection between the two Shechemites and Lucy's three assailants seems remote or perverse, though her attackers could be construed as fathers and son, and could well be said to "glory in their shame" of humiliating a woman whose ancestors had humiliated them. But Lucy's experience of disgrace, her withdrawal into a private world, does form an illuminating connection with Richard's portrait of Dinah as "that judgment" (48). This is not the more public judgment allegorized in her brother Dan, but a particular form of interior self-evaluation. Just so, Lucy's shame is of a particular, subtle kind: not the public shame of rape itself, as she might have had to endure in a fully patriarchal world, but a disgrace connected with the post-apartheid interregnum in which she lives, and which only she can feel.[8] Lucy's silent self-judgment castigates her own idealizations of a new, harmonious rural South Africa, where hard work and neighborly cooperation could leave both her commune days and apartheid's violence behind. Her naïveté is encapsulated in the novel's most suspenseful moment, when she chooses to lock up her two Dobermans while her assaulters look on. In her zeal not to be racist, to help bring about the new era through her trusting actions, Lucy exposes herself to the "personal hatred" of her rapists; she is not just an abstract "white person" or even "white woman" to them, she feels later, but an object of immediate, intimate hatred. Harassed by her father, who wants to control her life story as he had when she was a child (for example, 89, 105, 198), Lucy slowly, and quietly, develops her own well-tempered narrative, judging that she must endure the personal, inward shame of rape and untutored optimism in order to gain peace, continuation, and the Petrus-guaranteed safe boundaries of her house (208).

II, iv

In *The Mystical Ark* Richard isolates six modes of contemplation (I: 6) and develops a tropological (ethical, and also visionary) taxonomy of those modes. The lower stages outline the interrelationships of imagination and reason, the final two moving "above," then "beyond" reason to ecstasy. All are seen, finally, as manifestations of the divine, with the high spiritual world of the Trinity at the apex of the six stages. Further, any object whatsoever can become a proper object for contemplation.

At first this rapturous Christianity might seem to exclude David Lurie, who, a few undeveloped references to pre-existing souls and God aside, seems little drawn to the divine. Lurie's understanding of vision, further, is certainly mediated through "my master" Wordsworth and the Romantics, to whom he has devoted the largest part of his scholarship and teaching. Nonetheless, Richard's way of seeing, and his accounts of contemplative states, make their way into David's experience, and into the novel's texture. They flow along with, even anchor, the more familiar visionary company of the poets. They also present the life of contemplation as objective and universal, not simply personal and idiosyncratic: a making substantial that Coetzee hopes for in his fiction as well.[9] Finally, Richard's account of the visionary includes, but is not limited to, momentary epiphanies, the legendary "flash of insight"; the contemplative life also takes place in time and over time.[10] It is narrative as well as lyric, both of which will figure in David's history.

In his excellent introductory monograph to his edition of Richard's writings, translator Grover A. Zinn gives a concise summary of Richard's great subject: "By contemplation Richard means an attitude of mind, a state of beholding." He defines contemplation as ". . . the free, more penetrating gaze of a mind, suspended with wonder concerning manifestations of wisdom" (*The Mystical Ark*, I: 4). Zinn continues:

> Contemplation . . . is an attentive or eager looking at. Above all it must be clearly understood that contemplation is not some sort of mental process. Richard . . . is careful to distinguish thinking (a rather rambling consideration of many things without purpose) . . . from the act of contemplating. The contemplative act itself is an intent beholding focused upon a single object or cluster of objects presented to the mind by imagination, reason or the pure understanding that alone has access to divine things. . . . The purpose of contemplation is not thinking about something . . . but "adhering with wonder to the object that brings it joy" (I: 4). It is nondiscussive and unified. It enjoys rather than uses. It rests rather than acts. (23–24)

Once his conception of contemplation is clear, Richard goes on to posit biblical personifications, urging the novice contemplative to substitute himself for, imagine himself as, a great biblical figure. Each of these figures — and he includes a great variety, from Abraham to the Queen of Sheba — exemplifies a distinctive stage of contemplative realization. Richard also insists that at least some of the objects of contemplation, though not the highest, can be "brought down for the understanding of all" (IV, 12). In so claiming he continues his pedagogic emphasis from *Benjamin Minor*, establishing an ethical practice.

Beyond all this, however, lies the fundamental feature of Richard's inquiry into contemplation: the reservoir of erotic metaphors and allegories that charge and enliven his work. Beyond Jacob and his family, "The Song of Songs" suffuses much of Richard's writing, and the traditional figures of bride and bridegroom for the soul and God take on special savor in his formulations. Naturally this is a sublimated eros, an eros marking love, and also desire and longing, in their widest applications, but Richard doesn't shy away from the explicitly sexual in the rapture of his vision.[11] Here is a representative example, one that might almost serve as an outline of the later stages of David's difficult spiritual journey:

> And so when the soul enters with her Beloved into the bedchamber, she alone delaying and enjoying the sweetness with Him alone . . . she forgets all external things and delights in supreme and intimate love of Him. She sees herself, alone with the Beloved, when, after having forgotten all exterior things, she aims her longing away from consideration of herself and toward love of her Beloved. And on account of these things that she considers in her inmost places, she kindles her soul with such affection

and rises up with thanksgiving from the consideration of both her goods and her evils. . . . Think what is in your life that you have loved more ardently, craved more anxiously; what affected you more pleasantly and delighted you more deeply than all other things. Consider, therefore, if you feel the same force of affection and abundance of delight when you burn with longing for the supreme Lover and when you rest in His love. Who doubts that He does not yet occupy that innermost recess of your affections if the dart of intimate love pierces your soul less and excites it less fervently in divine affections than it was accustomed to penetrate and excite it sometimes with respect to alien affections? (*Benjamin Major*, IV, 16)

Also important for *Disgrace* is Richard's late treatise on the Trinity, whose third book develops an ingenious argument for a Three-in-One God based on the principle of active love, or charity:

When one person gives love to another and he alone loves only the other, there certainly is love [*dilectio*] but it is not a shared love [*condilectio*]. When two love each other mutually and give to each other the affection of supreme longing; when the affection of the first goes out to the second and the affection of the second goes out to the first and tends as it were in diverse ways — in this case there certainly is love on both sides, but it is not shared love. Shared love is properly said to exist when a third person is loved by two persons harmoniously and in community, and the affection of the two persons is fused into one affection by the flame of love for the third. From these things it is evident that shared love would have no place in Divinity itself if a third person were lacking to the other two persons.[12]

In order for God to be fully charitable, fully loving, he must be tripartite. Richard extends this interpretation to the human community, which also requires a third person to be complete. This recondite "vision as eros" with its "flame of love" and preference for threesomes will inform several of the novel's many triangular relationships, particularly the final one at the book's close.

Necessarily, Richard's overt allegories and unself-conscious erotic celebrations do not appear directly in Coetzee's rigorously self monitoring novel. Instead Coetzee gives us fiction in which the allegorical is fluid rather than fixed, and which constantly scrutinizes its own foundations. Fredric Jameson's succinct account of the first of these permutations of allegory, often endorsed by Coetzee's critics, can help us along:

The newer allegory is horizontal rather than vertical: if it must still attach its one-on-one conceptual labels to its objects after the fashion of *The Pilgrim's Progress*, it does so in the conviction that those objects (along with their labels) are now profoundly relational, indeed are themselves construed by their relations to each other. When we add to this the inevitable mobility of such relations, we begin to glimpse the process of allegorical interpretation as a kind of scanning that, moving back and forth across the text, readjusts its terms in constant modification of a type quite different from our stereotypes of some static medieval or biblical decoding.[13]

This account brilliantly summarizes an important part of Coetzee's practice in *Disgrace*. Think, for example, of the book's multifarious triangles, or of how our view of Bev Shaw shifts registers from just another "dumpy woman" in David's catalog to a rescuing angel. It is also consonant with the novel's refusal of finality in its characters' lives or in its own ethical position. Working in this mode, Coetzee turns the gap between Richard's spiritual universe and our own to his artistic advantage; any resonant eros-vision now surprises both character and reader, appearing dramatically in a world from which such things have long since been discounted by tough-minded realists such as Lucy, David, and, presumably, the reader. The surprise creates an authority, giving us a sense of a voice from elsewhere — not necessarily the "higher" elsewhere of traditional allegory — and that authority in turn sustains allegorical meaning. In this way Richard's visionary insights make their way into Coetzee's novel, further developing the similarities between religious and artistic visions. He draws on the "horizontal" allegory favored by postmodernism but in a way that maintains a shadow version of Richard's confident practice. Coetzee's allegory is arguably more important for his political and ethical purposes than for his exploration of the visionary, but it plays a vital part here as well. It also gives us a way to see the history of the visionary.

Within these frames I shall show that David's major visions are charged with the erotic energy Richard celebrated, and that the allegorical and intertextual triumphalism of his treatises leaves its mark on David's artistic and ethical life even as it once occupied his scholarly life. For example, he comes to re-see his imagined Teresa Guiccioli as an allegorical figure whom he tries to emulate; no longer the young girl he forcibly shaped in early drafts, she metamorphoses into a "dumpy little widow" who paradoxically becomes his teacher about love and longing (181–85, 213–14). Second, Richard's writings also touch *Disgrace* itself, not only its main character. As we have seen, Richard's elaborate "personification allegory" of Jacob's daughter Dinah — her shame via rape — underwrites Lucy's tragedy, and Richard's claims about the psychology of shame and disgrace color the novel's exploration of those subjects. Most important, however, are two related topics that lie at the heart of David Lurie and the fiction that gives him voice: love and the visionary. "Vision as eros": what David has sought his entire life, from his "womanizing" days and practiced urban gaze to the transforming visions near the end of his narrative, and where for David and

Disgrace itself the aesthetic, spiritual, and ethical come together — at least for a time.

III

> Stories, whether written as novels or scripted as plays, connect the visible with the invisible, the present with the past. They propose life as something with moral consequence. They distribute the suffering so that it can be borne . . .
> — E. L. Doctorow. From the introduction to
> *Creationists: Selected Essays, 1993–2006*

Throughout his writing career J. M. Coetzee has explored the visionary. His leading characters all experience powerful visions, from Jacobus Coetzee of *Dusklands* and Magda of *In the Heart of the Country* ("What I lack in experience I plainly make up for in vision . . ." [42]) through the Magistrate of *Waiting for the Barbarians*, with his recurring dream-visions of children and his fantasy of flying, all the way to Elizabeth Costello. The heroine of *Age of Iron*, Elizabeth Curren, has at least twenty such experiences over the course of her story. Many of these are brief and, to repeat, closely resemble other artists' accounts of the intuitions that launched their work. Others are more extended and intertextual, creating an overt or, more often, an unspoken dialogue with an earlier text. In *Youth* (2002) Coetzee narrativizes his own visionary experience as a young man in London, lying alone on Hampstead Heath:

> Tired out, one Sunday afternoon, he folds his jacket into a pillow, stretches out on the greensward, and sinks into a sleep or half-sleep in which consciousness does not vanish but continues to hover. It is a state he has not known before: in his very blood he seems to feel the steady wheeling of the earth. The faraway cries of children, the birdsong, the whirr of insects gather force and come together in a paean of joy. His heart swells. *At last!* he thinks. At last it has come, the moment of ecstatic unity with the All! Fearful that the moment will slip away, he tries to put a halt to the clatter of thought, tries simply to be a conduit for the great universal force that has no name.
> It lasts no more than seconds in clock time, this signal event. But when he gets up and dusts off his jacket, he is refreshed, renewed. . . . If he has not utterly been transfigured, then at least he has been blessed with a hint that he belongs on this earth. (117: see also 154)

In the face of *Disgrace's* pared-down style and strong skepticism about the metaphysical, such visionary experiences — both those that break into David's consciousness and those that he, following Richard, consciously sustains — yield our only access to a spiritual life beyond, or alongside, the quotidian. David claims to agree with his daughter that "there is no higher life. This is the only life there is. Which we share with animals" (74). In its conclusion the novel will take that "sharing with animals" and put it together with another way of seeing, certainly "different" if not higher (74), to bring David Lurie to a new beginning point for a future he could not envision earlier.

David's visionary life isn't as prolific as Elizabeth Curren's, but he has a number of such experiences during the course of *Disgrace*. Some are transitory, others — such as the vision of Lucy "struggling with the two in the blue overalls, struggling against them. He writhes, trying to blank it out" (97) — produce dark and painful knowledge.[14] But three in particular, in the last quarter of the novel, prove especially illuminating for the final turns in his character and the novel's outcome.

Ironically, however, David's understanding of "vision as eros" in the early stages of his story leaves us a long way from Richard's intricate religious hierarchies. Rather we're back with David's "womanizing"; Richard may passionately allegorize women and marriage, but David, evoking his unchangeable "temperament," largely denigrates and controls them.[15] His language and his "vision" seem, in the beginning, almost a repudiation of Richard's beloved *Song of Songs*: self-protection is his goal, not openness, or even alertness, toward the other. He is cool, bordering on cold. "He has always been a man of the city, at home amid a flux of bodies where eros stalks and glances flash like arrows" (6), and Cape Town, "prodigal of beauty, of beauties" (12), has always given him what he wanted. We have his quick, Pavlovian ranking of women's body parts, his "contented" account of carefully managed lovemaking with Soraya, his self-serving idealization of Melanie Isaac's young body, itself the latest of his many crushes on "one or another of his charges" (12). His perception of Melanie — indeed, of all his students — is habitual, canned: an "eye" that seems beyond "education." He claims that the "humility" he derives from his diminished academic position makes him a deeper learner than his charges, but his actions don't bear that out.

In addition, we have his anti-erotic account of his brief fling with his departmental secretary, Dawn ("Bucking and clawing, she works herself into a froth of excitement that in the end only repels him" [9]). This last encounter leads him to think of Origen and self-castration, and a particularly chilling vision spins into his mind:

> . . . a simple enough operation, surely; they do it to animals every day. . . Severing, tying off: with local anesthetic and a steady hand and a modicum of phlegm one might even do it oneself, out of a textbook. A man on a chair snipping away at himself: an ugly sight, but no more ugly, from a certain point of view, than the same man exercising himself on the body of a woman. (9)

This and several other sterile visions like it dominate the early sections of David's narrative. Directly beneath his account of the city's erotic glances lies his disgust with sexuality, women's and his own alike, and his acute sense that his life has become a "desert" (11) and himself a "ghost" (7), a self-parody of his earlier Byronic days. All expressions of desire and the erotic, not just the specifically sexual, are suddenly tainted for David, falling directly into decay and death; his "anxious flurries of promiscuity" (7) cannot cover his feelings of being newly undesirable and unlovable, and his exploitive seduction of the child-like Melanie represents a futile, narcissistic attempt to recover a power and beauty that has long since left him behind. Self-parody indeed.

Though dominated by these cold, measured narratives, other more hopeful features of David's psyche still break through on occasion. His frequent self-criticism, stinging and accurate, is part of this — though his inability, or refusal, to act on what he knows about himself shows its ethical impotence. But there are further signs that give us a more complex David early on, and lay the groundwork for his visionary experiences late in the novel. He does, first, find Melanie authentically beautiful, and is repeatedly astonished (19, 20, 25, 27) by the power of the feelings and desire she generates in him. He can also, however briefly, rightly perceive her suffering (for example, 27). Next comes a triangle of saints: Origen and Benedict (9, and also 66), and St. Hubert (84), who famously gave refuge to a deer. David, as his early book confirms, does know his way around religious history.[16] He does not mention Richard by name, but his celebration of erotic vision, twisted now but still resonant, will return strongly near the end as well. David can also see himself figured in the world as another, for example in the janitor who watches Melanie's play rehearsal with him in the darkness of an empty theatre (24). But this moment of insight — "the old men whose company he seems on the point of joining" — transposes instead into a familiar vision of aversion: "tramps and drifters with their stained raincoats and cracked false teeth and hairy earholes" and then of narrow self-justification: "Can they be blamed for clinging to the last to their place at the sweet banquet of the senses?" (24). This passage in turn points toward David's most serious and full account of eros in the book's first half: his parable of the male dog beaten for expressing his instinct for nearby females in heat (90). David's vision here is of his willing service to Aphrodite and Blake ("Sooner murder an infant in its cradle than nurse unsatisfied desire" [69]). A small sleight of hand allows him to substitute Blake's "desire" for the dog's "instinct": Desire is self-justifying, beyond ethical judgment or control. His conviction about his fixed "temperament" sustains him through the show trial that his ethically beleaguered institution imposes on him.[17]

As David defiantly endures his "inquiry" before his academic peers, refusing "a priest" and "repentance" (49, 58), and then sets out for the near-monastic isolation of his daughter's farm, he reenacts not so much the stages of Richard's taxonomy as the contemplative, ascetic spirit of his undertaking. But it is above all in his visions, unbidden and willed, that David achieves a measure of self-knowledge and aesthetic breakthrough that culminate in loving ethical action: "vision as eros." We see this process work itself out in the three central visions of his life: the re-envisioning of his opera; the fleeting images of all the women he has ever known; and in the Wordsworthian, Victorine sustained "spot of time" which finally shapes a new life for himself and his daughter. All point toward meaningful futures that David had despaired of achieving, and to an ethic that resituates desire in full recognition of the other.

IV, i

> Forgiveness but also unflinchingness: that is the mixture I have in mind, if it is attainable. First the unflinchingness, then the forgiveness.
>
> — J. M. Coetzee, "Interview" ("Beckett"), *Doubling the Point*, 29

> In Rousseau's mind one had only to be very honest with oneself, and brave . . . and one could tell the truth about oneself . . . [Dostoevsky] says that it simply is not good enough to look in your heart and write, that what comes out when you write is quite as likely to be some self-serving lie as it is to be the ruthless truth about yourself. I must say that, in this confrontation, my sympathy is wholly with Dostoevsky. The basis of his position is simply that the heart of our own desire is unknown to us and, perhaps even further, that it's in the nature of human desire not to know itself fully, to have some kernel of the unknowable in it. That, perhaps, is what animates desire, namely that it is unknowable to itself.
>
> — J. M. Coetzee, "A Conversation with Eleanor Wachtel," *Brick* 67 (2001), 45

> Strange how, as desire relaxes its grip on her body, she sees more and more clearly a universe ruled by desire. . . . Not the least thing, not the last thing but is called to by love. A vision, an opening up, as the heavens are opened up by a rainbow when the rain stops falling. Does it suffice, for old folk, to have these visions now and again, these rainbows, as a comfort, before the rain starts pelting down again? Must one be too creaky to join the dance before one can see the pattern?
>
> — J. M. Coetzee, *Elizabeth Costello*, Lesson 7

Disgrace's narrator makes it quite clear that David Lurie's opera, originally titled *Byron in Italy* (6), corresponds in revealing ways to his character;

indeed, David himself is more than half aware that its changing form mirrors his changing spirit. Begun as an account of the older Byron's last great affair, with the young Countess Teresa Guiccioli, David planned to contrast her full, youthful passion with the poet's ennui. She would plead to be carried away "to another life"; he too would long for another life, but one of retirement, even the peace of death. This conception re-presents the split David experiences between his own youthful ardor, now largely elegiac, and his increasing despair over his loss of passion, desirability, and even the semblance of love. Like one of Richard's contemplative novices, he imaginatively identified with Byron and made Teresa over into his own image. He did learn from this first version — "At the age of thirty-five he [Byron] has begun to learn that life is precious" (162) — but he can't get words and music together.

But by the time he takes up the opera again, during his final visit to Cape Town, those thematic lines — youth and age, passion and ennui — no longer arrest him. After long contemplation he recasts his heroine as an asthmatic, middle-aged "dumpy little widow" (181) resembling Bev Shaw more than Melanie. He wonders if he can have the requisite empathy with this "peasant" Teresa to sustain the work. He now finds her alone in the Villa Gamba, hoarding Byron's letters as her last hope for "immortality." In an echo of *The Aspern Papers* (and Dominick Argento's 1988 opera based on Henry James's short novel) David concentrates on his heroine's feelings.[18] Byron is now long dead, but not silenced; "from the caverns of the underworld" he sings pale, desiccated lyrics: "*It has dried up, the source of everything.*" His voice is so weak that Teresa must, Echo-like, repeat his words, doing her best to call him back to life and passion, even as David gives her voice in turn. But this is not a patriarchal conquest of her voice, for this time David is not fully in control of his material, or even sure how it will turn out. Instead she surprises him, and the act of composition enters into the visionary. Formerly he had planned to "lift" melodies from Gluck or another master, blurring the line between the intertextual and plagiarism; now that sort of consciously controlled, well-managed artmaking simply doesn't work. Rather he is "in the grip" of his revised character, eating little, following as she leads him (186), writing down new music. Sound-images for the work rise from beyond David's own limited musical palette (183). "Sometimes the contour of a phrase occurs to him before he has a hint of what the words themselves will be; sometimes the words call forth the cadence; sometimes the shade of a melody, having hovered for days on the edge of hearing, unfolds and blessedly reveals itself" (183). This "blessed revelation" arises from David's attentive, extended contemplation of his Teresa, and his channeling of her words and music.[19] Like his Teresa, David may "howl to the moon," but also like her, he begins to move beyond the narcissism and the paralyzing negativity that prevented him receiving anything "from the heart." She becomes his guide to a new purpose, and a new self-understanding.

And what does she reveal? That the elegiac and the youthful erotic are no longer central to her life, and that she is willing to risk all the disgrace and ridicule of becoming a comic figure: the seeker of "immortal longing" in a frumpy, long-forgotten body. The instrument to elicit that comedy is the old African township banjo that David turns to for her songs, a relic from Lucy's childhood. David will soon take the same risk, life following art, playing the banjo to the delight only of a crippled dog and the "whooping" amusement of three neighbor boys (212).[20] The banjo relocates David's relationship to Teresa and Byron; he plunks away, separate now from both and speaking for neither. Instead he discovers that he is "held in the music itself," every attempt to soar away reined back by the "ludicrous instrument . . . like a fish on a line" (184–85). No identification, no satire, but the wordless music itself "inventing him" (186), an ecstatic, out-of-body experience — but one leashed to irony, comedy, the modern. To learn aesthetic, visionary transport from the cracked kettle of the banjo: Victorine allegory has obviously been inverted, but its goal preserved. Some readers insist on the opera's failure because David knows he won't complete it (214), but it has been a contemplative and moral triumph, breaking David free of his granite temperament and self-regard. Unlike his Teresa, he is not trapped in a watchful house. But even so, by refusing to be dead, by singing her immortal longings (209), she carries him past the "honour" that has blocked his change, and brought him "back to this world" (212), a world in which he can act, in which, thanks to his disgrace, he can do the right thing.

Richard's Trinitarian vision as eros also lies beneath the almost inexhaustible series of triangles that have organized David's experience. Many of these are what his ex-wife Rosalind resolutely calls "disgraceful and vulgar too" (45): to be in bed with Melanie and Soraya at once, or with Melanie and her sister, or imagining Lucy and her recently departed lover Helen from a vantage point in their bedroom. It's true that, decades after Freud, readers may no longer be shocked by half-conscious feelings of desire between parents and children, or by male fantasies of multiple partners. But the triangles don't stop there. The opera began with triangulation between Teresa, Byron, and Count Guiccioli. Lucy has her hate-filled triangle of rapists. There's Bill and Bev Shaw with David. Lucy, Petrus, and David, and David, Lucy, and Pollux form other, increasingly problematic threesomes. It's hard to find scenes in the book that don't depend on this particular geometry.

Still, we are surprised, I think, by the late turns that David's triangulations take: Teresa, Byron, and David meeting in music; and the transformation that ends the novel: Bev, David, and "Driepoot," the three-legged "tripod" dog, a tableau with David standing between his two best teachers in love and ethical action. In Richard's terms, love can only fulfill itself if there are three persons, separate yet unified. Just as Richard's unusual theology made the Holy Spirit a full, acting Person in the Trinity,[21] so Coetzee makes Driepoot into a co-equal lover and beloved.

To be sure, this is no victorious, monologic allegory; human societies that permit so many "excess dogs" that euthanizing becomes an ethical act lie far from any City of God. Driepoot's death, even as it calls up a strong ethical vision, also calls to mind the vicious deaths of Lucy's dogs at human hands.[22] Only the old, unwanted, and angry bulldog Katy, David's female counterpart, survives. Yet David's ethical action grows out of the overwhelming feelings produced in him by the "theatre" of the dogs' impotence and suffering, and he sees himself as a *harijan*, the lowest of the low, doing ritualized work (146) whose deep ethical significance only Bev Shaw sees. So *harijan*, "disgraced" and untouchable dogs, in this "horizontal" allegory may become spiritual guides to authentic love, and frumpy animal activists may prove wiser than all, teaching self-sacrifice ("One gets used to things getting harder . . ." [219]) and responsibility. This is the erotic vision to which his disgrace has brought him: not to wallow in what he has lost, or in his own righteousness before his judges, or in his guilt before Melanie and her family, or even his self-regarding ideas of happiness, but to strip his old self away until only his "immortal longing" and a single act of selfless love shine through, transcending for a time what he had been. Giving up Driepoot, "bending to the tempest" (209), refusing the temptations of possession and control, and accepting his new future as a grandfather in rural South Africa are all related. The dog's love lives on in him as, perhaps, his love will live on in Lucy's child and in the country: desire without possession, desire that refuses possession, vision — and ethics — as eros. Teresa, tied to the Villa Gamba, has no way to take this final step. So David asks her "forgiveness" (214) because he cannot save her in the same way that she saved him. Immediately the novel takes us to the dogs' holding pens and the "generous . . . unconditional" love of an animal. Richard's claims that transcendence follows alienation of the spirit, and that "a virtue is nothing other than an ordered and moderated affection" (13) have been resituated, and affirmed (*Benjamin Major*, V, 2, and III, 23).[23]

IV, ii

> Morals have bedded with story-telling since the magic of the imaginative capacity developed in the human brain.
> — Nadine Gordimer

> We live in our own souls as in an unmapped region, a few acres of which we have cleared for our habitation; while of the nature of those nearest us we know but the boundaries that march with ours.
> — Edith Wharton, *The Touchstone*

The composition of the opera gives us the first of David's three decisive visions that round out *Disgrace*. The second — actually a small set of connected visions — comes shortly after he returns to the Dock Theatre to see Melanie Isaacs's ongoing performance in *Sunset at the Globe Salon* (190–94). Unlike all his other affairs, he still senses "something unfinished" about his relationship with Melanie, a "stored smell," while at the same time labeling any attempt to revive their affair as "crazy." This corresponds to the earliest stages of contemplation in Richard's hierarchy — the sensuous, imaginative perception of an object in the world: a beginning, but only that. He still sees Melanie selfishly as his last chance for youthful passion, for that "flash of feeling," but reluctantly affirms (in a witty alteration of mythic male leads) "The marriage of Cronos and Harmony: unnatural" (190).[24] This predictably launches another of his slightly bitter, self-regarding laments on old age, complete with phrases from Yeats and an audible sigh. But he knows that Melanie is back on stage, and he goes.

In an unusually straightforward piece of allegory, the Dock itself had been until recently a cold-storage holding bin for cattle carcasses headed for export, now revised into a "fashionable entertainment spot." Just so, *Sunset* has been revived in a newer, spiffier production, but remains a post-apartheid, "nakedly political," slapstick comedy with a multicultural cast. David still dislikes the play, whose too-easy achievement of cultural catharsis (23) Coetzee places his book against. But Melanie has found her voice in her reprised role as the novice hairdresser, and plays the part with an assurance and "deft timing" that she lacked before, either in performance or life. David speculates that perhaps Melanie has come through a trial of her own and been made stronger. Like his imagined Teresa, she has found a new self in an absurd part, asserted her independent voice in spite of the bad jokes and "vulgar" puns. Instead of a banjo or mandolin she wields a broom.

David, again in thrall to her youth and beauty, wishes for a "sign," and composes one: her clothes burning off in a "cold private flame" (echoing the flame he endured during Lucy's rape) and her standing "in a revelation secret to him alone," naked and perfect before him as she had in his daughter's room. It's a summary of his controlling desire to date, and a medieval vision out of Richard, charged with eros and idealization, repeating the enmeshing triangle of desire and incest, young lover and young daughter, both unavoidable and crippling. But David's eye has been educated by his reflections, and he moves past this appropriating vision of Melanie to see her not as an idealized young body but more as a blossoming actress (191) and independent daughter whose excellent performance he wishes to take pride in.[25] The transformation immediately yields two involuntary visions. A memory — perhaps the true sign he hoped for (191) — rises "without warning" of a young German tourist he had picked up years ago. He remembers her legs and soft hair, not in conquering, Byronic tones but with a warmth that leads to a second, deeper vision:

> In a sudden and soundless eruption, as if he had fallen into a waking dream, a stream of images pours down, images of women he has known on two continents, some from so far away in time that he barely recognizes them. Like leaves blown on the wind, pell-mell, they pass before him. *A fair field full of folk*: hundred of lives all tangled in his. He holds his breath, willing the vision to continue." (192)

Set against the opening catalog of "David's women" ("wives and mistresses" [7]), this set of streaming images from his deep time and space flows by quickly, yet each person is recognized. And the cumulative effect of all those faces is not more burnt-out exhaustion, more self-pitying retreat, but instead curiosity about their histories: an empathetic rather than narcissistic upwelling. Can the German girl be imagining him even as he imagines her? This experience does not offer unambiguous closure, but points the way to an erotic vision that draws on David's disgrace, comes out of that disgrace, and offers a sign. It turns on a word: *enriched*. David had "stupidly" used it to describe his relationship to Melanie to reporters during his trial (56), but now he's ready to "stand by it" as the right word for all his relationships with women: ". . . by each of them he was enriched, and by the others too, even the least of them, even the failures. Like a flower blooming in his breast, his heart floods with thankfulness" (192). The enrichment came from each woman to him, and he has carried it with him without knowing how to see it, until this moment. This comes close, I think, to Richard's claims for contemplation: its "enlargement (*mentis dilatation*) and lifting up (*mentis sublevatio*) of the spirit's vision," leading to its "adhering with wonder to the object that brings it joy."[26] The vision ends with questions: where do these "hypnagogic" moments come from; "what god is doing the leading?" Eros indeed: like Melanie in her play, David's "second act" of re-envisioning his chilling summary of the women in his life has been empowered by love.

David's overt literary associations with this vision are medieval, but with *Piers Plowman*, not Richard of St. Victor. Langland's dream-vision of "a fair field of folk" is slightly recast; the lives of these women folk are not occasions for satire, as are the men that pass before Piers in the poem, but, in a striking metaphoric sequence, their faces "pour down" on him, then ride the wind past him, before "tangling" (quite unlike scattered leaves) their lives (not just their images) with his.[27] In Richard's terms, David here sees more deeply into the "innermost part of things" because the "fog of error" and "cloud of sin" have been lifted from experience (*Major* IV, 4). That's not David's language, of course, but the description fits well; he does not stand apart to judge the fair field, but to embrace it. At the same time the "wives and mistresses" of David's early, callous catalog have become not some perfect, idealized, grace-filled vision of women — even in moments of visionary insight David will never entirely escape modernity or conventional maleness or South Africa — but the dream-memory of each woman has let him reclaim a word of great value: "enriched."

Then the vision is over, and Coetzee, like Joyce but in much more aggressive fashion, shows the limited impact of this epiphany on David's action. As a culmination of what he calls, without irony, his "*night of revelations*" (194) David eyes a leather-clad prostitute, a drugged girl even younger than Melanie, and has her service him on a dark cul-de-sac in his car. "*Why not?*" he asks himself, and experiences a post-orgasm "contentedness" just as he did with Melanie (19) and Soraya (5). This lacks the "anxious flurry" of his earlier promiscuity, and adds the "strangely protective" feeling he has toward the girl, but the whole encounter carries us back to his narcissism: Habitual old sex in the city. "*So this is all it takes*! he thinks. *How could I ever have forgotten it?* (194): Honest, true to character, but not a return to earlier "values" that anyone can admire, and hardly "enriching." The move from young love to protected daughter dissolves in David's familiar, destructive lusts. Sexual desire works in the present and imagines an immediate future; David knows this, and repeats a judgment he's expressed to the Isaacs, and to Rosalind: "Not a bad man but not good either" (195). He takes the benumbed girl back to her street corner, which may be more than he did for Melanie, but not much more. Plainly, even violently, Coetzee refuses any idealization of David's vision; by itself it is not enough. But it may clear the ground for a more important new beginning with his flesh-and-blood daughter, Lucy.

IV, iii

> Richard of St. Victor on the aftermath of an ecstatic vision: "For truly, we are led outside ourselves in two ways: At one time we are outside ourselves, but we descend below ourselves; at another time we are outside ourselves, but we are raised above ourselves. . . . But just as there is a two-fold going out, so there is also a two-fold return. From both goings out we return as it were to the dwelling place of our usual life, when after worldly labors or, preferably, after a manifestation of celestial contemplations, we bring the eyes of our mind back to the consideration of our morals, and through investigation of our innermost being we examine by studious reconsideration what sort of person we are ourselves. . .
>
> When Peter returned to himself he said: "Now I know truly that the Lord sent his angel." [Acts 12:11]
>
> — *Benjamin Major*, V: 8

Against the endlessness of skepticism Dostoevsky poses the closure not of confession but of absolution and therefore of the intervention of grace in the world. In that sense Dostoevsky is not a psychological novelist at all: he is finally not interested in the psyche, which he sees as an arena of game-playing, of the *middle* of a novel. To the extent that I am taken as a political novelist, it may be because I take it as given that people must be treated as fully responsible beings. Psychology is no excuse. Politics, in its wise stupidity, is at one with religion here: one man, one soul, no half measures. What saves me from a mere stupid stupidity, I would hope, is a measure of charity, which is, I suppose, the way grace allegorizes itself in the world. Another way of saying this is that I try not to lose sight of the reality that we are children, unreconstructed (Freud wouldn't disagree at this point), to be treated with the charity that children have due to them (charity doesn't preclude clear-sightedness).

— J. M. Coetzee, "Interview" ("Autobiography and Confession"), *Doubling the Point*, 249

David's final vision emerges out of his fifteenth and final exchange with Lucy, during which he begins to accept her choice to keep her baby. Lucy deliberately wills her future; she will, following nature, come to love her child, and shall choose to be "a good mother and a good person." David responds yet again with "it's too late for me" sourness, but a seed has been planted: "A good person. Not a bad resolution to make, in dark times" (216). Love and the ethical now interweave for Lucy, and David will struggle to achieve the same.

Returning uninvited to the farm a few days later, David leaves his truck at the last hillcrest and walks the remaining distance. The scene echoes his first view of his daughter months earlier, when he first arrived in the Eastern Cape ("From the shade of the stoep Lucy emerges into the sunlight. For a moment he does not recognize her" [59]). This time he gains an overview of the novel's central landscape in its "season of blooming," its "bees . . . in seventh heaven," before walking down the hill toward his daughter, engrossed in her gardening "among the flowers" (216–17). The ducks and geese are on the pond, "visitors from afar," but no other people are in sight. He halts at the border fence, honoring Lucy's independence, and watches her work alongside her "snoozing" watchdog, Katy. His imagination and reason work together to produce a remarkable four-part instance of Richard's second level of contemplation. The scene's mood matches his imagined music for the young Teresa: "lushly autumnal yet edged with irony . . ." (181).

David's eye goes first to "the milky, blue-veined skin and broad, vulnerable tendons of the backs of her knees, the least beautiful part of a woman's body, the least expressive, and therefore perhaps the most endearing" (217). Unsurprisingly, his vision begins at an unattractive low point; his curdled imagination isolates the "least beautiful" body part, as it often has when David sought to protect his isolation and superiority. Even the fact that he finds it "endearing" is ambiguous, since this could mark his characteristic condescension toward women as easily as a fresh turn toward grace and the future. Ditto the beginning of Lucy's transformation into a peasant that follows, a transformation repeating that of the imagined *contadina* Teresa (181) as she moved "beyond honor" to the disgrace that ultimately enabled her assertion of free selfhood. In Teresa's aria David listens to the voice of an authentic other, and the hidden, declining Byron completes the triangle; in this portrait Lucy and her hidden, waxing child are honored in their separate integrity in David's vision.

For all of the novel's controlled, clean prose, the scene follows the path of Teresa's monologue arias in yet another way, operatically soaring past loss and degradation to discovery. Here the "peasant" comparison sparks the idea of the "immemorial" that will expand as the vision unfolds. David then imagines, lyrically, Lucy's entire existence, from "tadpole" to the "solid" woman now before him that carries a future: a child who will continue a "line of existences." David knows that his "share" in the line will "inexorably" be forgotten, yet in another rising turn he sees himself "a grandfather. A Joseph. Who would have thought it!" (217). Like the Virgin's husband, David hopes to be a useful bystander in the birth of a new generation.[28]

Continuing the up-and-down rhythm of his vision, David then thinks, conventionally, of his inability to lure a pretty girl to his bed once more, but, as with his early reservations, this tired line of thought gives way to affirmation. Instead of imagining a blood grandchild, he imagines adopting and accepting Lucy's child, fathered in hatred and violence. As we have seen, Lucy's single description of her rapists concentrated on their look of utter hostility: she anticipated what the sexual assault would be like, but not the vision-as-hatred that came with it. So the weight of the passage falls instead on David placing himself in a new line of descent, one arising from a violent act that he abhors but which nonetheless creates a future ("What will it entail, being a grandfather?").

Ever the literary man, David muses on instructing himself in grandfathering by rereading Hugo, even as he had mused on being the "shadow-father" to Soraya's children (6). He tallies up the reasons for his predicted "below average" success; he lacks "the virtues of the old: equanimity, kindliness, patience" (217). Yet this vision, and the book's last scene, both show him to be practicing just these virtues: a wish fulfilled? Then he offers a strange idea: that the "virtue of passion" might fade as these more equitable virtues rise in him. It suddenly makes us re-see David's first "vision of eros": passion — its natural rightness in the face of the prejudiced judicial committee, its integrity as represented in the vision of Blake (69) and the fable of the male dog whipped for desire (90).[29] But now "passion" can no longer stand as a separate, self-justifying virtue, but must be integrated with love and forbearance and respect for the irreducible otherness of its object. It must be refigured in a wider notion of the "vision of eros," one that embraces all desire from the sexual to the selflessly loving.[30] The roots of his vision run right through the book, in every scene.

Then "the wind drops" and his vision climaxes in

> a moment of utter stillness which he would wish prolonged for ever: the gentle sun, the stillness of mid-afternoon, bees busy in a field of flowers, and at the centre of the picture a young woman, *das ewig Weibliche*, lightly pregnant, in a straw sunhat. A scene ready-made for a Sargent or a Bonnard. City boys like him; but even city boys can recognize beauty when they see it, can have their breath taken away. (218)

The setting is Wordsworthian, but the main weight falls on the pictorial as great painters might envision, and on David's involuntary associations with *Faust* and Richard of St. Victor, his aesthetic and visionary frames. Lucy metamorphoses from a thick-kneed unattractive woman to an archetypal peasant to Goethe's last, overriding archetype of the "eternal feminine," an oxymoronically "lightly pregnant" young woman that saves Faust from narcissistic passion and hatred and carries him to a higher world. Her "broad, vulnerable tendons" have become beautiful, transformed by contemplation into a vision worthy of two worldly painters (though not an imitation of them). The narration balances David's aesthetic self-consciousness and postmodern skepticism with his genuine rapture. Like the two veteran painters he too may be a sophisticated "city boy," but the vision literally took his breath away, translated him for a moment from our "breathing world" to the spiritual kingdom of Byron's fallen angel (32), or of Boito's Mefistofele, defeated by the *ewig Weibliche* and rose-scattering cherubim — and then decisively returned him to time, self-consciousness, and Lucy. The subjunctive verb "would wish" positions him perfectly; were it not for the finally more valuable quotidian reality of the scene, he might well wish for the vision's "timeless beauty" to never end.

David ends his meditation with a brief inquiry in which he tries to unite the good and the beautiful. He reviews the history of his own gazing — only "pretty girls" — and the paucity of that history leads to the pivotal ethical and aesthetic question: "Is it too late to educate the eye?" to see as I just have, and then to act on that vision? David begins an answer by calling out again to his daughter, who, in a final addition to the *ewig Weibliche* portrait, "looks the picture of health." After a dozen earlier accounts of her aging, unattractive body, the change is remarkable. Her formal but friendly offer of tea marks a new beginning of their relationship: "Visitorship, visitation: a new footing, a new start" (218). "Visitation" places us first in the realm of parents and children meeting on new footing after separation and divorce; then in religion, when the Virgin visited

Elizabeth, pregnant with John the Baptist (the second "joyful mystery" of the rosary). Elizabeth (or Mary) sang "The Song of Hannah," a poem-prayer (1 Samuel 2:1–10) giving thanks to Yahweh for the birth of her son, Samuel: A word, a contemplation, and an action worthy of Richard of St. Victor.[31]

Put thematically, grace may be present near this narrative's end, but disgrace does not vanish; David's self-pronounced sentence of "disgrace without term" (172) remains in force. Pessimistic? — perhaps, if by pessimism we mean a distrust of all fables of steady, upward human progress and any easy, settled connection between self-knowledge and action in the world.[32] Optimistic? — perhaps, if by optimism we mean that human change for the better is possible, if fitful; and that one's habitual actions can be altered, though rarely obliterated; that love in any form can proffer meaning. Richard of St. Victor's account of the "unknowing" that carries the visionary past rational knowledge, and then of the memory of that "unknowing," attains a Proustian subtlety that illuminates David's encounter:

> And although we may retain in memory something from that experience and see it through a veil, as it were, and as though in the middle of a cloud, we lack the ability to comprehend or call to mind either the manner of seeing or the quality of the vision. And marvelously, in a way remembering, we do not remember; and not remembering, we remember . . . (*Benjamin Major*, IV, 23)

V

> Don't you become like someone called in from the street, a beggar, for instance, offered fifty kopeks to dispose of an old blind dog, who takes the rope and ties the noose and strokes the dog to calm it . . . and as he does so feels a current of feeling begin to flow, so that from that instant onward he and the dog are no longer strangers, and what should have been a mere job of work has turned into the blackest betrayal . . . ?
> — J. M. Coetzee, *The Master of Petersburg*, 99

> It's as accurate a measure as any of a society: what is the smallest act of kindness that is considered heroic?
> — Anne Michaels. *Fugitive Pieces*, 162

> *Sunt lacrimae rerum, et mentum mortalia tangunt.*
> — *Aeneid* I, 461–62 and *Disgrace*, 162

As we approach the novel's final scene, and the hard questions about desire, ethics, and literary form that it raises, I want to round out this account of the visionary in *Disgrace* with one final way of reading its dynamics. I apologize for introducing yet another angle of vision at the eleventh hour, but I think that Charles Altieri gives us an important, specifically literary way to understand the ethical connection between lyric vision and David's actions with the dogs, between the visionary and ethical praxis:

> Literary modes like lyric often ask us to participate in states that are either too elemental or too transcendental or too absolute or too satisfyingly self-absorbed to engage ethical criticism. Yet these states can have enormous impact on how and why we are concerned with values of all kinds ... at their richest these works explore the limitations of all judgmental stances by requiring complex blends of sympathy and distance, and hence eliciting our fascination with extreme states of mind while complicating any possible grasp of how one might put such states into the categories of commensurability upon which ethical judgments may ultimately depend.[33]

While analyses of ethics in narrative almost always turn on questions of agency — a character's, an author's, a reader's — Altieri develops the idea that the lyrical experience can shape those states that typically come before any of our specific actions. So, at first, David's vision of a meaningful future as accepting father and loving grandparent — familial, life-celebrating, desirable — may seem to stand in sharp contrast to his future-erasing decision to euthanize Driepoot this week rather than next. Altieri's account, however, lets us see them as of a piece; David's visionary experiences prepare him, in Bev Shaw's "*condilectio*" company, to see Driepoot clearly as a doomed animal with a pain-filled life, not as his private pet or sentimental companion. Visionary love is not blind; it integrates and clarifies, and like great lyric prepares the way for action. David can at last separate his desire from the need to control the desired; making the dog an exception would be in the service of his old narcissism, not his love. He now desires not to desire in the old, narrow ways. This enables him to act on what he knows, even — especially — if that action is not self-gratifying. His love is what Richard of St. Victor called "violent": absolute, and ruthless, in a spiritual stage beyond the immediate "blackest betrayal" sensed by *The Master of Petersburg's* beggar in my epigraph. *Disgrace* shows us how lyrical envisioning provides a space in the spirit from which ethical choices can emerge without diminishing their painful complexity.

Finally, there's the significance of *Disgrace's* organization, the formal side of what Coetzee termed "grace allegorizing itself in our world." Its twenty-four chapters match the twenty-four dogs that Bev and David put down on the book's final day, with the limping, "incomplete" Driepoot matching the three-legged final chapter, seemingly incomplete in action and in meaning. It's a formal gesture that confirms the novel's uncompromising, austere conclusion. For some it's a disgraceful ending, leaving readers morally uncertain and aesthetically dissatisfied, just as its account of South Africa's still-divided and violent culture has angered other citizens anxious for brighter visions of their country's future. But a careful reading complicates these claims for frustrating incompleteness or defeatist cultural analysis. It's easy to imagine that David's future, "unreconstructed" life in the harsh new South Africa will include further backsliding as well as further *harijan* service; Richard's "virtuous shame" of disgrace remains, but it has enabled David's vision of a new family and loving loyalty to the unwanted dogs. His knowing visions align with Altieri's account of lyric's rich dynamic: greater sympathy and greater distance together. In *Age of Iron* Elizabeth Curren, seeking to aid the homeless Mr. Vercueil and the young black rebel John, describes herself as "full enough to give and to give from one's fullness," and claims that "One must love what is nearest. One must love what is to hand, as a dog loves" (7, 190). By stripping himself of distorted stories of desire, and by his openness to visions of animal love, "immortal longing," and his daughter's independent future, David arrives at a similar place. His final words, "I am giving him up," are poised in the present between intention and completion.[34] This abrupt finish, its "limping" incompleteness echoing David's opera, at the same time preserves openness to the future. We have concluded our journey through disgrace's many permutations, but David's future, like South Africa's, remains in suspension.

Coetzee's consistent reliance on the visionary throughout his fictions is part of his strong resistance to reductive materialism, and to any single-level, monologic accounts of subjectivity and ethics, politics and history. More particularly, in *Disgrace*, he probes the complex relationships between desire, vision, and the ethical. Desire is often at odds with the latter two, as in David's city-bred gazing or in his exploitation of Melanie. Unreflective gazing can make desire a self-justifying anchor of action, while the ethical may seem to refuse desire altogether. But *Disgrace* doesn't rest in a puritanical account of this subject; controlled or suppressed desire doesn't by itself lead to the good life. Instead it explores how the visionary and the ethical require desire's energy and drive toward an imagined future to meet their aims: vision *as* eros, understood in the widest terms. By showing this Coetzee makes a place for the visionary within his chastened, clear-sighted humanism. It gives him an allegorical route for preserving the discoveries of a medieval mystic and three Romantic poets in his writing without reviving them forcibly, or accepting them in an uncritical way. It also lets him explore "horizontally" the symmetries between artistic and religious vision, and to connect both to ethical action, to seeing things anew. It is still not too late to "take our breath away" (218), and to do so without taking away our skepticism, our convictions, or our educated eye.

Notes

[1] "Interview" (on Kafka's "The Burrow") in *Doubling the Point*, 203.
[2] "Interview" (on "The Poetics of Reciprocity") in *Doubling the Point*, 57. It's also worth mentioning that Coetzee, a Protestant by heritage, received his secondary education at a Marist high school in Cape Town.
[3] There is the tantalizing case of Richard's first Abbot, one Ernisius, who was accused of "misconduct" and eventually dismissed from the Augustinian monastery of St. Victor by a papal commission. The misconduct was apparently more administrative than erotic, but Ernisius's "disgrace" resonates teasingly for readers of David's story. The charges against him included "appointing his favorites to office and acting in prejudicial ways" (Zinn, "Introduction," 4), perhaps the monastic equivalents of David's institutional offenses. (Richard himself is credited with a work with another provocative title: *Liber Penitentialis I.*)
[4] By choosing these titles Richard places himself directly in line with his famous predecessor: Hugh of St. Victor's *On the Moral Ark of Noah* and *On the Mystical Ark of Noah* also trace the stages of the contemplative life.
[5] Matt. 11:29: quoted by Richard in *Benjamin Minor*, chapter 46.
[6] That shame counts as a virtue in Richard's scheme does not mean that it functions only in the righteous: "Even perverse men have shame, but if only it were good, if only it were ordered! For if they had good shame [what Dinah represents], perhaps they would not be perverse" (*Benjamin Minor*, 46).
[7] He treats disgrace as a subset of shame (*Benjamin Minor*, 67).
[8] South African writer Zakes Mda's novel *The Madonna of Excelsior* (2004) offers an intriguing parallel. Niki, the lead character, was raped and impregnated by an Afrikaner farmer thirty years earlier (the well-known "Immorality Act" trial of 1971). In the novel's present she accepts a ride from her attacker, and they discuss, without resolution, the possibilities of forgiveness.
[9] "Interview" (on "The Poetics of Reciprocity") in *Doubling the Point*, 63.
[10] David's theory of poetry, which he crassly uses to seduce Melanie Isaacs, rests on the equation between the poem's "flash of revelation" and the listener's "flash of response. Like lightning. Like falling in love" (13). But in practice his own language-focused interpretation of poetry concentrates on craft, not revelation.
[11] The recent book *Toward a Theology of Eros: Transfiguring Passion at the Limits of Discipline*, edited by Virginia Burrus and Catherine Keller, places this tradition in theology in a fresh context.
[12] *De Trinitate*, III, xix, in Zinn, 392. As C. S. Lewis's *The Allegory of Love* attests, "love" was a hot topic throughout the twelfth century.
[13] *Postmodernism*, 167–68. I'm equally indebted to Dominic Head's excellent discussion of postmodern allegory in his *J. M. Coetzee*. See also Bill Brown's remarkable *PMLA* essay on the religious and the medieval in Jameson himself: "The Dark Wood of Postmodernity (Space, Faith, Allegory)."
[14] Here, and in several other scenes, the reader remembers that St. Lucy is the patron saint of the blind.

[15] This is a familiar Coetzee theme: the Magistrate in *Waiting for the Barbarians* enjoyed the "easy morals of the oases" of Empire, "the long-scented summer evenings, the complaisant sloe-eyed women. Later that promiscuity modulated into more discreet relations with housekeepers and girls lodged sometimes upstairs in my rooms but more often downstairs with the kitchen help . . ." But the outcome was the same: "Desire seemed to bring with it a pathos of distance and separation which it was futile to deny" (45).

[16] David cites the Church Fathers' view of animals' souls (78), for example, in addition to these saints. St. Hubert's story, which David doesn't quite have right, gives us another womanizer brought to his full character by a remarkable vision. The gay blade Hubert (656–727), the eldest son of Bertrand, Duke of Aquitaine, and grandson of Charibert, King of Toulouse, married Floribanne, daughter of Dagobert, Count of Louvain, and seemed to have given himself entirely up to the pomp and vanities of this world. But a great spiritual revolution was imminent. "On Good Friday morn, when the faithful were crowding the churches, Hubert sallied forth to the chase. As he was pursuing a magnificent stag, the animal turned and, as the pious legend narrates, he was astounded at perceiving a crucifix between its antlers, while he heard a voice saying: 'Hubert, unless thou turnest to the Lord, and leadest an holy life, thou shalt quickly go down into hell.' Hubert dismounted, prostrated himself and said, 'Lord, what wouldst Thou have me do?' He received the answer, 'Go and seek Lambert, and he will instruct you" (C. F. W. Brown, *The Catholic Encyclopedia*). St. Hubert, of course, is a patron saint of hunters, but also animal lovers and caregivers; he cured dogs of hydrophobia.

[17] Several readers have commented on the similarities between David's trial and the hearings of South Africa's Truth and Reconciliation Commission. See, for example, Rosemary Jolly, "Going to the Dogs: Humanity in J. M. Coetzee's *Disgrace*, *The Lives of Animals*, and South Africa's Truth and Reconciliation Commission" in Poyner, 148–71.

[18] There are several other possible operatic sources for David's composition. For example, Virgil Thompson wrote a three-act opera on Byron. It has a simple melodic style, and uses pastiche and popular tunes, such as "Auld Lang Syne" and "Ach du lieber Augustine": banjo-friendly practices that David/Coetzee may have borrowed. Thompson's Teresa is a character, but Byron commands the stage throughout. Then there's the libretto "Lord Byron's Love Letter" (1955) by Tennessee Williams, set by composer Raffaello de Banfield. It features an old woman and her granddaughter who have one love letter of Byron's that they show only to paying customers. Its music is also a pastiche: Puccini, Strauss, and Menotti. *New York Times* reviewer Tim Page, after a performance at the 1986 Spoleto festival, remarked that Williams and de Banfield deserved equal credit for the work's obscurity.

[19] This strongly resembles Coetzee's description of his own artistic process: "Writing is not free expression. There is a true sense in which writing is dialogic: a matter of awakening the countervoices in oneself and embarking upon speech with

them. It is some measure of a writer's seriousness whether he does evoke/invoke these countervoices in himself, that is, step down from the position of what Lacan calls 'the subject supposed to know'" ("The Poetics of Reciprocity" in *Doubling the Point*, 65).

[20] Is this a suggestive symmetry with the three rapists, giving another, deliberately vague glimpse into the future of South Africa?

[21] Gervais Dumeige, *Richard de Saint-Victor et l'idée chrétienne de l'amour*, 90, 31.

[22] For admirers of Barry Lopez it also brings to mind his 1989 *Apologia*, a meditation on the many "road kill" animals he has removed from American highways and honored as best he could.

[23] Timothy Frances Strode's stimulating account of space and the ethical makes much the same point: "I will be much more interested in 'exteriority,' a term related implicitly to the idea of exile, to an orientation outward . . . toward a beyond that is ethically, domestically, and geographically opposed to, or better yet, other to propriety and possession. . . . In ethical terms, my focus will turn toward the idea of hospitality, an ethical orientation that could be said to begin to manifest itself to the degree that propriety — the moral form that best characterizes the ethical orientation of territoriality — absents itself" (178).

[24] Cadmus was a young rescuer of Zeus, while Harmony was the daughter of Aphrodite and sister of Eros; their wedding marked the last time, in myth, that all the Olympian gods and living men sat at the same banquet table and toasted one another. In old age their deep eros turned Cadmus and Harmony into intertwined snakes, an image that recalls David's totem animal (Calasso, 381ff.).

[25] Lucy Valerie Graham (2003, 438) reads this paternal feeling as a further instance of David's patriarchal claim on Melanie as "his property," and links his emotions solely to the satisfactions of power, not as genuine, if transferred, fatherly pride. By extension, this would level out David's vision and his subsequent pick-up of the prostitute, lumping them together as yet more examples of his claims of privilege and control. It denies, or rather reduces, any potentially praiseworthy feeling in David's psyche to an expression of dominance, sublimated or direct. Graham's David, like Farodia Rasool's David in the university "inquiry" scene, must remain representative, and can be made acceptable only in accordance with a certain script. His claim that with Melanie he experienced "something generous that was doing its best to flower" (89) cannot be accepted at face value.

[26] *Major* I, 3 and V, 2. Consider also this lovely passage from *Major* II, 5, which could pass as a description of David's character at this moment, and arguably of the novel as a whole: "We are easily able to grasp a working of nature. As in grasses, in trees and in animals: in grasses, how they grow and mature; in trees, how they leaf out blossom and bear fruit; in animals, how they conceive and give birth, how some grow and others die. . . . An artificial work is considered a work of human activity, as in engraving, in painting, in writing, in agriculture and in other artificial works, in all of which we find many things for which we ought worthily to venerate and marvel at the dignity of a divine gift. And so, because they cooperate mutually

with each other, natural work and artificial work are joined to each other on the sides, as it were from the side, and are united together in themselves by mutual contemplation."

[27] The leaves recall *Iliad* VI, and Glaucon's oft-quoted parable of the generations passing as leaves, but more pertinently the rose petals of love that the chorus of women (cherubim in Boito) cast down on the great negator Mephistopheles in *Faust*, driving him away with eros.

[28] Richard's typology in *Benjamin Minor*, chapter 70, gives us an allegorical Joseph embodying the "discretion" and "complete self-knowledge," the "care and keeping of all his brothers," and "the foresight of future things." Joseph knows "the vices of the heart and the infirmities of the body," knowledge hard-won by David as well.

[29] Elizabeth Curren extends this figure in a remarkable way in *Age of Iron*, Coetzee's novel preceding *Disgrace* and its spiritual twin: "This letter has become a maze, and I a dog in the maze, scurrying up and down the branches and tunnels, scratching and whining at the same old places, tiring, tired. Why do I not call for help, call to God? Because God cannot help me. God is looking for me but he cannot reach me. God is another dog in the maze. I smell God and God smells me. I am the bitch in her time, God the male. God smells me, he can think of nothing else but finding me and taking me" (137–38).

[30] Here is Faust himself, in the epilogue of Boito's *Mefistofele*: "Ogni mortal": Every mortal / mystery I have savored, / The real, the Ideal, / the love of a maiden, / the love of a goddess. . . . Yes. / But Reality brought suffering / and the Ideal was a dream. / Having reached the last step / of extreme old age, / my soul now delights / in a final dream: / king of a tranquil world, / of a boundless expanse, / I want to give life / to a fruitful people." Translation supervised by Gwyn Morris.

[31] See also Rita Barnard. "Coetzee's Country Ways," 390.

[32] See Joshua Foa Dienstag, *Pessimism: Philosophy, Ethic, Spirit*.

[33] Charles Altieri. "Lyrical Ethics and Literary Experience."

[34] See Mark Sanders, "Disgrace," 363–73, esp. 368.

4: *Disgrace* and the Neighbor: An Interchange with Bill McDonald

Kenneth Reinhard

IN HIS ESSAY, "'IS IT TO LATE TO EDUCATE THE EYE?': David Lurie, Richard of St. Victor, and 'vision as eros' in *Disgrace*," Bill McDonald is primarily concerned with the nature of erotic vision in Coetzee's novel, and the possibilities — and limitations — of the redemption that vision represents. The central character in *Disgrace*, David Lurie, is a literary critic, and McDonald has taken seriously the account we are given of Lurie's main scholarly works, in particular, his monograph on the twelfth-century Christian mystic, Richard of St. Victor. McDonald shows how this work, as well as Lurie's books on Boito's opera *Mefistofele* and Wordsworth's sense of history, informs the development of Lurie's character, as well as Coetzee's novel on a more structural level. McDonald describes the transformation of Lurie's "disgrace" into a kind of "grace," parallel with, as McDonald writes, "the contemplative, ascetic spirit" if not the precise stages of the soul's journey to redemption described in Richard's writings. Coetzee's novel, however, works in a modernist or perhaps postmodernist mode, with an ambiguous conclusion — ironic, ambivalent, indeed, according to McDonald, inconclusive. Although he does not discuss in detail the surprisingly harsh criticism *Disgrace* has received for the various perspectives on post-apartheid South Africa that some readers have attributed to it, McDonald makes it clear that the novel's politics must not be understood as either an independent issue or as an allegorical counterpart to the various sexual relationships presented in it. Rather, the politics of Coetzee's novel are *intrinsically* erotic. No "vision" that the novel may present for the future of South Africa can be separated from the varieties of violent sexual experience it represents or imagines, from seduction and rape to prostitution and adultery. Moreover, McDonald shows how this violence is not merely understood as associated with sexuality, as we might expect, but with *love*; such "violent love" may not only be inevitable in the traumatized landscape of South Africa, it may be the very condition of salvation. As McDonald indicates, such an account of love's salutary violence is central to Richard of St. Victor's thinking, especially in his *Four Degrees of Violent Charity*, as is evident from its title ("charity" of course is the translation of *caritas*, the Latin version of *agape*, used by early Christianity to signify non-erotic modes of love). McDonald's reading does not condemn Coetzee for the violence of his representations of eros, but sees that whatever political vision the novel may have must be understood as not incidentally but necessarily, and even *redemptively*, bound up with that violence.

I have two sets of related questions and comments about Bill McDonald's reading of *Disgrace*, both of which ultimately involve the role of Richard of St. Victor's writings in the novel. The first has to do with the nature of *vision* in the novel, and the possibilities of redemption that may or may not be available through it; the second has to do with the nature of social relations between people who are neither friends nor enemies, the question of the *neighbor* in the novel. Both vision and the neighbor are, finally, bound up with *love* in Richard of St. Victor's writings and Coetzee's novel. And for both Richard and Coetzee, love implies a certain violence that cannot remain merely contemplative.

First, what are the redemptive possibilities and limitations of *vision*? For Richard of St. Victor, in the tradition of the Pseudo-Dionysius and earlier Neoplatonism, contemplative "vision" is a spiritual tool that harnesses erotic drives for the purpose of mystical union with God. In St. Augustine's distinction, it is for the goal of the *enjoyment* (*frui*) of its object rather than instrumental "use" (*uti*) — an enjoyment that is for its own sake and, finally, only completely realized in the form of enjoyment of God.[1] For David Lurie in *Disgrace*, vision is not only the primary conduit for his sexual attractions but, as McDonald points out, the rhetorical lure that he uses to seduce Melanie Isaacs in (and out of) his literature class, in tendentious figures such as his description of poetry as a "flash of revelation and a flash of response. Like lightning. Like falling in love" (13). Lurie's question, which is taken up by McDonald, "is it too late to educate the eye?" could be reformulated as the question of whether Lurie can find in his own personal and intellectual history the resources to transform his erotic "use" of the object of vision into something closer to Augustine's notion of enjoyment. McDonald writes, "It is above all in his visionary life . . . that David achieves a measure of self-knowledge and aesthetic breakthrough that culminate in loving ethical action." The three central visions that McDonald describes in the novel — Lurie's "re-envisioning" of his opera; the stream of images of women from his past during Melanie's play; and, at the end of the novel, Lurie's vision of his daughter Lucy and the possibility of a new life — all point to what McDonald calls "an ethic that resituates desire in full recognition of the other."

My first question is not only whether or not it is indeed "too late" for David Lurie to redeem his vision, to transform it from sexual "use" to higher "enjoyment," for the sake of self-knowledge and ethical action, but whether it is possible at all. That is, can a transformation of the nature of vision — whether erotic, intellectual, or spiritual — constitute ethical transformation? Does it have such resources in the novel or is it fundamentally limited, bound up with a model of knowledge that remains spectatorial (and even specular) and without either sufficient passivity or activity to be transformative? And even if a certain possibility of subjective change were available to David Lurie by means of vision, would it really have any significance for political change in South Africa? Insofar as Lurie is the central character and consciousness of the novel, we might expect the question of whether or not his personal disgrace can lead to any kind of redemptive grace to be key to the novel's ethical or political significance. Indeed, I would argue that Lurie's personal path of penance as the loving Angel of Death for abandoned animals is merely personal — rather than an act meant to transform the world he lives in, it merely serves to change his relationship to that world. Finally, Lurie's subjective transformation, such as it is, is not what the novel — or the reader — really cares about. Lurie is a dead end, the last of a line. His grandchild will *not* be his, will *not* transmit his culture or values, but will be part of something completely unknowable and absolutely independent of him. I think it is clear that the character of David Lurie changes to a certain extent over the novel, at least in terms of his erotic objects; although he continues to frequent prostitutes when inclined, he also has had a less illicit and pathetic, if still not quite legitimate, relationship with a (married) woman of his own age, Bev, and we are inclined to doubt that there will be many more Melanies in his life. But all David has ever gained from relationships is "self-knowledge" as a mode of intellectual narcissism and that is all that he seems to achieve by the end of the book. It is fine for David to accomplish some measure of understanding of himself, but such knowledge is not the same as transformation, and may not be an indication of real change — either on a personal or on a political level. Indeed, it may be an *impediment* to change, an imaginary screen against a vision that David cannot face. "Love of the neighbor," we should recall, is not predicated on or conditioned by self-knowledge, but self-*love* — and "love" must be taken, as both Richard of St. Victor and Freud do, as intrinsically violent, ambivalent, and potentially not only self-transformative, but transformative of a world. As McDonald indicates, David Lurie's characteristic vision at the beginning is erotic in a detached, analytic mode; vision as sexual knowledge, we might say, whether in evaluating his regular prostitute Soraya or Melanie, the young student on whom he fixes his eye. Vision is the first moment of sexual penetration for Lurie, and the end is possession, consumption, and finally evacuation of the object. This kind of erotic vision is fully parallel with Lurie's literary critical methodology, which is again more about self-knowledge than knowledge of something outside of himself, something truly other. Lurie's sexual and critical vision are both, we might say, "jaded": he sees merely what he has already seen, and there is nothing new under the sun, merely variations on a theme (whether poetic, musical, or feminine).

The first of the three visions that McDonald describes in the novel centers on David Lurie's opera on Byron and Teresa Guiccioli; as McDonald indicates, Lurie finds himself surprised by his own rewriting of Teresa, who comes to resemble the middle-aged Bev, a comic figure, rather than the sort of suggestible younger woman that is his usual fare. Whereas Lurie had originally planned to "borrow" the melodies for his opera from a composer such as Gluck, this revised Teresa now acts as his muse for the composition of a simple, folk-based but original score. For McDonald, this transformation of Teresa-as-Bev represents Lurie moving "beyond the narcissism" that had prevented him from being open to something truly other than himself. Nevertheless, as McDonald also writes, "she becomes his guide to a new purpose, and a new self-understanding." However, I wonder if Lurie's "self-understanding" is anything more than that: *self*-understanding, a more intellectualized mode of his fundamental narcissism? Is he not a character who, in this scene of re-visionary understanding and the similar scenes that follow, merely comes to reflect more deeply on himself? Do his visions ever show him anything other than himself, that is, any *other* human being? Indeed, even his work at the animal shelter and crematorium does not directly involve him with other people; it is as if he does it for the sake of seeing himself as charitable, as relating to and offering loving service to another creature, even in a mode as violent as providing the mercy of an easy death to an unwanted animal.

The second sequence of Lurie's visions remains just as solipsistic. In his reading of the scene where David watches Melanie acting in *Sunset at the Globe Salon*, McDonald argues that "David's eye has been educated by his reflections," and he no longer sees Melanie as an object of sexual desire, but more as "a surrogate daughter whose excellent performance he wishes to take pride in." This leads to a visionary sequence in which Lurie suddenly is flooded with "images of women he has known on two continents," the women he has slept with and, sometimes, loved. McDonald understands this image as "an empathetic rather than narcissistic upwelling"; and even though he points to the irony in Lurie describing the women as having all "enriched" him, using the same infelicitous word that he had earlier used to justify his relationship with Melanie, McDonald nevertheless regards this sequence of visions as representative of authentic ethical or spiritual progress, along the lines of the path described by Richard of St. Victor. But once again it is simply Lurie himself who is the focus of this "enrichment": the women swirling in his vision like leaves, "a fair field of folk" as Lurie puts it, quoting *Piers Plowman* and alluding to a tradition of such visions in Homer, Dante, and elsewhere, are dancing on his private stage, as supporting actresses or foils for, again, his *self*-discovery. Once again, vision is a path of development, but one that has little to do with the encounter with other people; once again Lurie is working out his own psychodrama in a vision that is hardly his own, but borrowed from other writers and artists. Indeed, McDonald agrees that the vision has "limited impact . . . on David's action," insofar as, upon leaving the theater, he comes across a pathetic, drugged-out prostitute, even younger than Melanie, and has sex with her. McDonald writes, "Plainly, even violently, Coetzee refuses any idealization of David's vision; by itself it is not enough. But it may clear the ground for a more important new beginning with his flesh and blood daughter, Lucy."

There is little indication, however, that David Lurie's increasing self-knowledge, as demonstrated by this sequence of visions, has any consequences beyond, well, self-knowledge. Has he become more ethical? Has he changed in other than purely subjective ways? And even if his self-reflection has indeed transformed his sense of himself, should we care? Is Coetzee and the novel really very interested in David Lurie's personal transformation or lack thereof? Perhaps; but I believe that Lurie is something of a "lure" in the novel, a red herring that leads the unwary reader into the trap of identification and the illusory assumption that a change of vision is the same as a vision of change. We are likely to regard Lurie as debauched or at least foolish and strangely self-destructive at the beginning of the novel; but are not his attempts to connect with his estranged and damaged daughter, his relationship with Bev, and his growing care for abandoned animals, all presented to us as invitations to empathize and even identify with him? There is no doubt that he has been "enriched" as a character by these developments, but if we are satisfied by these signs of his ethical growth, aren't we also tacitly endorsing his unrepentant claim that he has "enriched" Melanie by seducing her? And further, doesn't this slippery slope become even more unstable when we realize that such a claim could similarly be made by Lucy's rapists, if they were as educated as Lurie — that they were merely "enriching" her? To understand the question of his development as an ethical individual or as a literary character as being central to the novel's mythos and ethos is to remain within a paradigm of subjectivity and responsibility that may not operate in the new South Africa. David Lurie, I believe, will be left out of whatever brave new world it is that Lucy's child will be born into.[2]

The third vision that McDonald describes involves a painterly scene of David watching his pregnant daughter, Lucy, working in her fields. Here Lurie seems to accept Lucy's decision to keep the child and to marry Petrus, even accepting the fact that she will become a member of the same family as the men who raped her. Lurie sees himself as the grandfather of a new lineage that will derive from the birth, and convert its violent origins into a new beginning, a new race mixing whites and blacks in South Africa even if his contribution to it will quickly dwindle and likely be forgotten. So what do we make of Lurie's vision of his daughter as a figure in a painting, "a Sargent or Bonnard"? No longer does he see her in more or less erotic terms, but as something more aestheticized and allegorical, "the eternal feminine" as he puts it, a sort of earth mother, or Principle of Generation. "The truth is," Coetzee writes, Lurie "has never had much of an eye for rural life, despite all his reading of Wordsworth. Not much of an eye for anything, except pretty girls; and where has that got him? Is it too late to educate the eye?" (218). I think that we must take this as a real question, not merely rhetorical; and I am inclined to respond, Yes — it *is* too late for David Lurie, but for Lucy, her child, and South Africa, and finally for us, the book's readers, the question of David's vision must be subordinated to larger questions and concerns. In contemplating the scene of the pregnant Lucy working in the fields, "becoming a peasant," David sees her world as a painting, a study in color and light, figure and ground; he may not have had much of an eye for rural life, but with his daughter at the center, allegorized and redeemed, he is happy to compose a pretty picture of the future. And what about Lucy in this painterly scene? Is she gazing into a brave new post-apartheid world on the horizon? No; she is *absorbed* in the world in which she is living and working; she is *making* a world, not painting one. After having watched his daughter from a distance, and self-consciously composing her as the subject of a painting, Lurie finally breaks the "spell" he had cast by calling out to Lucy, and she replies, surprised, "I didn't hear you"; but she might have said, I didn't *see* you. And as if to suggest just this, the narrator remarks that Lucy's dog, Katy, "stares shortsightedly in his [Lurie's] direction" (218). There is no real place of significance for Lurie in Lucy's future, in the future of South Africa; she simply can't see him. But more that this, she does not "see" in a visionary sense at all: she is not a subject who imagines possible futures, but she is fully caught up in the activities of making. And this may involve a certain degree of willful blindness, both to the terrible past and to the uncertain future.

The world that David Lurie gazes upon is what Heidegger calls a "world picture," an aestheticized and allegorically pre-interpreted image.[3] It is true that he is not "in the picture," but no matter: he is the artist who has *set up* the picture and the subject *for whom* it is composed. For David, vision always means *seeing himself seeing*: ultimately, whatever the object, his vision is always for the sake of establishing himself as Seer. Lucy and her offspring will always remain no more than an image for his eye, a moral for his story, rather than fellow creatures with whom he may share a history and a world. But this suggests another reading of the question "is it too late to educate the eye?": David's eye and his consciousness dominate the novel, and finally there is no redemption available for him. But it is perhaps not too late to educate the reader's eye, and this involves precisely breaking with the perspective determined by Lurie, realizing that it is not exemplary but a visual "lure," the lure, precisely, of the visual. Finally, vision by itself, no matter how redeemed or transfigured, no matter how spiritually or historically informed, is not adequate to the requirements of a new South

Africa; it is the visual opposition of "black" and "white," after all, that was the basis of apartheid's regime. To build a new world, or to bring something radically new into the world (a child?), what is required is not vision or knowledge, but, I would like to suggest, *love*, which, after all, is blind.

My second set of comments, which are connected with the first, have to do with McDonald's remarks on social love in the novel and on Richard of St. Victor's notion of *condilectio* and "violent love." McDonald describes Richard's account of the mystical journey as "a path that emphasizes relationships with others and the importance of full community where love may be enacted." What Richard calls *condilectio*, "shared love," or *neighbor love*, implies the need for a third party who, as a common object of love for two others, allows their love to achieve a more perfect union without solipsism. Just as the trinitarian account of God requires a triple unity of poles within the Godhead so that God can reflect on himself by means of a mediating element, and in turn be fully *loving*, so human relations need a third person in order to avoid specular dualism and to transform love from a private to a social affect.

In French psychoanalyst Jacques Lacan's terms, *condilectio* would be the love that breaks through the tendency to "imaginary" insularity for the sake of a more authentically "symbolic" relationship, one based on difference and mediation rather than the immediacy of fusion. But for Lacan, neighbor love ultimately aims at something else, a third element, neither imaginary nor symbolic, but *real*. The neighbor as "real" implies the traumatic alterity that the other embodies or includes within him or herself, as an "intimate exteriority" — the unfathomable desire of the other that is more fundamental to the subject than its sense of self. For Lacan, "to love our neighbor as our self" is to encounter what is most singularly strange and disturbing in the other person, what is most rageful, perverse, or disgusting, and unknowable, not available for empathy, not recognizable — yet to acknowledge that dark abyss as the figure of our own unconscious desire. In his seminar from 1959–60, *The Ethics of Psychoanalysis*, Lacan distinguishes the easy gestures of a "philanthropy," the charity (if not *caritas*) that imagines the other's desires and needs on the model of one's own, from a more radical possibility of loving the neighbor. Lacan draws on the example of the fourth-century bishop, Saint Martin of Tours, who famously shares his cloak with a naked beggar he happens upon, as a negative exemplum of neighbor love, beyond the ethics of the Good:

> As long as it's a question of the good, there no problem; our own and our neighbor's are of the same material. Saint Martin shares his cloak, and a great deal is made of it. Yet it is after all a simple question of training; material is by its very nature made to be disposed of — it belongs to the other as much as it belongs to me. We are no doubt touching a primitive requirement in the need to be satisfied there, for the beggar is naked. But perhaps over and above that need to be clothed, he was begging for

something else, namely that Saint Martin kill him or fuck him. In any encounter there's a big difference in meaning between the response of philanthropy and that of love.[4]

Lacan's critique of Saint Martin's gesture, as characteristic of a certain mode of ethical reason and moral utilitarianism, is that it remains at the level of the other's need, never touching on the question of desire — on what the other is lacking on a more fundamental level. It is of course of primary importance to recognize the purely animal requirements of every human being — clothing, shelter, food, etc. — but the response to the neighbor in terms of such needs does not require my encounter with what is truly other in the other, and in that sense is not really what Lacan means by ethical. In fact such a gesture risks acting as a screen designed precisely to conceal from myself what might be disturbing in the other, what Lacan calls the other's *jouissance*: its strange, unfathomable "enjoyment," intrinsically transgressive and singularly human, and profoundly more difficult to address than animal needs. Lacan's notion of the neighbor's *jouissance* is by no means identical with Richard of St. Victor's Augustinian account of *condilectio* as "enjoyment," but in both cases the relationship to the other is understood as non-instrumental, as an absolute end in itself, and as addressed to something that exceeds my possibilities of vision or knowledge and may in fact undermine my most fundamental self-certainties. The love of the neighbor that Lacan goes on to describe in the acts of other (women) saints involves incorporating the horror of the other: joyfully eating the excrement of a sick man, drinking water in which a leper's feet had been washed, etc. These are not acts of "perversion" according to Lacan, but on a fundamental level, acts of neighbor love, attempts to love the other person not in spite of what is most horrific and vile in them, but precisely for that horror, as the sign of their alterity, which is elevated to the status of a sublime object.

Can we see Lucy's response to her rape and impregnation as a version of neighbor love? Is her willingness to marry Petrus and to merge her life with those of her assailants a kind of loving-kindness that has nothing to do with religious obligation or social necessity, but enacts a fully conscious and self-willed *decision*? There is clearly no "identification with the aggressor" going on here; Lucy does not see herself as "like" Petrus's family, does not make herself one of them, will clearly always remain outside, even when she lives within Petrus's walls and sleeps between his sheets. Indeed, she does not will herself to see him as "my neighbor" — there is no act of charity, no Christian self-abasement in her action. Can we even suggest that her decision is a response to a call she has heard — a call not from some transcendental source, but from the boys who have raped her, a reply to their obscene, perverse, cruel acts of neighbor love?

In the post-apartheid South Africa of *Disgrace*, the relationship that best describes the situation of blacks and whites is that of *neighbors*, with all its complex ambivalence, and all its sense of ethical or political imperative. Already before the rape, the relationship between Lucy and Petrus was complicated; certainly not one of master and servant, nor exactly one of friendship. But after the rape, with David's lingering question of whether Petrus was in some way complicit with the crime, and Petrus's emerging independence and unpredictability, things have changed:

> In the old days one could have had it out with Petrus. In the old days one could have had it out to the extent of losing one's temper and sending him packing and hiring someone in his place. But though Petrus is paid a wage, Petrus is no longer, strictly speaking, hired help. It is hard to say what Petrus is, strictly speaking. The word that seems to serve best, however, is *neighbour*. Petrus is a neighbour who at present happens to sell his labour. He sells his labour under contract, unwritten contract, and that contract makes no provision for dismissal on grounds of suspicion. It is a new world they live in, he and Lucy and Petrus. Petrus knows it, and he knows it, and Petrus knows that he knows it. (116–17)

The relationship of neighbors is bound more by unwritten and tacit agreements than by written law or explicit rules. Its rules are local rather than universal, and are constantly evolving, constantly reformulated, for the sake of maintaining equilibrium and a certain possibility of openness between worlds that allows for the inhabitation of any particular world. The situation of a neighborhood is singular and contingent: one does not usually settle in a place because of one's neighbors, nor does one usually leave simply to escape particular neighbors. When violations of the unwritten agreements that regulate neighborhoods become intolerable, the level of aggressivity tends to escalate, since there is no clear path to outside adjudication. But the neighbor is also the object of an injunction in Judaism and Christianity, to *love your neighbor as yourself*; and this commandment confronts the ambiguous and ambivalent actual relationship with the neighbor, always provisional, always contingent, with a transcendental moral imperative — the imperative, precisely, to come closer to that strange contingency.

I think that McDonald is absolutely right in suggesting that Richard of St. Victor's writings on social love are central to Coetzee's understanding of the issues faced by his characters in his novel, and the novel as such. Perhaps the novel's central question for post-apartheid South Africa can be articulated most simply as a variation of the lawyer's question to Jesus in the parable of the Good Samaritan: who is my neighbor? What does it mean to love my neighbor? Neighbor love in post apartheid South Africa may indeed be a "violent love," one that is fundamentally ambivalent, essentially mixed with hate, but one that may lead to a new kind of social relationship. This is not to say that Coetzee has romanticized the violence of neighbor love as the "necessary" price that the white South Africans must pay for their long oppression of the black South Africans. Although it is never completely clear how Lucy herself regards her rape and marriage, it is never portrayed or imagined as a "just" violence that must be accepted as penance for the years of apartheid and other forms of institutional violence. Rather, as Lucy understands it, and Coetzee seems to concur, the rape is simply violence, motivated by pure, personal hatred, and as such unredeemable. It is not the price that must be paid, the retributive justice that will allow for the annealing of the country's wounds. But however non-signifying the event of the rape itself was, however blind was its fury, reasonless its commission, even with the weight of history and suffering that seems to unleash it, Lucy's decision to accept the child that has resulted from it has consequences. The outcome is unforeseeable, not without risk, not necessarily for the good; but her decision is absolutely her own. And it is not motivated, as far as we can tell, by anything like self-reflection, self-knowledge, self-interest, or any other mode of vision. It is as if Lucy gazes *blindly* into the future, neither confident nor despairing; she acts but does not know the consequences of her action. That is, her act exceeds calculation, its results are infinite, and in this sense it opens the space for something truly new to emerge in the world.

In Coetzee's recent book, *Diary of a Bad Year*, the opening section entitled "The Origin of the State" interrupts a meditation on the nature of citizenship and subjection with a series of encounters between the writer-narrator and his younger female neighbor. A half-imagined opening conversation between them centers on the question of urban neighboring: "I live on the ground floor and have since 1995 and still I don't know all my neighbours, I said. Yeah, she said, and no more, meaning, *Yes, I hear what you say and I agree, it is tragic not to know who your neighbours are, but that is how it is in the big city and I have other things to attend to now, so could we let the present exchange of pleasantries die a natural death.*"[5] The narrator becomes increasingly obsessed with this attractive neighbor, and his interchanges with her continue to punctuate his reflections on politics and ethics. In the section "On Machiavelli," Coetzee takes up the question of what it is that allows the common man, our most generic neighbor, to hold fundamentally contradictory political and ethical positions:

> The kind of person who calls talkback radio and justifies the use of torture in the interrogation of prisoners holds the double standard in his mind in exactly the same way: without in the least denying the absolute claims of the Christian ethic (love thy neighbour as thyself), such a person approves freeing the hands of the authorities — the army, the secret police — to do whatever may be necessary to protect the public from enemies of the state. (18)

The "typical reaction of liberal intellectuals" to this, according to Coetzee, is to simply see it as a contradiction, an impossible position, incoherent. But Coetzee argues that this belief in a *necessity* that can command incompatible moral and political positions is a defining characteristic of modernity. Yes, this member of the talk radio *hoi polloi* seems to insist, we *must* love our neighbor; and yes, this may include at times the necessity of *torturing* our neighbor, if he is also the enemy of the state. Coetzee argues that one cannot counter this by claiming higher moral ground or the virtues of political-ethical consistency. "Rather," he writes, "you must attack the metaphysical, supra-empirical status of *necessità* and show that to be fraudulent." The problem is not simply that we have ambivalent attitudes towards and contradictory beliefs about our neighbors, that we do not know the difference between "loving" and "torturing" them, but that we treat our relationships to other people as bound by one or another mode of *necessity*. Our relationship to our neighbor is *not* ruled by necessity, but is fundamentally contingent. If there is an imperative that verges on necessity in the command to love the neighbor, it is *the necessity of contingency* — that is, you *must* love your neighbor as yourself, *whatever that might mean in a particular situation*. And that is something that cannot be determined in advance, cannot be codified, any more than can the vagaries of neighboring. It is a universal rule, a categorical imperative, but one that does not operate according to the assumption that it will provide a guide to ethical behavior or a moral rule that could be predictive or prescriptive.

Finally, there is no room in the new world that Lucy is helping build for Lurie and his visions; there is no moral education that can redeem his eye — there is no place for the mode of vision and knowledge that are intrinsic to Lurie's way of being in the world. The neighbor love that Lucy has embraced, as a real possibility, a serious act and ongoing labor, requires a certain *blindness* or abandonment of vision, the knowledge it implies, and the subjective position it assumes. But this does not mean that Lurie cannot find personal redemption — it just doesn't matter to anyone, nor should it. Lurie's redemption comes in the form of the service he assumes of euthanizing sick or unwanted pets. Earlier in the novel, we are told that what the people who leave their dogs and cats with the Animal Welfare clinic really want is not for them to be "killed," but simply and naively that they "disappear": "What is being asked for is, in fact, *Lösung* (German always to hand with an appropriately blank abstraction). sublimation, as alcohol is sublimated from water, leaving no residue, no aftertaste" (142). This characterization of the desire to dispose of the animals as simply the need to find an answer, a *Lösung*, to their problem without nasty moral residue is clearly criticized as an ethical failure, an act of denial of the painful realities entailed by our responsibility for animals, and perhaps even hints at the "final solution to the Jewish problem" (*Endlösung der Judenfrage*) proposed by the Nazis. By the end of the book, however, Lurie has found another way of understanding his work of animal euthanasia; it is still the execution of a solution, a work of "*Lösung*" — but now he also understands that this is indeed a euphemism; now "he no longer has difficulty in calling [the killing] by its proper name: love" (219). For Lurie the killing is no longer a *Lösung*, a "solution," but an act of *Erlösung* — that is, *redemption*, in the sense of release, ransom, or even deliverance in a messianic sense. Whatever personal redemption Lurie achieves at the end of the novel is not by means of vision, but by love, a kind of *neighbor love* that does not exclude violence but, in his case, even requires it. But the mode of neighbor love that Lurie discovers does not involve him directly in the world of his daughter, her new family, and the new world they are creating (also not without violence). Indeed, that world remains only a picture to him. Lurie's neighbors are the animals to whom he gives a gentle death, and the world that he finds for himself in this work remains, as Heidegger would say, poor. This is not to scorn the work or the world that it involves; indeed, it is an authentic act of love, albeit a modest one. Not an act of world building, but perhaps for the first time in his life, something real.

Notes

[1] In *On Christian Doctrine*, Augustine writes, "Some things are to be enjoyed, others to be used, and there are others which are to be enjoyed and used . . . To enjoy something is to cling to it with love for its own sake. To use something, however, is to employ it in obtaining that which you love. . . . Thus in this our mortal life, wandering from God, if we wish to return to our native country where we can be blessed we should use this world and not enjoy it . . . The things which are to be enjoyed are the Father, the Son, and the Holy Spirit," 9–10.

[2] Mark Sanders suggests that Lurie's seduction of Melanie, as well as the rape of Lucy, can be understood as acts of "manic-reparative colonial phantasy." But these attempts at "reparations" are undermined not only by the violence that they necessarily involve, but by a resistance to closure that is expressed in the novel's grammer. Sanders traces the distinction in *Disgrace* between the functions of tense and "aspect" — the relative perfection or imperfection, completion or incompleteness, of an act, as in the series "burned, burnt, burnt up" — and argues that the novel uses imperfection to suspend closure and the possibility of a transcendental futurity. See Sanders 2007, 168–85.

[3] In his essay "The Age of the World Picture," Heidegger writes, "The fundamental event of the modern age is the conquest of the world as a picture" . . . "Where the world becomes picture, what is, in its entirety, is juxtaposed as that for which man is prepared and which, correspondingly, he therefore intends to bring before himself and have set before himself . . . Hence world picture, when understood essentially, does not mean a picture of the world but the world conceived and

grasped as a picture." To have a "world view," a vision of the world *as a picture*, is to see it as composed, ordered, and flattened; structured as a picture set up *for us*, framed and presented as an object for the speculative eye (Heidegger 1977, 134; 129).

[4] See Lacan, 186. Also see Reinhard 1997.
[5] *Diary of a Bad Year*, 5.

5: To Live as Dogs or Pigs Live Under Us: Accepting What's on Offer in *Disgrace*

Pat Harrigan

No Country, This, for Old Men

> As much as ever would we like to hold in our arms the beauty of all the world. It never wanes in us, that yearning. But the beauty of all the world does not want any of us. So we have to make do with less, a great deal less. In fact, we have to accept what is on offer or else go hungry.
>
> — J. M. Coetzee, *Slow Man*

IN *DISGRACE* WE ALL MAKE DO with a great deal less. The characters lose much certainly, but from the beginning the prose of *Disgrace* seems underpopulated. Through its free indirect style, we observe David Lurie clearly enough, with little else to distract us, but we observe him, as it were, telescopically, with each item in his mental inventory at the same middle distance from us. This is a narrative without close-ups.

What we discover in *Disgrace* are the limits of Lurie's ethical understanding, and possibly our own. The book proposes different methods of situating ourselves ethically — Romantic, institutional, aesthetical, allegorical — but eventually reveals all of these as inadequate. All of these methods rest on the illusion that other people are ultimately comprehensible to our own imaginative sympathy. The consequences of this, as played out in Coetzee's plot and language, are to collapse the grounds of our usual ethical methods. Without this foundation, the possibility of raising an ethical society (in post-apartheid South Africa or anywhere else) seems impossible. The book's ending seems to dramatize this, with David, isolated, among only the dogs, with nothing to look forward to except a hard future for himself, Lucy, and his grandchild.

But there is still a little room on this side of despair, if we resign our usual methods, our expectations of understanding. There is hope, if we treat one another as we would treat animals if we were kind. David's hard future is one in which he coexists, in sympathy, with his remaining family and an unending stream of doomed dogs. But this sympathy is not an imaginative one. We do not pretend to understand dogs or pigs, but there are understandable moral positions that we can take in our interactions with them. To realign human beings and animals onto the same moral plane, without compromising the dignity of individual men and women, is one of the unstated projects of the book.

Trailing Complications

> One of [Costello's] arguments is that philosophical reason has prevented us from entering the consciousness of animals. Once we decide that such access is limited, we tend to think that we are entitled to do what we want with such restricted life-forms.
> — James Wood, "A Frog's Life"

The planed-down language of this book keeps us at a distance; our access is limited, even to the human animal. It is astringent and cool; it lacks something: vitality, or passion. This is because the language arises entirely from David; the free indirect style is David's thought, evaporated. This language runs contrary to his self-image as the involuntary subject of passion:

> But he is in the grip of something. Beauty's rose: the poem drives straight as an arrow. She does not own herself; perhaps he does not own himself either. (18[1])
> . . .
> "My case rests on the rights of desire," he says. "On the god who makes even the small birds quiver." (89)

For all this rhetorical robustness, we wonder how seriously to take it all; the tones of passion seem to echo dispiritedly within the empty spaces of the book's language. The rhetoric might be self-justification, intellectual puffery allowing David to avoid a genuine self-criticism. Whether an evasive strategy or not, conscious or not, although we are allowed into his inmost thoughts, we find it difficult to parse them, accord them the relevant weights.

As the central engine of his "passion," David names Eros, but this middle-aged man (who will soon think of himself as old) seems an unlikely, not to say risible, choice for the god's visitation. Whatever hormonal rushes David may experience, and whatever he may tell himself, to us his sexual encounters with Melanie are passionless. Narrated action has rarely seemed so far from lived experience. Latched to David's rigorous point of view, the prose remains separated from all but the weakest physical shudders. Beyond David's body, our instruments can detect little of anything at all. Melanie is distant, practically nonverbal, her thoughts barely guessable, dark:

> When he made the first move, in the college gardens, he had thought of it as a quick little affair — quickly in, quickly out. Now here she is in his house, trailing complications[2] behind her. What game is she playing? He should be wary, no doubt about that. But he should have been wary from the start. (27)

Our instincts are to understand and to judge. But this may not be possible through the eyes of David Lurie, whose preferred technique for interpretive closure is allegory. He habitually allegorizes — it is one of the tools he uses to prise open the thoughts of others — and he is especially interested in his own role in these tenuous metaphorical dramas. He is at his most pathetic, in fact, when in full allegorical flower, at his most hubristic too, identifying himself with the Lucifer from Byron's "Lara":[3]

> Good or bad, he just does it. He doesn't act on principle but on impulse, and the source of his impulses is dark to him. Read a few lines further: "His madness was not of the head, but heart." A mad heart. What is a mad heart? (33)[4]

The free indirect style, only a few steps removed from omniscient narration, tempts us to accept David's judgments. Even as we inevitably grow suspicious of his narrowness, we still think that he is providing all of the necessary information. We think we can, for example, hover somewhere above him, and decipher the motives of the other actors by a trivial reach of imagination. David shares this delusion. In practice his interpretations are sometimes correct, sometimes not; often, we never know which:

> He does not dismiss the possibility that at the deepest level Bev Shaw may be not a liberating angel but a devil, that beneath her show of compassion may hide a heart as leathery as a butcher's. He tries to keep an open mind. (144)

This illusion that we can penetrate into the soul of others leads to much misery. Certainly it places an unwarranted obligation on the other party. If we say, *I can understand you*, we covertly add: *You are obliged to act in ways that I can understand*. This attitude, like Newtonian physics, has an everyday utility, as long as we operate in the usual gross physical world. But when extreme experience accelerates us further from familiar ground, a new approach is called for, and relativism, general or moral, won't do either.

We are in "darkest Africa," and however urbane we are, its inhabitants are alien to us. Through David, Melanie is among the first people we meet here, and between the two of them — and by extension, between Melaine and us — there is a profound gulf of communication and understanding. Her obscurity is representative of the people here. David's, and our, inability to understand these citizens of *Disgrace* will culminate in a state of moral terror when we must speculate on Lucy's and, especially, Petrus's motives:

> The worst, the darkest reading would be that Petrus engaged three strange men to teach Lucy a lesson, paying them off with the loot. But he cannot believe that, it would be too simple. The real truth, he suspects, is something far more — he casts around for the word — *anthropological*, something it would take months to get to the bottom of, months of patient, unhurried conversation with dozens of people, and the offices of an interpreter. (118)

This is a country seismically damaged, riven with gulfs of understanding. Between the races and the sexes we chart the most impressive chasms. Melanie and Lucy are in their individual ways indecipherable. Models of intergender relationships and prerogatives are postulated, changed, and warped: into "Eros," "tax collecting" (158).[5]

Even race is at first bleached entirely out of narrative description. As our ostensibly civilized narrator, David initially pretends that race is not meaningful. Petrus is not at first described as black, nor are the rapists. We cannot even honestly say for certain, for example, what color Melanie is. But as the narrative progresses, we are reminded of the persistent importance of race, even in this new country: "So that is it. No more lies. *My people*. As naked an answer as he could wish. Well, Lucy is *his people*" (201).

We need guides, signposts, instruction, if we are to claw our way further. Regarding David's relationship with Melanie, the question Rosalind asks him seems a legitimate place to start: "Really, how *could* you?" We have already heard much about his quasi-Byronic imperative; the working out of its dubious logic in response becomes, even more grandly, Shakespearean: "Why? Because a woman's beauty does not belong to her alone. It is part of the bounty she brings into the world. She has a duty to share it" (16).

This aesthetic imperative is not outweighed by the evident need for caution and self-protection. And David is not unaware that Melanie is "no more than a child," but even this modulates into some obscure parental or pedagogical impulse (which leads him, ridiculously, to show her a Norman McLaren video and lecture her about her attendance in class [20]).

David finds it morally distasteful to resist Eros — as he says, "No animal will accept the justice of being punished for following its instincts" (90) — and so brings Melanie and himself to disaster. David makes the questionable moral decision to pursue the affair with Melanie; other diegetic forces, no doubt following their own ethical calculus, make the moral decision to punish him for it. Where does this leave us? The caustic portrayal of the committee of inquiry does not inspire our confidence in them as an appropriate ethical arbiter. Though there is much that is troubling about David's treatment of Melanie and about his Romantic justification for it, we nonetheless feel the committee is missing the point.

The ethical nausea of *Disgrace* is profoundly disturbing. It is urgent that we find some firm ground. There is some hope, late in the book, that this stability might be found through artistic production. David's opera, for example, is composed for reasons not immediately apparent to anyone:

> Yet, first at Lucy's farm and now again here, the project has failed to engage the core of him. There is something misconceived about it, something that does not come from the heart. (181)

But then the opera begins to modulate through different modes of discourse, modeling something of David's own progression over the course of the book. In the beginning Byron is the opera's ostensible central figure:

> This is how he had conceived it: as a chamber-play about love and death, with a passionate young woman and a once passionate but now less than passionate older man; as an action with a complex, restless music behind it, sung in an English that tugs continually toward an imagined Italian. (180)

This is the tragic dwindling of Byronic heroism; here also the inhabitation of Eros, the requirements of feminine beauty. Later, as David is lurchingly compelled to feel compassion for his daughter, Teresa comes to occupy the opera's central place. She is ruined, an object of derision, her life among men is over, she sings for a vanished past. This is, we need hardly add, David's own shallow understanding of his daughter's new life. But the elegiac mode, with its elevated subjects and aspiration toward timelessness, does not honestly speak to life on the modern Cape. David, perhaps to his credit, recognizes this. So he turns finally to the comic, the ridiculous plunk-plink-plonk of the banjo.

Within these competing poetic imperatives, in David's desire to compose the opera in emotional parallel with his own experiences, we can hear a faint echo of ethics, even an embryonic morality. But it is still only an echo. Really, what difference does it make? The opera will never be finished, probably mercifully. Even if, against all likelihood, it was any good, what purpose does it serve if no one but David ever hears it? Some therapeutic value, we can compassionately hope. David eventually realizes how little the opera has to offer to the world at large:

> The lyric impulse in him may not be dead, but after decades of starvation it can crawl forth from its cave only pinched, stunted, deformed. . . . It has become the kind of work a sleepwalker might write. (214)

Aesthetics might form an ethics, but we will need to look elsewhere than in this purely internal composition.

Might we find our ethical ground in allegory, as David attempts? The overtones of possible allegory, as elsewhere, ring out again in Lucy's final words of chapter 22: "Yes, like a dog." Surely Coetzee must mean, by linking between Lucy and the pathetic, doomed dogs, to allegorize a moral code of behavior. Lucy's state is that of a dog, and we know what that means. Only David and Bev Shaw, themselves devoid of sentimentality, find the animals worthy of compassion, and can provide them with anything at all — a minuscule amount of love, at the end of life. Here is love, and a small sense of community, in the face of inexorability. We're coming close to understanding how it is possible to act at all, during this country's dry season. No longer eulogizing, as with Teresa and Lucy, but euthanizing, as with the dog: "Yes, I am giving him up."

> *It gets harder all the time*, Bev Shaw once said. Harder, yet easier too. One gets used to things getting harder; one ceases to be surprised that what used to be as hard as hard can be grows harder yet. (219)

Without a solid ground for our ethical understanding it is even more difficult to understand, for instance, Lucy's desire to stay on her freeholding. David speculates on her reasons. Is this a practical decision, or can we call it an ethical one? If ethical, then by which ethical principles does Lucy make her decision to stay? We, along with David, compile a possible inventory: Self-interest (this is her land)? Determination or stubbornness (she won't be driven off)? Why don't the principles of self-protection and justice lead her to a different decision? For his part, David tries to argue her through shifting levels of ethical responsibility:

> "[I] repeat: if you buckle at this point, if you fail, you will not be able to live with yourself. You have a duty to yourself, to the future, to your own self-respect. Let me call the police. Or call them yourself." (134)

But insofar as she brings herself to explain her decisions to her father, Lucy as much as says that he will never understand them:

> "This has nothing to do with you, David. You want to know why I have not laid a particular charge with the police. I will tell you, as long as you agree not to raise the subject again. The reason is that, as far as I am concerned, what happened to me is a purely private matter. In another time, in another place it might be held to be a public matter. But in this place, at this time, it is not. It is my business, mine alone." (112)

David, we might think reasonably, takes this to mean that she is viewing her own rape as a sort of penance for the historical crimes of South African whites — a misguided, if arguably ethical principle. Lucy grows angry, and denies this: "I don't act in terms of abstractions" (112). Contrasting herself with David, of course.

We might speculate that Lucy is making a practical ethical decision, deciding that it is more in the interest of the community to forego justice for her rape, and accept Petrus's offer of a more or less stable future — that this is, in effect a higher ethics, one that transcends her own self-interest. But if this is the case, David cannot see it, and as readers we are not permitted enough information to know. We will inevitably project our own desired interpretation onto Lucy's decision, but the narrative does not permit full understanding here. In fact it *cannot*, because *Disgrace*'s vision of ethical community, such as it is, is based on the impossibility of understanding others. Lucy's ambiguous choice is a dramatic instantiation of humanity's infinite incomprehensibility.

Lucy, who does not think in abstractions, is incomprehensible to David. Any further speculation by him on her motivations will tell us only more about his and our own ethical schemata, not hers. This might be personally instructive, but it is not the point of *Disgrace*.

Articulated a hundred and forty years before the publication of Coetzee's novel, and in one of Charles Dickens's darker frames of mind, *this* is the point of *Disgrace*:

> A wonderful fact to reflect upon, that every human creature is constituted to be that profound secret and mystery to every other. A solemn consideration, when I enter a great city by night, that every one of those darkly clustered houses encloses its own secret; that every room in every one of them encloses its own secret; that every beating heart in the hundreds of thousands of breasts there, is, in some of its imaginings, a secret to the heart nearest it! Something of the awfulness, even of Death itself, is referable to this. (Dickens, 9)

Disgrace is about the inexorable consolidation and perpetuation of the secret.

The End of Roaming

> The 20th century permanently cured us of the illusion that being well-read has any connection with being good.
> — Adam Kirsch

In connection with *Disgrace* we might remark that the more we try to understand other people, the harder it becomes. Where does the fault lie? In ourselves, or in the tools we use to gather understanding, such as David's internalized Romantics,[6] or in our own internalized literary theorists? It's tempting to put the blame onto the other people themselves, to blame them for being obscure.

Whomever we might blame, it does not solve the problem. The suspicion arises, as it did for Dickens, that it is insoluble. And if so, there are two rational responses. We can crumble into despair, or we can stop the search, deliberately give it up. This is a moral choice. This bears thinking on. What, really, do we lose when we do this? Irreplaceable things? Well, we put aside our expectations. We relinquish hope. Without hope, we say farewell to fear, an unexpected bonus. If we are lucky, even the dread of nonexistence can be shrugged away:

> So: once [Lucy] was only a little tadpole in her mother's body, and now here she is, solid in her existence, more solid than he has ever been. With luck she will last a long time, long beyond him. When he is dead she will, with luck, still be here doing her ordinary tasks among the flowerbeds. And from within her will have issued another existence, that with luck will be just as solid, just as long-lasting. So it will go on, a line of existences in which his share, his gift, will grow inexorably less and less, till it may as well be forgotten. (217)

There is something to be said for retreating from the imagined lives of others into our own selves, even our own biology, which in fact we *do* share with the rest of humanity. We know, at least, what to expect from that:

> "Do you love him yet? . . .
> "The child? No. How could I? But I will. Love will grow — one can trust Mother Nature for that. I am determined to be a good mother, David. A good mother and a good person. You should try to be a good person too." (216)

To find our human connection only on the common genetic level, in the shared realities of body inhabitation, brings a sort of comfort. But more than enough horror, too, in realizing the fact of this common biology: "They were not raping, they were mating. It was not the pleasure principle that ran the show but the testicles, sacs bulging with seed aching to perfect itself" (199). Still, where else *can* we go, if we can no longer pretend to enter the private worlds of others, if their obligations to us, their obligations to demonstrate themselves, are forgotten? How do we act, here in the dark? *Disgrace* will tell us, if we care to listen.

To break away from an ethical interpretation of the characters in *Disgrace* will wreak havoc on any traditional view of narrative progress, which depends on the deployment of competing ethical principles on their way toward aesthetic resolution. Like the fact of evolution itself, the narrative of *Disgrace* has no necessary endpoint. It expresses no teleology. It responds only to the conditions of the moment. It is adaptive. By contrast, a fully realized future ethics could only be the result of something like a quantum evolutionary leap:

> [A] constant theme of [Robert Musil's]: the unbridgeability of the gap between the rational and irrational, between the moral, based always on the example of the past and therefore on calculation, and the ethical, calling for a leap into the future. (Coetzee 1986)

When David envisions the future, it is in the form of his daughter becoming a peasant, birthing a new tadpole. Near the end, David may indeed enter the realm of Coetzee's "irrational," if we understand that term to mean something outside of reason, not the negation of it. Following the trail laid by the quotation above, we can refine the concept of moral decisions: they are those based on calculations we have developed through experience, a possibly unacknowledged but ultimately comprehensible choice of ethical principles. But if so, a leap into the future seems unthinkable; a new form of ethical choice which cannot be based on previous forms of understanding is a new form of life indeed.

In *Disgrace* at least, the wished-for society is not in fact the necessary endpoint of the literary narrative. Within the logic of the book it is only a fantasy of a future understanding, where motivations can be deciphered through sex (Melanie), love (Lucy), and art (Lara), and it is hardly even glimpsed in this book before its status as fantasy is uncovered. We are left with just the stuff of mortal matter: bodies in germination, aging, and death. We remain hopeful for the future of our embryonic, peasant morality, but to our realistic eyes it looks due for a hard life.

In this permanent ethical space, there are no certain good choices. Deprived of ethical understanding, lacking the grounds we are accustomed to use to reach our moment of moral decision, we can only hope to make the least bad choice. For David, this is to wait, and watch Lucy tending her own garden, to be there, giving whatever he can of love, to Lucy and the child, to the death of dogs. Our new ground for ethical understanding is one in which men and women are recognized as incommunicatively private and permanently internal. Imaginative sympathy cannot bridge this gap, and humans remain as secret from us as dogs — and in fact coequal with them in dignity.

This is what we share: you and I, what we share. This world, our culture. We can find the space to love here, but it is an irrational, circumscribed love, one that does not pretend to understand the secret. It can only sit and watch, with limited access, unhappy but resigned. We live, in David's words, "as dogs or pigs live under us" (74). We might wish for more, but wishing only brings further grief. This is acceptable, must be acceptable, because the alternative is too terrible to think on. Do not think on it. The choice is between the operating table and the floor. There is no other choice. This is truly a great deal less.

Notes

[1] All quotations from the Viking edition of *Disgrace*, unless otherwise noted.

[2] The echo of "trailing clouds of glory" is in no way accidental. When, like David, all you have are books, everything looks like a poem.

[3] Lucy recognizes something absurd in David's self-Romanticizing, as when she compares him ironically to Byron himself: "Mad, bad, and dangerous to know" (77).

[4] But this is signally meaningless to anyone but himself, a completely internal process. David even seems to recognize this, a little. Over the course of the book his Erotic self-justification modulates in tone from seductive (to Melanie) to indignant (the committee) to supplicatory (Melanie's father). Byronic heroism turns out not to be a rock-solid way of running one's life.

[5] Most terribly, and with awful implications for the future of Lucy and the country, rape is even hinted at, rhetorically, as a sort of migratory or natural rhythm, as the arrival of the three rapists is prefigured by the benign visit of the three ducks: "'Aren't they lovely,' she says. 'They come back every year. The same three. I feel so lucky to be visited. To be the one chosen'" (88).

[6] And occasional Romantic Modernists: Yeats, Rilke.

6: Tenuous Arrangements: The Ethics of Rape in *Disgrace*

Kim Middleton and Julie Townsend

FOR TEACHERS CONCERNED WITH THE ETHICS of the classroom, the moderation of a discussion about rape activates an array of concerns. *Disgrace* — with its representation of an unethical teacher-student relationship, an acquaintance rape, a problematic father-daughter dynamic, and a violent and racist rape scene — seems bound to provoke charged responses from contemporary college students. At two different colleges, we read the novel with two very different sets of students. In Kim's class at the College of Saint Rose in Albany, New York, for example, after the first day of discussion, a student refused to return to class until the group had finished the novel. Julie participated fully in Bill McDonald and Matt Gray's "Coetzee" seminar in the Johnston Center, where students negotiated to read *Disgrace* at the beginning and again at the end of the semester. Some responses bridged the geographic divide between the two classes. On the subject of Melanie's relationship with David, for example, some students condemned her actions while others fiercely defended her; some judged David Lurie for his interactions while others sympathized. All of the students were appalled by Lucy's rape. None was able to fully articulate a defense of her refusal to file a police report or her willingness stay on the land and marry Petrus.

As feminist readers and teachers, we felt unmoored, and this essay traces our collaborative work toward a reading of rape in *Disgrace*. While the two of us had met briefly in the summer of 2006, we were virtual strangers to one another when we accepted the task of co-authoring this essay on rape in *Disgrace*. In the fall of 2006, we began our discussion by sending questions, tentative readings, and interpretive frustrations back and forth. Through this correspondence, we discovered that our mutual interest lay in the desire to understand Lucy's decisions, and those of survivors of rape in general, as complex and considered interventions within the particular affective contexts that govern their individual lives.

From our earliest discussions, we both felt that the crux of the dilemma was to develop a viable reading of Lucy. Initially, we both felt that the novel abandoned Lucy's character and relegated her entirely to an allegorical "fix" for the conflicts in the new South Africa. Neither of us felt that such a reading adequately answered the questions posed by the personage of Lucy. Our chapter, then, discovers how *Disgrace* makes visible and interrogates contemporary Western expectations of rape. By disrupting the viability of our culturally accepted "rape narratives," the novel calls us to develop alternative ways of reading. To this end, we look closely at the representations of rape in the novel and put these in conversation with current theory on cultural scripts. We then excavate the ancient intertexts suggested by the novel and look to them for new ways to read the motivations and effects of rape. Our chapter ends with a discussion of the ethical implications of these new ways of reading rape via theorist Judith Butler's work on an ethics of non-violence.

I. Narrating Rape

As a novel that features disturbing and controversial depictions of rape, *Disgrace* calls readers to acknowledge and bring to bear a number of competing contexts. We are certainly required to reflect upon the national and historic specificity of South Africa and the disturbing trends that mar the post-apartheid landscape: according to Mary Robertson at the Centre for the Study of Violence and Reconciliation, South Africa has "one of the highest rape statistics in the world" (http://www.csvr.org.za/articles/artrapem.htm). A number of literary critics look to the history of South Africa and the unintended consequences of the Truth and Reconciliation Commission to provide (particularly for women) a means with which to parse the ethics of representing rape in the novel. Lucy Valerie Graham argues that *Disgrace* inscribes a double bind: it avoids a colonial cliché in dwelling on the rape of a white woman, but it also revisits a rape genre trope in which the victim is silenced. Anne Reef's article, "Representation of Rape in Apartheid and Post-Apartheid South African Literature," maps what she calls the "ethical minefield" of representing rape in literature, a minefield made more dangerous by the historical and political particularities of South Africa. Both critics describe the difficulties of representing rape in a way that does justice to those who experience it, and both evince deep ambivalence about the possibility of inscribing rape in a South African narrative. Graham and Reef urge readers to acknowledge the local context as a primary lens; in doing so, they gesture toward the necessity of a postcolonial theoretical framework for interpretation. Meg Samuelson takes up this challenge; she interrogates the construction of female subjectivity vis-à-vis colonized/slave subjection and juxtaposes the novel's representation of sexual violence with that of Zoe Wicomb's *David's Story*. For Samuelson, the revelation of racial and gendered dynamics surrounding post-apartheid rape offers cold comfort — a new, prosperous future for South Africa purchased with the coerced/cooperative silence of victimized women. Doubtless, the socio-political/historical context and its associated body of post-colonial theory provide keen insights with which to problematize the position of a given audience. This necessary context, however, may be less immediate and/or viscerally affecting than the matrix of personal, cultural, and philosophical associations specific to each reader, particularly those who are less familiar with the mythologies and histories at the forefront of studies like Samuelson's.

Countless popular and scholarly studies map not just the experiences that define individual instances of rape but also detail reactions to those instances from a range of sources: friends and family; law enforcement representatives; educational or legal officials; and medical personnel. The diversity of and intensive contestation among these studies indicates the degree to which ideas about rape circulate across any number of social arenas. The subjects of contributions to one oft-cited volume of essays on rape, for example, range from pornography to workplace harassment, from fraternities to church culture. First published in 1980 and now in its second edition, *Transforming a Rape Culture* explicitly makes the case that the societal conditions that engender rape exist in federal institutions, family dynamics, leisure activities, and religion. In essence, the editors make the case that Western culture (primarily American) is itself a culture of rape, and one that "will continue . . . until our society understands and chooses to eradicate the sources of sexual violence" (Buchwald, et al. 9).

If the editors of the collection are correct, then what we know about rape emerges from the multiplicity of activities and institutions we experience daily. This resultant body of knowledge, accumulated across time and societal space, comes into play as we read *Disgrace*. The novel calls the reader to activate his/her own matrix of contexts in order to understand rape, whether that rubric is formulated as a reasoned political position or a loose body of unacknowledged, perhaps unexamined, beliefs. In its representations of rape, *Disgrace* reminds us of some of our most deeply ingrained ideas about what constitutes the act: who is at fault, to what extent, and why; how does it affect victims and perpetrators; and, what are the possibilities and/or applications of justice in the aftermath? In ways that have confounded many readers, the novel refuses to give a definitive account of its own stance on the issues above.

To begin, we'd like to look carefully at the ways the novel's first depiction of rape (and, not surprisingly, the first mention of the term) activates the questions above. At the moment we witness this scene, David Lurie's relationship with Melanie Isaacs is still young. As it transpires in narrative time, they've had perhaps three conversations outside of class. One of these conversations ends in sex on the floor of David's living room. Days later, he abruptly appears at her flat, unbidden.

> He has given her no warning; she is too surprised to resist the intruder who thrusts himself upon her. When he takes her in his arms, her limbs crumple like a marionette's. Words heavy as clubs thud into the delicate

whorl of her ear. "No, not now!" she says, struggling. "My cousin will be back!" But nothing will stop him. (24)

Suddenly, David is no longer the one who critiques, but instead has become the one described and judged — and with a surplus of violent language. He is the "intruder who thrusts," the one wielding "words heavy as clubs." Melanie, on the other hand, is described as exhibiting vulnerability, comparable to a child's toy. Despite this, she resists him and (an important point here) says "no." A familiar dynamic of rape emerges in this paragraph: the fragile young woman struggling against the aggressive intruder, voicing her refusal of his actions.

We read this scene carefully because of the reverberations its elements create. Social psychologists chart a socially constructed process of cognition that comprises a series of what they refer to as "rape scripts," which condition the way we understand and interpret rape. These schemas "contain information about props, roles, and rules regarding the sequence of events" (Fiske & Taylor, 1991, quoted in Littleton, 1). When test groups are asked to script scenes of rape versus those of seduction, they most often cite male violence and female resistance as the key differentiating factors.[1] This scene in *Disgrace*, then, provides, up front, the fundamental information — the requisite elements of the rape script — that resonates with readers qua rape. Subsequent language in the scene, however, complicates the ease of those initial references to the predominant script. While David admits that "nothing will stop him," he kisses Melanie's feet as his thoughts turn toward mythic love, which comes to him "from the quiver of Aphrodite . . . no doubt about that" (25). Readers have no access to Melanie's thoughts; instead, we only witness her actions as seen by David and described by the narrator: "She does not resist. All she does is avert herself: avert her lips, avert her eyes. She lets him lay her out on the bed and undress her: she even helps him, raising her arms and then her hips" (25).

Gone, in this section, are the similes that inscribe violence in David's actions; likewise, Melanie has abandoned active resistance. Without these markers, are we to assume that the scene has shifted? Now that the characteristic language has disappeared, has the moment transformed from rape to something else? Just as we begin to reassess the dynamics, the word itself appears, along with its immediate negation:

> Not rape, not quite that, but undesired nevertheless, undesired to the core. As though she had decided to go slack, die within herself for the duration, like a rabbit when the jaw of the fox close on its neck. So that everything done to her might be done, as it were, far away. (25)

Even as the term is denied, that denial is qualified: "not rape, not quite that, but . . ." The text moves through a dizzying set of fine-grain distinctions in this sentence: a negation leads to a differentiation between rape and "undesired" intercourse, yet at the moment that it establishes the second term, it intensifies the degree ("undesired to the core") and reveals a hint of self-disgust in David as he repeats the word. It returns to a simile of violence between prey and hunter, and ends with an evocation of a coping mechanism for trauma — the dissociation from the body.

As a whole, then, this second half of the scene diverges from the immediacy of violence and resistance, but introduces, for a careful reader, additional associations with rape scenarios — additional narratives that indicate the complexity of victim and perpetrator responses. The difficult distinction between rape and undesired intercourse, for example, mirrors a larger phenomenon wherein these two terms compete and overlap. In a 2006 study, Darcy McMullin and Jacquelyn W. White cite and confirm earlier statistics in which nearly half the women whose experiences meet the legal definition of rape choose not to label it as such.[2] Public perception of the distinction between rape and not-rape is no less cloudy. Situations in which the woman knows her attacker often go unreported to authorities and friends as they raise questions about the degree of her culpability — a narrative element that has, historically, neutralized the offenses of the perpetrator.[3] The short paragraph that closes the description of David and Melanie's intercourse, then, plays through an array of elements that reference some of the most significant narrative schemas activated in association with rape: those that assess the responsibility of the victim and of the perpetrator. In this way, the paragraph works metonymically for the entire scene and, in addition, anticipates what the reader will bring to the interpretation of the second rape later in the novel.

Even after the ambiguities contained in this scene, the novel continues to exert pressure on readers' definitions of culpability. Many students who refuse to categorize this scene as rape use the instance of Melanie's return to David as proof. While in narrative time "she stays away the whole of next week" (26), her return appears mere paragraphs after the scene described above. For these students, Melanie's request, "Can I sleep here tonight?" is tantamount to an admittance that she actively participated in the act above. David is careful to note the ways that Melanie is sexually complicit this time: "she presses herself tighter to him, her face arm against his belly. The sheet slips aside; she is wearing only a singlet and panties. Does she know what she is up to, at this moment?" (27). His question is as ambiguous as the descriptions above, and rhetorically compels the reader to answer it. That Melanie comes to David and asks to stay with him, that she makes love to him again is undeniable. Moreover, the narrator takes great care to describe a particular act that signals her willing engagement: "she hooks a leg behind his buttocks to draw him in closer" (29). And yet all of this is framed by an array of evidence about Melanie's state when she appears at David's house. She comes at midnight (26), "Her face is strained" (26), "she whispers, avoiding his eye" (26). She falls asleep in her clothes, exhausted, and when he returns to her room in the morning, "she is awake . . . looking haggard" (26). As he holds her, she "begins to sob miserably" (26). For some readers, the myriad possible reasons for Melanie's return are elided by an all-too-common rape script: the victim would never return to the perpetrator. While this belief is convenient and supportive of widespread devotion to the integrity of an autonomous individual, it ignores reams of data that document women who, on social, economic, and personal grounds, are compelled to return to abusive partners or husbands, and, in a similar theme and for like reasons, women who return to their rapists.

It's crucial to acknowledge the active presence of rape scripts or rape narratives in the reader for two reasons. First, as seen above, the text clearly calls out to them; they appear seeded throughout, juxtaposed in ways to make them either compete or collude. The effect is, in part, to create a troubling interference with an easy qualification of the event and simplistic characterizations of both Melanie and David. Second, it conditions the reader to acknowledge his/her own expectations of the work that these narratives do and, by extension, to be cognizant of his/her insistence that a narrative appear *to do* that work. In Sharon Marcus's "Fighting Bodies, Fighting Words: A Theory and Politics of Rape Prevention," she contends that an important way to understand rape is extant in its form as a narrative:

> [A] way to refuse to recognize rape as the real fact of our lives is to treat it as a linguistic fact: to ask how the violence of rape is enabled by narratives, complexes and institutions which derive their strength not from outright, immutable, unbeatable force but rather from their power to structure our lives as imposing cultural scripts. To understand rape in this way is to understand it as subject to change. (388–89)

Our lives, Marcus explains, are shaped by a powerful set of cultural scripts, or stories. She sees narrative as one component of a triadic structure that produces these; and like the editors of *Transforming a Rape Culture*, she sees the materials to engender rape within that system. Narratives create scripts to live by, yet these scripts themselves are narratives: myth-like texts invested with the authority to explain the ways that rape happens, the kinds of characters that are involved, the ways in which the plot can believably unfold.[4] As Marcus very carefully points out, however, these are narratives — or scripts — that maintain the aura of reality even as they can be changed to reflect and structure new realities.

"Reality" in rape narratives is the veritable double-edged sword. On the one hand, it is absolutely necessary to interrogate widely held beliefs — shared cultural narratives — about rape.[5] On the other, there is a long and devastating history of utilizing interrogation as a strategy of victim intimidation to prevent prosecution, institutional embarrassment, and social change. The scene with David and Melanie indicates the complex interlocking system of these beliefs and the ways that they can disproportionately condition our reading of the novel, just as they can our interactions with scenes of rape in the real world. One of the most powerful tools used to scrutinize these narratives is the public speech of rape survivors describing their experiences. Susan Brownmiller positions it as central in a long-standing conflict: "In making rape a *speakable* crime, not a matter of shame, the women's movement has already fired the first retaliatory shots in a war as ancient as civilization" (445). Later, she lists the legislative, social, and grassroots initiatives that sprang from the act of women articulating rape, thus cementing the central role of these public narratives. In this way, the verity of cultural narratives of rape is challenged and made visible by the rape narratives of survivors. Nothing here, however, reveals the ways in which the narrative, regardless of ideological bent or consequence, is the privileged approach to understanding rape. And for feminists, *speaking* that narrative is a necessity of the first order.

Carine Mardorossian, in "Toward a New Feminist Theory of Rape," makes a claim for the absolute necessity of public articulation: "Through . . . speak-outs, women come to understand that an experience they might previously have perceived as interpersonal in nature is in fact rooted in historical and social relations . . . What ultimately empowers survivors of sexual assault at speak-outs is not the process of reclaiming a unified self so much as the production of narrative itself" (764–65). Mardorossian's contention is emblematic of a large body of feminist critique that cites positive ramifications for both individuals and communities in the event of a speak-out. Even in those few works that investigate the possible negative consequences of this speech act, the authors nonetheless continue to draw the same pervasive conclusion: narrativizing the experience of rape is a necessary act of personal reclamation of autonomy.[6]

In sum, narratives are crucial to the ways that we understand rape. Rape narratives may not themselves be inherently political, but they enter into the public space with the power to shape material effects. As such, there is a powerful public compulsion for a narrative that makes a scene of rape comprehensible; arguably, any scene may engender multiple narratives that make motivations, events, and identities contested territories. Regardless of this contestation, however, exigency rests on the narrative of rape: we require it to speak, and to speak through a victim. This expectation comprises a weighty reading formation that we bring to bear on representations of rape.

So what do we do with one of the most troubling aporias in *Disgrace*: the unarticulated experience of rape from the victim's perspective? In the scene above, we witness Melanie's actions, but are not privy to her thoughts. Later, when David is brought before the university tribunal, he declines to read Melanie's statement, and there's no guarantee that it would address his trespass of her flat. If this silence is troubling, the attempts to narrate Lucy's rape — and her refusal of those attempts — are even more disquieting.

The silence surrounding Lucy's experience begins with the men's intrusion into the house. What happens to Lucy happens in a room that the narration does not approach. After the men leave the house, Lucy releases David from the bathroom, tends to the dead and dying dogs, and "wriggles loose" from a hug that David attempts to give her (97). She closes herself in the bathroom. Here, the narrative gives the reader access to both David's speech and his thoughts, just as it did in his interaction with Melanie. "'Are you all right? Are you hurt?' Stupid questions; she does not reply" (98). Neither David nor Lucy has verbalized the word "rape" yet; it will be many pages, many weeks in narrative time before David does. David had been frantic about Lucy while he was locked in the bathroom ("whatever is happening to her will be set in stone . . ." [94]; He can burn, he can die; and if he can die, then so can Lucy" [96]), but rape remained in the category of the unarticulable — a "whatever" to be feared and prevented, and of a lesser concern than that of death. In the aftermath, however, David becomes increasingly dedicated to the idea of Lucy talking about her experience. Above, his first question inculcates, by habit of association, a narrative of trauma. "Are you all right?" is a question we often ask after hearing about or directly witnessing an event of harm, whether physical or emotional ("I fell off a ladder. / Are you all right?"; "My favorite aunt died. / Are you all right?"). The second question is more likely to be asked following physical harm than emotional ("I fell off a ladder. / Are you hurt?" seems more likely than "My favorite aunt died. / Are you hurt?"). While the questions may function as a verbal means of instigating a discussion that acknowledges trauma, David immediately dismisses their utility. They are stupid, he may think, because they are rhetorical questions. As he begins to contemplate what Lucy has experienced, he realizes that these questions will preclude rather than enable further discussion. The punctuation here signals a motivation behind this classification. David's assessment of his speech and Lucy's reaction share a more direct, even causal relation (via the semi-colon) than the questions and the assessment itself. More than his independent apprehension, however, Lucy's *refusal to engage* conditions David's judgment of his questions. In either case, this is the first instance of Lucy's unwillingness to discuss her experience on David's terms. The chapter ends with Lucy's request to David: "when people ask, would you mind keeping to your own story, to what happened to you . . . you tell what happened to you, I tell what happened to me" (99). Here, Lucy requests that she be able to narrate her own experience. The second part of her speech moves from the form of a request to that of a statement, if not an order. In it, she makes a clear delineation between David's experience and her own. Further, she connects the act of telling to the object of the specific experience and that object alone: one can tell only what happened to him/her. Also notable: whatever happened, it happened *to* her — she becomes the object of the action, not a participant in it. Only in the telling would she become the active subject.

David and Lucy establish a pattern of reactions to her experience here, a pattern that they continue to engage in during the weeks after the invasion. David searches for the rape narrative that will make sense of Lucy's experience and thereby dictate their respective appropriate responses. Lucy negates these narratives and refuses to provide David with the one he (and, by extension, the reader) is so desperate to have. David first attempts the narrative that Lucy reshapes above — the one in which the experience of rape fixes her as an object. He explains: "Why don't you want to tell? It was a crime. There is no shame in being the object of a crime. You did not choose to be the object. You are an innocent party" (111). Meant to comfort, David's story of her experience eradicates Lucy's integrity as a subject in any number of ways: she is not just an object, but an object without choice, an innocent object, and one for whom shame is assumed, even in the process of negating that reaction. Later, David and the narrator further the characterization of victim-as-object when they configure Lucy as an unnamed thing that has been tainted by her experience. Horrified by news of Lucy's pregnancy, David imagines that the rapists meant "to soil her, to mark her, like a dog's urine" (199). Likewise, the police officers who take Lucy's statement appear to view her as "a creature polluted and her pollution could leap across to them, soil them" (108). Whether a territory to be marked or a contaminated animal, Lucy — through her experience and reactions to it — activates powerful rape narratives.

This attempt to characterize Lucy as object after the fact, however, is contradicted by the simultaneous pressure for her to speak. "Why don't you want to tell?" (111) David asks Lucy above. The question — again phrased as a negative (not, for instance "why do you want to keep silent?") — is one of many attempts to compel Lucy to narrate her experience. In this instance, as that question precedes the script about innocence and objectification, we might wonder if the latter is designed to compel Lucy's "confession." Just as narratives condition the interpretation of the experience of rape, so too do they structure the array of reasons why a victim must speak. Again, the question of shame enters the fray as David imagines the responses of the perpetrators: "Too ashamed, they will say to each other, too ashamed to tell . . . Is Lucy prepared to concede them that victory?" (110). And again: "She would rather hide her face, and he knows why. Because of the disgrace. Because of the shame . . . Like a stain the story is spreading across the district. Not her story to spread but theirs: they are its owners. How they put her in her place, how they showed her what a woman was for" (115). In both of these instances, Lucy's silence is wedded to her supposed shame. David seems to imagine that speaking — publicly narrating her experience — would counteract this in some way. In an ironic association, David here takes up the argument of feminist critics like Mardorossian: the act of telling is the one that eradicates the shame of the act.

When these schemas (so present in David's mind) fail to compel Lucy to speak, he invokes a convincing social narrative to persuade her. "[I]f you buckle at this point, if you fail, you will not be able to live with yourself. You have a duty to yourself, to the future, to your own self-respect" (134). Summoning the specters of regret, personal integrity, and implicitly, social responsibility, David attempts to coerce Lucy to report to the authorities. The emotion-laden terms he utilizes acknowledge the narratives many hold to be true: that to remain silent is to fail oneself and others, and that such a failure cannot be borne by a subject with strong self-worth.[7]

Despite the range and force of David's appeals, however, Lucy adamantly refuses to report to the authorities or to narrate her experience at all. "What happened to me is a purely private matter," she says. "In another time, in another place it might be held to be a public matter. But in this place, at this time, it is not. It is my business, mine alone" (112). In an oft-quoted passage, Lucy gestures at the historical-material context of her experience, even as she asserts that the space for that experience is in the private sphere. Claiming it as something that belongs solely to her, Lucy rejects David's insistence on the exigencies of public confession. By doing so, she simultaneously appears to ignore the battle for public ownership of that experience and the concomitant characterizations of shame and soil. This continued refusal to narrate the story of her rape subtends one of the few privileges that Lucy ever claims for herself: "What happened to me is my business, mine alone, not yours and if there is one right I have it is the right not to be put on trial like this, not to have to justify myself — not to you, not to anyone else" (133). In the face of David's continued appeals and the reemergence of one of her attackers, Lucy insists that she not be compelled to narrate. In keeping with Lucy's re-evaluation of her place in her community, she phrases this in the conditional ("if there is one right I have . . ."). The strength of her claim to this right, however, materializes via the repetition of negations: not to be put on trial, not to have to justify, not to you, not to anyone. Throughout the novel, then, Lucy forbids the application of familiar rape narratives — the ones that would render her experience easily comprehensible and prescribe her reactions to it. In a certain light, the force and stamina of her refusal registers as agency; Lucy looks like a subject who performs resistance, with full knowledge of the prohibitions against it and the consequences one must suffer. At the same time, resistance via silence is a particularly tenuous path (as witness/reportage is the central component of our justice system), and one that conflicts quite significantly with the feminist approaches to rape charted above. As readers with a commitment to ethics, what do we do with a victim/survivor who refuses to craft a narrative — and who will not, like Melanie, disappear from view?

II. Classical Contexts

Given the cultural weight placed on scripts of rape, especially on college campuses, and the extent to which this novel challenges those narratives, we felt that the development of viable readings trod dangerously on our values as feminist teachers. We took several interpretive approaches in order to sort out readings of Melanie and Lucy. Although neither of us could clearly articulate why, we were not willing to throw up our hands and see Lucy as a sacrificial victim in the allegorical construction of the new South Africa.[8] We were, indeed, convinced that further examination would yield a more complex and profound reading of rape and its aftermath in the novel. The text's invocation of and resistance to familiar ways of reading rape demand that the reader seek new narratives — not in the text but via the text. We finally made some progress when we looked beyond *Disgrace* itself and far from our current understanding of rape into intertexts that evoked rape in tandem with conflicts over land, property, and kinship.[9]

The biblical story of Dinah (Genesis 34, 1–31) situates rape as part of a negotiation of land, relationships between longtime inhabitants and new arrivals — intercourse and trespass. This story provides us with one of a few rich intertexts that informs our reading of Lucy's experiences. The story in Genesis is as follows: Jacob and his family arrive in Shechem and purchase land from the children of Hamor, including the eponymous Shechem, the son of Hamor. When Dinah, daughter of Leah and Jacob goes to "visit the women of the land," she is "seized" by Shechem, who "lay with her and humbled her," and who then wants to marry her. Although Jacob's sons are outraged, Jacob hears Hamor's argument for the marriage: "I pray you, give her to him in marriage. Make marriages with us; give your daughters to us, and take our daughters for yourselves. You shall dwell with us; and the land shall be open to you; dwell and trade in it, and get property in it" (Revised Standard Version, Genesis 34: 8–10). Jacob's sons Simeon and Levi "deceitfully" agree to the marriage as long as all the men of the city agree to be circumcised. Hamor returns to the city and argues for the circumcision of the men; "these men are friendly with us; let them dwell in the land and trade in it; for behold, the land is large enough for them; let us take their daughters in marriage, and let us give them our daughters" (Genesis 34: 21). After the mass circumcision, Simeon and Levi slaughter the incapacitated men of the city. Jacob fears that the inhabitants of the region will destroy him in turn, but the brothers ask "should he deal with our sister as with an harlot?" (Genesis 34:31).

Dinah's story, like Lucy's, explores the complex ethical ground of sexual trespass in the context of land, kinship, and trade. And, as is the case in *Disgrace*, the biblical version does not give us Dinah's account of her rape. Different translations give alternative readings of the relationship: in the RSV text he "lay with her and humbled her" (Genesis 34:2), whereas in the New Jerusalem Bible he "saw her, seized her and forced her to sleep with him" (Genesis 34: 2). The negotiation between Hamor, Jacob, and Jacob's sons sets up an astonishing split between prosperous peace and genocidal revenge as the two possible social/cultural responses to Dinah's rape. There seems to be no middle ground, no venue for juridical evaluation or restitution. In Lucy's refusal to tell the story of her rape even to her father, might we conjecture that she sees the outcome of her own choices as equally stark? While we cannot know what, if any, role Dinah might have played behind the scenes, we do know that Lucy's refusal to report the rape and her directions to David on how to handle the negotiation with Petrus drive the situation solidly in the direction of a "prosperous peace" with no stipulation that would account for the violence done to Lucy. Her solution not only denies the narrativization of her rape but goes so far as to give Petrus the role of author: "Say he can put out whatever story he likes about our relationship and I won't contradict him. If he wants me to be known as his third wife, so be it. As his concubine, ditto" (204).

Echoes of this same link between rape, land, and trade between different peoples appear in accounts of the rape of the Sabine women in Plutarch's *Life of Romulus* and Livy's *The History of Rome, Vol. I*. In *Disgrace*, David recalls finding a painting called *The Rape of the Sabine Women* in an art book when, as a child, he was trying to understand what rape meant. This memory becomes yet another of David's own intertextual series in which he draws dubious distinctions between types of rape:

> men on horseback in skimpy Roman armour, women in gauze veils flinging their arms in the air and wailing. What had all this attitudinizing to do with what he suspected rape to be: the man lying on top of the woman and pushing himself into her? He thinks of Byron. Among the legions of countesses and kitchenmaids Byron pushed himself into there were no doubt those who called it rape. But none surely had cause to fear that the session would end with her throat being slit. (160)

David does not, at this moment, come back to an image of his own rape of Melanie (or "not quite that" [25]), in these musings, nor does his mind wander down an alternative intertextual path, one that would connect the rape of the Sabine women to issues perhaps closer at hand than Byron's philandering: land, the state, and citizenship in South Africa. Without dwelling on too much detail, the Plutarch and Livy accounts do set up several potentially rich paradigms through which to read Lucy's rape.

From the outset, the kidnap and rape of (and the *de facto* marriages to) the Sabine women were part of a plot to build the Roman state, which suffered from a shortage of women with whom to marry and reproduce. Neighboring peoples would not allow intermarriage with the Romans.[10] So Romulus invents a celebration and invites the Sabines to join the party. On his signal, Roman men kidnap and carry away the unmarried Sabine women. The grieving girls are assured by Romulus, "that none of this would have happened if their fathers hadn't been so inflexible in not letting them marry with neighbors. But now they would have the status of wives with all the material rewards and civil rights of citizenship and they would have children, than which nothing is dearer. . . . A good relationship often begins with an offence" (http://www.stoa.org/diotima/anthology/wlgr/wlgr-privatelife233.shtml). When the Sabines demand the return of the daughters, Romulus refuses and demands instead "that the Sabines should allow community of marriage with the Romans" (Plutarch 16:2). In his attempts to persuade the Sabines, Romulus cites the fact that the women, since the rape, have entered into marriage with their rapists, have been treated well, have become citizens, and have borne children. These negotiations end in both sides preparing for war, but the raped women intervene to stop the violence, claiming that they now love their husbands and children as well as their fathers and brothers. Like the Sabine women, Lucy insists on peace and rejects punishment, revenge, or even an abortion.

As unsavory as it may be in our contemporary context, the narratives of the Sabine women and of Dinah suggest that we could read Lucy's response to her rape within an allegorical context that places rape at the beginning of a negotiation of kinship. These intertexts provide a way of seeing Lucy's rape not as an ethical and bodily trespass conditioned by scripts,[11] but instead as an event that focalizes the future of a community vis-à-vis the economies relevant to the other: land, exchange, kinship, etc. In the context of these classical texts, rape is a trespass that opens a negotiation. The novel gives us only small glimpses of that negotiation: "'Go back to Petrus,' she says. 'Propose the following. Say I accept his protection. . . . But then the child becomes his too. The child becomes part of his family. As for the land, say I will sign the land over to him as long as the house remains mine. I will become a tenant on his land'" (204). Our reading suggests that the novel conjures, though never elaborates, a far more subtle ethical negotiation.

III. Reading Lucy

The work above positions us, we think, to look specifically at Lucy as the key figure "fixed" by rape — through a system of trespasses informed by local historical-political, as well as literary, contexts. The work of this section, then, is to see how a hybrid form of analysis, with attention to the necessity of the intertextual frames, can address Lucy's choices. Is any schema capable of positioning Lucy as something other than a sacrifice for a future that might resolve the post-colonial situation? Can we imagine a reading of Lucy as feminist? These questions remain conundrums for us. On the one hand, Lucy does set her own terms for how she will deal with the invasion and rape; on the other hand, her negotiations seem to relegate her to a traditional patriarchal form of protection through the marriage to Petrus.

If Lucy's refusal to tell her story to David or the police and her decision to marry Petrus cause problems in terms for a feminist reading, it might be because most feminist narratives of rape subscribe to models of identity that the novel finally seeks to critique. In this section, we want to interrogate Lucy's response to the rape. Earlier, we explored the ways in which Lucy rejects one after another of the available feminist narratives of rape and rape victims. We wonder if the course that Lucy does take, namely to keep the child and marry Petrus, might engage with a different narrative of identity, specifically, a narrative of social bonds rather than a narrative of justice.

In this reading, we suggest that Lucy's rejection of certain modern privileges such as property ownership, an independent identity, and a self-directed narrative comes with a (re)instatement of a set of privileges based on kinship and social bonds. This exchange of a modern identity for a hybrid arrangement that seems to draw from an ancient past while it points towards an uneasy future presents readers with a shaky, but tenable, contract. In one sense, this system of conflict resolution avoids some of the problems posed by a colonial history in which the rights of the self — specifically the privileged colonial self — are central. Lucy's guiding force seems to be a reaction to the rape that allows her to stay on the land that she loves. "I am the one who has to live here," she says to David when he wonders aloud why she did not "lay *real* charges" against the attackers (133). Lucy's solution, proposed by Petrus, replaces David's model with one of kinship, perhaps exchange, in which Lucy receives limited basic protections by becoming bonded by marriage to the traditional local population. Her decision, though, excludes recourse to the state. Lucy seems to reject almost all institutional forms, so it shouldn't surprise us that she turns to a "community" solution rather than to the "state." As critical readers we must interrogate this deal that Lucy makes with Petrus, though perhaps not the same way or for the same reasons that David does. We must consider the extent to which the marriage to Petrus represents a different kind of social institution. And what stake, we might ask, does Lucy — or the novel — put in this alternative resolution?

In order to sort out a reading of Lucy's decision to marry Petrus, we may have to temporarily set aside most feminist narratives of rape. In Judith Butler's *Giving an Account of Oneself*, we came across an argument that helped us construct a reading of Lucy's decision — not a reading that makes us entirely comfortable, but one that seems consonant with the novel. Butler's inquiry examines works by Emmanuel Levinas, Theodor Adorno, and Adriana Cavarero to consider the state of responsibility, and finally ethics, in the context of an "I" dispossessed of a self-sufficient narrative. What initially drew us to this text was Butler's question: what does it mean to respond to violence with non-violence? Her contention that "the first-person perspective assumed by the ethical question . . . [is] disoriented by [a] fundamental dependency of the ethical sphere on the social" (25) suggested to us that Lucy's solution to her rape, as incomprehensible as it is to David and perhaps to the reader, might be read in the context of social bonds.

When David leaves the city and the university to enter Lucy's world of the rural frontier, he leaves behind a world with clear, if problematic, social structures and enters a terrain of social flux. Lucy's relationships to Petrus, Bev, and even Helen in her absence are shrouded in opacity. Although he does make some effort to engage in Lucy's world, it is with suspicion and even irony that he approaches most of these interactions. The attack and rape, of course, force David, the reader, and perhaps even Lucy to reexamine the structure of social bonds. When Bill and Bev Shaw take in Lucy and David after the rape, David has the following rumination:

> Bill Shaw believes that, because he and David Lurie once had a cup of tea together, David Lurie is his friend, and the two of them have obligations towards each other. Is Bill Shaw wrong or right? . . . Does the drinking of tea seal a love-bond, in the eyes of Bill Shaw? Yet but for Bill and Bev Shaw, but for old Ettinger, but for bonds of some kind, where would he be now? On the ruined farm with the broken telephone amid the dead dogs. (102)

Though David does not entirely forgo his cynical irony in this passage, the structure of one question after another suggests that he is both entirely out of his element and that he is reconsidering a point of view well outside of his own. David does not easily acquiesce to this unfamiliar structure of being with others. He departed from the world of the university in disgust, but he has not entirely rejected the social structures of that world to become a part of Lucy's community. Although David left his university post, having refused to speak within the rhetorical confines of justice, authority, and agency, these are precisely the narratives that he insists are most relevant to Lucy's experience. His arguments for why she ought to narrate her experience, and to whom, become part of a shift — in David and in the novel — from one world to another. Although the novel certainly critiques the formation of bonds in David's world, Lucy's choices point toward a world that is far from idyllic. This shift emerges slowly out of conversations between David and Lucy; however, as we move from one set of social values to another we are offered neither comfort nor reassurance.

Although it might seem, from what little we get from her perspective, that Lucy has clarity about what she wants to do with her situation, she also seems to be struggling in uncharted waters. Here is Lucy in a conversation with David on their drive home from New Brighton:

> "It was so personal," she says. "It was done with such personal hatred. That was what stunned me more than anything. The rest was . . . expected. But why did they hate me so? I had never set eyes on them."
>
> . . .
>
> "It was history speaking through them," he offers at last. "A history of wrong. Think of it that way, if it helps . . ."
>
> "That doesn't make it easier." (156)

This exchange engages with existing feminist narratives on the subject of rape victims and perpetrators; at the same time, though, it seems to reveal the failure of those narratives to provide any meaningful response for Lucy. While her sense of the rape being personal certainly fits with the narratives of privacy and shame, this rhetorical move from the personal to a broader political schema does not address Lucy's experience in a meaningful way. David persists, though, to express to Lucy that he "understands" what happened to her, and he ends with "Because you were nothing to them" (157). This, it seems, is the one thing that Lucy connects to. She says, "But you are right, I meant nothing to them, nothing. I could feel it" (158). Her response to that "meaninglessness" is *to forge* and finally *to trust in* links with others. In her life on the farm, Lucy has made meaning despite the fact that her friends left the commune and that her relationship with Helen seems to have dissolved. Lucy has made her existence meaningful through the work with Petrus, the trips selling her produce in the local market, her friendship with Bev Shaw, and especially the boarding of dogs. While we are right to wonder, with David, whether Petrus was complicit in Lucy's rape, we must also consider the meaning of the day-to-day work and the bonds that Lucy has already created with him. She trusts that in taking a bond of marriage (kinship on his terms) he will be honorable in his relation to her.[12]

Lucy's experience of being *without meaning to* and *hated by* her attackers may, as David argues, be a function of colonial history and injustice. However, we'd like to suggest that Lucy's reaction to the rape points to a broader encounter with the violence of others. If she resents being but a minor character in David's life (198), Lucy seems devastated at the experience of being even less than that to her attackers. Butler's discussion of feminist philosopher Adriana Cavarero's theory of exposure may be of help here:

> Cavarero argues that we are beings who are, of necessity, *exposed* to one another in our vulnerability and singularity, and that our political situation consists in part in learning how best to handle — and to honor — this constant and necessary exposure . . . If I have lost the conditions of address, if I have no "you" to address, then I have lost "myself." . . . *This* exposure that I am constitutes, as it were, my singularity. I cannot will it away, for it is a feature of my very corporeality and, in this sense, of my life. Yet it is not that over which I have control . . . no one can be exposed for me, and I am, in this way, nonsubstitutable . . . I become recognizable through the operation of norms. (31–33)

Although Butler here is working through Cavarero in order to think specifically about identity formation, we can also engage with these ideas politically — and, in the case of Lucy, quite literally. She is indeed exposed in the most concrete way, and her agreement to marriage can readily be seen as participation in a social norm that will allow her to negotiate (not negate) her exposure.

For Lucy to report the rape and identify her rapists would be, in a sense, to continue a narrative in which she would not be "seen" or be "meaningful" — she would become a "rape victim" — a recognizable narrative but one that utterly circumscribes her within a set of discourses (political, feminist, juridical, colonial) that preclude the formation of social bonds in her world. So, while Lucy could, through laying "real charges," seek recourse to the state, an institution that offers to record her narrative, execute a judgment, and finally provide her with "justice," Lucy's world allows for an alternative path, one that will forego the promise of conventional justice but provide instead the promise of meaning.[13] Lucy's commitment seems to lie in a different sphere than does David's ("Am I wrong to want justice?" he asks Petrus [119]). Though David may not be "wrong," Lucy's interest lies elsewhere. Here, again, Butler helps us with the shift from the juridical to the ethical:

> Although I am certainly not arguing that we ought never to make judgments — they are urgently necessary for political, legal, and personal life alike — I think that it is important, in rethinking the cultural terms of ethics, to remember that not all ethical relations are reducible to acts of judgment and that the very capacity to judge presupposes a prior relation between those who judge and those who are judged . . . Moreover, judgment, as important as it is, cannot qualify as a theory of recognition; indeed, we may well judge another without recognizing him or her at all . . . Condemnation, denunciation, and excoriation work as quick ways to posit an ontological difference between judge and judged, even to purge oneself of another. (45–46)

Butler's work on the value of recognition above and beyond the value of judgment poses a problem in the face of existing feminist narratives of rape and recovery from rape. The incommensurability of these stems from two very different notions of the position of the self. While feminist rape narratives rely on the value of first-person narration and a community that can then confirm the validity of the first-person perspective, Butler suggests that the maintenance of such a "coherent" narrative relies upon non-recognition of the other and a denial of one's constitutional exposure to the other.

For Lucy, the kinship bond — with Petrus, his extended family, and her child — might function as a replacement for the pitfalls of an individual identity seen in David's world. We might consider it a structural repair for the impossibility of forging an identity that is satisfactory within the context (historical, geographical) of her life.[14] Withholding accusation and judgment, along with the establishment of kinship, play out as an effective example of responding to violence with non-violence. To return to Cavarero, Lucy's "exposure" to the other is a condition of her existence and a condition perhaps exacerbated by her historical/geographical situation on the frontier in post-apartheid South Africa; her solution is not to deny the "unfreedom" of that exposure but rather to accept that her "unfreedom" comes with the recognition of her relation to others and hence her ability to create a bond to Petrus and his family.[15]

Of course, it is one thing to forego revenge, but Lucy's response seems to forego justice as well in favor of mutual recognition. In her thoughts on meeting violence with non-violence, Butler asks:

> What might it mean to undergo violation, to insist upon *not* resolving grief and staunching vulnerability too quickly through a turn to violence, and to practice, as an experiment in living otherwise, nonviolence in an emphatically nonreciprocal response? . . . It might mean that one does not foreclose upon that primary exposure to the Other, that one does not try to transform the unwilled into the willed, but rather, to take the very unbearability of exposure as the sign, the reminder, of a common vulnerability, a common physicality and risk. (100)

This common vulnerability, though, is not without some regulation. Rather than remaining utterly vulnerable to violence, Lucy can connect with others and mitigate the immediacy of violence, even if she cannot abolish her vulnerability. In order to do so, she must engage with a set of norms that seems perhaps unfamiliar to western readers: polygamy, a dowry, and a marriage of convenience. But in Lucy's situation, these social structures render her recognizable. Butler writes of how, in the context of "unfreedom," norms must adjudicate between inevitable and reversible forms of impingement (107). In Lucy's context, marriage to Petrus is the available option. Petrus says to David of Lucy's situation, "it is dangerous, too dangerous. A woman must be marry" (202). By not being married, Lucy is operating outside of the norm. Instead of being a place of "more" freedom, perhaps the frontier is precisely a dramatization of the limits of our freedom (control, safety, etc.).[16] Her sexuality, her status as a loner, and her landowning are not recognized by the social norms of this world. As readers, we might ask: to what extent do we expect Lucy to challenge or, in the face of colonial history, accept the kinship norm? The novel, like Butler, seems to acknowledge that without accepting a limit to our freedom (rights and protections) we deny the fact of our susceptibility, exposure to others, and, in turn, we do violence to those others.

In her discussion with David, Lucy says that she will "start at ground level. With nothing. Not with nothing but. With nothing. No cards, no weapons, no property, no rights, no dignity" (205). Yet, the kinship model that Lucy agrees to does offer a level of status and protection as well as a guarantee that a certain set of rules will be respected. Although Lucy does not have the kinds of social guarantees we might usually associate with kinship laws, she and Bev both trust that Petrus will protect Lucy and allow her to stay on the land with her child and the dogs. So, if we, like Lucy, trust in the potential for this marriage to provide a route to the future and, more broadly, if we read this as allegorical on some level, what does this marriage mean for the "new state"?

Not "truth and reconciliation." Lucy refuses to narrativize her rape — and she accepts the formation of bonds that hold no illusion of retrieving some idyllic past. Lucy gives up justice in favor of peace. In a sense, the novel renders obsolete the narrative of the past in favor of a founding violence that opens up the possibility of a peaceful future. Is this not, ironically, the story of anthropological modernism? Though it offers no promise of justice, in this world, David receives grace as an antiquated figure; his generation, though, did not construct a narrative that would make the future nor did he form the kinds of bonds required by the new world. Lucy, in order to forge those bonds, must reject a model of identity, a subject position — that is, she must reject narratives of justice and healing — in favor of a tenuous arrangement. As readers and as teachers, we remain disconcerted by Lucy's response to the material and communal implications of rape and the futures it creates, and yet, we concede that it introduces new terms with which to critique our own bedrock beliefs. The power of particular narratives (colonial, racial, feminist) is never so visible as in those contexts that render that power insufficient. *Disgrace* calls us to acknowledge that subject status, autonomy, bodily integrity, ownership, are in fact modern privileges borne to us on the backs of cherished scripts we are compelled to reproduce, whole cloth, despite new situations which call their relevance into question. The novel's attention to the ancient and modern narratives surrounding the foundational trespass of rape highlights our cultural compulsion for telling certain tales, which, to our detriment, may prevent new, ethically challenging arrangements between ourselves and others, tenuous as these may be.

Notes

[1] A significant body of social psychology research studies "rape scripts." Littleton and Axsom describe it thus: A script is a type of schema, which is a cognitive structure that represents organized knowledge about a given domain (Schank & Abelson, 1977). Specifically, a script is a schema for a particular type of event, such as eating a meal at a restaurant or going out on a first date. Scripts contain information about props, roles, and rules regarding the sequence of events (Fiske & Taylor, 1991). They often operate unconsciously and are highly resistant to change (Demorest, 1995). In addition, schemas serve to influence cognitive processing. They influence attention, organization, interpretation, and recall of information (Baldwin, 1992; Zadney & Gerard, 1974), (1). In their study, Littleton and Axsom note the dominance of certain conventions in college students' rape scripts as opposed to their seductions scripts: "In the rape scripts there also was overt violence on the part of the man and resistance of the man's advances on the part of the woman (though sometimes in seduction scripts the woman was described as wanting to resist). Rape also was viewed as leading to clear negative outcomes for the woman" (6).

[2] McMullin and White 2006, 96–105. Again, it should be noted that one of the significant variables affecting a woman's likelihood to label her experience as rape is the presence and extent of physical injury.

[3] Even Susan Brownmiller, in her canonical feminist treatise *Against Our Will: Men, Women and Rape*, describes acquaintance rape as partially the fault of the victim: "Upon hearing such cases, even with my feminist perspective, I often feel like shouting "Idiot, why didn't you see the warning signs earlier?'" (284).

[4] Meg Samuelson closely attends to two narratives or "rape myths" in *Disgrace* that condition the existences of black and white women: "both rape myths have shaped the ways in which racialized gendered bodies have been produced and regulated the ways in which sexual violence has been conceptualized, and the political projects to which rape has been harnessed" (141).

[5] Martha Burt's 1980 study "Cultural Myths and Support for Rape" instigated two decades of research documenting the dominant "rape myths" in various communities and the material effects of these myths.

[6] Wendy Hesford, for example, analyzes the documentary *Rape Stories* and questions whether it is able "to not reproduce the spectacle of violence or vicitimization and to not erase the materiality of violence and trauma by turning corporeal bodies into texts" (193). In the end, however, she insists that the film is able to transcend these challenges as it tells the story. Likewise, Linda Alcoff and Laura Gray's article "Survivor Discourse: Transgression or Recuperation?" likens the societal compulsion

to narrate rape to Foucault's technology of sexual confession and agonizes over the manifold ways in which first-person rape narratives are used for entertainment and ideological purposes. They too, however, insist that speaking is the answer: "The applicability of Foucault's analysis to survivor discourse thus ends here: what we need to do is not retreat . . . from bringing sexual violence into discourse but, rather, to create new discursive forms and spaces in which to gain autonomy within this process" (287).

[7] Madorossian glosses Brown's *States of Injury*. "Besides fixing women's identity as 'wounded,' the effort to seek legal redress for injuries also 'legitimizes law and the state as appropriate protectors against injury' while obscuring the masculinist state's own power to injure (759).

[8] Although she laments this conclusion, Gillian Gane indeed interprets Lucy's actions in this very way: "If we believe that women can hold out hope for the future of the New South Africa, we must surely hope that they will do so in a ways that go beyond silently suffering rape, torture, and betrayal and sacrificing their violated bodies for the sustenance of others" (110).

[9] In her article "Ethics and Politics in Tagore, Coetzee, and Certain Scenes of Teaching," Gayatri Spivak argues that *Disgrace* fosters an intertextual reading by way of its interpolation of the reader: "The literary text gives rhetorical signals to the reader, which lead to activating the readerly imagination. Literature advocates in this special way. . . . Literary reading teaches us to learn from the singular and the unverifiable" (22–23). Spivak cites the conversation between Lucy and David in which Lucy articulates that she will "start from nothing"; this scene, she contends, "focalizes" the reader on Lucy's narrative without providing the reader with the entire story. Although we are only given what David is privy to, Spivak suggests that the text and intertext lead the reader to seek beyond the novel.

[10] Although the terms are certainly different in *Disgrace*, we do have a structure in which the colonial group, although willing to hire and, in Lucy's case, trade labor for land with the historically local population, but we do not see examples of a real engagement between cultures. And, while there may not be an absence of marriageable women for the black African population, we do get the sense that the acquisition of land is tricky business.

[11] Samuelson interprets Lucy's silence as a means of avoiding a rape script that confines her to a set role within a "racialized patriarchy." She writes: "The (un) spoken response to her rape that Coetzee grants Lucy may be read as an attempt to negotiate the treacherous ground of a patriarchal society that names 'woman' as the fundamental unit of exchange . . . she both highlights and refuses the construction of white women's bodies as 'property to be defended' through the ritualised 'black peril panics that cast black men as rapists, white men as protectors, and white women as bounty'" (148).

[12] The ambiguities of Petrus's relationship to Lucy and his potential complicity in her rape are elaborated on pages 116–18. David considers Petrus as a "neighbour" rather than as an employee but then notes that this new role implies a kind of "unwritten contract" with no provision for "dismissal on grounds of suspicion"

(117). While Lucy seems prepared to forge an arrangement with Petrus, David remains "anthropological" in his approach (118); this, it seems, is a fundamental difference between David's and Lucy's approaches to the situation, but we do think that David's attachment to an anthropological approach is important.

[13] Coetzee's 2007 novel *Diary of a Bad Year* begins with a diatribe against the state that might provide a window into Coetzee's view of the limitations of state solutions and the possibility of opening up new avenues of social organization in a post-apartheid South Africa.

[14] "what happened to me is a purely private matter. In another time, in another place it might be held to be a public matter. But in this place, at this time, it is not . . ." (112).

[15] See Butler 91. Responsibility here is an avowal of my relation to the other and hence an avowal of my "unfreedom."

[16] Gareth Cornwell, in fact, sees geography as key to what he terms the "pastoral solution" (54) of the novel.

7: Dis(g)race, or White Man Writing

Sandra D. Shattuck

> How are they to be figured, this man and he? As master and slave? As brothers, twin brothers? As comrades in arms? Or as enemies, foes?
>
> — J. M. Coetzee, "He and His Man"

MY INTRODUCTION TO J. M. COETZEE'S WRITING began with *Disgrace*, and a first reading of the novel did not dispose me kindly towards the author. I found the rendering of black South African characters truncated and skewed, Lucy's silence on her rape offensive: in short, I thought *Disgrace* was sexist and racist, an indulgence of a self-absorbed narrator. I fell into the camp of readers described by Derek Attridge as condemning Coetzee "for painting a one-sidedly negative picture of post-apartheid South Africa, representing blacks as rapists and thieves, and implying that whites have no option but to submit to their assaults."[1]

My ignorance of Coetzee's oeuvre was by design; I boycotted his writing precisely because he was Afrikaner and I rooted for the underdog, whom I saw as under-acknowledged black South African writers like Bessie Head, Alex la Guma, Lewis Nkosi, Ezekiel Mphalele, and Miriam Tlali, writers I began reading in graduate school in the 1980s at Coetzee's alma mater, the University of Texas at Austin. (My literary apartheid, however, did not extend to women writers, since I read the works of Nadine Gordimer, Olive Schreiner, and Doris Lessing.) In the 1980s, UT Austin was home to *Research in African Literatures*, then edited by Bernth Lindfors; the English department featured a new Third World Literature program; and replicated township shanties constructed on the quad testified to a resurgent student activism, galvanized by protests against South African apartheid and attempts to get the university to divest.

In retrospect, my refusal to read Coetzee's work was an empty political gesture, both uninformed and also racist in its own way, even as its impetus was to address ignorance of and racism towards black African writers. After all, of the 104 writers awarded the Nobel Prize in Literature since 1901, only four have been African; of those four, only one is black. Nigerian writer Wole Soyinka, the first African to receive the prize, did so in 1986, eighty-five years after the initial prize was awarded. As Gertrude Makhaya mentions in her review of *Disgrace*, "The Trouble with J. M. Coetzee," many readers of African literature expected Chinua Achebe (often referred to as the grandfather of the African novel) or Ngugi wa Thiong'o to be similarly honored, but they were not; Naguib Mahfouz, Nadine Gordimer, and J. M. Coetzee were. (Of course, this tally of black and white African Nobel Laureates only works if Egyptian Naguib Mahfouz is positioned closer to the white side of the color bar.) And although the 2007 Nobel Laureate's national affiliation is with the United Kingdom, readers often view Doris Lessing as an African writer, not only because she lived in Zimbabwe (then Southern Rhodesia) from age six to thirty, but also because her work is marked by the land and the issues of southern Africa. Lessing, therefore, could be considered the most recent addition to the list of white African writers who have won the Nobel Prize in Literature.

Lest the above inventory seem a dry calculation, let me contextualize it with a personal anecdote. Just a few years ago, in 2003, as I sat in the faculty lounge of the English department in a historically black university and discussed my upcoming presentation on Chinua Achebe's *Anthills of the Savannah*, a highly educated white colleague asked me: "Is there any good literature in Africa?" This story echoes the beginning of "An Image of Africa," Achebe's groundbreaking lecture of 1975, which became the classic piece of criticism faulting Joseph Conrad's *Heart of Darkness* for its racist depiction of Africans. In this article, Achebe describes hurrying across the campus of an American university at the start of the fall semester, when an older man crosses his path and comments on how young the students seem. The man then asks Achebe if he, too, is a student. Achebe corrects the man's assumption, says he teaches African literature, and reports the man's response: "Now that was funny, he said, because he never had thought of Africa as 'having that kind of stuff, you know'" (782).

Three decades later, my colleague articulated the same sentiment. Had the department where I worked offered any courses on African literatures, this professor most likely would not have posed the question. But putting aside the complicated relationships between race, culture, diaspora, and the canon at underfunded historically black colleges such as mine, we still must acknowledge a western benightedness that cultivates the ground for such a question as: "Is there any good literature in Africa?" The list of Nobel laureates might indicate that the answer is, "Yes — if the writer is white." For Coetzee and Gordimer — both white, both South African — international acclaim complicates their reception at home. As Gertrude Makhaya explains in her review of *Disgrace*, "The fact that black South African viewpoints and portrayals of the new South Africa are rarely given a platform outside Africa cannot be ignored and heightens tensions around what white South African artists and intellectuals, with easier access to international audiences, have to say about democratic South Africa."

This discussion of the context for my studied detour around Coetzee's novels does not excuse my intellectual wrongheadedness, especially since such contrariness contradicts my own pedagogy. In my classes, students have told me, they learn to persevere with difficult texts by reading again and again through the challenges. Thus, participation in this project on *Disgrace* has allowed me a chance to rectify my willful ignorance. As a former anti-reader, I also recognize my culpability in creating what Coetzee has described as his "disabled, disqualified" status:

> In the first half of this [Coetzee's life] story — a story spoken in a wavering voice, for the speaker is not only blind but, written as he is as a white South African into the latter half of the twentieth century, disabled, disqualified — a man-who-writes reacts to the situation he finds himself in of being without authority, writing without authority. (*Doubling the Point* 392)

One might argue that Coetzee's international fame no longer qualifies him as either disabled or writing without authority, but such an argument makes it easy to overlook Coetzee's own investigations into the complexities of power and language, history and fiction.

After further readings of *Disgrace*, I still find the novel troubling. I still find the depiction of black South African characters circumscribed (especially the unnamed and unvoiced rural female characters) and Lucy's refusal to report her rape disturbing. This event — the rape of a white South African woman by three black South African males, often described in the novel as two men and a boy — at the heart of *Disgrace*'s contentious reception is also the inflammatory turning point of the novel. An astute student of history, Coetzee would be well aware of the ways in which this extreme trope has figured in the instigation and justification of violence by whites against blacks.[2] Why, then, does he employ such an incendiary plot event in his first novel published and set in post-apartheid South Africa? Derek Attridge phrases this concern as follows: "The overriding question for many readers is: does this novel, as one of the most widely disseminated and forceful representations of post-apartheid South Africa, impede the difficult enterprise of rebuilding the country?" (*Ethics of Reading*, 164). Attridge argues in the same chapter against reading *Disgrace* for its "political efficacy," claiming that all readers "may find the bleak image of the 'new South Africa' in this work hard to take" (164).

My distress with Coetzee's novel steered me to an initial project of comparing *Disgrace* to a contemporary novel by a black South African woman writer. I chose Sindiwe Magona's *Mother to Mother*, which takes as its impetus the murder of American Fulbright scholar Amy Biehl in Guguletu in August, 1993. Published a year before *Disgrace* and written in part as letters from the killer's mother to Amy Biehl's mother, Magona's novel also takes up post-apartheid violence committed by young black men against a young white woman; the novel also traverses urban and rural settings primarily through the experience of the South African mother, whose history of poverty and displacement constitutes much of the story. And while I found in *Mother to Mother* the voices that Coetzee's novel elides, I could not find a way to write about the two novels in one piece.

I went back to *Disgrace* and re-read; I read other works by Coetzee and researched the scholarship. This study led me to interpret the novel more carefully as David Lurie's story and to shift my attention to the following question: What can the character David Lurie teach us about post-apartheid South Africa? In other words, instead of sticking with my impatient and frustrated first reading criticizing the novel for what it lacks (full portrayals of black South African characters, Lucy's denunciation of her own rape), I have become more curious about what the novel does put before us.

My shift in perspective began in earnest when I was musing over the unusual name given to the boy rapist in the trio: Pollux. The name invites speculation about twinning and doubling, subjects Coetzee takes up in many of his writings, and provokes the question: Where in the novel is his twin and inseparable companion, Castor? The two older and unnamed rapists seem the obvious choice, but their relationship in the novel begins and ends with the house invasion and the rape scene imagined by Lurie. The violence to Lucy's home, her dogs, her father, and her self is possibly Pollux's initiation into a life that will allow him to act on his wild adolescent threat: "We will kill you all!" My thinking about the character Pollux and his shadow brother led me to wonder if David Lurie himself could stand in for Castor. Both are rapists (mythologically and in the novel), and both must be educated about the new South Africa. If we read Lurie as Pollux's twin, then this quiet undercurrent in the novel might enrich our understanding of Lurie and of Coetzee's textual strategies of twinning, doubling, and mirroring in (and beyond) *Disgrace*.

Disgrace is marked by several instances of mirroring or twinning: the father-daughter constellations of Isaacs and Melanie, Lurie and Lucy, Byron and Allegra; Lurie's rape of Melanie and the gang-rape of Lucy; and David's silence during his hearing and Lucy's silence after her rape, to name a few, but the character of Pollux provides one of the most intriguing and least examined instances.

Pollux is an easy character to overlook, not only because Petrus overshadows him, but also because he is a boy frequently described as mentally or emotionally off-kilter. Nevertheless, Coetzee invites us to pay close attention to Pollux, who is the only named participant in the rape, and in fact the only other rural black South African character besides Petrus with a proper name. Pollux's name doesn't appear until late in the narrative: after the rape, after Lurie confronts him at Petrus's party, after Lurie has left the Eastern Cape and returned, and even after Lucy reveals her pregnancy. While Lurie and Lucy sit at the dinner table, Lucy tells David that "the boy is back" (199), and then she names him. Lurie reacts to the name

Pollux by saying, "Not Mncedisi? Not Nqabayakhe? Nothing unpronounceable, just Pollux?" (200). Lucy responds by spelling out the name and then reprimanding her father for his culturally insensitive comment: "P-O-L-L-U-X. And David, can we have some relief from that terrible irony of yours?" (200). Lucy's spelling out of Pollux's name in capital letters highlights the name both aurally and visually, and Lurie's repeated sarcastic comments about the name (later, after Lurie kicks the boy, he says, "Pollux! What a name!" [207]) further alert us that the character's name requires a closer look. Pollux has been named by a colonial Master, or by a person steeped in the European classical heritage. Did he perhaps have a twin, a boy from whom he's separated by events or even death? Petrus may know, but on this, as on many topics, he's silent. But the name, in one sense an alias for any African boy who bears it, in another enables the narrative to put forward, in a manner appropriate to its post-1994 suppression, the ongoing force of race-hatred in South Africa.

In searching for the twin suggested by Pollux's name, we find one important clue in the repeated description of Lurie's head bandages as a skullcap (115, 120, 128, 135). In the traditional Greek story Castor and Pollux are hatched from eggs fertilized by Zeus in his rape of Leda. The shattered shells become their "skullcaps."[3] Like the characters Lurie and Pollux, the mythical twins were involved in rape, depicted for example in Rubens's painting *The Rape of the Daughters of Leucippus*. After Lurie finally utters the word "rape" in the first conversation in which he and Lucy discuss the attack, he remembers trying to understand the word as a child when he encountered it in newspapers. Lurie then recalls another of Rubens's paintings, *The Rape of the Sabine Women*, which mystified him.

Lurie and Pollux encounter each other three times: during the house invasion and rape, at Petrus's party, and when Lurie beats Pollux after he finds the boy playing peeping Tom. These three encounters depict confrontations that indicate the characters cannot share the same space and time, just as versions of the Castor and Pollux myth state that the Dioscuri alternated being mortal and immortal: either Pollux is in ascendancy, as he is during the attack and with Petrus's intervention at the party, or Lurie wields power, as he does during his beating of Pollux.

Petrus's party begins with intimations of healing race relations, since David and Lucy, the only whites invited, represent the possibility of interracial communication. Lucy's ability to speak Xhosa and to observe customs properly also demonstrates the gulf between her and her father's positions in post-apartheid South Africa. Lurie disturbs this exchange of hospitality when he confronts Pollux, but Petrus's entire community is endangered when Lurie twice threatens to call the police. Once they've returned to the farmhouse, David and Lucy fight again over his desire to call the police, and Lucy insists yet again that her father take no action.

This encounter calls forth violent emotions from both Lurie and Pollux; Lurie hates Pollux as the perpetrator of violence against himself and his daughter, while Pollux hates Lurie for being white and thus an oppressor. The incident sharpens the mirroring between the two characters:

> In front of the boy he plants himself. It is the third of them, the dull-faced apprentice, the running-dog. "I know you," he says briefly.
> The boy does not appear to be startled. On the contrary, the boy appears to have been waiting for this moment, storing himself up for it. The voice that issues from his throat is thick with rage. "Who are you?" he says, but the words mean something else: *By what right are you here?* His whole body radiates violence. (131–32)

When David returns to the party, he disturbs it one more time as he lurks on the fringes of the audience listening to an elder's speech. Like Pollux's name, the patriarch's gold chain with Victoria's image stamped on one side represents colonialism; the gold chain is one of many duplicates manufactured in an English foundry. Thus, the patriarch wears a symbol that distinguishes him as a chieftain, but the distinction is false, since the medal was mass-produced and sent to all corners of the empire. The new South Africa inherits this history of colonialism and must deal with that legacy.

Standing at the edge of this audience listening to the patriarch's speech, Lurie sees a nervous and wary Pollux nearby, and stands defiant against the group that shelters the boy: "Let them know I am still here, he thinks, let them know I am not skulking in the big house" (135). Lurie will not hide in the "big house," and Lucy has just told David during their argument that Petrus isn't some native laborer in the old dispensation that she can fire on a whim. She adds, decisively, "That's all gone, gone with the wind" (133). These references to colonialism and American slavery deepen the historical layers of racial conflict portrayed in *Disgrace*. The party scene ends with a gesture by Lurie that links him to and distinguishes him from Pollux as he "lifts a hand to his white skullcap. For the first time he is glad to have it, to wear it as his own" (135).

We learn more about Pollux from Lucy in the scene in which she relates his name. Pollux is a brother of Petrus's wife, and although Lucy is unsure if he's a blood brother, she still lectures David that Petrus has real family obligations toward him. Lucy advises David to steer clear of him, in part because she "suspect[s] there is something wrong with him" (200). Even the tolerant, culture-savvy Bev Shaw doesn't like the look of him.

All of this material coalesces in the final scene between David and Pollux, a pivotal scene that yokes the two characters together in a final outburst of violence. If Lurie is a liberal-minded intellectual, then his latent twinning with Pollux in this final encounter dramatizes the naked racist violence just below the liberal surface. David and the now companionable bulldog Katy return from a walk to see the boy watching once more, spying on Lucy through her bathroom window. An "elemental rage" sweeps over Lurie; he curses the boy twice (*"You filthy swine!"*), and the boy falls down as he tries to escape. Lurie thinks: "Phrases that all his life he has avoided seem suddenly just and right: *Teach him a lesson. Show him his place.* So this is what it is like . . . to be a savage" (206). David — also a voyeur, also a rapist — sees the mirror without quite recognizing himself in Pollux.

Katy joins the assault, replicating the day of Lucy's rape, when Lurie first commanded the bulldog to attack the boy he was determined to keep an eye on. The parallel is inescapable: the terrifying use of attack dogs by minority whites against their black neighbors, a truth which makes the rapists' shooting of the penned guard dogs at least partially understandable. Katy does little damage this time until David gives the fallen boy "a good, solid kick." Then Katy, "mounting the boy's body," gets her grip: "There are score-marks from the dog's fangs; as they watch, pearls of blood emerge on the dark skin" (207). "As they watch": again, Coetzee gives us a dark yet clear representation of South African whites administering violence, watching the blood.

The barely clad Lucy emerges to rescue the boy, but Pollux doesn't distinguish between her and her father: "We will kill you all!" he shouts, swept up again in the same "elemental rage" (206) and violence that consumed Lurie. The scene repeats Pollux and Lurie's previous encounter almost exactly: as Lucy and David blundered through the potato beds as they fled Petrus's party, so now the boy tramples the same patch as he flees toward Petrus's protection. And to underline Pollux and Lurie's first encounter at the rape itself, Lucy's robe opens as she ministers to Pollux, revealing her breasts. "A stillness falls" — a frozen moment — as the wounded boy and Lurie stare in tandem at Lucy's exposed body, and David's rage returns, not only because the boy sees, but also because David sees his pregnant daughter, pregnant through rape committed in part by Pollux and unprevented by Lurie. As Lurie thinks, "Something about Pollux sends him into a rage: his ugly, opaque little eyes, his insolence, but also the thought that like a weed he has been allowed to tangle his roots with Lucy and Lucy's existence" (209).

Hours later, his hand still tingling from the blows, Lurie discovers some difficult self-truths; he understands that his violence has taught neither himself nor the boy anything at all. Like Pollux, David is a school dropout, and his angry description of the boy has become a revealing mirror: "I don't trust him. He is shifty. . . . In the old days we had a word for people like him. Deficient. Mentally deficient. Morally deficient" (208). David, too, appears "deficient," cracked and eccentric, to others — think of the three boys who laugh at him as he lurks in the compound behind the clinic, "a mad old man who sits among the dogs singing to himself" (212). And although Lurie is ashamed of his violence, he knows he will attack Pollux again if the boy insults Lucy. A phrase from Rilke's poem "Archaic Torso of Apollo" leaps into his mind: "*Du musst dein Leben ändern*!: you must change your life" (209), and he tries to fend off this challenge with his oft-heard claim that he's too old to change without losing his "honour." But change is already well under way, as "honour" soon falls out of David's lexicon. Lurie remains near the smallholding, sharing yet another similarity with Pollux: neither of them is going anywhere. As Lucy says of Pollux, "he is here, he won't disappear in a puff of smoke, he is a fact of life" (208).

And so if something about Pollux sends Lurie into a rage, it may be the unexamined knowledge that they are more alike than they are different. It is perhaps significant that their "roots" are tangled and not their branches. Coetzee's twinning of the two characters asks us to consider what Lurie does not: that he and Pollux grew from the same South African soil and that their roots have always been entangled. In the myth, after all, Castor and Pollux are not merely rapists: they are themselves the product of rape. Even as we may condemn both Lurie and Pollux for their unforgiveable crimes, Coetzee insists that we must also recognize that they have both been shaped by the legacy of South Africa's history, a birthright of racism and violence that remains despite the momentous political changes, despite the work of the Truth and Reconciliation Commission. The feelings may be buried, harder to detect, but the shadow twinning of Lurie and Pollux, the tangling of their roots and their eyes, invite the reader to question easy polarizations. This invitation to consider complex intertwinings is precisely what David Lurie's character teaches us about post-apartheid South Africa.

This dark history has also produced Coetzee, his novels, and all South African literature — a fact of which Coetzee himself is fully aware. The cost of apartheid for all South Africans has been a stunted and deformed inner life, Coetzee says, an observation "that applies to myself and my own writing as much as anyone else" (*Doubling* 98). This is why the writer in South Africa is "disabled, disqualified" and writes "without authority"; this is why Coetzee describes South African literature as a "less than fully human literature, unnaturally preoccupied with power and the torsions of power, unable to move from elementary relations of contestation, domination, and subjugation to the vast and complex human world that lies beyond them" (*Doubling* 98).

My initial reading of *Disgrace* relegated it to this dustbin of fractured writing. Like other readers I faulted the novel for its failure to be "fully human" — to encompass the full human reality of rural South Africa, to fully embody the African characters, to do full justice to Lucy's dilemma and decision. But if we examine Lurie as Pollux's hidden twin, then the two characters — neither fully human nor immortal — embody this failure and elucidate both the limitations and the possibilities of post-apartheid South Africa. We might view David Lurie and Pollux as the last rapist of the old order and the first rapist of the new: oppositional factions caught in mirrored, cyclical violence — one always in ascendancy, one always in descent. Or, more generously, even if we detect glimpses of grace in David Lurie, and if we are able — like Lucy — to view Pollux as a "disturbed child," we must recognize that neither is able to change entirely. Perhaps the future of South Africa lies with neither shadow twin, since each is lost in the post-apartheid period and must find his place on the shifting ground claimed by the new, represented by the characters of Petrus and Lucy.

In the end Petrus and Lucy may illustrate another example of mirroring or twinning, as the new parents — or business partners — of the new South Africa. Lucy and Petrus both work hard to prevent further violence between David and Pollux. Willing to change and compromise, Lucy and Petrus try to accommodate past crimes, to transcend obsession with the "tensions of power," and to achieve a peaceful synthesis between black and white, between oppressor and oppressed. This uneasy coalition is further represented by — and represents the only hope *for* — Lucy's child, a product of violence whose place at the table will be provided through Petrus's and Lucy's labor. As the possible child of Pollux and the grandchild of Lurie, this new citizen further entangles the shadow twins in relationships neither can possibly want. Nevertheless, Lurie chooses not to turn his back on this unwanted being.

And although Lurie denies he can change his life, he nevertheless offers us a model of transformation. He absolutely disagrees with Lucy's choice not to report the gang-rape, but he abides by her wishes not to pursue her rapists legally. He hates Pollux but still stands by Lucy and the child, even though the father may be Pollux. He commits himself to the opera, itself a speaking-back to the classics he used to teach in the university. Lurie finds the art he has been seeking through a woman's voice accompanied by his daughter's toy banjo, an indigenous instrument bought at market near the land where Lurie now waits, committed to a new generation, "a child of this earth" (216). As Lurie says, "There may be things to learn" (218).

Notes

[1] Attridge 2002, 317. Several South African writers have denounced the book, notably Breyten Breytenbach and Athol Fugard. Fugard was quoted in the *London Sunday Times:* "We've got to accept the rape of a white woman as a gesture to all of the evil that we did in the past? That's a lot of bloody bullshit"

(cited in Attridge, *Ethics of Reading*, 164n). More important, politically, was an African National Congress-commissioned report on racism in the media that held up *Disgrace* as illustrative of white racism in South Africa today. Entitled "Blackboard Bungle," it claims that "[I]n the novel, J. M. Coetzee represents as brutally as he can, the white people's perception of the post-apartheid black man. . . . It is suggested that in these circumstances, it might be better that our white compatriots should emigrate because to be in post-apartheid South Africa is to be in 'their territory,' as a consequence of which the whites will lose their cards, their weapons, their property, their rights, their dignity. The white women will have to sleep with the barbaric black men" (cited by Rosemary Jolly in "Going to the Dogs: Humanity in J. M. Coetzee's *Disgrace*, *The Lives of Animals*, and South Africa's Truth and Reconciliation Commission" in Poyner 2006, 149). See also Lucy Valerie Graham 2003, 433–44, and the essays by H. P. von Coller and J. Van Der Elst in Sikorska 2006, esp. 33 and 43. Peter McDonald (2002) and David Attwell (2002) offer excellent, though differing, analyses of the complexities of race in the novel, complexities that extend beyond South Africa.

[2] *Disgrace* is not the first fiction in which Coetzee presents the rape of a white South African woman by a black South African man. His early novel *In the Heart of the Country*, published in 1977, offers us an intertextual mirror of *Disgrace*. Both novels invert and critique the traditional Afrikaner *plaasroman* or farm novel, which Coetzee has stated imprisons women (*White Writing* 9). The women in both novels own and manage their farms, however ineffectively: Lucy gives up her smallholding to Petrus, while Magda allows the land to reclaim her farm. Both Magda and Lucy are bisexual or lesbian; both struggle with controlling fathers. Magda's and Lucy's rapes are both described as payment exacted. Hendrik rapes Magda after his long trip to the bank reveals that Magda will not be able to make good on her promises to pay his wages, while in a statement that has provided much of *Disgrace*'s controversy, Lucy asks David, "What if . . . what if *that* is the price one has to pay for staying on?" (158). However, Magda is not Lucy; she shoots and kills her father, sees her rape as a path to sexual awakening, and unreliably narrates the novel in numbered sections that offer alternate imaginings. By the end of the novel, Magda has become an insane and marooned Robinson-Crusoe-witch figure who sexually threatens a young black South African boy who strays onto her land.

[3] Our earliest written source for this in Greek mythology is the fourth-century B.C.E. playwright Lykophron, in his *Alexandra* (506–7). The earliest written source for the widely accepted story of Zeus taking the form of a swan to rape Leda is Euripides' *Helen* in the late fifth century. The eggshell skullcaps are also recorded in Lucian's *Dialogues of the Gods* (25). See Gantz, 318–28, esp. 321. The birth narrative of Castor and Pollux is also a tale of uncertain fatherhood — Zeus or Tyndareus — and the result of Leda's rape is a further rape: Helen is abducted and taken to Troy by Alexandros.

8: Clerk in a Post-Religious Age: Reading Lurie's Remnant Romantic Temperament in *Disgrace*

Gary Hawkins

NO, THIS CHRONICLE OF A FALL is not written to enlighten. Nor is schadenfreude sufficient to compel a modern reader's descent into the unraveling life of a middle-aged man who will show little inclination to stave off his own disgrace nor much ability to mend its collateral effects — a young woman, his student and his lover, chief among the dire complications. Instead, J. M. Coetzee's *Disgrace* draws us into unyielding witness of a man's pathetic fall via Coetzee's unwavering gaze.[1] Within this perspective David Lurie is repeatedly exposed: as a professor of Romantic literature marooned in a post-Romantic age — then as an exile from even that reconstituted academy; as a pale intellect in harsh rural post-apartheid South Africa; as a father consigned to the role of roommate; as an amateur composing opera on a banjo. In every case, Lurie presents a quaint and lonely figure who is set upon a vast Modern plain — and who holds little hope of rescue or even self-preservation. At times the prospect is unbearable. I would rather close the covers of the book on him than face an exposed and vacant Lurie dangling the props of Romanticism — its poetry, its promises of transcendence — as lures in his parlor seductions. I would much rather hear his bloodied confession confirm my prejudices than watch him defend the contents of his heart at the secular tribunal assembled to judge his indiscretion.

But *Disgrace* itself operates not in judgment but in inquiry. To conduct its inquiry the book follows a man emerging late from the time capsule of apartheid, dragging his European literatures and colonial proclivities into a post-apocalyptic landscape of upheaved cultural realities: post-apartheid, post-structural, post-Romantic, post-modern. Seen as a story of this man responding to this predicament by modulating between his Romantic ideals and his world of arranged efficiencies, *Disgrace* seems fraught with opposing questions. Is Romanticism under critique for its self-delusion? Or is the post-Romantic world under critique for its inability to find that "glimpse of the invisible" which Lurie still seeks (22)? Coming to terms with fallen ideals, particularly the Romantic, may seem the old news of Modernist literature, yet *Disgrace* asks us to consider this as a persistent postmodern predicament.[2] Lurie's thickened skin and ironic distance — by which he first shrugs off archaic pursuits of transcendence like love or atonement — may align him in the pews of common dissent that line our present age of doubt. But even in his rigidity and refusal, his temperament, which he professes to be "fixed," still moves occasionally to seek a transcendent light, only to have his refusal of ideals harden again around him (2). If we track the core of his disgrace into a fallen Romanticism and witness it most profoundly in his failing romance with his student Melanie Isaacs — as I intend to do — then we are also likely to locate, amid the ruins of this temperament, Lurie's remnant Romantic belief that there is more to this world than petty pleasures and more to it than earthly marks of success (or failure). This news flickers only briefly into his present view, and when the flame dwindles he proceeds freely (and too often immorally). In navigating Lurie's troubled descent and questioning his attempts to right himself, *Disgrace* takes seriously the dilemmas of a post-religious age. It asks what gestures — if any — are sufficient or legitimate strokes of meaning; and it shows, via a most disgraced citizen, the persistent and desperate human impulse to make such gestures.

In charting David Lurie's unwillingness to fully yield his collapsed idealism to cynicism, Coetzee provides a means to consider an alternative to the flattening skepticism that remains a primary intellectual posture of the post-colonial age. To achieve this alternative David Lurie will not undergo a dramatic transformation: he will not retreat to atavistic Romantic ideals nor will his final gesture of "offering up" the lame dog constitute an emblem of some new order. Rather, viewed through the lens of his Romantic temperament, the figure of David Lurie — still no less pathetic as his heart leaps up toward Melanie — becomes tinged with trouble and tragedy. In Wordsworthian terms that might still describe a contemporary fallen world, Lurie at his lowest with Melanie inhabits that complex state of dejection where to inhabit loss means to be near an upward presence of hope, however brief and where any glimpse of invisibility is fleeting and suspect. Or, as Wordsworth concludes his "Elegiac Stanzas," claiming the uncomfortable complexity that Lurie could also proclaim: "not without hope we suffer and we mourn" (60).

Indeed, transformation is not an arc that Coetzee would ever allow. At his hands any clear lines of genre or history fissure into intricacies where a character will act on competing motives and react contradictorily. Yet significantly, much debate on the novel critiques the extent to which this is a narrative of *Bildung*, and this debate tends to assume that the novel follows contours of development even though the novel's many readers will follow the premise of "education" in the book to starkly different conclusions.[3] In tracking change in this way, most commentators at least implicitly acknowledge the bipartite structure of the book: from urban Cape Town to the rural Eastern Cape; from Lurie's marginally intact professional life before the Board of Inquiry to his professional disgrace after; from his seductions and transgressions with Melanie, which are racially marked and likely conclude in rape,[4] to the aggressions and rape which he and his daughter Lucy later suffer on the farm. In taking seriously the novel's depiction of David Lurie as a Romantic, I, too, will see the book as a journey (a romance) and Lurie as a changed character through it — but his trajectory will be indefinite and his change far from unambiguous.[5] My primary interest will be the start of this journey and particularly the circumlocutions of his relationship with Melanie which extend into the latter part of the book. Through this focus I'll have the means to present a complex and unruly David Lurie, a man finally arriving in a troubled place of fallen ideals and persistent dreams.[6]

Part one introduces David Lurie in all his duplicities. We witness his peculiarly willful ability to moderate his experiences into discrete compartments, a practice that runs simultaneously with and counter to his remnant Romantic desires for transcendence and bliss. For instance, the opening paragraph orchestrates Lurie's perennial "pleasant-smelling and softly lit" romantic rendezvous at the regal-sounding Windsor Mansions where his contracted mate, Soraya, is perfectly placed, "waiting for him at the door," and their commerce is afforded the highest recommendation: "they make love" (1). But this description of the encounter cuts both ways when necessarily read in the context of the novel's first line: "For a man of his age, fifty-two, divorced, he has, to his mind, solved the problem of sex rather well." [7] Having assigned this logic to Lurie and "his mind," the deadening impact of this initial declaration suffuses the claimed tranquility that follows. Framed between "the problem of sex" and "mak[ing] love" this first paragraph initiates the novel's ambivalence. Their tryst includes all the trappings of romance, including the appropriate sensuous atmosphere and script of vacancy and fulfillment ("Have you missed me?" she asks; "I miss you all the time," he replies), but when cast as the solution to a "problem," these trappings arrange as the simulacra of romance (2). Indeed, these scenes may be more remarkable for what they show Lurie to be missing than for what they show him to contain.

Love is also glimpsed only through the cracks of this presentation of the affair (and often suggested by Lurie's refinements of what this *isn't* with Soraya), and love remains a conception which he continues to recognize and to sanctify as a higher ideal, even when it is absent. So his self-correction that this "may not be love" saves "love" from his present inauthenticities. Yet if this is a sign that he has not calcified to cynicism, he soon initiates a complicated inquiry in which he will dissect the body of non-love in a calculation that will ultimately serve his self-deception. Lurie decides that if this is not love then his experience may be "at least its cousin," namely "affection" (2). For Lurie, affection seems to be rooted in a surfeit of pleasure and when this pleasure is reciprocal, a relationship ascends to "affinity" (3). And as moderator his calculations with his escort fail to take into account (even though he acknowledges that "no doubt with other men she becomes another woman") how all of Soraya's own actions are calculated to respond to him. What he calls "affinity" is the nature of the transaction of the prostitute. He gets what he pays for and then elevates it to an epistemology of a new kind of bliss. In a blissful afternoon with an escort, he pockets the sublime like a souvenir, a purchased postcard of Mont Blanc.

In constraining the vast and turbulent realm of human relationships into a "problem" that he has "solved" with arranged afternoons, Lurie has parceled out affection as a portion of love, a portion which seems to offer a low and reachable horizon. So even if love evades his mastery he has arranged the world so that he can at least complete one of its minor transactions. Thus, even as the catastrophes of the novel unfold, Lurie is shown to be a man who actively creates his life *within* a set of defined lines — "he lives within his income, within his temperament, within his emotional means" (2). If this were all there was to Lurie we likely wouldn't give him much more thought. Even written into the charged cultural and political landscape of the late twentieth century, a merely low-horizoned and manipulative Lurie would be little more than a traumatized artifact of the past. But this man still looks upward, still aspires, still holds some expectation of the heights. And his upward vision is not mere nostalgia — Coetzee promises to open it up into a visionary light.

So the guidance of temperament need not be rigid even if it is "fixed." If the dictum, "follow your temperament" charges Lurie's life, he is careful not to ascribe it the level of "a philosophy," but rather, he will forward this as "a rule, like the Rule of St Benedict" (2). In adopting a rule rather than a philosophy here Lurie minimizes its jurisdiction over him. And in opting for a comparison to the Rule, Lurie does not necessarily align himself with the regimen of monks, but he evokes St Benedict's strategy by which laymen, too, might live a life according to the Gospels, a social life of work and prayer, a life more moderate than ascetic. That a life of "moderate bliss" with prostitutes — and with faculty wives, department secretaries — might be at all consummate with St Benedict's moderation is among the several moments of slapstick flatly observed by the novel. Yet the irony also reveals Lurie's troublesome self positioning: he wants to ascribe limits to his life; at the same time the novel hints that such a life might still afford contact with God.

But Lurie is more likely to conduct his worship in the classroom than in church; and Wordsworth is more his saint than Benedict. So the hobbled vision quest he conducts with Soraya on Thursday afternoons will be better understood in terms of how it remarkably maps to his often truncated visionary pursuits in teaching Romantic literature, an avocation which Lurie would like to equate to a kind of ministry. With its calls for work, material self-denial, and daily prayer, the Rule of St Benedict instills diffidence by submitting a parishioner to a consistent recognition of his place beneath a higher power. David Lurie credits his work as a teacher with similar correction. He believes that his teaching "teaches him humility, brings it home to him who he is in the world" (5). Moreover, the scholarship which still forms "the core of him" and which can still bring him closest to ecstasy is Wordsworth's chronicle of The Poet humbled beneath the sublime. "For as long as he can remember," he admits, "the harmonies of *The Prelude* have echoed within him" (15). Yet lately David Lurie's full-blown Romantic temperament is largely under duress because the re-forming world finds little space for visionary pursuits. His home institution has been constrained from its previous liberal identity of Cape Town University College to become the procedural Cape Technical University. At CTU he teaches within the gutted interior of the former academy as a result of South Africa's "great rationalization," which dismantled the department of Classics and Modern Languages and left him an adjunct professor teaching "communication skills" (4). Opting for necessity over idealism, a docile, protected, and aging Lurie accepts the change and patiently "earns his living" according to this technical curriculum. He adapts — too easily it seems. He adapts in a way that shows neither conviction toward the new order nor any fighting commitment toward older ideals. Were this, again, our final depiction of David Lurie — without future vision or even a whiff of nostalgia for the old ideals — his merely moderate willingness would seal our distaste and assure our disinterest in him.

Yet what compels about *Disgrace* is its refusal to be contained. Much as we might want to do so, David Lurie cannot be dismissed because this would be our own act of containment, a participation in one of the epistemologies the book critiques. The state of disgrace, the book contends — even this early and rather benign sort of nostalgic pedagogical idealism — has no palliative. Rather, disgrace forms a postmodern pathology, a severe and persistent discomfort as experienced by Lurie in his painful betweenness: on the one hand too skeptical and too aware of the world as construct, and on the other hand, desperately in search of the world's secrets, for flashes of its design. Some sparks of revelation yet leap, briefly, in front of Lurie. Yes, his contempt for the tenets of his newly assigned field of Communications zeroes in on a "preposterous" statement in a departmental handbook which ascribes language the quotidian duties of "communicat[ing] our thoughts, feelings, and intentions to each other." But Lurie counters this with a theory of language that is more transcendent, if also more abject. For him "the origins of speech lie in song, and the origins of song in the need to fill out with sound the overlarge and rather empty human soul" (4). Unfortunately, this opinion Lurie "does not air," as his notion of a mechanistic temperament seems to have trumped the presumption of a soul. Or, if he does allow the possibility of a soul, his Romantic aspirations to fill it lie collapsed.

If Lurie does not assert the worth of song within the politics of his department, there are some signs of his faith and his vision — even evidence of this teacher's past glory — within the classroom when he lectures on the Romantic poets. One Wednesday he is reciting from Book VI of *The Prelude*, the poet finally coming upon Mont Blanc only to face the disappointment of the actual sight of the mountain:

> From a bare ridge we also first beheld
> Unveiled the summit of Mont Blanc, and grieved
> To have a soulless image on the eye
> That had usurped upon a living thought
> That never more could be. (1850: VI.523–529)

For Lurie, the profundity of the Mont Blanc moment turns on the recognition of an unusual verb form. "Usurped upon," the imperfective, meaning "to intrude or encroach upon," an action hinting toward but not yet reaching the complete, perfective usurpation of imagined idea by sense image; and this, Lurie exalts to his class, "is one of the deeper themes in the Alps sequence" (22–23). This Wordworthian theme seems easily to be a Lurian theme as well. Although details of the low slopes of Lurie's life are sketchy, we meet him on the far side of several completed ascents, each of which has left a palpable grief upon this traveler. We can imagine that as a young scholar Lurie once stood like Wordsworth in the valleys, out of view of the summits of the alps of intellectual discourse, yet still their imagined "mighty forms, seizing a youthful fancy, / Had given a charter to irregular hopes" (1850: VI.334–5). But after early hope that his criticism, including one "critical opus" on *Wordsworth and the Burden of the Past*, might reconcile, like Wordsworth, "the truth of young and old" (1850: VI.476), Lurie has instead been wearied by the failure of this work to elicit "a stir or even a ripple" among fellow scholars, and he has grown "tired of prose measured by the yard" (4). Referred to in this way, the scholar's quest of creating new theses becomes a distancing activity to fill one's days in the academy (and one's CV), and when the status-seekers surpass the truth seekers, Lurie is discharged from both ranks. In a similar way, we can begin to imagine Lurie the young wanderer in love who once took the "mighty forms" of "a wife, a home, a marriage" as summits of kind assurance but now finds a reunion with his ex-wife like a gathering of "war veterans" (5, 43). But if we read on in *The Prelude*, past the passage covered by Lurie in his class, we recall that Wordsworth's Mont Blanc episode does not terminate in grief. Instead, as the "soulless image" usurps upon his own "living thought," Wordsworth experiences a sense of perfect fittedness with his loss — he sees how the sense image itself is in part crafted by his original hopes, which themselves persist and constitute our truth, however fictive:

> Whate'er in this wide circuit we beheld,
> Or heard, was fitted to our unripe state
> Of intellect and heart. With such a book
> Before our eyes, we could not choose but read
> Lessons of genuine brotherhood, the plan
> And universal reason of mankind,
> The truths of young and old . . . (1850: VI.541–547)

We have no choice, concludes Wordsworth, but to "abound / In dreams and fictions" (1850: VI.550). What's more, coming to terms with our creations, as the poet does here, even given the discomforts incumbent in such revelations, is a gift. We cannot ignore our fictions, Wordsworth argues; but neither should we use them as cause to dismiss transcendence. Rather, we must cultivate the troubling middle ground of "dejection taken up for pleasure's sake" (1850: VI.551).[8]

Right now, at this troubled but rarified moment in the classroom, Professor Lurie, who has surely internalized the whole passage, allows his hopes to rekindle at the prospect that his students might experience some of Wordsworth's truths and breathe dejection infused with pleasure. Moreover, in asking them to understand that they live inevitably in fictions, he wants them to cultivate the uncertainty of an imperfective state. Only here will they have a chance to grasp Wordsworth; only in bringing them here will Lurie have his chance to claim victory of transcendent literature over skilled communication. All this may be too much to expect of his students. But in a dedicated attempt to help them to access this state, Lurie asks his students to hover here, at one of Wordsworth's famed "spots of time," a moment when the duration of the poet's "living thought" is waning while that "soulless image" threatens — but does not yet eclipse — his imagined ideal of the peak. Lurie's joy in this small lecture erupts from the revelation which a minor but precise attention to language has the power to reveal. In the grammar of the imperfective, Wordsworth's poem fills out with complexity in a way that exceeds any technical transaction or mere "communication . . . of feelings and intentions." His maneuvering to bring his students into contact with grammar of a different sort has been a valiant attempt but one that falls short. He has, perhaps, been too technical in leading them toward transcendence. On the heels of his best attempt to lift his students into this revelation, Lurie fixes on the vacancy of their lack of response. Now, the silence and vapidity of undergraduates are not by themselves wholly indicative of the lowered stock of Romantic tropes. Even an unjaded professor knows that. But this behavior strikes Lurie severely. Within a growing sense of isolation, he takes responsibility for failing to stir them with his own words; the effect of his lecture he describes as both deathly and domestic: "the very air into which he speaks hangs listless as a sheet" (21). Still, faced with his students' persistent silence he continues to search for a way to reaffirm the greater value of what they are missing, both that pleasure of revelation that Wordsworth recounts and the pleasure of revelation he wants them to find in Wordsworth. Where his workaday teaching at Cape Technical University has become a mechanized duty in which "month after month he sets, collects, reads, and annotates their assignments," here his students' dull awareness of Romantic pleasure sparks a pedagogical inspiration in Lurie that exceeds any mere uplift of faculty "morale" (4). More conspicuously, his initial response to their listlessness is sympathy. He kneels down from his seniority to meet them at their ages and to meet them in their Ironic Age by asking himself their questions: "A man looking at a mountain: Why does it have to be so complicated?" (21). He takes their skepticism to heart, takes seriously their call to relevance. "What answer can [I] give them?" he further asks himself. In his desire to provide a relevant answer he still holds Romantic ideals within reach.

But for Lurie the Romantic, the potential for a Wordsworthian flash of revelation has been largely replaced by the flicker of desire, which he further mistakes for romance. In tracking the way that he shunts his Romantic ascendancies into romantic ones we are witness to the charge of those former high beliefs grounding into lust. Yet if we transpose Romantic trajectories onto Lurie's next romantic encounter, we may discover his spark is more than mere lust. With Melanie Isaacs, desire forms the vector by which Lurie manages the business of his residual Romantic might. And in recognizing that this work includes cultivating not only pleasure but also dejection, we may find that his enthrallment also leads him toward the visionary. In this, the encounter with Melanie is not only the most recent in a string of romantic indiscretions but also a signal departure from them. Indeed, at the moment of his classroom inspiration his thoughts turn to Melanie, lured to his house a few nights before with his seductions of wine and Wordsworth. Through this plot we have been made to follow Lurie's willful and moderate seduction of Melanie. We have watched from the conspicuous beginning when Lurie overtakes his student walking in a campus garden. We have watched him conflate lazy interpretations of Wordsworth with the hopeful machinations of his latest parlor romance. And there, within his parlor and faced with Melanie's lukewarm response to the poet who for Lurie remains "one of my masters," the professor has extracted a lesson, a gesture designed more to force sexual tension in the room than to allow entrance to the poetry. ". . . in my experience poetry speaks to you either at first sight or not at all. A flash of revelation and a flash of response. Like lightning. Like falling in love" (13). Awkwardly, distastefully, he has conflated poetic revelation with the thrill of desire. Just so, now in the classroom, he ostensibly aims to elicit that literary "flash of revelation" to help his students identify the prospect of being thrilled by Wordsworth. But in fact Melanie alone becomes the subject of his lecture. Asking himself broadly, "Where is the flash of revelation in this room?" Lurie overlooks the room to focus on Melanie and finds "her head is bowed[;] she is absorbed in the text or seems to be" (22).

Just as his afternoon trysts with Soraya followed a script, this seduction of Melanie has shown Lurie steering the young woman into her part. Inviting her to stay for an impromptu supper, he commands, "say yes"; after supper he "takes her by the hand and leads her to the sofa" where he plays a tape of modern dance and "wills the girl to be captivated" (13, 15). Here in class he wants to cast Melanie as a dutiful student searching for the flash of inspiration in lines from *The Prelude*, and he reads her bowed head as absorption rather than distance or shame. If it were sufficient to his purposes to steer her toward the poetry while privately thrilling at the prospect that the sensation of being thrilled by Wordsworth might transfer onto him, Lurie might at this point be inspired to continue leading the class through the intricacies of Wordsworth and the "far different dejection" at Simplon Pass. Or he might likewise take his own pleasure from the dejection that must come once he realizes the rift between what he wants of Melanie and what she is capable of giving. But this is where this one of Lurie's seductions differs from all the rest. The script Lurie employs here is less the cinematic (and, frankly, pornographic) fairy tale he used with Soraya and more the one that seems to direct his own life. A life which has moved to the "harmonies of *The Prelude*" moves along a Romantic plot. Thus Lurie casts himself as The Poet who eagerly seeks a summit by marching himself — and Melanie — along his chosen route. All along he is no stranger to the fact that upon sight of the "top" (which is an acme, the poet knows, that is not often recognizable as such) he (and Melanie) will grieve to have this pathetic affair matched to any "living thought" of love. So, too, he may hold out the hope that they might survive this dejection. He surely also has the next Alpine scene in Wordsworth in mind, and just as the poet crossing Simplon Pass only realizes his accomplishment while making his descent, so the Romantic script may play out unexpectedly. Even the plot he creates might lift him to another state.

Given Melanie's proximity to his Romantic interest as a student in his class, Lurie hopes to elevate his romantic activities to those of Romantic poetry, but instead those actions fall so much more flat. He cannot survive the parallel with Wordsworth.[9] And even if Melanie doesn't recognize as much, he knows it. Still, to his own personal, professional, and poetic disgrace, he persists. Just now he responds to Melanie's bowed head with even greater attempts to have her recognize the parallel between Wordsworth's moment in the Alps, the poet wedded to Nature, and the moments he has staged between the two of them, David Lurie "wedded to" Melanie Isaacs. The class becomes an attempt to get Melanie to notice him — not the soulless image of an aging man momentarily thrilled by youthful desire but the sustained "living thought" of her Prince Charming arrived behind her in the college gardens. Going off book and into an analogy which he admits is "hardly in Wordsworth," Lurie proposes that the dilemma of *The Prelude* is "like being in love," and suggests that any lover does not wish to see the "cold clarity" of his paramour but would rather "throw a veil over the gaze, so as to keep her alive in her archetypal, goddesslike form" (22). Lurie's operations here are impossible to defend. Is his awkward advocacy of veiled affection meant to justify their clandestine rendezvous? Is his entire not-in-Wordsworth argument a circuitous means to self-justification rather than love's transformation? These questions are unanswerable, even when consulting a Romantic paradigm. In fact, Lurie is less approaching a state of transcendental Romantic rapture and more devolving into fantasy; his own classroom analogy — and the calculated need "to bring her" to him — leads him to think now of that night on the floor of his living room, his hands up the shirt of his "goddess." And if Melanie reacts to any of this and finally looks up so that "her eyes meet his and in a flash see all," the "all" that she absorbs can only be the private ecstasy of a man enrolled in fantasy. Rather than erupt in revelation or even recoil in disappointment, she stares back merely "confused" and simply "drops her glance" again (23). He has gained her neither as his student nor as his lover. Worse, the whole episode is transparent to Lurie. Melanie's newly downcast eyes form their own soulless image for Lurie, now seemingly more aware of how caught up in displaced desire he has become. He quickly shuts down: "Enough! He is sick of the sound of his own voice, and sorry for her too, having to listen to these covert intimacies." But the very worst, perhaps, is that Melanie has exceeded the bounds of Lurie's script. "A week ago," he reflects, "she was just another pretty face in the class." Now she is a "breathing presence" in his life, a "living thought" made flesh, although we can hardly accept this elevation of her stature considering the fact that at no point in these episodes are we given access to Melanie's inner life. Lurie's indiscretions, committed against Melanie's rising subjectivity, disgrace the Romantic by confining it to a script and disgrace Melanie by inflicting similar constraints on her transcendent possibilities.

In fact, the novel's early narratives of desire rise along the development of scripted characters and Lurie's dictatorial practice of confining them there using a variety of sources in addition to his Romantic favorites. In this way any analysis of the affair with Melanie is impacted by our initial introduction to Lurie, his temperament, and his behavior with Soraya. Indeed, early in his time with Melanie, while waiting for her to come to the phone, he decides that Melanie is "not a good name for her" and proposes instead to "shift the accent" and name her "Meláni: the dark one" (18). He recasts her as his next exotic. Likewise, our memory of his behavior with Soraya leaves us highly attuned to the evident calculations that are central in Lurie's seduction of Melanie and to suspect that his turns of desire with her are little different from the "moderated bliss" he managed with his escort. Chief among these suspicious moments — moments in which he claims an earnest and uncontrollable desire but when we are more likely to suspect him of continued calculation — is his reading of Shakespeare for his own benefit. That first evening in the living room with Melanie, Lurie remains self-conscious of the "ritual that men and women play out with each other" as he progresses the evening — easily it seems for him — from wine to music; the recitation of Shakespeare inevitably follows (12). Indeed, the early sonnets are expert, often ruthless, arguments of seduction, and Lurie cannot afford to pull any punches at the moment that he asks Melanie to "do something reckless" and stay the night with him. When Melanie asks "why" she should, he crafts the obligation, "because you ought." And to further explain this obligation against her doubt, Lurie asserts: "a woman's beauty does not belong to her alone. It is part of the bounty she brings into the world"; and then, increasing the stakes, he adds, "It is her duty to share it" (16). Always self-aware, Lurie recognizes these "smooth words" of seduction, but he finds that "at this moment he believes in them." If Lurie already has Shakespeare in mind, we might take his argument to parallel Sonnet 1, which accuses the beloved addressee of holding within himself, "making a famine where abundance lies"; and the poet must "pity the world" for this loss of beauty. But where Shakespeare expects the pitiful state of the world to subtly rouse his beloved, Lurie has opted for a more aggressive call to "duty." Moreover, beneath these "smooth words," his internal dialog shifts from an emphasis on sharing her bounty to a more imbalanced and aggressive commerce: "She does not own herself. Beauty does not own itself." In Lurie's recent experience beauty can be purchased in segments of one afternoon a week; and in his mind he is again on his way to situating Melanie as his next discrete beauty. Her bounty has become a price he is willing to pay to get to her. These base notes of duty and ownership infect the authenticity of the lines of Shakespeare that Lurie quotes at the end of this exchange: "From fairest creatures we desire increase / that thereby beauty's rose might never die." The sonnet is, he realizes, "not a good move" and their conversation immediately breaks off; Melanie quickly gathers her things, he embraces her, and then he tempers her evasion, noting how she merely "slips his embrace and is gone" (17). In Lurie's final analysis, the recited Shakespeare estranged her by revealing him as bookish, as "a teacher again," but he may also have just been revealed as an opportunist, using whatever words might afford him his selfish desires (16). And again he sets up a twofold fall in this affair: he will disgrace a young charge by opportunistically employing his poetic expertise, and in doing so he'll leave poetry — and the Bard himself — in disgrace.

Later in the affair Lurie will overlay Melanie with yet another genre, this time marking his scripts during her dramatic pursuits.[10] Following his botched Wordsworth class, Lurie attends a rehearsal of the contemporary social comedy *Sunset at the Globe Salon* in which Melanie plays a bungling, inelegant Kaaps-speaking woman forced to seek a job as a hairdresser's assistant, a role which essentially makes her a gay hairdresser's maid.[11] For the larger audience, this play operates by displaying stock characters and "coarse old prejudices" to be "washed away in gales of laughter" (23). For David Lurie, this is what he has fantasized before with Melanie as "reversals: the stuff of bourgeois comedy" (14). Only now, rather than giggling over reversed gender roles, he gets to witness a young woman playing the dark servant, a titillating prospect following the demise of his arrangement with Soraya, the "exotic." On stage in a first run-through, Melanie's entrance falls flat, but she is a quick study who nails the slapstick in her next attempt, tangling a broom in an electrical cord to create "a bang, a flash, screams of alarm" and the scripted subservient lament, "It's not my fault" (24). Such pyrotechnic special effects provide meta-commentary against those flashes — both Romantic and romantic — which Lurie has worked so hard to get Melanie to practice. Lurie's whole Romantic "flash of revelation" subplot is illuminated as a painful farce. But even with these transparencies, Melanie's comedic but still transgressive role-playing is sufficient to arouse this spectator. The very next afternoon, "astonished by the feeling she evokes . . . the apparition on the stage," he unleashes another scripted encounter with her, this time a violent and abbreviated version of his Windsor Mansions trysts (and, it is worth noting, the abbreviated "plot" here echoes the transparent plots of pornography). He surprises her at her front door, carries her into her flat, and, as "her limbs crumple like a marionette's," he takes her on her bed and then makes a quick exit to his car outside. Meanwhile back in the auditorium, too aware that his posture of "sitting in the dark spying on a girl" puts his activity in the category of "letching," Lurie re-casts himself (and all "the old men whose company he seems to be on the point of joining") as men who were "once upon a time children of God." This forced re-application of Wordsworth's "blessed be the Infant babe" argument allows Lurie to reinterpret lechery as an act of "clinging to the last to [one's] place at the sweet banquet of the senses," for which none can be blamed. If he can't contain the unruly give-and-take of the classroom, he can still moderate in monologue from the back of a dark auditorium.

Seen in these ways to be overpowering Melanie, even overpowering our conception of her via the novel's confinement to his view, David Lurie deserves our harsh assessment. But is having an affair with a student — surely a violation of the academy's valid codes of ethical conduct — the full basis of the level of disgrace to which Lurie ultimately sinks with Melanie? And what does the context of the Romantic do to complicate our judgment of Lurie and of the book's post-Romantic propositions? A quiet thread in the book, rarely glimpsed and only barely defended by Lurie, reaffirms the presence of a greater force driving his attraction to Melanie and rendering his behavior beyond his control. Lurie points most often to this force as "desire." This desire often wells up and overcomes him, drawing him to a brief insight in the afterglow of sensual luxury — there might, he thinks, be more to it with Melanie than only quick sex on the floor, "there might, despite all, be a future" (29). This more profound vector of desire arrives with Melanie one Sunday night. Following the incident at her flat, he largely expects "a scene" but instead decides that Melanie is merely "strained" and, dressed all in black, she asks to stay the night. Her immediate motive is not sex but sleep — and perhaps comfort. Still, Lurie suspects that she is preying on his more base desires to get the safety and comfort that she needs. Or is she learning her part — not the preferred version of "a quick little affair" as Lurie would try to contain it, but rather is she playing her full part as desire must have it, "trailing complications behind her" (27)? Even with complications he still "feels a tingle of desire" at her presence and at the prospect of her "stay[ing] for a while." These feelings of desire no level of suspicion can erase. At this moment it is impossible to tell who is playing whom. Lurie's speculations — for instance, "Does she know what she is up to, at this moment?" — trail off unanswered. And her pressing against his belly reflects an intimacy that cannot be easily dismissed as coerced. Still, Lurie is "vexed, irritated" by what he diagnoses as her "behaving badly, getting away with too much." He pauses to put the scene into perspective:

> She is behaving badly, getting away with too much; she is learning to exploit him and will probably exploit him further. But if she has got away with much, he has got away with more; if she is behaving badly, he has behaved worse. To the extent that they are together, if they are together, he is the one who leads, she the one who follows. Let him not forget that. (28)

But he quickly forgets and instead, in his thinking about Melanie, he falls into his own Romantic analogy and returns to terms he used for Wordsworth in the Alps. In describing the sublime experience to the class, he had paraphrased later lines of Wordsworth for his own purposes. He had pointed to the moment when the senses of the poet reach their limit of perception and finally "a light leaps up one last time like a candle-flame, giving us a glimpse of the invisible" (22). Now, stretched out on the guest bed next to her, Lurie experiences "the last leap of the flame sense" as he focuses on the larger prospect of having her "take up residence with him" (27). Yet if this moment in the guest room reflects a transcendence of their relationship — perhaps lifting it into the realm of "relationship" for the first time in the novel — it falls short of the sublime. And rather than taking a leap to a higher realm, Lurie at the very end of the scene is poised mostly for a last hurrah, a proposition of "intoxicating" earthly delights: "Every night she will be here; every night he can slip into bed like this, slip into her."

At times, his surfeit of desire terminates merely in "blank oblivion," a post-coital blackout that garners no heightened perception and from which Lurie wakes to the hard facts of his desire: Melanie is beneath him, "her eyes closed, her hands slack above her head, a slight frown on her face" (19). Immediacies outpace transcendences, and if these are the slopes rising to something larger, the terrain between these lovers is uneven. At other times this imbalance is more precipitous and any insight afforded by desire arrives more darkly in the aftershocks of his desirous misbehavior. It can even take the form of a recognizable downward plunge into a state of dejection, that realm of the imagination's decrepitude which drew the aging Wordsworth to lament, "Whither is fled the visionary gleam?" Back in his car outside Melanie's flat after he has overtaken her in a fury of his own desire and found his advances "undesired to the core," David Lurie collapses, naming his state as "such dejection, such dullness," such a failure of sensation (25). If desire is in part a superior and euphoric energizing of the body, even to the effect of existing purely as body, without rationality or self-conception, then dejection is the body as dead weight. Here, Lurie "sits slumped over the wheel unable to move." Unfilled desire, such as that he cultivated on his third (and rainy) day with Melanie, led him to tepid questioning ("What am I doing?" he asked himself while giving Melanie a ride home from campus) (20). Yet that was easily offset by desire's potential (his line of self-questioning cuts off when "his heart lurches with desire"). Now, having claimed and acted upon his desire, his dejection leads him to a kind of brute assessment. His act was, he now tells himself, "a mistake, a huge mistake," underscoring it in repeating it and facing one of the few moments of such certainty (25). The most revealing and complicating effect of his dejection, however, is the rare vision it births of Melanie acting on her own. As a part of his brutal self-assessment, he conjures the image of Melanie still back in her flat "trying to cleanse herself of it, of him," and in doing so he judges his actions as rape by conjuring the clinical and ritual bathing that often follow such an event. But within a plot solely at Lurie's direction, this vision affords Melanie a degree of subjectivity. Significantly, her activity in the vision asserts herself free of him. And this limited gesture of liberation heralds a later and substantial vision in which Lurie breaks a bit more free of his moderating and dominating, in which he will break into an affirmative Romantic position. Just now we can use this moment to assess Lurie's journey. In his earliest desirous aspirations (with Soraya and even with Melanie), Lurie sought to capture in a quasi-visionary ecstasy something like Wordsworth's "serene and blessed mood," a bulwark of feeling in a muted world of postmodern contingencies. At the same time, his pursuit of such serenity was revealed as a more base acquisition, a simplification of love that was also all he could expect to obtain. In his later relationship with Melanie, David Lurie has come to inhabit both critiques. His gestures at transcendent states are failures; and in the midst of failure, his perceptions loosen to insight.[12] In my final analysis I'll consider how he exists beyond critique, as a figure of the book's guarded advocacy.

But first, we must wade through serious duplicities in the overlapping and simultaneous critiques that make it considerably difficult to read David Lurie at the Inquiry Hearing. Ostensibly a situation in which he is called to face an assembly of colleagues to address the nature of his relationship with "Ms Isaacs," this event is largely a showdown around the book's main inquiry, pitting radical skepticism against belief in inner truth (34). Lurie himself begins to take both sides; he no longer exists (comfortably or uncomfortably) between but rather shifts radically across the extremes. The result is a farce that seems to take seriously neither critique nor belief. And for the duration of this uncertainty the novel seems to have lost its arc: David Lurie neither triumphs nor falls apart. On his entrance to the hearing, Lurie seems poised to manipulate the proceedings. He has, he confirms to himself, "slept well," and his confidence rises to the point of "vanity" as he steps into the room, sure that he will be able to deliver to the committee the plea he thinks it wants so that they all can quickly "get on with our lives" (47–48). As he sees it, this bureaucracy (a "secular tribunal" he calls it) can only hope to address the facts of the case which are succinct to him and deserve a succinct reply: "I am guilty" (58, 49). But for the committee the situation is not so simple. They repeatedly press Lurie for more than a plain admission of guilt, asking him to "state his position," to clarify "what it is exactly that [he] acknowledges" in his guilt, and are adamant in their pursuit of clarity (49–50). The chair of the committee frames the dilemma this way: "In our own minds I believe we are crystal clear . . . The question is whether Professor Lurie is crystal clear in his mind" (51). That any statement — any words — could penetrate the depths of a mind could not be more absurd to Lurie. That anyone could call out for "crystal clarity" in this day and age can be nothing but Coetzee's comedy. And indeed with deadpan calls for clarity like this Coetzee means to stage the Inquiry as another social farce, a comedy of stereotypes, *Sunset at the Great University Salon*. Assembled here are: the feminist evoking a panic of "overtones" and "abuse"; the junior faculty member asking Lurie if he would "be prepared to undergo counselling?"; the Dean of Engineering advocating the tool of a public statement by which Lurie could "work out a compromise"; and the silent student observer (49–54). In all this, Lurie, too, seems to have abandoned his

Romantic energies to follow the stereotype of the postmodern academic who can only scoff at the prospect of a "verifiable" confession. Pushed to add to his one brief admission of a mistake ("I regret it") by Professor Rassool who asks, "Does [this] reflect your sincere beliefs?" Lurie retreats and dismissively "shakes his head" (54–55). His confidence devolves to defensiveness and he retorts, "What goes on in my mind is my business, not yours" (51). But this is also a devolution of transcendent belief. In his adamancy against their repeated requests, it seems that Lurie will see no further than the bare facts, that there is — for all intents and purposes — nothing more to consider. When pressed to present a more probing statement which would address the "overtones" in the case, Lurie is direct: "There are no overtones in this case" (50). There is nothing to see except what is right in front of them. Confusingly, he yields slightly to offer a contained confession, telling the story of crossing paths with Melanie in the college gardens and the point at which "something happened," although the specifics of this he begs off: "not being a poet, I will not try to describe" (52). What happened between them exceeded his control; he confesses, "I became a servant of Eros." Lurie, who entered the inquiry seemingly divorced from further beliefs in invisible truths, who seemed positioned against the potential of revelation, now has a different argument. Revelation might be possible and there might be something behind the facts — and his heart might contain them — but he cannot trust this venue or these people to plumb those depths. Oddly, the greatest faith that there are overtones or other hidden intricacies comes from his judges — those who would neglect Lurie's half-hearted evocation of Eros as an inadequate excuse of "ungovernable impulse" still hold out hope that they will arrive at the bottom of Lurie's soul. A member of the committee follows her pursuit of the "crystal clear" by proposing: "The statement should come from him, in his own words. Then we can see if it comes from his heart" (54). But this is the farce, that authenticity could be verified by committee. Here Lurie returns to his own brand of skepticism. He sneers and calls this proposal on its face: "And you trust yourself to divine that, from the words I use — to divine whether it comes from my heart." Still, if the depths of the heart have no place in these proceedings, they have not been dismissed from the realm of *Disgrace*. But it will take more than a committee — it will take something with more access to the divine — to plumb them. Lurie will never claim the divinity of the poet himself; he is a student and scholar of poets. Worse, he is, by his own self-description, the "disgraced disciple" of Wordsworth at this point. Unable to see into the life of things by himself, his journey, seemingly stalled or circling through the course of the inquiry, will require a different vector. David Lurie will undergo further confusion before stumbling along one of his perverse habits of desire to come to his tentative reckoning.

The inquiry points to David Lurie's exhaustion, a low point in a novel of low points: his weariness of age and his retiring physical appeal; his withering prowess and trailing glory. Where have they fled? His tedium peaks with a final reconciliation attempt by the Chair which Lurie dismisses as "splitting hairs" (58). The pre-drafted statement which Mathabane promises would allow Lurie to maintain the dark recesses of his soul and still allow him to "acknowledge [his] fault in public and take steps to remedy it" is untenable at best and more likely absurd, even for Lurie who has navigated much of the novel on the razor's edge between belief and its critique. Thus the Inquiry that largely creates the division between the first and second parts of the novel marks that transitional space with a flatness in Lurie's fate. It is unclear where he can go from here. Moreover, a reader through the Inquiry is left with no gauge of the novel's trends. All points of view from the Romantic to the anti-Romantic — theatrically represented by the various members of the committee as well as Lurie — are equally farcical. And yet this failure of bureaucratic means cannot table the novel's larger themes; they are yet to unfold as the book explores other avenues of inquiry.

After the calculated attempts of the committee of inquiry to create the terms by which David Lurie might properly reveal his inner truths in the case of Melanie Isaacs, those later scenes when Lurie visits the Isaacs family in George offer intriguing counterpoint. Significantly, the scenes are remarkable for the way in which they compile a series of gestures of meaning (not strictly Romantic and ranging from explanation to atonement) that Lurie seems compelled to make as follow-up to the vacant result of the Inquiry itself. Yet despite their number and Lurie's apparent compulsion to engage in them, these gestures, both Lurie's and the reciprocations from Isaacs himself, repeatedly and patently ring empty. The meal which Mr. Isaacs wants to present as an occasion to "break bread with us" must be muscled through (167). When Lurie attempts to leave, realizing he is "causing upset in your home," Isaacs commands him: "Sit down, sit down! We'll be all right! We will do it! . . . You have to be strong!" (169). Later, actually moving toward his exit, Lurie enters a room where Mrs. Isaacs and her daughter Desiree have retreated and conducts what he terms a "careful ceremony" of lowering to his knees in front of them and touching his forehead to the floor — a tragicomic prostration in a suburban bedroom (173). Even Isaacs's evocation of God raises mostly doubts. Lurie's response is confusingly both that of the academic agnostic and the God-fearing believer. And if the character of Isaacs is meant to function as witness of deeply held belief, his call to Lurie's hotel room later that night in which he wishes Lurie "strength" along "the path . . . that God has ordained" mostly aligns him with stock-phrased televangelists (174).

After the formal inquiry and then these further inquiries we are left ever more torn by the tenor of the book. On one hand these episodes constitute further questions into the legitimacy of making claims for understanding. On the other hand, *Disgrace* at this point makes the result of such persistent questioning look pretty bleak. We might be inclined to ask repeatedly what Lurie asks himself while getting up off the floor following his "ceremony": "Is that enough? he thinks. Will that do? If not, what more?" (173). Repeatedly, our answers would have to point to insufficiency. These gestures are not enough; they will not do; and we seem to have lost access to anything more. Not only are these individual gestures of meaning each called into question, but they are the hollow inventory of a structurally significant event in Lurie's journey. Here where the script of a romance would have the disgraced man contritely seek forgiveness, we are given only the shell of that act. This emptiness can in fact be witnessed with a re-reading of the premise of Lurie's visit to the Isaacs. For a reader the encounter is inspired and unexpected. At the end of chapter eighteen, Lurie is contemplating his departure from the farm to return directly to Cape Town; chapter nineteen begins abruptly at the front door of the Isaacs home in George. Lurie's initial narrative confirms the visit as an inspired detour, the result of having been "at a loose end" ever since the Inquiry (163). Later Lurie confesses the untruth of this. He visited George by design. Even the story of being spontaneously inspired to stop in is only Lurie's latest calculation. In this, Lurie first claims to "drop in" primarily in order to "say what is on my heart" (165). Having scoffed at the attempts of the committee to ascertain the contents of his heart, Lurie now returns to offer those secrets himself. Still, his abilities to plumb the depths are suspect and limited. He questions himself: "That much is true. He does want to speak his heart. The question is, what is on his heart?" (165). In truth, his heart still eludes him. It evades even his calculated efforts. He begins the story of himself and Melanie, which he affirms "began without premeditation on my part." But quickly this explanation is consumed by an overwrought metaphor in which Melanie is a spark that "struck up a fire" in him, a fire that he felt obliged to kindle the way the ancients worshipped a "flame-god" (166). Soon, Lurie admits that his story-making here is not driven by some higher cause but consists mostly of "self-defence."

Before dismissing every gesture Lurie makes in George, we should look at one hopeful portion of those scenes, his most pointed (and Romantic) confession. After supper, Lurie, finally alone with Isaacs, feels "he can prevaricate no longer" and delivers this speech:

> "It could have turned out different, I believe, between the two of us, despite our ages. But there was something I failed to supply, something" — he hunts for the word — "lyrical. I lack the lyrical. I manage love too well. Even when I burn I don't sing, if you understand me. For which I am sorry." (171)

Juridically, Lurie conspicuously does not apologize for what he might have done to Melanie; rather, he claims what he failed to do. Lurie's argument again is that he is not the poet: he lacks the lyrical. The lyrical aspect of poetry comes in its unmanageable leaps. In the lyric, through song that is not restrained by the plodding prose of speech, the poet can rise past earthly concerns, past the simple experiences of the senses to leap — yes, past that candle flame again — toward the invisible, the lost, the apocryphal. The disgraced disciple of Wordsworth knows what it is to be lyrical — he has poured over the leaps in the poems, he has fallen for many women, in acts he takes to be equivalent — but the full trajectory eludes him. Is this because he is not a poet? If so, must the failures of all second-class citizens of this sort merit the fate of disgrace? No, David Lurie is as much poet as any of us. But being a poet guarantees nothing, least of all consistent access to lyric heights. Lurie may be inclined to dream of Wordsworth only for his accomplishments. *Disgrace* reminds us of a Romantic truth: the penalty for striving higher is consistent ruin. Lurie's dark heroism emerges at not resisting that fate but in attempting to recognize this double-state. As he names his fate: "I am . . . trying to accept disgrace as my state of being" (172).

Finally, David Lurie returns to Cape Town, to an overgrown garden and a ransacked house, and to an unsettling sense that "there is something unfinished in the business with Melanie" (190). Whether Lurie as character can be said to be conscious of creating a parallel experience, the book offers to finish the business with Melanie via a scene that parallels that earlier theater moment: Lurie in the audience and Melanie back on stage. Her play, *Sunset at the Globe Salon,* has been revived at the Dock Theater, a new and, according to Lurie, "fashionable entertainment spot" where "the set is more stylish, the direction more professional," but the play's base humor and obvious politics are still, especially for him, "hard to endure" (191). Yet endurance is the theme of Lurie's return. He assures himself that Melanie — especially the crude intimacy of "the smell of her" — endures "deep inside him," and he wonders, should they meet again, "Will there be a flash of feeling, a sign that the affair has not run its course?" (190). Unwilling to leave such a question entirely up to chance, one night he buys a ticket and takes his seat just as the curtain is rising. Though he finds her lines themselves are "predictable," her performance is superior. Indeed, Lurie, in a moment of authentic praise that would have been highly rare early in their affair, pronounces her "positively gifted" and ascribes her improvement to her perseverance through their shared trial. "*Whatever does not kill me makes me stronger,*" he affirms, congratulating both Melanie and himself with the status of veterans. But as usual, Lurie is not content to merely perceive sympathies between himself and others in the world, not content to allow things to take their course. Here in the dark of the theater he wills Melanie, wills the world to move in response to his desires: "He wishes he could have a sign." And lacking a sign, he imagines one. He imagines the "absurd clothes" Melanie wears for her costume "burn[ing] off her body in a cold, private flame" where, exposed, the girl stands "in a revelation secret to him alone, as naked and as perfect as on that last night in Lucy's old room." In this vision, the comedy of Lurie's vaunted "flash of revelation" literalized into a pyrotechnic wardrobe malfunction signals Lurie's pornographic tragedy — a girl's immolation and exposure all for his "private" glory. If his "business" with Melanie were to end here then we could safely assign him the status of socially disgraced "imposter" that he already feels in the midst of all his fat, self-congratulatory, fellow theatergoers, his "countrymen." And what follows this vision — an unbidden memory of another seduction, a single night with a German hitchhiker in a hotel room — serves mostly to further implicate Lurie by confirming what Rosalind had earlier accused him of when she called Melanie "another of your quick flings, your peccadilloes" (189). Lurie returned to his old position in the back of a theater is a man once again on the prowl. Yet this memory of an old lover is more catalyst to Lurie's second auditorium vision:

> In a sudden and soundless eruption, as if he has fallen into waking dream, a stream of images pours down, images of women he has known on two continents, some from so far away in time that he barely recognizes them. Like leaves blown on the wind, pell-mell, they pass before him. *A fair field full of folk*: hundreds of lives all tangled with his. (192)

Initially extending the catalog of his inconsequential flings, the vision transforms into something more profound (albeit no less painful). In this "stream of images," the women are distinct; they are subjects (even if he "barely recognizes them," he registers their differences as distinction, enough to know he does not know them). But at the same time there is little delineation between the beginning and the end of each of his affairs. This love is not discrete. This love is a tangle — not a dramatic arc from seduction to climax to denouement of avoidance and hurt looks. It is something altogether less neat. And as Lurie exits this vision, he comes again to a rare moment of sympathy. Rather than fix exclusively within his own perspective, his own desires and desires for signs, he wonders if any of these women ever experiences a parallel vision — which would not focus exclusively on Lurie but place him, too, within what he sees as an "ocean of memory" (192).

The tides of memory are, of course, Wordsworth's central theme in *The Prelude*. And while Lurie, in his teaching of Book VI, focused on the climactic present-tense Mont Blanc episode and its immediate experience of "dejection taken up for pleasure's sake," Wordsworth next recalls an earlier experience in the Alps which (in the 1805 edition) the poet introduces by claiming that "far different dejection once was mine" (1805: VI.491). Understanding this differently dejected state will help us come to terms with the final position Coetzee posits for David Lurie, which reconstitutes the Romantic to become a fitting vision for the late-twentieth-century condition. In this later Simplon Pass episode Wordsworth and his hiking party, in great anticipation of marking the moment when they finally cross the Alpine divide, set out after lunch "up a lofty mountain" to achieve it (1805: VI.506). But when they become aware during their short and unremarkable journey that the route they are on is not the main track over the pass, they stop a peasant to ask the way to the top. From him they learn the painful truth: "that we had crossed the Alps" (1805: VI.524). That is, they had already crossed them and "thenceforth all [their] course was downwards" (1805: 518–19). Upon this realization, Wordsworth exclaims:

> Imagination! lifting up itself
> Before the eye and progress of my song
> Like an unfathered vapour, here that power,
> In all the might of its endowments, came
> Athwart me. I was lost as in a cloud,
> Halted without a struggle to break through,
> And now, recovering, to my soul I say
> "I recognize thy glory." (1805: VI.525–32)

In his script of mountain accomplishment, Wordsworth had anticipated his triumphant achievement of the summit. Instead, the actual summit has become tangled in the "eye and progress" of the course of his life, the script of his epic "song." Remembering the event he faces the confluence of the discrete narrative he anticipates and the sensory experience that refuses to fulfill that narrative. And the moment of contact between the two — the moment the imperfective passes into the perfective "usurpation" — he anoints as "imagination" — a tangle of vision and life, an unruly response to rules (1805: VI.533, 525).[13] This exalted moment Wordsworth further describes as "when the light of sense / Goes out in flashes that have shewn to us / The invisible world" (1805: VI.534–6). The continued anticipation of such a summit has sustained David Lurie in both academic and amorous pursuits. Unfortunately, his attempts to achieve the flash of the invisible world have, to this point, been all too directed. His temperament, prone to containment, has tightened the shutters on the unruly work of imagination and cut off its potential to enlighten. Just so, we could see his opera as stalled; it is "going nowhere" and it will never arrive anywhere by the end of the book. Teresa sings and sings for rescue, and Byron groans impossibility. Lurie laments that "the lyric impulse in [me] may not be dead, but after decades of starvation it can crawl forth from its cave only pinched, stunted, deformed . . . [becoming] the kind of work a sleepwalker might write" (214). Coetzee's critique of Romanticism throughout *Disgrace* is clear: there is no place for mere dreamers in our current world. Nor can we allow the hope of pending lyric perfections to blunt our perception of atrocities. *Disgrace* does not declare the death of lyric, nor the death of love — nor of transcendence. And David Lurie, then, is never the victim of this change but is often portrayed as its outlaw, alternating between skepticism and vision at will, and too often employing whatever serves his secular pursuits in a kind of supernatural naturalism. But for all his dark strength of will, there is a contrary and revitalizing image of this man, a brief but indelible image of him that cannot be dismissed simply because it operates within what is in many cases an outmoded Romantic paradigm. Here in the theater he has finally lost control; he is lost in a sea of memories, a vision, and he fights not for shore, not for air, but "holds his breath, willing the vision to continue" (192). Extensive participation in the world of sense is not Lurie's crime. Nor do his previous false attempts toward vision shut down the curative realm of the visionary now. *Disgrace* insists on an imperfective Lurie, an intractable man only briefly set free. To be put to sleep, at someone else's hand, as the novel's final scene seems to say, is an option only for animals. For the rest, such as Lurie coming out of his theater reverie, the book offers no promises and substantial grief. Desire, which can flower to recognition — an uplift of hundreds of intermingled lives — can quickly erode to sexual desire, which Lurie cultivates solitarily in another prostitute. Even in asserting vision, *Disgrace* offers little solace from grief and no bulwark against error. Our disgrace, as witnessed by David Lurie, befalls us not through some one grave act but in our shuffling through the middle of the world, tepidly refashioning mere pleasures into falsely imaginative pursuits.

Notes

[1] In the ANC's view, Coetzee unflinchingly "reported on" the conditions on the ground in South Africa to become a witness who "represents as brutally as he can the white people's perception of the post-Apartheid black man" (qtd. in McDonald 323-24).

[2] Leading with a litany of references to Rorty which caution against those who have become "immune to romantic enthusiasm" and ask us to "put a moratorium on theory," Ortwin de Graef begins an analysis of the "familiar friction" between the Wordsworthian sympathetic imagination which forms Lurie's roots and theory (311, 314). Noting Lurie's background in English studies, Graef locates a conspicuous use of the term "theory" as turning point late in the novel and will proceed to conduct his investigation of these "incommensurable universes of discourses . . . beyond propriety, and at the expense of an actual reading of *Disgrace*" (314).

[3] As a cross-section of the criticism on the novel, the special *Disgrace* issue of *Interventions* (2002) remains a good representation of the range of critical views. Here we find David Attwell speaking to the "ethical turn" in the racial aspects novel that he pinpoints in Lurie's relationship with Bev Shaw who "extend[s] his ethical horizon" and precipitates a "metonymic chain of immolations" that reach "fulfillment" in Lurie's treatment of the dogs (339). In his Introduction to this issue, Derek Attridge recalls his own earlier article which concerns Lurie's "growing involvement with animals," but for Attridge this growth must be very carefully construed (318). He finesses his reading of Lurie at the end of the book: "These activities of Lurie's are not presented, I would argue, as the achievement of redemption or as a prescription for ethical behaviour, but rather as an instance of a commitment that signals, in its very irrelevance to larger programmes and practices, its integrity in a world of calculation and accumulation" (318). Elleke Boehmer's important feminist reading of *Disgrace* also outlines the book's "structural symmetries" and the implications of these which so many other critics follow (344). Noting the many "silent parallels" that divide the book into two "halves of the narrative," with Lurie's seduction of Melanie organizing the first and the gang rape of Lucy the second, Boehmer sees the novel as a "diptych" (344). And though this structure works "largely by implication," it leads us to "the question of Lurie's achievement of kindness and redemption" which will be weighed by a comparison of his behaviors in the two halves of the book (344, 347). Each of these readings ultimately — and understandably — devotes the bulk of its argument to the "second half" of the novel. In doing so, these articles find unexpected company in the immediate responses of the ANC and South African intellectuals (such as Jakes Gerwel) writing in the popular press, which, as Peter McDonald notes, focused on the incidents of rape and race relations in the second half to assert an allegorical reading of *Disgrace* as "a powerful witness to contemporary realities" (324). At the same time, it is important to note that many of these commentators — especially McDonald and Boehmer — as well as many important others beyond the *Interventions* issue rely on this two-part developmental schematic while still asserting a subtle reading of Lurie's final state. For McDonald, Lurie's "understanding of redress remains partial at best, even at the end"; Boehmer asserts Lurie's accomplishment as a questionable and complex "secular atonement"; Mike Marais ("Ethical Action") follows his strong claim of a "development from monadic subjectivity to self-substituting responsibility in the course of the novel" with the caveat that any such claim of development will "require fuller exposition"; and Attridge's subtly reads the end as noted above. Elsewhere, Marais ("Task of the Imagination") calls the book an "anti-*Bildungsroman*, a novel which involves the forfeiture rather than the consolidation of the protagonist's sense of self" (79).

[4] Boehmer speaks of how "significant verbal resonances bring the novel's two acts of violation into chillingly close parallel" but stops short of calling Lurie's overtaking of Melanie a rape (344). Lucy Graham is unequivocal: "Lurie's relationship with Melanie in *Disgrace* is depicted as a betrayal of ethical responsibility, as he violates and will not take responsibility for her as an embodied human being.

Although Lurie protests to the contrary, the act that he commits is rape, it is 'undesired' by the girl and involves an abuse of her self" (438).

[5] Likewise, Marais insists: "the ethical trajectory of *Disgrace* is by no means clearcut. If anything, its movement is chiastic and involves a doubling back on itself that disputes what it seems to assert even as it is asserted" (79).

[6] Elleke Boehmer's belief that Lurie's gestures constitute a "secular atonement" is a unique argument of the "personal political ramifications of refusing to make a confession," but her description of the condition of that atonement emphasizes its troubled state (342). For Boehmer, Lurie undergoes "the far more painful process of enduring rather than transcending the degraded present . . . [a] flawed, highly subjectivized, and also gendered process of coming to terms" (343).

[7] In his syntactical analysis of the novel in *Interventions,* Mark Sanders scrutinizes this first sentence to determine its ambivalent effects. In parsing the sentence, Sanders first points to the "transcendent aspect" within the perfective "has solved" which he believes "secures the narrative present"; in consistently harnessing that present, Lurie pitches toward perfect. But at the same time, this syntax of the perfective is conspicuously interrupted by Lurie's willful subjectivity — "to his mind" — which renders his perfective state "premature" (364).

[8] Although his avenue into Romanticism in *Disgrace* is primarily via Wordsworth's Lucy poems, Marais also reaches "the ambiguity at the heart of Romanticism" (85). "The Romantic project," Marais reminds us, "celebrates the power of imagination [and] its ability to grasp" transcendence; and at the same time "[the Lucy poems] evince a fine sense of the possibility of failure of this faculty's" power (85).

[9] McDonald tracks the fall of Lurie's "male Romantic literary heroes," particularly his lowered estimation of Byron (328).

[10] Michael Holland considers the incident of the play at some length as part of his argument of Coetzee's "total commitment to that aesthetic imperative" in which the play draws Lurie's attention to Melanie's unexpected aesthetic beauty as Gloria (395). What is remarkable to Holland is that although Lurie's reaction to her beauty is parodied (in the slapstick and malfunction of the rehearsal) and also "unsynchronized" (to the extent that he "becomes uneasy" and leaves the theater), the delayed result is that "seeing the play has transformed Lurie's perception of Melanie" (a truth which Holland is aware results in Lurie advancing on Melanie "more or less against her will)" (396).

[11] Kaaps is an Apartheid-era designation of the dialect of Africaans spoken by "coloured" Cape Town residents, often Muslim, including those known as Cape Malay.

[12] For Holland, the incident of the play remains the crux that creates Lurie's "in-between position": as "a seducer" he has experienced "a division which renders him powerless" and leaves him with "two entirely opposed responses": ecstasy and dejection (396–97).

[13] Marais's reading of Coetzee's Romanticism works to merge Wordsworth and Coleridge. First, he affirms the reciprocal act of imagination as Wordworth puts it in *Tintern Abbey*: the combination of "what they half create, / And what perceive" (ll. 106–7). But next Marais emphasizes his view of the Coleridgean Coetzee. In

Marais's view, Coetzee "would add that the Primary Imagination is located in the self who is in the world and, accordingly, that the imaginative expression of this self is worldly, rather than a repetition of the transcendent 'eternal act of creation in the infinite I AM' (Coleridge, *Biographia* 167)" (2006, 81).

9: Saying it Right in *Disgrace*: David Lurie, *Faust*, and the Romantic Conception of Language

Patricia Casey Sutcliffe

> Two souls, alas! reside within my breast,
> and each is eager for a separation:
> in throes of coarse desire, one grips
> the earth with all its senses;
> the other struggles from the dust
> to rise to high ancestral spheres
> — Faust in Goethe, *Faust I*, 30, lines 1112–17

Introduction

THE TITLES OF BOOKS DAVID LURIE WROTE when his scholarship still commanded "his heart" (162) are among the few things we know about his past life. And, just as McDonald shows us that the subject of *The Vision of Richard of St. Victor* has continued to influence Lurie's consciousness, so too has his critical study entitled *Boito and the Faust Legend: The Genesis of* Mefistofele. Its inclusion in the backdrop to Lurie's present likewise deserves more explication. The title offers intriguing ambiguities for interpretation: does the book focus on biography, literary history, or more narrowly on the stages of *Mefistofele*'s composition? Are we to infer that Lurie emulates Boito, or perhaps the Mefistofele of the title, or even Faust?

There are some teasing, suggestive parallels between Arrigo Boito and David Lurie, and between the grandiose *Mefistofele* and *Byron in Italy*. Like Lurie, Boito was first and foremost a man of letters, steeped in European literature from adolescence, and better versed in it than in music. He wrote essays, comedies, poems, and journalism throughout his life. His first music teachers termed his work "mediocre." Bernard Shaw called *Mefistofele* the product of "an accomplished literary man without original musical gifts, but ten times the taste and culture of a musician of only ordinary extraordinariness."[1] Like Lurie, Boito perennially lacked confidence in his abilities, and in fact left several works unfinished. During his first visit to Paris the nineteen-year-old decided, brashly, to undertake a "Faust" opera; meeting Hugo, Verdi, Rossini, and especially Berlioz no doubt influenced him. Like Lurie, he began his opera not in his familiar Milan but in Poland, while visiting his mother's aristocratic family. Just so, Lurie has begun the actual composition of his opera not in Cape Town but in his homeland of the Eastern Cape, where Lucy had been raised and now lives. In contrast to Lurie, whose progress is so halting, Boito finished his first version quickly (1868), but it suffered from an inverse fault: not too short and half-formed, but way too long and unmanageable (over five hours). Revisions and shortening took years, culminating in a successful premiere in Bologna in 1875. Again like Lurie, Boito sought to escape traditional operatic forms such as that of Gounod's *Faust*, favoring a new form entirely appropriate to the material of the libretto and achieving that form via the greatest tonal and rhythmic development. The title of his work shifts the focus to Mephisto, and to the mockery and parody at which the devil excels.

Boito had a long history as a parodist — he re-set "La donna è mobile" as a polka when he was only nine — and his work creates deliberate tension between the extraordinary power of its enormous choruses and their mocking by Mefistofele. Some of the devil's lines, such as his caricature of humans, sound like Lurie at his most despairing: "The tiny God of the tiny earth / degenerates steadily and strays / and, hopping like a cricket, by chance / pokes his nose among the stars, / then with haughty and tenacious fatuity / chirps away in the grass" ("Prologue in Heaven"). He terms Faust "a poor panting devil"; it's easy to imagine him reaching for a banjo. And even when Mephisto is "showered with roses" by the Cherubim and feels his "limbs eaten away by / the rays of light and the flowers," he never ceases to mock. The final chorus may drown him out, but his mockery remains: "The Lord triumphs, / but the reprobate whistles! Eh!" Boito himself oscillated between self-doubt and a visionary Germanic Romanticism; Lurie's self-mockery contrasts with his admiration for, and even emulation of, the Romantic poets Byron and Wordsworth, and with his moments of vision.

So, *Mefistofele* makes fun of the bombast of grand opera in the middle of a grand opera that can still sweep us away; Lurie becomes increasingly an object of parody, and especially of self-parody, to the citizens and children of Salem, but we are still caught up in the drama of his "salvation," of his finding grace via love of those "beneath" him. His chamber opera seems a failure at every turn and Lurie himself guilty of recovering Teresa's voice only to magnify her suffering, yet he hopes — and with reason — out of these sorry conditions "there will dart up, like a bird, a single authentic note of immortal longing" (214). Coetzee, like Goethe but in a radically more critical age, looks for the small traces of "grace" in a desolate world while rigorously removing all sentiment, religious fervor, and ready belief from his novel.

One way that Coetzee effects this search for grace without sentiment is by combining, in this postmodern recasting of the Faust legend, the inexhaustible mockery of Mefistofele with the lofty, Romantic aspirations of Faust in one character: David Lurie. Lurie's mockery, also self-directed, is never far below the surface. It begins on the first page, when he recognizes the unnaturalness of his relationship with Soraya ("Technically he is old enough to be her father; but then, technically, one can be a father at twelve") and continues throughout the novel, emerging even (and especially) during his visionary moments. Consider his vision of pregnant Lucy working in her garden just before the novel's close: "A grandfather. A Joseph. Who would have thought it? What pretty girl can he expect to be wooed into bed with a grandfather?" (217). When he interprets Byron's poem "Lara" for his class, his desire to evade it arises not only because of its closeness to the unspoken tension in the room ("Scandal. A pity that must be his theme" [31]) but also because he identifies with the devil who is its protagonist. Like Byron's Lucifer, he is a stranger among his "[p]ost-Christian, posthistorical, postliterate" students (32); he is filled with the same haughty pride; and he follows his impulses without regard to their morality, as the presence of Melanie's menacing boyfriend so clearly reinforces. But Lurie's embodiment of Faust is less obvious, not least because Coetzee, like Boito, parodies and inverts Goethe's Romantic conception. This chapter focuses first on the parallels between Goethe's *Faust* (the primary source of Boito's libretto) and *Disgrace* while noting Coetzee's parody of the Faust tradition. The second part dwells on one of Lurie's Faustian characteristics — his Romantic conception of language — because his adherence to this allies him with Faust and the devil yet again as one who brings his downfall, or disgrace, upon himself through an absolute Romantic idealism, in spite of his self-mockery.

Coetzee's graduate training certainly made him familiar with both the Faust tradition and the Romantic conception of language. He earned a PhD in English, Germanic languages, and linguistics in 1968 from the University of Texas at Austin,[2] where he would no doubt have engaged deeply with Goethe's drama and likely would have encountered the premises of Romantic and structuralist/generativist linguistics, a more pragmatic approach than its nineteenth-century predecessor.[3]

I. David Lurie as a Faust Figure

Two direct allusions to Goethe's *Faust* that occur simultaneously and shortly before the close of *Disgrace* encourage us to read Lurie as a Faust figure. First, Lurie experiences "a moment of utter stillness which he would wish prolonged forever," (216) the kind of moment Faust is willing to sacrifice his soul for. Faust agrees to give up his soul if Mephistopheles can make him content:

> If I should ever say to any moment:
> Tarry, remain!   You are so fair!
> then you may lay your fetters on me,
> then I will gladly be destroyed! (44, lines 1699–1702)[4]

Indeed, Faust dies when such a moment arises, just before the end of *Faust II* (and in Boito's final scene) (292, lines 11,582): Faust perceives a selfless love for humanity, especially for his subordinates, envisioning himself as a benevolent king in a fertile and prosperous land of his own creation.

The second allusion is the cause of Lurie's moment of contentment, which helps us to understand the first more fully. Approaching his pregnant daughter unnoticed as she works in her garden, he sees her as *das ewig Weibliche*, Goethe's phrase: the Chorus Mysticus, part of the panoply of spirits welcoming Faust into heaven, sings it in praise of the Mater Gloriosa, the Virgin Mary, who represents the selfless love that ultimately redeems Faust.

> All that is transitory
> is only a symbol;
> what seems unachievable
> here is seen done;
> what's indescribable
> here becomes fact;
> Woman, eternally,
> shows us the way.[5]

Gretchen, too, appears as a Penitent in the Chorus, grateful to see "the love of her youth" find happiness now loosed "from all the bonds / that once enveloped him on earth" (304, lines 12,073, 12,088–89). Faust is free; "Eternal Love" effectively "disunite[d]" his spirit from the distasteful "remainder of earth," his body (301, lines 11,954–11,965).

These allusions invite us to compare Lurie's and Faust's experiences. Lurie's moment of contentment occurs just before the novel closes, begging the question of whether Lurie, too, has become "good," selfless, benevolent. The final act of the novel, his sacrifice of Driepoot, actually offers another oblique allusion to *Faust* by reversing one of Faust's misdeeds: At the close of *Faust I*, Goethe's hero continues to act out of selfish desire by attempting to save Gretchen from the executioner's axe against her will. Here, instead, Lurie gives over a creature that he loves *to* the executioner. The Faustian inversion suggests that we understand this not as killing, but as freeing Driepoot from misery and torment, an act of selfless love towards one who is weaker ("he no longer has difficulty calling [it] by its proper name: love" [219]), so that Lurie shows a turn to goodness similar to Faust as a benevolent king. Whereas Goethe's Faust experiences an absolute transcendence, and Boito's Faust rises to heaven as Mefistofele jeers at the host of angels, Lurie as Faust, ever undermining his own goodness, cannot help but poke fun at the helpless creature even as he gives it his heart. The dog, he thinks to himself, will not be able to work out what is happening "*in a month of Sundays!*" (219).

Lurie's vision of Lucy as *das ewig Weibliche* also inverts Goethe's original conception. Far from being the Virgin Mary, Lucy is a victim of rape. But her child, a product of violence and hatred, as well as a union of black and white, suggests a world of potential for South Africa. Most importantly, though, by viewing Lucy as the eternal feminine, the embodiment of selfless love, Lurie establishes that he has, at that moment, come to accept the choices Lucy has made and acknowledge their value. She will be a mother, grow to adore her child, and continue to work the land — all acts requiring forgiveness, self-sacrifice, and, of course, love.

Together with the novel's early mention of Lurie's monograph on Boito, these direct allusions form a frame around the narrative and underscore the significance of the Faust tradition in interpreting not just these scenes but the whole novel. Indeed, a careful analysis reveals compelling parallels between the characters, plots, and especially themes of the works that make Goethe's and Boito's works indispensable to an intertextual understanding of *Disgrace*.

Consider first Faust and Lurie as characters, professors who have grown disillusioned with their calling. Never a passionate teacher, Lurie finds his new discipline, Communications, "preposterous" (3). Faust, too, laments the meaninglessness of his field:

> I well may know more than all those dullards . . .
> but I get no joy from anything, either,
> know nothing that I think worthwhile . . .
> No dog would want to linger on like this! (13, lines 366–76)[6]

Their disillusionment leaves them feeling bereft of a Romantic sense of passion they feel is essential to life, and especially to teaching and understanding, as they both instruct their students. Faust teaches Wagner that passion is crucial to the rhetorical art:

> unless you feel some passion,
> unless there's something bursting from within
> . . . unless your heart is where all starts,
> your efforts won't affect the hearts of others (17, lines 533–44)

Lurie's conversation with Melanie about her "literary passions" faintly echoes this. He tells her that understanding or being moved by poetry requires "A flash of revelation and a flash of response. Like lightning. Like falling in love" (13).

Both Faust and Lurie use women to try to rekindle the Romantic flame of passion. At first, Faust attempts to conjure spirits to escape his frustration. Then Mephistopheles appears and promises to entertain him with sensual delights in exchange for his soul. After signing a pact, Faust almost immediately falls in love with Gretchen, who ignites a fire in his heart (64, lines 2461); after her death, he pursues Helen of Troy. Lurie, too, distracts himself with women, and usually just with sex, though, like Faust, he tends to romanticize his encounters. He convinces himself that the prostitute Soraya feels affection for him and even believes that Melanie and he really could have been lovers. Regarding their empathy with their "victims," Faust and Lurie differ somewhat, but again because Lurie has internalized "the Great Deceiver."[7] While carousing with Mephistopheles, Faust has a vision of Gretchen's suffering and wants to return to her, but Mephistopheles lures him away from his conscience. Lurie, on the other hand, blinds himself to his undesirability and the suffering he causes Soraya and Melanie, at least some of the time, though his conscience, and his goodness, overcome his self-deception with increasing frequency as the novel unfolds; for example, when watching Melanie upon his return to Cape Town, he acknowledges that "perhaps she too has suffered, and come through" (190).

Arrogant and isolated, Faust and Lurie also both believe themselves superior to their students, neighbors, and colleagues so that they prefer little or no company. As we saw above, Faust thinks he knows more "than all those dullards" and is filled with contempt for Wagner, whom he perceives as the most superficial of scholars. Faust refers to Wagner alternately as "that humdrum plodder" (line 519) and "you sorriest of mortals" (line 609) and is annoyed by Wagner's intrusion into his study:

> How can a person still have any hopes
> who is addicted to what's superficial,
> who grubs with greedy hand for treasures
> and then is happy to discover earthworms!
>   Is it right to let that voice be heard
> where inspiration compassed me about? (18, lines 602–607)

We have already seen Lurie's sense of superiority over his "[p]ost-Christian, posthistorical, postliterate" students, but his antipathy extends to the people of Cape Town as well, and especially to Bev Shaw, whom he initially regards as "an ugly little woman" (84). Like Faust he lacks male friends, but, unlike him, Lurie has actually tried to live with others — all women

— yet must now labor to get along, even temporarily, with his daughter. He thinks of himself, somewhat ironically but unapologetically, as "too old" for his temperament to change (2).

In their aging bodies Faust and Lurie also resemble one another, and both struggle to come to terms with the limitations age brings. Tormented by desire, Faust wishes for death and is, in fact, on the brink of suicide when Mephistopheles enters his study. He bemoans his misfortune to Mephistopheles: "I am too old to live for pleasure only, / too young to be without desire. What can I hope for in this world?" (40, lines 1546–48); Lurie, for his part, laments the gracelessness of aging and contemplates castration in sordid detail as an alternative solution to the problem of sex (9). Yet loathsome as their aging bodies become to them, both Faust and Lurie share the universal longing to achieve immortality. Lurie tells Lucy regarding his opera, "One wants to leave something behind" (63), and he ponders his ever-present though diminishing contribution to the stream of lives that will issue forth from the tadpole in Lucy's womb (217). Faust's highest moment of joy occurs not just when he envisions a vibrant world of his creation but when he recognizes the immortality that this kingdom brings with it: "the traces of my days on earth / will survive into eternity!" (292, lines 11,583–84).

Faust's and Lurie's fundamental similarities already hint that the plots of *Faust/Mefistofele* and *Disgrace* will run along roughly parallel lines. After all, both will necessarily involve chasing after young women. Nonetheless, the number of structural congruences between the works is striking. In *Faust*, the aging hero, having consciously chosen a fall from grace by signing his soul over to the devil, first regains his youth with help from a witch's potion and then pursues Gretchen, a young maiden less than half his age, whom he encounters by chance. With Mephistopheles's assistance, he eventually seduces her in her garden (81). In a similar though less mystical manner, Lurie attempts to recapture his youth by seducing his young student Melanie, whom he encounters in the college gardens (11). Yet his desire, unlike Faust's, which was at least partly induced by magic, is not uncontrollable; he merely wants to cling to the last to his place "at the sweet banquet of the senses" (24). And so, in chasing Melanie, and especially in dealing disastrously with the public fallout from that affair, Lurie consciously chooses his fall from grace, just as Faust does. Both Faust's and Lurie's affairs end badly, with Gretchen's execution and Lurie's disgrace bringing the first part of each work to a tragic close.

The second part of each work offers a fresh start in a new world, and, though the stories diverge considerably, Faust and Lurie follow a common path of development. Faust, "paralyzed by Helen" (169, line 6568), pays court to this paragon of beauty in the world of classical antiquity, and Lurie begins anew on his daughter's farm. After some time in these new worlds, they revisit their old homes as changed men. Faust returns to his study, too sick with love to rise from his bed, and Mephistopheles takes in the surroundings, remarking that "Nothing, no matter where I look, / has changed or suffered harm; perhaps the window panes are more opaque . . . but everything is where it was before" (169, lines 6570–75). Lurie's homecoming again inverts Faust's. Not lovesick but disfigured and psychologically transformed by the attack on his daughter's farm, he "cannot imagine" returning to this home and this life "in the shadow of the university" (175). In contrast to Faust's merely time-worn study, Lurie's home has been ransacked; he becomes "too depressed to act" and sinks into a chair (176).

Later, Faust and Lurie each experience a *"night of revelations"* (Coetzee, 192): Faust accompanies Mephistopheles to Walpurgis Night, still in search of Helen, and Lurie goes to the Dock Theatre to revisit his "mate," Melanie Isaacs, at least from a distance (190). Faust watches a parade of mythical figures and beautiful nymphs, unsure whether he is awake or asleep:

> This is not sleep! O may they never vanish,
> these forms beyond compare
> that I envision in a miracle
> of all-pervasive feeling!
> Can they be dreams? Or are they memories? —
> I have already, once before, been so enchanted. (186, lines 7271–75)

Faust remembers the spectacle because he has been to Walpurgis Night, "the sphere of dreams and magic" (97, lines 3871–72) with Mephistopheles once before. Lurie, too, experiences "a waking dream": "a stream of images . . . of women he has known" passes before his eyes.[8]

Finally, both Faust and Lurie learn to embrace the world in a spirit of selfless love. As we saw above, the blinded Faust as a benevolent king imagines the prosperity of his people and experiences his "highest moment" (292, lines 11,586) and expires. Although Mephistopheles thereby wins the bet and should own Faust's soul, Faust is redeemed because of his striving and love; as the angels sing,

> This worthy member of the spirit world
> is rescued from the devil:
> for him whose striving never ceases
> we can provide redemption;
> and if a higher love as well
> has shown an interest in him,
> the hosts of heaven come
> and greet him with a cordial welcome. (301, lines 11,934–41)

Lurie, however, after his selfless moment re-envisioning his daughter, does not expire but goes on to sacrifice Driepoot. The direct allusions to and structural parallels with Faust encourage us to see this ending as a kind of redemption for Lurie, a final act of selfless love, yet, at the same time, the inversions of the Faustian paradigm call this interpretation into question. Unlike Faust, Lurie carries on after his vision, which means he will not be able to maintain his "goodness" or "selflessness" infinitely. Though the novel concludes with a selfless act, it can easily be seen as cutting off love (cf. Boobar's interpretation in this volume, 58) rather than celebrating it. Glimmers of the old, mocking Lurie who eschews any kind of transcendentalism shine through; he ridicules Driepoot's cluelessness and acknowledges the meaninglessness of his "love": "He will do all that for him when his time comes. It will be little enough, less than little: nothing" (220).

Coetzee thus foregoes the simple, binary conclusion that was available to Goethe in the Age of Romanticism. Romanticism was, in so many ways, grounded in binary oppositions such as good and evil, emotions and reason, nature and civilization, ideal and real, and even Romantic and pragmatic. Boito, as a post-Romantic, necessarily oriented *Mefistofele* around these oppositions as he sought to relativize them. His Faust, for example, declares the inadequacy of the Real and the Ideal of the mortal world as he departs for the infinite, and therefore non-oppositional, realm of heaven in the epilogue:

> All mortal mysteries I have proved —
> The Ideal, the Real;
> The love of simple maidenhood,
> And of the higher goddess —
> Yet the Real was sorrow, and but a dream the Ideal.[9]

Coetzee, too, orients *Disgrace* around these oppositions as he strives to subvert them even further, combining the opposites in a single consciousness and transforming the dialogue between Faustian and Mephistophelian elements into an internal contradiction in Lurie's character. Lurie may be a Faust figure, but he is also a Mephistopheles, and the tension between the two poles will remain.

II. David Lurie's Romantic Conception of Language

Another parallel between Goethe's *Faust* and Coetzee's *Disgrace* is the prominence of the Romantic–pragmatic binary in their overall structure. Goethe uses the Romantic–pragmatic binary as an external frame. In the "Prelude on the Stage," the theater manager, the poet/playwright and a player of comic roles debate the significance of the performance as it is about to begin. The poet, a true Romantic, extols the permanent value of true poetry and disregards the public. He wishes for "some celestial refuge / where nothing blights the poet's quiet joy" (63–64). The pragmatic manager views the theater as an "enterprise"; he is willing to sacrifice quality only if he can bring in large crowds. The player then offers a third category that we could call the comical: he sees the greatest value of theater not in art or money, but in entertainment. Coetzee, too, uses this opposition as a framing element for his novel. Lurie, a disciple of the Romantic poets Byron and Wordsworth and a Romantic spirit in his own right, finds himself in the newly "rationalized" university, which is characterized by pragmatism. The disjunction between his Romantic world view and the pragmatic world he inhabits reveals itself especially in language. As a Romantic, Lurie adheres to a Romantic conception of the nature of language that comparative philologists contemporary to his favorite poets held, whereas the university promulgates a pragmatic view of language through Lurie's new discipline, "communications." His unwillingness to accommodate this alternative view in the committee of inquiry's hearing essentially constitutes a conscious choice to bring about his own disgrace, just as Faust chooses to fall from grace. The comical that Goethe uses to mediate the two poles emerges in Coetzee's novel as well, as Lurie transforms from a Romantic idealist into a comical figure, an old man plucking away at a banjo behind Bev's clinic. This image, though almost pathetic, presents a relativization of Faust's transcendence.

To clarify how Lurie's Romantic view of language brings about his disgrace, I will summarize the primary characteristics of Romantic language theories and illustrate them at work in Lurie's reflections on language throughout the novel, particularly in relation to Lurie's behavior at the committee of inquiry. Pitting the Romantic against the pragmatic conception of language, Coetzee again calls these absolute categories into question. Finally, I shall suggest that Lurie's Romantic conception of language itself is yet another characteristic that allies him with Goethe's *Faust*.

Romantic Theories of Language

Romantic language theory predominated in the embryonic field of comparative philology from about 1800 to 1860, spurred by the larger phenomenon of German Romanticism; it thrived primarily in the German-speaking world. Sir William Jones's discovery in 1786 that Sanskrit was related to Ancient Greek, Latin, Gothic, Celtic, and other European languages motivated the new discipline, but not until Friedrich von Schlegel (1772–1829), a Romantic poet and philosopher, had combined it with Romantic thought in *On the Language and Wisdom of the Indians* in 1808. In this programmatic treatise, Schlegel called for a systematic analysis of the relationships among the ancient languages in order to access "a distant past when language was still an organic whole and exhibited perfections that were lost in later stages of development" (Amsterdamska 35).

Schlegel inspired not one unified theory but a host of theories of language that shared certain features shaped by Romanticism. These included the idealization of a perfect past with a perfect *Ursprache* whose roots organically connected to their meanings. Modern linguistics, by contrast, maintains an arbitrary relationship between signs and their meanings. The focus on ancient languages made the new field diachronic rather than synchronic; in consequence, etymologies took precedence over modern meanings. Similarly, root meanings prevailed over speakers' intent. Because ancient languages only survived in written records, written language was privileged over spoken language to the extent that many theorists removed speakers from discussions of language altogether. Jacob Grimm (1785–1863) and Franz Bopp (1791–1867) most prominently advocated the view that language was an organic being that existed independently of humans; not a tool for communication, it comprised an entity with its own internal life force — modern tendencies signaled decay brought on by the interference of human society. Others like Schlegel and Wilhelm von Humboldt (1767–1835) conceived of this internal life force not as divorced from humans but rather existing in harmony with them; the more civilizations interacted and adopted features of one another's language, the less connected with their own languages they became. Humboldt formulated a principle of linguistic relativity as a correlate of this view: each nation's language had a peculiar form that best expressed the character of its people, which no other language could adequately express.

Before Romantic comparative philology emerged, however, philosophers had long been fascinated with language origins. During the Enlightenment, the issue took on new urgency as thinkers grappled with the relationship between language and reason, so much so that in 1770, the Berlin Academy of Science held an essay contest on the subject. The prize-winning essay *Treatise on the Origin of Language* was written by Johann Gottfried Herder (1744–1803), one of Goethe's mentors, whom he met in Strasbourg in October 1770 and remained friends with throughout his life.[10] German theologian and philosopher Günter Jacoby (1881–1969) dedicated a monograph to the argument that Goethe not only modeled Faust on Herder, but that, in fact, Faust represented "the aggregate of the human impression Herder [made on Goethe]."[11] Consequently, Herder's essay deserves a closer look in our investigation of Lurie's language theory and his relationship to the Faust tradition. Herder wrote the essay in December 1770 (Moran and Gode 171), and Goethe read it and commented upon it (Jacoby 13). We will see that some of Herder's philological ideas, as well as ideas he refuted in his essay, made their way into *Faust* and also Coetzee's *Disgrace*.

An Enlightenment thinker, Herder begins by rejecting two theories of language origin popular at the time: that of Étienne Bonnot de Condillac from his *Essay on the Origin of Human Knowledge* (1746), and that of Jean-Jacques Rousseau.[12] Both Condillac and Rousseau associate the origins of language with natural cries, though in slightly different ways. Condillac assumes that two children without any language left to their own devices would learn to associate their needs with the natural cries they emitted, and thus invent language (in Moran and Gode 99–100). Rousseau, however, assumes that language arises not from physical but from emotional needs, so he associates language with music and the passions (Moran and Gode 11–12). For Herder, however, true human language cannot emerge from these natural cries, remnants of "the language of nature" that man has in common with animals. Rather, the origin must be sought in a quality that distinguishes men from animals, the uniquely human characteristic of *Besonnenheit*, or reflection. A solitary child with no language, upon encountering a sheep, would use reflection to find a distinctive feature in it — its bleating. The sheep would thus become "the bleater" in the child's mind, and even without a sound to represent it, this concept already would constitute language: "He recognized the sheep by its bleating: This was a conceived sign through which the soul clearly remembered an idea — and what is the entire human language other than a collection of such words?" (Moran and Gode 116) In contrast to Condillac with his two social children, Herder gives us a solipsistic child who names things not to communicate his needs to others or express his emotions, but to fix objects in his consciousness according to his own perceptions.

Of these three theories of language origin, it will become clear that David Lurie agrees most heartily with Rousseau, although there are certainly some Herderian qualities to his view of language. Moreover, as I will show, he adheres to several other features of Romantic language theory, including a focus on etymologies and root meanings, believing in an intrinsic power of words and names, privileging written over spoken language, and Humboldt's linguistic relativity.

The Origin of Language

> It is written, "In the beginning was the *Word*."
> ... I cannot concede that words have such high worth
> and must, if properly inspired,
> translate the term some other way.
> It is written, "In the beginning was the *Mind*." ...
> Can it be *mind* that makes all operate?
> I'd better write: "In the beginning was the *Power*!" ...
> Yet even as I write this down,
> something warns me not to keep it.
> My spirit prompts me, now I see a solution
> and boldly write: "In the beginning was the *Act*."
> — Faust in Goethe, *Faust I*, 33, lines 1224–37

At the very opening of the novel, Coetzee juxtaposes a pragmatic conception of language, as exemplified by Lurie's "rationalization" as a communications professor, with Lurie's own, Romantic view of the origin of language.

> Although he devotes hours of each day to his new discipline, he finds its first premise, as enunciated in the Communications 101 handbook, preposterous: "Human society has created language in order that we may communicate our thoughts, feelings and intentions to each other." His own opinion, which he does not air, is that the origins of speech lie in song, and the origins of song in the need to fill out with sound the over-large and rather empty human soul. (3–4)

His new discipline conceives of language merely as an instrumentality, a view that began to dominate linguistics in the late nineteenth century in explicit rejection of Romantic language theories. Moreover, the handbook authors presume that this obvious but not sole function of language is responsible for its origin. Lurie's take on language origins, on the other hand, clearly echoes Rousseau's and marks him early on as an adherent of a Romantic conception of language. Whenever Lurie thinks about the particular sounds of words, as when he reflects on the what "the letter p, usually so gentle" is doing in the middle of the unspeakable word "rape" (160), and whenever he considers the interplay of music and words as he writes his opera (the plink-plunk as the only possible musical tone for his comic diva), his view of the musical origin of language in creative expression resonates in the narrative.

Etymologies and Root Meanings of Words

> Faust (*shuddering*): The Mothers! It's a shock each time I hear their name!
> What is this word I so dislike to hear?
> Mephistopheles: Have you some prejudice against new words?
> Must you only hear what you've heard before?
> — Goethe, *Faust II*, lines 6267–68

With the advent of structuralism, linguists acknowledged a distinction between what signifiers are supposed to mean within the system of language and what they actually mean within a given context. Saussure recognized that speakers make mistakes, and developed the difference between the system of language (*langue*) and actual speech (*parole*) to account for them. Later, in speech act theory, linguists came to recognize that speakers' intentions are determined by nonverbal cues and context as much as by the denotations of their words. But the Romantic philologists, for the most part, did not yet admit of such variations of meaning and contextual understanding (Humboldt was a notable exception). Seeking the core inherent meanings of the earliest roots of language, they gave priority to etymologies and root meanings of words and ignored the illocutionary intentions of speakers. In fact, focusing on dead languages, they often forgot about speakers altogether. David Lurie does the same. In numerous instances, he refutes (if only in his head) the ideas of his conversational partners with reference to the "true" meanings of words as understood by their etymology.

Several examples betray this focus on etymology as an unbridled habit of thought for Lurie. When Lucy refers to him as a "scapegoat" in the scandal at the university, he reminds her of its original sense within its pagan/religious context, when people literally "loaded the sins of the city on to the goat's back and drove it out, and the city was cleansed" (91). But when the gods died, he continues, this symbolism was no longer enough and the "censor was born, in the Roman sense," that is, one who watches over the morals of the people, and "Purgation was replaced by the purge" (91), where a ceremonial cleansing or purification was replaced by an actual cleansing or rooting out of dangerous elements. His etymological precision, thus, rejects Lucy's (perhaps not fully understood) assertion that he was a sacrificial victim and implies instead that he is a dangerous element who was rightfully eliminated. This little lecture, however, only separates him from Lucy, who had perhaps only intended to console him by taking away some blame. In the same way, though silently, Lurie cuts himself off from Bill Shaw, who, as a "friend," has gone out of his way to help him after the attack, by calling up the etymology of the word friend, specifically, its relationship to love, to reinforce his condescending notion of the local man's naïveté (102).

But does Bill Shaw mean that there was a love-bond between Lurie and himself, or just that they are friends, in the modern sense?[13] Lurie's focus on historical meaning makes him read unintended meanings into what other people say and do. For example, he chooses to read Petrus's use of English according to historical contexts Petrus cannot possibly understand. He dislikes Petrus's use of the word benefactor (129) because of its negative connotations. Even as he acknowledges Petrus's inability to sense the distastefulness of the word, Lurie cannot help but interpret it with the full weight of its history. In the same manner, Lurie sees in Petrus's gesture of rubbing thumb and forefinger together the European tradition of referring to Jews that way. Lurie cannot leave the old meanings of words and other significations behind to make room for new, unburdened intentions.

Finally, Lurie's defensive reaction to the words of Melanie's boyfriend Ryan, when he drives Lurie out of the play by telling him to stay with his own kind, shows the older man retreating into etymologies and learnedness to dismiss the painful truth of his own undesirability:

>   *Your own kind*: who is this boy to tell him who his kind are? What does he know of the force that drives the utmost strangers into each other's arms, making them kin, kind, beyond all prudence? *Omnis gens quaecumque se in se perficere vult.* The seed of generation, driven to perfect itself, driving deep into the woman's body, driving to bring the future into being. Drive, driven. (194)

The Latin phrase here has been debated but translates roughly as "Every nation whatsoever wants to perfect itself in itself," which Lurie freely glosses to justify his *contra naturam* behavior. In fact, like the Romantic philologists before him, Lurie forgets about the speaker: he loses himself momentarily in this etymologizing and thus shuts out the confrontation altogether, realizing only at the end of this internal digression that Ryan is still speaking to him. In all of these examples we see that Lurie's focus on root meanings leaves him self-contained within his idealized linguistic world, unreceptive, for the most part, to the real intentions and ideas of his interlocutors, or to new meanings.

The Intrinsic Power of Words and Names

> Faust: What is your name?
> Mephistopheles: That seems a petty question from one who
> is so scornful of the Word
> and who, aloof from mere appearance,
> only aspires to plumb the depths of
> essence.
> Faust: The essence of such as you, good sir,
> can usually be inferred from names
> that, like Lord of the Flies, Destroyer, Liar,
> reveal it all too plainly.
>   — Goethe, *Faust I*, 35, lines 1327–33

A corollary of the Romantic preoccupation with etymologies is the notion that the forms of words are not arbitrary but somehow natural, emerging from the life force of a language. This belief is diametrically opposed to one of the fundamental tenets of modern linguistics, the arbitrariness of the linguistic sign. As formulated by Saussure in *Course on General Linguistics*, signifiers have no true meaning but only *value*, determined solely within the system, and solely in relation to other signifiers. Thus, the form words take has no bearing on the real world; they have no power in themselves but only within the system of signification. Since Romantic language philosophers believed in inherent meanings, though, they also held that the form of words was powerful and grounded in the nature of things.

Lurie's Romantic conception of language thus announces itself in his fascination with names and the significance he gives them. Often when hearing a new name, he first reflects on its form and the "inherent" meaning that it carries. He knows, for example, that "Soraya" is not the real name of the two prostitutes that he sleeps with, but a popular *nom de commerce* meant to designate their exoticness (7). He finds Melanie's name inadequate, a "meretricious rhyme" with the word "melody," and wishes to shift the accent to the second syllable: Meláni. Unlike the "cheaply ornamental" and "insincere" rhyme, his new name for her is symbolic, derived from the Greek word for "black."[14] When he hears her sister's name, Desiree, he dwells again on the meaning, this time of both names: "Melanie the firstborn, the dark one, then Desiree, the desired one. Surely they tempted the gods by giving her a name like that!" (164). His own lurches of desire in the course of the evening with Desiree and her parents suggest the power of the name to evoke its inherent meaning. Bev's name calls forth his contempt; he'll work with her, he tells Lucy, "Provided that I don't have to call her Bev. It's a silly name to go by. It reminds me of cattle." It is impossible to know why Lurie makes this bizarre association with the short form of "Beverly," but his contempt seems to arise from its sheer meaninglessness.[15]

In these examples, Lurie only has to reflect on names. But giving names is an act laden with meaning. Following Herder's example, Lurie considers naming a way of getting at the essence of things, or at least one's perception of that essence. Fixing one's perception of an object in a name establishes ownership of or control over it in a particular and personal rather than arbitrary way. Lurie's shift of accent in Melanie's name essentially *renames* her to make her his own. It is certainly a power play, a way of asserting his subjectivity. Lurie also uses it to distinguish her from Soraya (not meretricious, not a prostitute), and to bestow upon her a "real" name with inherent meaning, as opposed to a false one, like Soraya's, or the pretentious one she actually possesses. Most importantly, though, he bestows a name that relates specifically to *his perception* of her. When Melanie first appears in the novel, Lurie sees her as "small and thin, with close-cropped *black* hair, wide almost Chinese cheekbones, large, *dark* eyes" (11, emphasis mine). The mere shift in accent gives her name a meaning that is not arbitrarily connected to her but derived from a salient feature of her appearance. That his sense of ownership over her continues long after the affair is over is evident not least in the fact that he continues to think of her using his own designation: "With the best will in the world he could not find wit in Meláni" (78).

It is this sense of ownership implied in naming that Lurie apparently wants to avoid in the case of the dog with the withered left hind quarter that *Bev* calls "Driepoot" ("three-footed" in Afrikaans). "It is not *his* in any sense; he has been careful not to give it a name" (215). He even refers to it in his mind with the neuter pronoun, whereas most people, including Bev Shaw, call dogs, and in her case, even goats, "he" or "she," making their relationship with these gendered animals somehow more personal.[16]

The contrast between Lurie's sense of ownership through naming Melanie and his avoidance of it here is important. It reinforces a redemptive reading of Lurie toward the close of the novel as a man undergoing profound change, learning to relate to the world around him in a more open, less judgmental and directive way. Lurie does, however, grow attached to Driepoot: he begins referring to him as "he" the day he gives him up (219), which underscores the personal sacrifice entailed in this act.

While these two examples involve Lurie giving or refusing to give proper names, he takes even greater care in naming everything else. One could almost say he is obsessed with finding exactly the right word to define people and events. He often meditates explicitly on word choice, even though most of these thoughts are for his mind alone. Significantly, such meditations become more frequent when he goes to Lucy's farm. Although he certainly labels things in the opening Cape Town portion of the novel (consider his reference to the hearing as a "secular tribunal"), the thought processes behind this labeling increase in prominence once he goes to Salem. It makes sense that in his routinized life in Cape Town, Lurie had, for the most part, already found labels for compartmentalizing his day to day experiences. Encountering a new environment, however, he first has to go through this process, which gives us a glimpse of this mental habit.

Arriving at the farm, Lurie does not recognize Lucy because she has put on weight — in other words, she no longer conforms to his idealized mental representation of her — so the first thing he has to do is find the appropriate word: "Her hips and breasts are now (he searches for the best word) ample" (59). Later, he revises this assessment: "*Ample* is a kind word for Lucy. Soon she will be positively heavy" (65). Seeing her growing attachment to the place he helped her buy, he also finds a label for her new status, "a countrywoman, a *boervrou*," and shortly thereafter lists for himself some qualities essential to this phrase: "Dogs and a gun; bread in the oven and a crop in the earth" (60).[17] Soon he must decide what to call his "visit" with Lucy, and it is she who suggests *an alternative word* so that he can reconcile himself with the idea of staying on a while. "'What if we don't call it a visit? What if we call it refuge? Would you accept refuge on an indefinite basis?'" Significantly, he corrects her, "'You mean asylum? It's not as bad as that, Lucy. I'm not a fugitive,'" but he does stay on, accepting her offer.[18] At the end of the novel, his return to the status of visitor is explicitly marked with a double label, "Visitorship, visitation," and he feels secure in the foundation, "a new footing, a new start," that this restored concept brings.

In labeling things, Lurie attempts to intellectualize, control, and fix his experiences into an ideal, or idealized understanding. His class lecture on Book VI of Wordsworth's *Prelude*, and particularly the distinction in it between "usurp" and "usurp upon," provides the model for reading

Lurie's precise usage and its relation to his Romantic theory of language. Importantly, he first points out the dictionary definition of the two expressions. Then, he interprets the difference between them as central to the meaning of the passage:

> From a bare ridge we also first beheld
> Unveiled the summit of Mont Blanc, and grieved
> To have a soulless image on the eye
> That had usurped upon a living thought
> That never more could be. (21)

The actual sense perception of the summit encroached upon, but did not take over, the living thought, the pure idea. Thus, though the poet grieves for the sense of encroachment, the pure idea is not lost. The difference between the two verb forms "usurp upon" and "usurp," therefore, alludes to the balance between living "in a realm of pure ideas, cocooned from sense-experience" and being overwhelmed and disappointed by the "matter of fact clarity" of the sense-image (23).

Within Lurie's Romantic conception of language, a word represents a living thought or pure idea. Although he has to acknowledge that meanings change over time, he, like the Romantic philologists, resists such change by adhering to the letter to the dictionary definition of words.[19] So Lurie's habit of precisely labeling things points to his lack of true interaction with his environment and to his solipsistic idealization of the world. He tries to keep his sensory experiences "as fleeting as possible," just long enough to "activat[e] the idea that lies buried more deeply in the soil of memory," where the *bon mot* crystalizes it (22).

Lurie particularly attends to defining people's roles, often with irony; these labels clarify their essence for him. He sums Bev up to himself: "Bev Shaw, not a veterinarian but a priestess, full of New Age mumbo jumbo" (84). Likewise, he struggles to find an appropriate term for Petrus, although Lucy had referred to him as her "new assistant" and even "co-proprietor" on first mentioning him; this vagueness sincerely irks him:

> But though Petrus is paid a wage, he is no longer, strictly speaking, hired help. It is hard to say what Petrus is, strictly speaking. The word that seems to serve best, however, is neighbour. (116)

Though he finds a pseudo-solution in the word "neighbour," it fails to satisfy him as it captures only one aspect of their relationship to Petrus (his proximity). It is significant that Petrus cannot be summed up in a word — again, Lurie's intellectual patterns of thought, his quest for linguistic precision manifested in the repetition of "strictly speaking" cannot help him in this new world any more than his knowledge of French and Italian can during the attack.

An intriguing twist on Lurie's labeling is other characters' overt resistance to it. Petrus seems to be as fascinated with labels as Lurie is. He calls himself "the gardener and the dog-man" when he first meets Lurie and is pleased by the phrase (64), but later, at the party celebrating his new status as a homeowner, he is only too happy to have overcome this designation: "I am not any more the dog-man" (129). Of course, it is with full awareness of this renegotiation and the power shift it entails that Lurie ironically thinks of himself as the new dog-man: "A dog-man, Petrus once called himself. Well, now he [Lurie] has become a dog-man: a dog undertaker; a dog psychopomp; a harijan" (146). Having established himself on his own land, Petrus then resists becoming "the *farm manager*" when Lurie proposes this role. The term is italicized as if to mark it as foreign to Petrus. Lurie thinks, "He pronounces the words as if he has never heard them before" (152). Apparently, this concept of bearing responsibility without possession is alien to Petrus, and he rejects the offer.

Lucy, too, challenges Lurie's labels. She tells him to stop calling her "piece of land" where she grows things "the farm" (200), as if this designation raises her humble aspirations to an unreachable ideal. She does, however, call it the farm herself the next day: "[Petrus] is after the farm. The farm is my dowry" (203). Her father's idealized understanding rather than the word itself is problematic, it seems. In a powerful act of rebellion, she even rejects Lurie's most fundamental and, indeed, indisputable, label for himself: father. He signs the letter he places under her door "Your father," and she replies not only by referring to him as David, in keeping with her standard practice, but also by explicitly rejecting his status as her father: "You cannot be a father forever" (160–61). Strictly speaking (the only way of speaking that Lurie knows), he must remain a father forever. But Lucy is rejecting an idealized understanding of fatherhood rather than doubting his paternity. She will not let him be her guide, mentor, adviser. These battles over mere labels betray the power with which the words are imbued, at least for Lurie. Designation means control.

Curiously, Lurie often derives his labels from other languages. He favors Afrikaans, no doubt because of his familiarity with it in South Africa; perhaps he is fluent. Lucy becomes a *boervrou* (60) and later Petrus a *bywoner* ("squatter" 204), and he calls himself Petrus's *handlanger* (literally, "hand long-er" but defined as "helper" [136]).[20] He also uses Italian, which he knows from his studies, as well as a stay in Italy as a young man (Bev's *tessitura* of hair [81], Teresa, a *contadina* [181]). He turns to German, too, for example, to find "an appropriate blank abstraction" to capture the essence of his killing sessions with Bev Shaw: *Lösung*. His gloss, "sublimation, as alcohol is sublimed from water, leaving no residue, no aftertaste" (142), significantly, is not entirely accurate. *Lösung*, historically loaded by association with Hitler's *Endlösung* ("final solution"), means "solution," both in the concrete (liquid) and abstract sense. Lurie subtly alludes to the word's history by selecting it in the context of extermination but shifts it to "sublimation." This change conveys his ambivalence about the sessions: "sublimation" carries a second, figurative meaning that exalts the act of killing, yet Lurie immediately undercuts this interpretation by connecting the word to the chemical process and emphasizing its apparent inconsequentiality — as well as the process he and Bev engage in.

Like his numerous literary allusions, Lurie's use of non-English terms reinforces his understanding of himself as an intellectual, but it also profoundly broadens his repertoire of choice words for labeling and controlling his experiences. It allows him to utilize not only etymology for a more nuanced understanding of words but also comparison across languages. *Lösung*, for example, is such a common word in German that, without *End* in front of it, it now evokes no particular emotions in everyday contexts among German speakers. But as an English speaker, Lurie can use it to call up the darker connotations nearly always associated with it outside the German-speaking world. Even more importantly, however, Lurie's use of foreign words resonates with his Romantic conception of language because it acknowledges linguistic relativity, the impossibility of equivalence across languages. He must use foreign words because these ideas cannot be adequately expressed in English.

For the Romantic language philosophers and Lurie, the intrinsic power of words means that the right word discloses the true nature of a person, event, or thing, and renders it manageable, controllable. But it also means that words are agents not always under the speaker's control. For all Lurie's conscious contemplation of words, they sometimes come "unbidden" ("letching," for example [24]), or in other ways that suggest their agency (the word "lubricate" comes "reluctantly" [168]). Sometimes, words even seem to speak themselves, as when Lurie asks Lucy if she loves her child yet: "Though the words are his, from his mouth, they startle him" (216). The power of words is, thus, a dual one — they give the speaker power to control, but they can also control.

Privileging Written over Spoken Language

Mephistopheles:	I must request a line or two in writing.
Faust:	So you want something written, too, you pedant? . . .
	And yet, a parchment document that bears a seal —
	that is a spectre that all people shun.
	— Goethe, *Faust I*, 44, lines 1715–27

With their intense focus on ancient languages, the early Romantic comparative philologists gave precedence to written over spoken language, and

Lurie does too. He focuses on written words perhaps more than mere thought words. For a narrative relatively sparse in descriptive passages, it is telling that written signs are often reproduced in full as having entered into Lurie's consciousness, far more than nonverbal aspects of his environment. He notes the SAPPI Industries sign with its (later) ironic declaration that trespassers will be prosecuted at the boundary of Lucy's farm (69), her advertisement for cut flowers and cycads (70), the sign at the animal welfare league (80), the casualties sign at the hospital (100), the address on Melanie's home (163), the signs on the middle school (164), and the new name-tag on his old office door (177). Only the "emphatic signs" forbidding parking at the police station are not actually spelled out (153). To be sure, Lurie does not concentrate exclusively on written words. He also notices the art and posters on both Petrus's and his successor's walls, for example (128, 177). But even then, he perceives these images not in their detail but in their representation. They stand for something, or at least he assumes that they do. Treating these images and words as representations, Lurie privileges them over other, nonrepresentative features of his environment and over spoken language, as did his Romantic predecessors.

Written words are more powerful than spoken ones, and Lurie, like the Romantic language philosophers before him, recognizes that power. They store memories for the individual from one point in life to another: Byron's love for Teresa lives on for her in his letters, the only physical evidence she possesses of their affair; thus, they become her *reliquie* (181). But they also call what they represent into being; Lurie recalls, somewhat ironically, Wordsworth's visit to a play in London, in which the word "invisible" renders Jack the Giant Killer so when written across his chest (178). Although this is a theatrical device, it is significant that Lurie remembers it as Wordsworth's (a Romantic poet's) experience. Words also make ideas that exist only in the mind concrete, real, and perceptible to others. Lurie's meditations concerning the complaint form Melanie filled in underscore this quality of the written word. At great length, he contemplates her hand writing the "careful block letters" of their names and the "arabesque" and "flourish" of her signature. Even more important, he reflects on what those words, and the "x" in the correct box, stand for — her accusation and the formalization of their relationship for all to see. This passage is all the more remarkable because Lurie merely imagines the complaint form, almost as though he needs to conjure the written word to believe the turn of events. Just as the putative complaint form broadcasts Lurie's affair, Byron's letters will disclose his affair with Teresa to her grand-nieces one day (181).

Like these love letters, written words reanimate what is long dead. They carry love stories and the stored knowledge of whole civilizations across generations; they are remnants that represent the totality of individuals and cultures after they are gone. For Lurie, a writer, this is exceptionally important: his opera, whether or not it will ever be performed, is what he wants to leave behind (63), and he wonders what the "verdict" of the universe, "with its all-seeing eye," will be (195).

With their longevity, written words have a greater capacity than spoken ones to *misrepresent*. Though Lurie uses words to penetrate to the essence of things, he is also aware that not all words "ring true" (in Herder's sense). Significantly, Lurie is misrepresented in all three newspaper articles that refer to him. In the first two on the harassment allegations, his age is incorrectly given as 53 (46, 57). In the second, moreover, the camera perspective makes him appear to be wearing a dunce cap, and his remarks are misconstrued to convey that he had slept with several students (56). In the third, the report of the attack, he is called Lourie (115). Lurie has no control over these reports, but he, too, engages in such misrepresentations when he does have control — he gives his name as Lourie when hiring a room (211) and deliberately falsifies his student records (26), for example. Recognizing the intrinsic power of words to shape perceptions, Lurie also recognizes the power words can give him to manipulate others' perceptions through misrepresentations. Controlling the way that stories (condensed representations of events) are told thus becomes an important leitmotif of the narrative.[21]

Humboldt's Linguistic Relativity

> Mephistopheles: When people hear some words, they
> normally believe
> that there's some thought behind them
> — Goethe, *Faust I*, 165–66, lines 2565–66

Although Wilhelm von Humboldt (1767–1835) is often categorized as a Romantic language philosopher, his theory of language was much more complex than those of his contemporaries. In part, this derived from his focus on the relationship between language and its speakers, in contrast to others (such as Grimm and Bopp) who concentrated solely on establishing the structures of and reconstructing the relationships between languages. As a result, Humboldt first formulated principles about language that did not gain currency until much later. The idea of linguistic relativity, now often called the Sapir/Whorf hypothesis, is one of these.

In Humboldt's version, linguistic relativity expresses the interrelationship of language structure and speakers' mentality: a nation's language affects the way its people think, and the mentality of the people also influences the language structure. As he stated in his final work (1836), *On the Diversity of Human Language Construction and its Influence on the Mental Development of the Human Species*, "The *comparative study of languages*, the exact establishment of the manifold ways in which innumerable peoples resolve the same task of language formation that is laid upon them as men, loses all higher interest if it does not cleave to the point at which language is connected with the shaping of *the nation's mental power*" (1999: 21). The hypothesis entails two correlates: concepts exist that can only be expressed within a particular language, and some languages, by the elegance of their structure, reflect a superior mental capacity of their peoples — the Indo-European languages represent the highest cultural attainments. The unique "inner form" of a language expresses "the whole mental capacity, related to the structure and use of the language" (in Arens 211, translation mine). At the same time, Humboldt believed that the forces of civilization, especially language contact, interfere with the natural resonance between a language and the mentality of its people, so the less civilized languages and people are somehow more pure, the inner form of these languages less compromised or, in his Romantic organicism, "decayed."

Three of Lurie's reflections on language convey his belief in linguistic relativity. First, he would like to hear Petrus's story, "but preferably not reduced to English," because "Pressed into the mould of English, Petrus's story would come out arthritic, bygone" (117). Moreover, he considers English an unfit medium precisely because of its history — it has been a language of advanced civilization for too long. Although Lurie does not believe English will die off, he likens it to "a dinosaur expiring and settling in the mud" (117), its vitality or, in Humboldt's terms, its inner form, destroyed. Elsewhere, he regards English as "tired, friable, eaten from the inside as if by termites" (129). Here, he also alludes to a Humboldtian language hierarchy. The monosyllables, characteristic of the more primitive (and purer) languages, are the only reliable parts of English that remain, "and not even all of them." Only "starting all over again" — that is, returning to a prehistoric state of linguistic primitiveness, can remedy the situation, or "reconstruct" and "purify" the language. Finally, Lurie conceives of his opera as "sung in an English that tugs continually toward an imagined Italian" (180). This is partly about the sounds of the two languages for the sake of his music, and for authenticity; the English should at least sound Italian; Teresa should sing with an accent and also interject Italian phrases like "Mio Byron." But it also implies that English alone, because of its sound *and structure*, could not adequately express this love story.

Another sort of linguistic relativity Lurie shares with Humboldt is the relativity of meaning, at least concerning understanding. On one level, this contradicts the Romantics' belief in the inherent meaning of words so central to their quest for the *Ursprache*. It is, in fact, one of the internal contradictions of Humboldt's theory, arising from his conception of the dual nature of language: it possesses an inner form that shapes speakers' perceptions, yet speakers also each individually contribute to its shape. Without rejecting the inherent meaning of words, Humboldt believed that a word's meaning depends on the whole language of which it is a part.[22]

Moreover, because he recognized that language does not exist independently of its speakers, he realized that meaning depends on speakers' experiences. No two speakers possess *exactly* the same language or understand *exactly* the same meanings because they have unique (and constantly changing) experiences with language. As a result, communication is a process of approximation involving both understanding and misunderstanding.[23] It is as though the inherent meaning of words resides in the resonance between them and the ideas of the individual speaker, a concept reminiscent of Herder's solipsistic child reflecting on the persistent qualities of a sheep, whereas the relative meaning of words resides in the necessity and impossibility of communicating one's individual perceptions to others.[24]

Lurie's belief in the relativity of meaning is most evident at the university inquiry when he twice draws attention to the disparity between words and how they are meant. When Farodia Rassool demands a sincere statement from him about his wrongdoing, he ridicules her for assuming she will be able to "divine" from his words whether it comes from his heart (54). Shortly thereafter, he finds it "preposterous" to demonstrate the sincerity of his words (55), emphasizing the impossibility of truly knowing what another person means. To be sure, Lurie's skepticism relates to words' power to misrepresent, but above all, his remarks point to the tenuous relationship between words and their intent, especially between speakers' meaning and listeners' understanding. At the same time, Lurie manifests his ambivalence about the relativity of meaning. He could easily have provided an insincere but well-acted statement to save his position, but he chooses not to lie to preserve the integrity of his own Romantic view of life and language — even though he knows that others will fail to understand him. It is an idealistic gesture to keep from compromising his Romantic "idea of the world" (146).

III. Lurie's Romantic View in a Pragmatic World

Mephistopheles:		We simply have to make a proper deposition to the effect that [Martha's] husband's limbs have been laid out in consecrated ground at Padua.
Faust:		How clever! Now we have to make the trip there first!
Mephistopheles:		*Sancta simplicitas!* There is no need of that; just testify without specific knowledge!
Faust:		I must reject the scheme, if that is your best suggestion . . . You'll always be a liar and a sophist.
		— Goethe, *Faust I,* 78, lines 3033–39, 3050

Lurie's Romantic idea of the world, reinforced by his Romantic conception of language, renders him out of sync with the post-apartheid, rationalized society he inhabits, both at the university, where he cannot come to terms with his new role as a communications professor and especially with the legalistic demands of the committee of inquiry, and on Lucy's farm, where he reflects on the uselessness of his linguistic skills, his knowledge of Italian and French specifically, during the attack (95). He is aware of his marginality and the uselessness of his knowledge and ideas here and elsewhere, as when he realizes that only he cares about the dead dogs (146). When he returns to Cape Town, the marginalization of his Romanticism has turned into complete exclusion: young Dr. Otto, a language learning specialist, has replaced him, and his former ID, a representation of his identity, fails to gain him access to the library (177). He is literally shut out. "So much for the poets, so much for the dead masters," he sighs to himself, fully cognizant that the ideals to which he has devoted his life no longer matter in this larger world.

Despite this awareness, however, Lurie is unwilling to relinquish or bend his Romantic idealism, even to save himself from disgrace. It seems as though a part of him, as with Faust, actually seeks out disgrace as a catalyst for change in his moribund existence. For a while he survives, teaching his communications classes, but without conviction; he remains devoted to the Romantic view of language origins in song and fails to connect with the new generation of students. But the disjunction between his views and the new, rationalized order comes out into the open when he confronts the legal system in the hearing; his inflexibility becomes his own undoing.

In contrast to Lurie, his lawyer and his ex-wife Rosalind have a pragmatic view of the legal system as a set of significations whose value obtains only within the system itself. In suggesting that Lurie try "'Sensitivity training. Community service. Counselling. Whatever you can negotiate,'" the lawyer essentially gives Lurie necessary but empty signifiers for communicating within this system. Lurie cannot see them as empty and tries to get at their possible meaning, "'To fix me? To cure me? To cure me of inappropriate desires?'" but this is irrelevant ("Whatever," the lawyer replies [43]). Later, when Lurie tells Rosalind that he was standing up for the principle of freedom of speech, freedom to remain silent, she admonishes him that trials are not about principles (188). At the hearing, Lurie has no legal challenges, but philosophical ones, which are not admitted within the discourse (47–48); his claim to have become "a servant of Eros" — a Romantic ideal expressed in Romantic language — is likewise disregarded (52). Thus, Lurie brings his state of disgrace upon himself not by pursuing Melanie, but by adhering steadfastly to his Romantic ideal and language, despite knowing he should not. Just as Faust elected to fall from grace by signing a pact with the devil in his quest to find meaning, Lurie chooses his disgrace — public humiliation, loss of his job, his pension, and his reputation — over signing his name to a statement he does not agree with.

But does this make him the dunce in the newspaper? Is there nothing noble in his unwillingness to sacrifice a principle to save his job? Although the juxtaposition of his Romantic view with the pragmatic view lays bare his shortcomings, it also shows us what is lost in the rationalized world. On the negative side, his idealism leads to self-delusion. He objectifies Melanie, seeing in her an ideal of beauty rather than an individual, and when he rapes her, he refuses to acknowledge it as such. He engages more with words and ideas than with real people. At the same time, he cultivates beauty, art; he pursues, in Lucy's words, "a higher life," though he admits that the life they are living is the only one there is (74). Molding the people and events of the world around him in his Romantic idealism, he imbues them with deep meaning, deriving a sense of enrichment and appreciation of life absent from the rationalized world.

Though Lurie remains a true Romantic to the end, he does undergo significant development, expanding his understanding of beauty and especially love, so that he begins to take and love things as they are rather than pressing them (violently) into the service of his own desires. Indeed, experiencing for the first time a selfless love towards his daughter, Driepoot, and his new conception of Teresa, he finds a private redemption, however relativized and muted it may be compared to the transcendence of Goethe's and Boito's Faust.

Where does Lurie's Romantic conception of language fit in with our interpretation of Boito's *Mefistofele* and Goethe's *Faust* as models for *Disgrace*? Does Faust, too, view language in this way, as suggested in Jacoby's argument that Faust is a fictionalized version of Herder? In fact, while Goethe read and enjoyed Herder's *Treatise on the Origin of Languages*, it would be too much to claim that Goethe's drama presents a coherent Romantic theory of language. Goethe made use of, but did not thematize, language issues he encountered through Herder and others, as these issues were prevalent in his day. Nevertheless, I think it fair to say that Goethe's Faust is sometimes preoccupied with language in ways similar to Lurie, as the quotations interspersed above indicate. Faust wants to "plumb the essence of things," which he can't believe merely consists of words, yet he acknowledges that names can embody essence. He distrusts unfamiliar words, which in themselves have the power to make him shudder. Like Lurie contemplating Melanie's complaint form, Faust recognizes the potency of "a parchment that bears a seal," and, consequently, the lasting value of the written word. He struggles to derive meaning from utterances, even when they have none. Finally, like Lurie, he is not (at first) willing to lie because it is practical. Faust's comments on language thus offer another suggestive link between Goethe's drama and Coetzee's novel. Lurie's Romantic theory of language is more important in a Faustian reading of the character as a mark of his uncompromising idealism and the direct cause of his disgrace. Yet altogether, the structural and thematic similarities, as well as common characteristics of Faust/Mephisto and Lurie, and of Lurie and Boito, offer compelling insight into the construction of Coetzee's *Disgrace*.

Notes

[1] George Bernard Shaw, Review of Boito's *Mefistofele*, *The Star*, 29 May 1889.
[2] http://nobelprize.org/nobel_prizes/literature/laureates/2003/coetzee-bio.html (accessed June 21, 2007).
[3] The University of Texas Graduate School Catalogues for this period confirm that the Germanic Languages Department offered a course on Goethe's *Faust* during this time, as well as "Studies in Germanic Linguistics and Philology" with the rotating topic of comparative Germanic grammar. For its part, the Linguistics Department offered "Comparative Linguistics." *Catalogue of the University of Texas at Austin, Part VII: Graduate School* (Austin: University of Texas at Austin, 1962–64; and 1964–66), 143, 164; 160, 180–81.
[4] The original reads as follows:

> Werd ich zum Augenblicke sagen:
> Verweile doch! du bist so schön!
> Dann magst du mich in Fesseln schlagen,
> Dann will ich gern zugrunde gehn! (lines 1699–1702).

(http://gutenberg.spiegel.de/goethe/faust1/Druckversion_faust009.htm, accessed September 6, 2007).
[5] "Woman, eternally" does not entirely capture the original, "das Ewig-Weibliche," as it renders an "appropriately blank" German abstraction, in Lurie's parlance (142), "the eternal-feminine," more concrete. The original in rhyme reads

> Alles Vergängliche
> Ist nur ein Gleichnis;
> Das Unzulängliche,
> Hier wird's Ereignis;
> Das Unbeschreibliche,
> Hier ist's getan;
> Das Ewig-Weibliche
> Zieht uns hinan. (lines 12,104–12,111)

[6] Another common leitmotif, if not a theme, surfaces here. Dogs, so peculiarly central to *Disgrace*, recur throughout *Faust*. Mephistopheles appears to Faust as a

poodle in Goethe's version of the story (34–35), and Faust and Wagner, like Lurie and Lucy, doubt the presence of mind or soul in them. Faust asserts, "I see no trace of mind — it's only training" (32, lines 1172–73).

[7] Rosalind calls Lurie something close to this epithet for Satan: "'. . . you were always a great self deceiver, David. A great deceiver and a great self deceiver'" (188).

[8] The dedication at the beginning of *Faust I*, written in the poet's voice, offers another model for Lurie's waking dream: "Images of happy days accompany you [elusive shapes], / and many dear familiar shades emerge, / first loves and early friendships, too, / like ancient tales whose words are half forgotten" (1, lines 9–12).

[9] The Italian original reads "Ogni mortal mister gustai / Il Real, l'Ideale, / L'Amore della vergine, / L'Amore della Dea Si / Ma il Real fu du dolore, e l'Ideal fusugno" (Boito 36).

[10] In fact, Goethe secured a position for Herder in Weimar so that Herder could come live there (Lilje 118).

[11] My translation. "Herder selbst ist Faust, und . . . im Faust [haben wir] die Verdichtung des menschlichen Eindrucks Herders . . . zu sehen" (Jacoby 1).

[12] In Rousseau's *On the Inequality among Men*. Rousseau's *Essay on the Origin of Languages which treats of Melody and Musical Imitation* was not published until 1781, after Herder wrote his essay, though it was written as early as 1755 (Gode 171). Nevertheless, Rousseau's general thesis was already well known.

[13] Although the first definition of "friend" in *Merriam-Webster's Unabridged Dictionary* maintains a tenuous link with the etymology of the word ("one that seeks the society or welfare of another whom he holds in affection, respect, or esteem or whose companionship and personality are pleasurable: an intimate associate especially when other than a lover or relative"), the second is far more pragmatic, and may be the one that Bill Shaw has in mind: "one not hostile or not an enemy . . . one that is of the same nation, party, or other group and whose *friendly* feelings are assumed or from whom sympathy or cooperation is expected" (http://unabridged.merriam-webster.com).

[14] "Cheaply ornamental" and "based on pretense or insincerity" come from Webster's second definition of "meretricious." The first definition, curiously, is "of or relating to a prostitute: having a harlot's traits" (http://unabridged.merriam-webster.com). Could Lurie wish to introduce a qualitative distinction between his affair with Melanie and his previous liaisons with prostitutes by changing her name in this way?

[15] One intriguing suggestion is that this association comes from J. M. Coetzee's time as a student at the University of Texas at Austin, whose Longhorn mascot is known as "Bevo."

[16] Compare Lurie's use of "it" with Bev's use of "him" (80–81), and "him" for the goat (83).

[17] This means "farmer's wife" or, literally, "farmer woman" in Afrikaans.

[18] Again, dictionary definitions offer insight into this exchange and reveal Lurie's etymological rather than pragmatic understanding of words. "Refuge" and "asylum" are very nearly synonymous. "Asylum" is defined as "a place of refuge and protection"; "refuge" is "shelter or protection from danger or distress," but curiously, the second definition is "a home for those who are destitute, homeless, or in disgrace." The difference in the words lies not in their current usage but in their etymologies: *refuge* from Latin *refugere*, to run away; *asylum* ultimately from Greek *asylos*, inviolable. Connecting "refuge" with its relative "fugitive," Lurie rejects the notion that he is running away from anything (or that he is in disgrace).

[19] We have already seen this tendency in his predilection for etymological interpretations, especially in his lecture to Lucy about her imprecise usage of the word "scapegoating." The two processes are closely related.

[20] Afrikaans definitions from http://www.rieme.co.za/woordeboek.asp.

[21] Consider, for example, Lurie's reflections on the story of Lucy's rape, which he realizes is not hers to tell, as well as the various newspaper articles about the robbery and the charges against him in Cape Town.

[22] Humboldt wrote, "to understand a single word, the whole language needs to be understood" (in Arens 182, all translations mine).

[23] "When one hears a word, no one thinks directly and exactly what someone else does, and the tiniest difference quivers, like a circle in water, throughout the whole language. Thus, all understanding is always at the same time a not-understanding, all agreement of thoughts and feelings also a divergence" (Humboldt in Arens 210, translation mine).

[24] This is quite different from Saussure's concept of linguistic value wherein words are mere ciphers whose meaning is solely determined by their relationship to other elements in the system.

10: The Dispossession of David Lurie

Kevin O'Neill

> Our craft is all in reading the other: gaps, inverses, undersides; the veiled; the dark; the buried, the feminine; alterities.
> — J. M. Coetzee, *White Writing*, 81

> . . . those who have indulged in gluttony and violence and drunkenness, and have taken no pains to avoid them, are likely to pass into the bodies of asses and other beasts of that sort. And those who have chosen injustice and tyranny and robbery pass into the body of wolves . . .
> Plato, *Phaedo* 81E–82A

WHAT HAPPENS TO DAVID LURIE IN *DISGRACE*? Having been dispossessed of his place and identity in the world of reason, he discovers, or rediscovers, a new way of knowing, as well as a new way of being, that exist, and have always existed, beyond the reach of traditional Western categories of mind and body.[1] Coetzee, through Lurie, privileges the body and the senses as vehicles for knowing and being, and in so doing he reveals a profound connection between his protagonist and the animals whose bodies, passions, and senses traditional philosophy has devalued or ignored, and among whom Lurie, dispossessed, spends more and more of his life.[2] I will argue further that Coetzee's rejection of Western rationalism and his emphasis on embodiment and on the human connection to animal bodies and feelings is anything but celebratory. It is, rather, tragic. Coetzee privileges the body without a glimmer of the hope that marks other contemporary approaches that see the rediscovery of the body as a cause for celebration.[3] If they find a principle of life and liberation in the body, Coetzee finds only death and obloquy, albeit a death and an obloquy that evoke and sustain a hard kind of love. He believes in an embodied soul for all living things, and in unique subjectivity for all animals, but he rejects the idea that such a soul can live past the death of its body.[4] Still, he believes that once we know about these embodied souls we must honor and mourn each passing one. On one level, we can read *Disgrace* as a sketch for a new metaphysics and epistemology based in the body, and on another as a primer for the care of souls, an ethic of care for subjectivities that have no hope of transcendence. Coetzee himself puts this succinctly:

"It is not possible to deny the authority of suffering and therefore of the body" (248), and in *Disgrace*, Lurie finds no way to deny it.

But Lurie discovers this world of the embodied soul only after he has become a scapegoat, driven out of his city environment and his country refuge by his inability to make himself clear to anyone. This is a deviation from the theme of the *Bildungsroman*, because rather than developing Lurie seems to devolve. This is a story in which the protagonist comes to deeper self-understanding not by *transcending* his situation, but by sinking beneath it. As Marais (2006) puts it, "there is much evidence in *Disgrace* to support the claim that Coetzee has furnished *Disgrace* with the structure of an anti-*Bildungsroman*" (79). He loses every rational argument in which he attempts to maintain his status in the human lifeworld. Lurie cannot think or speak as others think and speak, and is therefore thrust "down" the scale of being to the world of animals, where he learns new lessons about the nature of the soul and the meaning of identity.[5]

By the end of the novel Lurie has lost his name — he is "a mad old man who sits among the dogs singing to himself" (212) and "simply a man who began arriving on Mondays with the bags for Animal Welfare" (145). He, like the dog he refuses to name (215), has become anonymous. What little self-understanding he ever thought he had is gone. He tells Bev Shaw, "I don't know what the question is, anymore" (210). He has lost whatever *idea* he ever had of himself, and become like the dogs among whom he lives, a body among other bodies. However, his defeats and exclusions do not wholly silence David Lurie, or extinguish his desire, but redirect that desire and reshape that voice. Desire becomes love and speaking becomes a musical keening, or perhaps a canine howl.

We get at what happens to Lurie in three stages. First, we remind ourselves of ideas about knowledge and identity that have shaped the Western tradition. Having done that we will sketch Lurie's path, from a beginning in which he thinks he knows exactly what is going on in his world, through a series of disastrous arguments, the loss of which drive him out of the world of humans and into the putatively lower world of animals. It is not the lost arguments exclusively, of course, that drive Lurie toward the abject, devalued world of animals. His own unprincipled passions, the home invasion and rape, the times, with their shifting power vectors and political displacements, contribute to dispossessing David Lurie of the world he once occupied. But the lost arguments matter because they give voice to Lurie's understanding of his own actions, the rape and the changing historical scene. The arguments chronicle in a precise way exactly how and why Lurie comes to misunderstand his world, and they provide benchmarks for the stages of his dispossession. Conversely, we can argue that none of these events, the arguments or his actions, or what he suffers, simply *cause* his devolution into the world of the animals.

Despite everything that world is always already *there*, fully formed, and it is just barely conceivable that Lurie could have found it without external provocation.[6] Third, we will visit Lurie in that world and see what truths he learns from his sojourn there.

I. The Platonic/Cartesian Background

In the *Republic* Socrates likens the human situation to that of people imprisoned in a deep cave. We are chained so that all we see are images cast on a wall in front of us. But what we "know" in this way lacks accuracy and, as a set of mere images, lacks proper being (*Republic* 514C–515B). Socrates suggests that what we know and what is can be deployed along a "divided" line, in which the lower segment represents knowledge based on shadows and reflections, and which is farthest from the light of the Sun of true Being. "One subsection of the visible consists of images. And by images I mean, first, shadows, then reflections in water and in all close-packed, smooth and shiny materials" (*Republic* 509e). Just above it on the line are visible things: "In the other subsection of the visible, put the originals of these images, the animals around us, the plants and the whole class of manufactured things" (*Republic* 510a). Such images are mere copies of what is real (*Republic* 514a–517a).

In *Phaedo*, Socrates tells us that people think of the body as a prison, from which the soul escapes at death (*Phaedo* 7b). "Now the doctrine that is taught in secret about this matter, [is] that we men are in a kind of prison, and must not set ourselves free or run away." "The soul is invisible" (*Phaedo* 80D), "it goes away into that which is like itself, into the invisible, divine, immortal and wise" (*Phaedo* 81A).

> But, souls that fall prey to the body's passions return to earth, or cannot leave it when the body dies: we must believe that the corporeal is burdensome and heavy and earthly and visible. And such a soul, . . . interpenetrated with the corporeal . . . is weighed down by this and is dragged back into the visible world, and so, it flits about the monuments and the tombs, where shadowy shapes of souls are seen. (*Phaedo* 81 C, D)

Souls "who have indulged in gluttony and violence and drunkenness are likely to pass into the bodies of asses and other beasts of that sort. And those who have chosen injustice and tyranny and robbery pass into the bodies of wolves and hawks and kites" (*Phaedo* 81E). The souls that are most attached to their bodies becomes predators like wolves or ruminants — asses, goats, and sheep. Souls return to earth in animals because they took the senses literally and followed the bodily passions that such experience provoked. There is an indissociable connection between being an animal and being trapped in the senses and the passions they provoke.[7]

Descartes wants to pull down the edifice of inherited belief and find a foundation for certainty. He knows that beliefs he held when he was younger are not true. The only way to protect himself from self-deception is to subject all his beliefs to doubt. We are all in the same position with respect to beliefs based on bodily experience. We cannot be certain that the images that our bodies provide are the way the world is, or dream-generated fantasies. Only reason, which can exist without its body, can know the truth about how beings are.

Descartes believes that animals are biological automata that lack what makes humans, human. They cannot think because they cannot use language properly. By "think" Descartes means reasoning, that is, making and testing hypotheses. Animals are like clocks that tell the right time but that cannot "know" that they are doing so. They have no internal conscious states. There is no inner way that it is to be a dog. Animals are machines that process and act on sense impressions and the passions they provoke, much like Plato's wolves and asses.[8]

Plato and Descartes believed that the world of animals is that of the senses and the passions, and therefore of appearances, not the world of reasoning and true being, which, in the Western tradition, often becomes, as Jane Taylor attests, a world of Leibnizian monads, each one a living consciousness separated totally from every other living consciousness (paraphrased in Marais [2005], 78). This is the world in which Lurie ends up living. And, rather than finding nothing but passion and lower levels of knowing, Lurie finds there a rediscovered way of being and knowing that might be deeper and morally finer than the "higher" world of reason. But how does he get to this world, and what does he find when he gets there?

II. Lurie's Dispossessions

The First Dispossession: Lurie Loses His Place in the City

David Lurie begins the novel as a scholar of the British Romantic poets, in particular Wordsworth and Byron. Wordsworth is represented as Plato's spiritual ally. We find Lurie teaching Wordsworth's *The Prelude* the day after he first sleeps with his student Melanie Isaacs. Wordsworth laments that he is arriving at Mont Blanc, which cannot live up to the *idea* of Mont Blanc, a better and more perfect thing than the actual Mont Blanc (21).

> . . . we also first beheld
> Unveiled the summit of Mont Blanc, and grieved
> To have a soulless image on the eye
> That had usurped upon a living thought
> That never more could be.

Lurie teaches that Wordsworth believes in a higher and better world of Ideas, and that art, especially poetry, makes such perfect things present. "The great archetypes of the mind, pure Ideas, find themselves usurped by mere sense images" (22); and we will never find these ideas unless we "climb in the wake of the poets" (23) with an "eye . . . half turned toward the great archetypes of the imagination we carry within us." This attitude extends to how Lurie sees his attraction to Melanie, allying Lurie with Wordsworth and, indirectly, with Plato. When we love someone we want to get beyond his or her physical appearance: "do you truly wish to see the beloved in the cold clarity of the visual apparatus? It may be in your best interest to throw a veil over the gaze, so as to keep her alive in her archetypal, goddesslike form" (22). Wordsworth seeking the perfect archetype of the mountain, Lurie seeking a perfect archetypal beauty that does not belong to those who bear it: both attest to the reality of a realm of pure ideas, in which the platonic soul and/or Cartesian *cogito* can know pure archetypes.

Lurie is not, however, a pure Platonist because he is also a sensualist who believes in the power of the imagination. He teaches that, however appealing pure ideas might be, "we cannot live our daily lives in a realm of pure ideas, cocooned from sense-experience. The question is not, How can we keep the imagination pure, protected from the onslaughts of reality? The question has to be, Can we find a way for the two to coexist?" (22).

Lurie argues that Wordsworth means, in line 599 of *The Prelude*, to strike such a balance between ideal and actual by privileging the "sense image," which is halfway between "the pure idea, wreathed in clouds" and "the visual image burned on the retina" (22). But even this "sense-image" appears to privilege the Platonic idea: these images are to be "kept as fleeting as possible, as a means toward stirring or activating the idea that lies buried more deeply" (22), because as "sense-organs reach the limit of their powers, their light begins to go out." And at the moment such a limit is reached, "that light leaps up one last time, giving us a glimpse of the invisible." What matters to Lurie, Wordsworth, Plato, and Descartes is the invisible, the ideal, which Plato and Descartes both associate with the soul, which animals can never have.

The Double Expulsion

Lurie's journey to the edges of knowing and being is not something he either wills or expects. He begins the novel in a state of self-deception, filled with epistemological and ontological *hubris*. He is a man who thinks he knows, the sort whom Plato used as Socrates's foil.[9] Lurie's downfall begins when he is excluded from the urban environment, in which he occupies a position of power as professor of communications, because he sees the world differently from everyone around him. His epistemological obtuseness leads to ontological exile, that is, to a radical change of state.

The Urban Exclusion Phase One: Lurie Is Driven from the City into the Country

The first hint we get that there is something wrong in Lurie's world is the first "argument" he loses, with his weekly "escort," Soraya. He believes that his assignations with this woman have "solved the problem of sex." It becomes clear how wrong he is about "Soraya" when he sees her in public with her children, and imagines himself with her as a couple. He assumes that he has seen into the depths of their relationship, that he *knows* how Soraya sees him.

> Because he takes pleasure in her, because his pleasure is unfailing, an affection has grown up in him for her. To some degree, he believes, this affection is reciprocated . . . they have been lucky, the two of them: he to have found her, she to have found him. (2)

He becomes, fleetingly, "father: foster-father, step-father, shadow-father"(6).

But Lurie feels Soraya transforming herself "into just another woman and him into just another client" (7). He does not understand that he was always "just another client." Lurie has crafted an idealized Soraya in an idealized relationship. This becomes clear when he calls her at home. Soraya reacts angrily: "'I don't know who you are,' she says. 'You are harassing me in my own house. I demand you will never phone me here again, never'" (9–10).

Lurie missed what was going on — he did not *know* something he could have known. Soraya denies that she even *knows* who Lurie is. Since she was using a false name, he has no idea who she is and conversely, she has no idea who he is. Whatever she "knew" about him was circumscribed by the client-prostitute relationship in which neither party is bound to tell truth.

This rebuff to his sense of knowing what goes on has little effect. He moves quickly to a sordid liaison with a departmental secretary and then, as quickly, to the disastrous "affair" with Melanie.

The second argument that Lurie loses in the city is with his ex-wife, Rosalind. He has dinner with her after Melanie brings harassment charges. Lurie's template for interpreting the affair is radically different from Rosalind's. She tells him that he is "too old to be meddling with other people's children." He "should have known" that what he did was "stupid" and "disgraceful" (45), and he must "expect no sympathy, . . . no mercy, in this day and age." He has done something indefensible, "meddling" with "children" when he is himself a parent. Rosalind assures him that no one will take his side.

Lurie tries to change the "language game" from child molestation to the erotic.[10] He tells Rosalind: "'You haven't asked whether I love her. Aren't you supposed to ask that as well?'" Rosalind responds with deflating irony. "'Very well. Are you in love with this young woman who is dragging your name through the mud?'" (45). Rosalind never considers the possibility that love had anything to do with the matter, just as Soraya never thought there was any affection between Lurie and her. Lurie's attempt to idealize the relationship, which would lift it out of the slough of "meddling with other people's children," falls on deaf ears.

The third and most important argument Lurie loses in the city is the meeting with the University's committee of inquiry.[11] Again, the problem hinges on a disjunction between the way he wants to talk about the event and the way they do. The committee is interested in whether he accepts their membership. Lurie wants to raise what he calls a "philosophical objection" to the committee's right to call him to task. The committee chair says that this cannot be done because the committee is required to address only the "legal sense" of the events under discussion (47). Somewhat inconsistently, Mathabane, the chair, then adds that this is an "inquiry" rather than a "trial," which means it is more therapeutic than legal.

Lurie, following his lengthening list of misunderstandings, promptly pleads guilty to both charges, as if it *were* a trial. But since it is an inquiry, an attempt to find out the truth, not decide guilt or innocence, the committee is not satisfied with Lurie's plea. They want him to do something different, namely to "state his position" (49). His only position is that he is guilty, which requires no further statement. But the committee is not satisfied because, to put the matter crudely, Lurie is speaking the wrong way. They want to know: "Guilty of what?"

Lurie's answer, that he is guilty of everything that Melanie charges, is exactly what they do not want to hear. He is warned that his approach, which seems to the committee like "talking in circles," is "not prudent" but "quixotic." He is not playing the correct language game. Even if the chair of the committee stated that the inquiry was strictly about legal matters, and Lurie has stuck to strictly legal responses, the committee wants something more, and the more they want becomes clear when one of the female committee members asks, "'Would you be prepared to undergo counselling?'" (49). For Lurie, counseling "belongs to another world, to another universe of discourse" (58). The disjunction arises because the committee understands the proceedings, but also Lurie's inner life, differently than Lurie does. Even though the chair claims that what goes on in Lurie's "soul" "'is dark to us'" (58) and that they do not want repentance but a public statement that *expresses* repentance, the suggestion about counseling belies this claim. The committee sees Lurie's inner self, his "soul," as a territory open to inspection and correction. In calling for an intervention into his soul they are implying that his motive — what he calls Eros — was not an autonomous force but some version of mental unfitness. They reject the idea that souls can be visited by anything but their own urges and delusions, and argue, in effect, that references to Eros are purely psychological and political rather than indications of a form of possession.

They reject the idea that there is anything transcendent in the human soul, anything not subject to therapeutic intervention. Against this "idea of the world" Lurie is defending two ideas: first the primacy and irreducibility of the invisible soul, and second the legitimacy of the invisible motive force, Eros — the legacies of his Romantic mentors, Wordsworth and Byron.[12] The nub of his argument is that the invisible Eros, Eros as metaphysical, not biological, force, can move the invisible soul. But Eros has no currency in the paradigm used by the committee, just as what Lurie considers a religious category, repentance, should, in his opinion, have no currency in the supposedly purely secular, legal guidelines under which the committee *should* operate.

The committee *can* reject the language game in which his confession is couched just as they are implicitly rejecting the "language game" of Romantic poetry in which such figures as Eros are considered real, as Rosalind rejected the language game of love, and Soraya that of affection. The committee can impose its logically mixed, even inconsistent, language game on Lurie. They can reject "philosophical objections" in favor of purely legal procedural standards. They can call for quasi-religious "repentance," and public statements accepting moral blame. They can require therapeutic intervention because their templates for discourse, no matter how internally inconsistent, are currently hegemonic. Lurie's are "quixotic" and "subtly mocking" because the committee says they are.[13]

Lurie loses this third argument, and his job. He also loses his place in the city. Ironically the Professor of Communications has been read out of the University because of a profound breakdown in communications between him and his colleagues.

The Second Exclusion: Lurie Is Driven Off the Farm

This breakdown seems to have followed Lurie into the country, where he and his daughter immediately clash over the proper language to discuss his visit, and argue about the meaning of his firing. Lurie acts as if his appearance at the farm is voluntary, part of a "long ramble." Lucy thinks she knows more about his status than he does, and refers to the farm as a "refuge." But Lurie contests her description because if he is a refugee his status is reduced. The farm is not a refuge. He says that he is not (66) "a fugitive."[14] Lucy counters by saying that Rosalind told her that he had been let go under adverse circumstances. He says that he brought it on himself — he sealed his own fate because he would not accept what he describes as "Re-education. Reformation of character. The code word was *counselling*" (66). He associates such a proposal with "Mao's China. Recantation, self-criticism, public apology" (66). He rejects this because it belittles his claims about Eros and reduces his invisible inner self to a therapeutic site that needs correction. Such a redescription makes the invisible completely visible, something Lurie consistently resists. As Jane Poyner writes, "He refused to accept the university's version of the truth" (68). And if he was fired for defending a principle, then he left voluntarily, and is not a refugee.

He summarizes this position: "'These are puritanical times. Private life is public business. Prurience is respectable, prurience and sentiment. They wanted a spectacle: breast-beating, remorse, tears if possible. A TV show, in fact. I wouldn't oblige'" (66). In these times, the soul is turned inside out. What was once invisible is now made visible, becomes a spectacle and a "show," inauthentic in its visibility.

Lucy tells him, "You shouldn't be so unbending, David. It isn't heroic . . ." (66). She, too, is rejecting his self-characterization. He is not being a hero; he is not the protagonist in a battle between freedom and repression. He is just being rigid. Once more his "universe of discourse" is rejected in favor of a psychological interpretive scheme. Lurie loses this argument because Lucy does not accept his definition of who he is and of what happened to him. She might or might not agree with the committee's description of the world, but she definitely does not agree with his.

After this initial argument Lurie begins to live up to his daughter's characterization. He "devolves" from the role of citizen/professional to family member and aging parent, a visitor/refugee on Lucy's smallholding, and things seem to settle down. But life does not remain stable for long. There is the attack, the rape, Lurie's humiliating helplessness and injuries, the murder of the dogs, and Lurie's position begins to erode. The change of status expresses itself in a second series of lost arguments with his daughter. These arguments occur as a series of clashes through the second half of the novel. I present them one after the other, without reference to other events that occur between the clashes, to give the reader a sense of where these arguments are leading and also to highlight the fact that they have certain themes, such as what Lurie and Lucy respectively know, and the role of ideas in both Lurie's and Lucy's decisions about what shall be considered real.

These arguments follow a pattern. Lucy begins to forge her own version of what happened, and what she and Lurie respectively know about it, one that is sharply at odds with Lurie's views on both issues. Lurie and his daughter grow as far apart in their respective conceptual schemes as Lurie and the committee, or Lurie and Soraya, or Lurie and Rosalind. In the series of arguments with Lucy the issue seems once again to be one of *knowledge*. Lurie and Lucy have wildly different understandings of what happened.[15]

Lucy accuses Lurie of either not knowing, or not understanding what is going on, even of not being on the scene of events at which he knows he was present. Lurie persists in telling his daughter to be "sensible," and offers a series of "explanations" that involve Lucy being driven to act by a variety of what she contemptuously dismisses as "ideas": vengeance, history, guilt. He also advances the further "idea," or rational principle, that she is not acting with honor, another idea to which Lucy does not respond. If the arguments with the committee were about which language game to employ, the arguments with Lucy are about what we can know and about what is real, which also amounts to assigning different terms to what appears to be the same set of events. Lurie tries to show that he does understand by advancing a series of *ideas* about what Lucy is doing and should do, while Lucy keeps arguing that she has no ideas, only the brute facts of her current life. Lurie is finally asked to leave, only to find, among the animals, a place where the arguments cease and both a new language and a new sense of what is real emerge.

The first argument breaks out when Lucy and Lurie are preparing to speak to the police. Lucy tells him that there will be two stories — hers and his. She wants to control her narrative, intends not to tell the police that she was raped. Just as Rosalind and the committee invalidated Lurie's story of his relationship with Melanie Isaacs, so Lucy invalidates whatever story Lurie was planning to tell about her rape. "'You tell what happened to you, I tell what happened to me.'" Lurie disagrees: "'You're making a mistake.'" Lucy does not offer a counter-argument but says, "'No I'm not'" (99). Lurie returns to the subject the next day. "'Lucy, my dearest, why don't you want to tell? It was a crime. . . . You are an innocent party'" (111). Lurie is invoking "ideas" such as "innocence" and "crime." But Lucy is a realist who denies that there is "another world," that invisible realm of ideas that made Wordsworth disappointed at his view of Mont Blanc, or that drove Plato's freed prisoner up out of the cave into the sun. Lucy abjures the notion that ideas drive action, that there are invisible principles that move people to do things. For Lucy, there seem to be no "shoulds" but only "ises," to coin a barbarous term. Linda Seidel captures this: "Rejecting abstractions as irrelevant to her life, Lucy appears to embody the immanent, . . . like some well-tested female Candide, all theoretical optimism long spent" (19).

Lurie also assumes that Lucy is not telling because she feels ashamed of what happened. "Shame" is another "idea." She tells him the real reason for her silence. She says that "'as far as I am concerned, what happened to me is a purely private matter. In another time, in another place, it might be held to be a public matter. But in this place, at this time, it is not. It is my business, mine alone'" (112). This response can be read as a variant on Lucy's earlier rejection of ideas as explanatory entities. In the world she inhabits, public rules are inoperative. They are *ideas*. What matters and what works are private accommodations to particular circumstances.

When Lucy says that she is going back to the farm, Lurie tells his daughter to "be sensible," that going back is too dangerous, not a "good idea" (105). She responds that going back is not an idea at all, but what she is about to do. "'I'm not going back for the sake of an idea'" (105). Not only does Lurie lack "sense," he is accused of being an out-of-touch idealist, "quixotic": there is no guiding principle in Lucy's return. She is "just going back."

Lurie responds that Lucy cannot deceive herself into thinking that keeping the rape secret will protect her. "'Vengeance is like a fire. The more it devours, the hungrier it gets'" (112). But Lucy rejects the idea that the rapists are driven by an abstraction, "vengeance." What moves the rapists is an economy of assault followed by protection that has nothing to do with vengeance. Lurie counters with another possible explanation, another hypothesis: if Lucy is not trying to buy safety through meekness, she must be paying off an imagined debt. "'Do you hope you can expiate the crimes of the past by suffering in the present'" (112)? Again Lucy rebuffs him. She rejects "guilt" and "salvation" as explanatory concepts. These, like vengeance, are "abstractions," and abstractions do not describe Lucy's acts. "'I don't act in terms of abstraction'" (112). As Rosemary Jolly states: "But notice that Lucy has never subscribed to metaphysical moral values: her forte is refusing her father's habit of seeing the world through metaphysical glasses" (Jolly 164). She is not seeking salvation; she does not want to expiate past crimes with her silence.

Later, Lucy offers a fuller explanation:

> "But isn't there another way of looking at it, David? What if . . . what if *that* is the price one has to pay for staying on? Perhaps that is how they look at it; perhaps that is how I should look at it too. They see me as owing something. They see themselves as debt collectors, tax collectors. Why should I be allowed to live here without paying? Perhaps that is what they tell themselves." (158)

Lurie's response is succinct. "'Really, Lucy, from beginning to end *I fail to understand*'" (133). Agreeing with this, Lucy tells him: "'*There are things you just don't understand.* . . . To begin with, you don't understand what happened to me that day . . . You think you understand, but finally you don't. Because you can't'" (157: italics mine). This echoes something Bev Shaw told him earlier. He tells Bev he knows what Lucy was going through because "'I was there.'" Bev answers: "'But you weren't there, David. She told me. You weren't'" (140).

Lurie is baffled. The question is, what does "there" mean? For Lurie being "there" meant he was in the home when the rape took place. "Being there" meant being present. For Lucy, however, being "there" means experiencing, feeling, and understanding what it is to be attacked by three men who "'*do* rape'" (158), and who have "marked" her, as a dog might mark its territory. Lurie has *ideas* about what happened. Lucy has immediate experience, which she wants to keep private, and to which she thinks ideas do not apply.

Exasperated by his inability to get through to her, Lurie writes a letter that tells Lucy that she wants to "humble (her)self before history" (160), but that this is the "wrong" road and that if she continues she will be "strip[ped] of all honour." Lurie once more applies ideas to the situation. Perhaps he is referring to apartheid and arguing that Lucy mistakenly feels that she owes her rapists something because of past injustices. But Lucy never suggested such a thing, and nothing in her remarks about tax collecting indicate such a stance. As to honor, she has never mentioned "honor," another abstraction like "principle" or "history." These terms may be, as Rosalind suggested in an earlier conversation, "too abstruse." They do not seem to have anything to do with Lucy's decisions, and Lurie seems to get things wrong again.

Lucy's response makes this clear. She writes: "You have not been listening to me. I am not the person you know" (160). She is "a dead person" who does not have the luxury of entertaining ideas and who has made a deal to survive. She offers Petrus an "alliance," whereby Lucy will give him her land in return for his protection. She will "creep in under his wing" as a wife; he will be father to Lucy's child. Lurie thinks the proposal is "preposterous," a form of "blackmail" by whose terms Lucy is allowed to stay in her house unmolested in return for giving up her farm and her dreams of an independent rural life. But Lucy thinks that Lurie just does not get it. "'I don't believe you get the point, David'"(203). She knows the situation is humiliating but she takes the humiliation differently and sees the end of her hopes as a possible starting point. "'Perhaps that is what I must learn to accept. To start at ground level. With nothing. No cards, no weapons, no property, no rights, no dignity. . . . Like a dog'" (205).

Lurie does not grasp this, which becomes clear in the final argument, when Lurie attacks Pollux with the bulldog and Lucy comes to the boy's defense. It is Lurie and the animal against the emerging dominant culture. Lurie must leave. Once more his reasoning was not acceptable, and he leaves a second world, the one in which he hoped to find a refuge. Lucy is "prepared to do anything, make any sacrifice, for the sake of peace," and the argumentative David is part of what she is prepared to sacrifice (208). As this final series of arguments testifies, *Disgrace* can be read as a novel in which, as Salman Rushdie somewhat testily observed, no one understands anything about anyone else in the novel (cited in Wright, 98).

Ironically, as often as Lucy rails against Lurie for being a man of ideas, out of touch and lacking sense, it is finally Lurie who becomes one with "Africa," with the land, in the person of its rejected, exploited, and dying animals. Becoming a scapegoat for a second time, he is exiled from the realm of culture and full being and relegated to the place to which he has always already belonged: the world of animals against which Plato and Descartes have warned us.[16]

Lurie and the Animals

The world of animals has been lurking at the edges of this story since its beginning, when Lurie compares himself to a serpent in his sexual episodes with Soraya, and as a "worm," "fox," and "snake" in his affair with Melanie Isaacs. *Disgrace* is filled with more than one hundred figurative and literal animal references — including more than sixty references to dogs — but it is the literal meetings with animals that provide Lurie a new "home" on the margins of the world.[17]

His entrance to that world properly begins *before* he is cast out of his daughter's house. It is almost as if this world is waiting for him, waiting to take him in, as if this world is waiting patiently for Lurie to lose all his arguments, all his other homes, so that he can finally join this one. When he and Lucy go to town he meets Bev Shaw, who, with her husband, runs the Animal Welfare League clinic, with little or no government assistance. Lurie is put off by Bev's lack of attention to her appearance, by how tastelessly her house is furnished, and by her back yard, where he will eventually spend so much of his life. The clinic, with its odors of urine and mange and cleaning fluid, puts him off (72). Lucy asks him what he thought of Bev and her clinic. Lurie is impressed but has reservations. "'I don't want to be rude. It's a subculture of its own.'"

> I'm sorry, my child, I just find it hard to whip up an interest in the subject. . . . [T]o me animal-welfare people are a bit like Christians of a certain kind. Everyone is so cheerful and well-intentioned and after a while you wish to go off and do some raping and pillaging. Or to kick a cat. (73)

Lurie does not take people like Bev seriously. They are earnest do-gooders whose focus on animal welfare is admirable but unimportant, something a certain kind of (failed) person would spend time on. "He has nothing against . . . animal lovers. . . . The world would no doubt be a worse place without them" (72).

Lucy understands this perfectly. She says, "'You think I ought to involve myself in more important things. . . . I ought to be doing something better with my life.'" Lucy knows that Lurie believes in a "higher life," which is better than the life she and Bev are leading. Such a life would include things like "'painting still lives or teaching myself Russian'"(74). Lucy counters: "'. . . there is no higher life. This is the only life there is. Which we share with animals. . . . That's the example I try to follow. To share some of our human privilege with the beasts.'" Lurie agrees with her, but makes some significant exceptions. "'I agree, this is the only life there is. As for animals, by all means let us be kind to them. But let us not lose perspective. We are of a different order of creation from the animals. Not higher, necessarily, just different'" (74).

Lurie demonstrates a certain inconsistency. He agrees with Lucy that "this is the only life there is." Still, Lurie argues that animals and humans are of different "orders of creation," which presupposes hierarchy of lower and higher lives, echoing his earlier Platonizing view of the world.

Despite his views, Lurie volunteers at the clinic. Lurie evinces skepticism. "'It sounds suspiciously like community service. It sounds like someone trying to make reparation for past misdeeds'" (77). Lurie does not want to do anything that hints that he has a moral obligation to animals, or that he has done something wrong for which he must compensate.[18] There is no justice involved, only generosity. He agrees to help "'only as long as I do not have to become a better person'" (77).

Before he begins, Lurie has an interaction with Lucy's dogs that hints of what is to come. The younger ones recognize him; he has become part of their world. But the old abandoned bulldog, Katy, pays no attention (62). She, like Lurie, has found a refuge with Lucy. Lurie crawls into the pen with her, "stretches out beside her on the bare concrete" under the blue sky, and "His limbs relax." He falls asleep next to the abandoned dog. His daughter finds him and asks whether he is making friends. Lurie says this is not easy: "'Poor old Katy, she's in mourning'" (78). The nap is an incipient connection in which Lurie and the animal share a space of being, a single bodily location. When Lucy said that she did not believe in higher things and that we share this single life with the animals she might have had something like this in mind, and this is what Lurie rejected in words, even though he finds himself doing it, in practice. He has, perhaps, despite his protestations that we are of a different order of creation, begun to accept Lucy's egalitarian metaphysic, at least in respect to how he lives in his body.

However, Lurie's view of the world differs from his daughter's in unexpected ways that will have a bearing on his future relationships with animals. He mentions having a soul, and Lucy says, "'I'm not sure that I have a soul. I wouldn't know a soul if I saw one.'" Lurie, who agrees that there are no "higher things," puzzlingly tells her that she is wrong, that "'You are a soul. We are all souls. We are souls before we are born'" (79). Even in a world in which there are no higher things, there are still "souls" which pre-exist their appearance in bodies. He appears to be a dualist but we are not sure which sort, especially since he later tells Mr. Isaacs that he does not believe in God (171).

We are also not sure what he means when he says, "We are all souls." Does he mean all humans are souls, or is the mourning Katy, for example, included? If the latter is true then Lurie *has* changed his metaphysics. Perhaps he is not thinking about consistency, or is still in the process of working things out. As Ian Hacking reminds us in his review of Coetzee's work, things aren't always consistent when one is working out one's views.

"I imagine that Coetzee feels the force of almost all the ideas and emotions that his characters express. He is working and living at the edge of our moral possibilities about animals. Much is fluid, changing, being created. One positively ought to hold incompatible opinions as one works and lives one's way through to their resolution" (22).

When Lurie goes to the clinic the first thing he does is help Bev hold down a dog with an abscessed tooth. She has no anesthetics or antibiotics. She is not a veterinarian and can only relieve what pain she can, with her small resources and her thoughts. She instructs Lurie, "'Think comforting thoughts, think strong thoughts. They can smell what you are thinking.'" Lurie thinks this last idea is ridiculous but Bev tells him that he is "'a good presence. I sense that you like animals'" (81). Bev lives in and by her body, in a world in which thoughts have an odor, where one's bodily presence matters, where beings *feel* each other, in touch and smell and sound. She inhabits her body as if she is *not* of a different order of creation than the animals whose bodies she treats. Lurie has already foreshadowed this embodied metaphysic in his nap with Katy, and might, whether he knows it or not, be enacting it as he holds the terrified dog. Lurie might be moving into a different world, unrelated to the world of Platonic or Wordsworthian ideals, or to the world of argument in which his ideas were consistently rejected.

Right after the dog with the abscessed tooth, a woman brings in a grand old goat that has been savaged by dogs. His scrotum is badly infected. The wound has been left too long and there is nothing Bev can do to save him. But as she treats the goat, Bev does something extraordinary:

> She kneels down again beside the goat, nuzzles his throat, stroking the throat upward with her own hair. The goat trembles but is still. . . . She is whispering. "What do you say, my friend? What do you say? Is it enough?" The goat stands stock still as if hypnotized. Bev continues to stroke him with her head. (83)

Bev tells the woman she can euthanize the animal. "'He will let me do that for him.'" And she adds, "'I will help him through, that's all'" (83). The woman does not want this; the local people have their own way of slaughtering animals. Bev describes him in human terms: "'What a pity! Such a good old fellow, so brave and straight and confident!'" Bev sees the goat as a subject, an agent who has a right to control his fate, and she "consulted" with him by stroking his hair with hers and by speaking with him.

Lurie finds himself trying to comfort Bev by offering a theory, one made up or realized on the spot, about what goats do and do not know. This is a Goat Epistemology proposed as consolation and also perhaps a disquisition on the goat soul. He says:

"Perhaps he understands more than you guess. Perhaps he has already been through it. Born with foreknowledge, so to speak. This is Africa, after all. There have been goats here since the beginning of time. They don't have to be told what steel is for, and fire. They know how death comes to a goat." (83–84)

What is Lurie saying here? Is he claiming that goats have a bodily version of Platonic innate knowledge, an embodied Form of the Goat, always already imbedded in their consciousness, so that they *know* when death approaches as the slave boy in *Meno knows* the Pythagorean formula once he is reminded of it in the right way? Lurie is not advancing a biological theory about genetic coding, but says that goats *know* how they are going to die and also therefore *know* what it means to *be* a goat, to have a goat body and goat consciousness living in a goat world controlled by humans.

Bev half believes him but disagrees about one point. Even if the goat knew that he was to die she does not think knowing is sufficient. For Bev, dying is an essentially *social* act. Rejecting Heidegger's characterization of death, in *Being and Time*, as *Dasein's* "ownmost non-relational possibility" (294), Bev asserts "'I don't think we are ready to die, any of us, without being escorted'" (84).[19]

Lurie begins to understand what Bev is doing. Bev cannot be a healer because she has neither the skill nor the means. Bev, like St. Hubert, offers a last refuge to the hunted and harried. "Beverly Shaw, not a veterinarian but a priestess, full of New Age mumbo jumbo trying, absurdly, to lighten the load of Africa's suffering beasts" (84). There *is* something "absurd" about Bev's trying to give these animals their own deaths. But Lurie has just contributed to "New Age mumbo jumbo" with his theory about goat foreknowledge. Perhaps this could be read in the register of the darkly comic, but Lurie *is* taking part in this "absurd" activity of serving as dog psychopomp and he might be learning something in the process. Despite his characterization of what Bev does, he finds himself doing it too, and becoming exactly what he once mocked. Existing in this paradox marks Lurie's journey from outsider to insider.

The next stage in Lurie's education comes when he watches as the dogs in Bev's clinic eat. Despite their hunger and their numbers, they share access to the food without snarling and biting. "'They are very egalitarian, aren't they?'" Lurie applies, almost automatically, an abstract ethical concept to the dogs' behavior. A Dog Theory of Justice is added to the Goat Theory of Knowledge.

It is for these reasons — that Lurie imagines that goats know their place in the world, that dogs have a theory of justice, that sheep have souls, that dogs love — that I find myself ultimately rejecting the view, advanced most fully by Michael Marais and Rosemary Jolly but also present in some form in Laura Wright, and even in both Derek Attridge and Lucy Graham, that Lurie relates to the animals as to the wholly Other, and that this Other is beyond the limits of language, non-representable and mysterious.

Marais argues that it is precisely because animals are entirely other, and the act of sympathetic imagination fails (here Wright agrees), that animals have a serious ethical presence. It is their persistence on the limits of our understanding that makes us take them seriously. I think that Marais and Jolly, and by extension Levinas and Blanchot, have a serious point in arguing that the ethical demand comes from outside the exclusionary space of the conscious self, and that the demand is limitless, unending. But I tend to agree more with Derek Attridge, who, despite some flirtations with the Levinasian position, argues that Lurie remains consistent through the novel, always believing in the primacy of the subject and its knowing, and that what Lurie is honoring is the animals' singularity, which he knows as a subject knowing other subjects. Attridge puts the matter this way: what Lurie is honoring is "the singularity of every living and dead being, . . . In this operation we find the operation of something called *grace*" (117). Rita Barnard sums up the position nicely by connecting infinite Levinasian responsibility with a continuing concern for the other as a known single individual: "In refusing to single out the special dog, Lurie is accepting, perhaps helplessly, perhaps resolutely, the claims of an infinite number of other creatures with whom he has no special connection — who are neither his own kind nor his historical victims. . . . the claims of the "*menny*" — too many — suffering others. They are all equally urgent, and they are by definition excessive and incalculable; yet we seem obscurely bound to these forgotten creatures" (40). Yet, to enrich this idea, which could have come from Marais or Levinas, she adds a moderating citation from Derrida's *The Gift of Death*: "But of course, what binds me thus in my singularity to the singularity of the other, immediately propels me into the space or risk of absolute sacrifice. There are also the others, an infinite number of them, the innumerable generality of others to whom I should be bound by the same responsibility, a general and universal responsibility [what Søren Kierkegaard calls the ethical order; italics mine]. I cannot respond to the call, the request, the obligation or even the love of another, without sacrificing the other other, the other others" (Derrida 68).

Here, Barnard and Derrida invoke the idea that there is a universal ethical order, funded on reason, that assigns responsibility because of the shared being of humans and animals. It is not impenetrable difference, but penetrable sameness, that creates the bond and the obligation.

The dogs' problem, says Bev, extending this point in an oblique way, is not a lack of morals but that there are too many of them. Dogs do not understand, and as Bev says, we cannot tell them that there are too many dogs, "'by our standards.'" If dogs had their way they would do exactly as we have done — "'They would just multiply and multiply, until they fill the earth.'" (85). As he listens Lurie allows a dog to smell his face. He enters the dog's world on a *bodily* level, squatting by the cage, letting the dogs touch him, *feeling* them, falling for and into the world in which Bev Shaw lives, a world in which dogs share so many values with humans.

The attack sharpens Lurie's new awareness about animals even further. First, Lurie reacts to the execution of the boarded dogs as if the animals were humans who had been murdered. Lurie has been "bled dry" by the attack, and is "without hopes, without desires, indifferent to the future," like "an old man, tired to the bone" (107). Yet he still cares for dogs by burying them (110) as if they warranted an almost-human burial.

Second, Lucy goes to the dogs and holds them, calling them "'My darlings, my darlings'" as if they were human lovers, or her children. Although they will disagree about everything else, Lucy and Lurie are coming closer on the question of what animals mean. Here, despite earlier reservations, Lurie seems to *know* that the dogs matter in a way they did not matter before.

Lurie now begins to notice animals in a new way. Petrus is planning a party to celebrate the completion of his house, and purchases two sheep to be slaughtered for the event. He stakes them out in the sun with no grass and no water. Lurie moves them to a better location. When Petrus moves the sheep back Lurie ponders how he can help them. He has no way to take care of sheep. He is a refugee himself living on a half-ruined farm. Even if he bought them, Petrus would replace them with others. Lurie understands that he cannot be an animal savior because animals are, to use Thomas Hardy's phrase from *Jude the Obscure*, "*too menny*" (146).

This incident takes him a step closer to a new relationship with animals. Even Lucy argues that there is nothing to be done about the sheep. She and Lurie are, surprisingly, on the way to exchanging positions. This is Africa, after all, says Lucy, and the country besides. This is how people do things. Even though he tells his daughter, "'I haven't changed my ideas'" in the sense that he "'still do[es]n't believe that animals have properly individual lives'" (126), at the same time "'in this case I am disturbed. I can't say why.'" In ways he does not understand, "a bond seems to have come into existence between himself and the two Persians" that makes him regard their treatment as "indifference, hardheartedness." He purports not to feel emotions for the sheep: "The bond is not one of affection." And, denying that individual animals matter, he says, "It is not even a bond with these two in particular, whom he could not pick out from a whole mob in a field" (126).

However much he denies animal individuality, and claims no affection for these particular animals, he approaches the doomed animals and tries to connect with them. He says that he is "looking for a sign" — of recognition?[20] Of shared being? Attridge concurs: the sheep exert what can only be called an ontological pull: "The powerful but baffling claim made by the sheep on him is, it seems, far from either the emotional pull experienced by the animal lover or the ethical demand acknowledged by the upholder of animal rights" (108). And when he does not get that sign — the animals shy away — he remembers Bev Shaw with the goat, "nuzzling [him], stroking him, comforting him, *entering into his life*" (126: italics mine).[21] Even though he is not able to pick out the sheep in a field, and even though they offer no sign, they still, like the old goat, possess "souls," individual identities.

Lurie develops a Sheep Theory of the Soul, to go with his Goat Theory of Knowledge: "Sheep do not own themselves, do not own their lives. They exist to be used, every last ounce of them, their flesh to be eaten, their bones to be crunched and fed to poultry" (123). Having denied sheep value and sheep individuality, he then mentions the sheep's "soul," evidence that his claims about the difference between people and animals is shifting. "Nothing escapes, except perhaps the gall bladder. Descartes should have thought of that. The soul, suspended in the dark, bitter gall, hiding" (126). Whether Lurie means "soul" in a traditional sense, he does describe it as "suspended in the dark" and as "hiding," as if the animal soul — and perhaps the human soul, too — were a bodily being, something between visibility and invisibility, but distinct from the body nonetheless. Is it, like the "sense image" in his discussion of Wordsworth, a visible sign of invisible presence?

This theme of animal individuality reasserts itself when Lurie thinks about the people who bring dogs in to be euthanized. These people want something like what the Nazis wanted in the Holocaust, a *Lösung*, or "solution," a quick disappearance of the animal/person, "leaving no residue, no aftertaste" (142). Is this way of dealing with animals a willing *not* to see their individuality, as the Nazis' treatment of the Jews was a similar refusal? And are both, equally, sins?

It is to these "excess" dogs for whom people want a "final solution" that Bev Shaw as priestess/escort gives her attention, as if each individual dog had an importance, as if each one were a subject, had a *soul*. Lurie thinks that he impedes this process because he still lacks that "communion with animals" that Bev has. It is "Some trick he does not have" (126).

But he participates in the killings and the animals become more and more important. "His whole being is gripped by what happens in the theater" (143). Despite his claim that he does not know "whether by nature he is cruel or kind" and is, in a moral sense, "simply nothing," the pain gets worse. He lacks what he calls "the gift of hardness," and he finally breaks down: "The more killings he assists in, the more jittery he gets. One Sunday evening, driving home, he actually has to stop at the roadside to recover himself. Tears flow down his face that he cannot stop; his hands shake" (142–143). This, from the man who said, "Which among them get to live, which get to die, is not . . . worth agonizing over" (127).

He becomes convinced that the dogs sense/know what is about to happen. "[T]he dogs in the yard smell what is going on inside. They flatten their ears, they droop their tails, as if they too feel the disgrace of dying." Once inside, none will look at the needle, "which they somehow know is going to harm them terribly" (143). The dogs *know.* A Dog Theory of Knowledge is added to the Goat and Sheep Theories. As when Lucy called the dead dogs "darling" and when Bev Shaw speaks softly to the goat, or to dogs about to die, Lurie is beginning to speak about the animals as if they were *not* on a different level of being than the humans. Each dog, each goat, *knows*; perhaps each, as Lurie earlier conjectured, also has foreknowledge, a sense in their embodied soul what it means to be a dog or a goat, and what that means with respect to how they will die. Each dog, perhaps, has the soul that Lurie earlier said that we all have, and that he then extended to the sheep, even though he does not believe in God and believes, with Lucy, that this world is all the world there is.[22]

Though he is powerless to save the dogs, Lurie can attend to them after they have died. He might not have Bev's gift for entering into the lives of animals, but he might be able to act as both psychopomp and *harijan,* on one hand a guide and escort, on the other, an undertaker. He is not a dog whisperer who can live immediately with them and escort them in their final moments, but rather a dog undertaker, one who escorts them, when they are dead, to their resting place.

Lurie describes his emerging vocation. "The business of dog-killing is over for the day, the black bags are piled at the door, each with a body and a soul inside" (161). Each dead dog is both body and soul. He has extended his beliefs about souls to animals and moved beyond his claim that animals do not have "properly individual lives"; with these realizations Lurie has entered a new society, beyond both the city and the country — the world of ensouled animals.

This is indicated by his behavior and especially by his explanations for it. Lurie will not leave the bodies with "the weekend's scourings" of hospital waste. The dogs' bodies are not waste, but bodies, and Lurie "is not prepared to inflict such dishonour upon them" (144). When he first left them, rigor mortis had set in, making the bodies difficult to fit into the incinerator. The hospital workers break the legs so the bags would fit into the incinerator easily and the burning would be more complete (144–145). Lurie shows up early Monday mornings and places the dogs on the conveyor into the furnace himself, making sure that they fit. He knows that the dogs are dead and cannot care what happens to them. As Meg Samuelson notes, echoing Marais, "teleological plotting is thus forsaken" (153). His ideas on animals' souls do not extend to claims of immortality. Why does he trouble?

He does it "for himself. For his idea of the world, a world in which men do not use shovels to beat corpses into a more convenient shape for processing" (146). What world is this? We get images of death camps and genocidal massacres and mass graves — instances in which men *did* use shovels to beat corpses into shape for "processing." We also get images of industrial plants that "process" chicken and steer and pig corpses, of animal control centers that "process" unwanted cats and dogs.

It is neither accurate nor useful to push this reminder further. Lurie is not an animal advocate with a developed theory. He is the nameless old man, the "mad old man" (212) who brings the dogs in bags to the incinerator. He is not clear about what he is doing or even confident that it is not "daft" or "wrongheaded." But there is some principle involved. Lurie seems to believe that it is just wrong to show such disrespect to the dead, and he does not want to live in a world where such practices go unchallenged. He has an "idea of the world," of the *whole* world, in which there ought to be a rule: do not use shovels to beat corpses into convenient shapes, or, do not dishonor the corpses of the dead.

This is where Lurie ends up — as both Louis Tremaine and Travis Mason argue — like a dog, and among the dogs, honoring the dogs. He begins to live, more or less, at the clinic. The yard that he described with such distaste and condescension when he first saw it has become his preferred residence: "In the bare compound behind the building he makes a nest of sorts, with a table and an old armchair from the Shaws and a beach umbrella to keep off the worst of the sun" (211). This is the yard that he once described as "an apple tree dropping wormridden food, rampant weeds, an area fenced with galvanized-iron sheets, wooden pallets, old tyres" (73).

Lurie has nothing but his gas stove and canned food, and of course his banjo. He lives on the very edge of the human world. He has become a true dog-man. Living by their cages, in his own "nest," he has become more than a psychopomp. He feeds them and cleans out their pens. He talks with them. He is in their world, as lacking in dignity and almost as lacking in property as they are. Like a dog, he sits quietly, dozing in the heat. He has left the world of men, entered the world of dogs, and found there a new vision of the soul — temporal, embodied, unnamed — and real.[23]

Yet, this "idea of the world" also sounds suspiciously like a universalist rational principle based on the judgment that if both dogs and men have something important in common (bodies? souls? subjecthood?) then in both cases — dogs and men — we should not live in a world in which either one is dishonored in death by having his or her body beaten to fit into a crematorium opening.

I side with both Susan Neiman in *Moral Clarity* and Gillian Rose in *Mourning Becomes the Law* in believing that subjectivity and reason have a *sui generis* legitimacy that transcends historical conditions, and I believe that a case can be made that Lurie does as well. Tremaine agrees, stating that "David maintains from beginning to end his 'idea of the world,' his obstinate assertion of the "integrity of the self," an integrity that survives even after death" (605). It is this subjecthood, and this thinking, that Lurie shares with the animals and it is this *sameness*, as opposed to an absolute difference, that enlists his ethical regard and his love. With Neiman and Rose I believe that it is this shared subjecthood and rationality that provides a foundation for a hopeful politics. The Levinasian loss of faith in reason and subjecthood is as debilitating and as devastating as the Marxist reduction of all thinking to ideology, or Foucault's analogous and equally catastrophic reduction of all knowledge to an exercise of power.

I do not claim that, for Lurie, animals reason in just the same way that humans reason — Elizabeth Costello makes clear that she sees reason as a purely human adaptation, and one of ambiguous value when it is used to oppress others. Nyman, Jolly, Attridge, and to a degree, Samuelson share a diffidence about reason, for different reasons. What I want to argue is two things: first that, *pace* Costello, reason can operate independent of narrow self-interest, as it does in Lurie's no-shovels principle, and second, that humans and animals do share bodies, souls, and thinking, in which case the last need not be confined to our form of reasoning. I think Laura Wright is correct in arguing that all of Lurie's conclusions are revisable, dialogic, dynamic. Lurie advances the principle diffidently and has the decency and common sense not to try to defend it — a sense Elizabeth Costello, disastrously, lacks. He puts it out as a possibility, something to be discussed, if there were anyone interested enough to listen to what he has to say, which there is not. This is a good example of reason working in a non-oppressive, non-reductive way.

And, in finding this new understanding of the soul and subjectivity, Lurie discovers that he has both, too:

> Sunday has come again. He and Bev Shaw are engaged in another one of their sessions of *Lösung*. One by one he brings in the cats, then the dogs: the old, the blind, the halt, the crippled, the maimed, but also the young, the sound — all those whose term has come. (218)

Lurie works silently alongside Bev, putting the bodies in the plastic bags. He "has learned by now, from her, to concentrate all his attention on the animal they are killing" (219). Lurie's obligation is to focus all his attention on the individual animal that is dying. He expends his emotion in paying attention to each animal as it dies.

The importance of what he does becomes clear when he goes to Cape Town and does not do his job: "From Monday onward the dogs released from life within the walls of the clinic will be tossed into the fire unmarked, unmourned. For that betrayal, will he ever be forgiven?" (178) Who is he betraying? Lurie is groping toward a new principle — that the animals he helps to kill *do* have individual identities, are subjects, and are therefore worthy of honor, and as deserving of post-mortem respect as any dead human, the same level of intense respect for the dead that Ian Hacking notes: "a profound care for the dignity of the loved body after death, seems quite universal" (20). Lurie believes that every dog — and by extension every sheep, every goat — should be "marked" and "mourned" in its passing, should be escorted across the line between life and death and then honored after its death by someone like himself — a nameless, mad old psychopomp who lacks the "trick" of communing with animals while they are alive. And he should do this because in his new view of things *animals have exactly the same claim on being treated honorably in death as humans do because animals have souls and individual identities,* thus establishing, as Rita Barnard writes, an ethic that has "nothing whatever to do with kinship, labor, ownership, or debts — or anything else that can be made sense of in the moral economy of the colonial or postcolonial pastoral" (40).

The most powerful evidence that animals possess a nameless and unmarked subjectivity is that, in addition to being able to suffer and to know that they suffer, they love. "Of the dogs in the holding pens, there is one he has come to feel a particular fondness for. No visitor has shown an interest in adopting it. Its period of grace is almost over; soon it will have to submit to the needle" (214–15). From this dog with its withered haunches that is wanted even less than the other dogs, "he is sensible of a generous affection streaming out toward him from the dog. Arbitrarily, unconditionally, he has been adopted; the dog would die for him, he knows" (215). The dog loves him.

Sometimes Lurie lets this dog out of the pen. It plays and sleeps at his feet, although he will not name it. He even considers allowing the dog to "sing" alongside Teresa in his opera. They are, after all, equals in their sorrow: "Would he dare do that: bring a dog into the piece, allow it to loose its own lament to the heavens between the strophes of lovelorn Teresa's?" (215). The dog never contributes to the opera because Lurie allows it to go under the needle. But he almost included it, included it in principle, because it had a lament as individualized and as legitimate as the human Teresa's.

This might be the key. This dog unconditionally loves Lurie. It also likes music and might want to sing a lament in his opera. These are particular "personal" facts about this young crippled dog for which Lurie has developed affection. But Lurie's connection to the dogs is more severe and principled. As he makes sure that each dead dog is bundled up carefully and enters the flames intact, Lurie knows that he is "giving it what he no longer has difficulty in calling by its proper name: love" (219). In honoring the dead he is asserting that each of them, individually, had love to give, that each might or might not have liked music, and might or might not have wanted to, or been capable of, adding a lament to the opera. Lurie's "idea of the world" includes honoring — and loving — each of these anonymous, powerless animals that were capable of suffering, loving, and singing. His pledge is to all of them, and for this reason he cannot select one as more important or valuable than the rest. A man who has lived by selecting women for his private enjoyment has moved beyond all selection and become a guardian of all the dead, which excludes him from selecting any one of them to live.

But it is also true that in the last lines of the novel, if only for a moment, Lurie moves beyond his role as the one who honors all the dead equally, and appears to achieve what once he lacked: Bev's gift for entering animal lives on an individual level. As he carries the young dog to the needle, there is no question but that he enters *its* life. At the same moment his identity as undertaker reasserts itself and he relinquishes this connection, becoming once more the mad old man who gives up what he loves in particular so that he can honor and love all the dead in general.

Cast out of the city, out of the country, out of all human societies, a scapegoat who never wins an argument, who lost his human name and his voice, save the part which replicates the keening of ghosts and the howling of dogs, Lurie has "descended" to the world of the animals and ghosts and found, if not salvation, then a new way to love and, certainly, a new way to be.

Notes

[1] The existence of such a "counter-world" is suggested in several critical sources, but differently characterized in each source. Derek Attridge thinks of this world of Lurie and the animals as a place of grace ("Age of Bronze"). When he discusses Lurie's principle (*Disgrace* 145–46) about not wanting to live in a world where people use shovels to beat corpses into shape, he writes that "It is this experience of finding oneself personally commanded by inexplicable, unjustifiable, impractical commitments to an idea of the world that has room for the inconvenient . . . that I am calling *grace*" (116). Attridge then states that the political challenge, which Lurie does not take up, but which his work poses, "is to find a way to build a new just state that is not founded on the elimination of unpredictability, singularity, excess. We might call it, if it ever comes into existence, a state of grace" (118).

Mike Marais thinks of this alternate world as a kind of charmed Levinasian space beyond history in which the ethical can flourish outside the march of events. In "Imagination" he writes, "What is required of the imagination is not simply relocation of the self from one subject position to another position that is already presupposed and defined in opposition to a position it itself has vacated. Instead, the imagination must divest itself of all subject positions and language" (2006, 80). He then cites Coetzee himself, in "Erasmus' *Praise of Folly*": "The imagination must enable itself to occupy an uncommitted non-position, . . . a position not already given, defined, . . ." (2). Marais then characterizes this position "as a space in which the writer and reader encounter that which is beyond language." He further defines this space in "Little Enough" when, agreeing with Simon Critchley, he talks about a "double structure" in society, one level of which is "the ethical relation that transcends history, and may never become a part of history, [but which] nevertheless constantly interrupts and so mediates those contestatory relations extant in history" (173).

Laura Wright, in her *Writing "Out of All the Camps"* sees this counterworld as a space of "interregnum," borrowing the idea from an essay by Nadine Gordimer, and recycling it through its redefinition in Antonio Gramsci. South Africa, according to Wright, exists "between social orders but also between two identities, one that is known and discarded, and the other unknown and undetermined" (9). She also believes that for Coetzee, this interregnum is never a series of temporal events tied to a particular historical space and time, but as "conceptual, illustrative of the idea that any time two or more people can conceive of the mere possibility of disrupting the binaries that define their relationships and thereby engage reciprocally with one another, the secular limbo of the interregnum may (possibly, potentially, but certainly not probably) give way to the unknown and unknowable future" (9–10).

My characterization of the space of ghosts and animals as a "new world" privileges the idea that in entering the world of animals Lurie is opening up new possibilities and a new ethical universe, something also suggested clearly in Attridge (2006), Marais (2006), Barnard (2007), and Wright. At the same time, as the above citations suggest, Rita Barnard, in *Apartheid and Beyond*, is right to suggest that this new emerging parallel world is the child of crisis: in *Disgrace*, "all established oppositions and boundaries seem to be under threat of collapse, . . . A crisis of definition, relationships and responsibilities lies at the heart of *Disgrace*" (35).

[2] This privileging of the body is articulated with a great deal more theoretical detail in *The Lives of Animals* and later in *Elizabeth Costello*. There, in two essays, "The Philosopher and the Animals" and "The Poet and the Animals," putatively based on talks delivered by Elizabeth Costello, she sketches out a view of the world in which she rejects Cartesian dualism and the hegemony of reason and talks about "embodiedness" and the "embodied soul," ideas to which David Lurie will glancingly allude in his own non-theoretical way in the later parts of *Disgrace*, as we shall soon see (*Lives of Animals*, 33).

[3] See, for example, Susan Griffin's *Woman and Nature*.

[4] Travis Mason, in "Dog Gambit," concurs in this assessment that Lurie believes in an embodied, non-mortal soul. Tom Herron in "Dog Man" goes even further: he says that David Lurie "is attending to the death of a fellow being who may just possess what for so long has been attributed only to human beings, one of the marks of the absolute limit between the human and the animal, an eternal living soul" (487–88). Tremaine rejects any claims to immortality as "delusion" in "The Embodied Soul" but does assert an embodied but non-transcendent "salvation" "that can reside in no one and nothing beyond his own animal being" (609).

[5] In "Imagination" Marais also alludes to the fact that *Disgrace* is an anti-*Bildungsroman* (76), and Seidel, in "Death and Transformation," points to the fact that

Lurie, even as the novel begins, is a man who has already lost much of his status and identity, and certainly much of his power. As a white male intellectual in post-apartheid South Africa he is definitely living under revision (under Wright's interregnum), although at the beginning of the novel he does not seem terribly aware of this fact.

[6] This emphasis requires clarification. It has become almost a commonplace, and a perfectly justifiable one, to connect Lurie's fall and transformation to changing historical conditions and to his continuing to act in ways that fail to take those conditions into account (see, for example, Attridge [2000], Barnard [2007], Poyner [2000], Samuelson, Graham [2002]). In this essay I have chosen instead to concentrate not on the conditions but on the arguments Lurie advances in response to those conditions, as well as to the arguments with which he is countered by people who embrace different understandings of the world they share with Lurie. The committee, Soraya, his ex-wife Rosalind, Lucy, Petrus, Bev — all disagree with him in significant ways, although all come at the disagreements from different perspectives. This "democracy" of voices is noted especially by Wright in her discussion of the dialogic character of the novels, and her use of the concept of "interregnum." Wright argues that Coetzee's writing contests the role of what she terms "the monologic insider," that "textual presence that has access to untested notions of the truth" (100). Barnard sees "the times" as a period in which all relationships and definitions are under threat and being reshaped. This indicates, as Tremaine notes, an epistemological ambiguity, even a relativism, in Coetzee's writing, indicated by the free indirect discourse that he uses. Nyman, citing Huggan and Watson, concurs in "Postcolonial Dogs" (137). If this is right then the coexistence of, and contention among, many worldviews are part and parcel of the fundamental structure of the novel.

[7] It is however important to reiterate that Plato, unlike Descartes, *did* allow the possibility of souls living in animal bodies. Clearly, for Plato, the soul was something that could migrate from one species to another and from this we have to conclude that he did not entertain the same level of dualism as did Descartes, that is, between the human and the animal levels of being. David Lurie, when he first seeks refuge with his daughter Lucy, is much more a Platonist than a Cartesian.

[8] For a more detailed account of Descartes' ideas about animals, and excellent arguments about why it is misguided to see Descartes as entirely insensitive to animals and their feelings, see Cottingham and Harrison.

[9] The difference between David Lurie and the typical protagonist/victim in Plato's dialogues is that Lurie, unlike the Platonic characters, is not securely positioned within his society.

[10] I think the rubric "language game" (*Sprachspiel*), as that phase was coined and used by Ludwig Wittgenstein in his *Philosophical Investigations* (#2, 7, 23, *inter alia*), works here because in his arguments with Soraya, Rosalind, and the committee, Lurie is trying to do with language what Marais (2000) says that Blanchot and Levinas both think that people try to do with language, that is, use it to impose their own view of things, and especially to control and subjugate the things they encounter. I am proposing a version of Wittgenstein's "language game" allied to

Foucault and Blanchot's theories that connect knowledge, and naming, to the exercise of power. Lurie, under this description, is trying to nail things down, to make them *be* a certain way by thinking and saying that they are that way. He is trying to assert his epistemological and ontological priority over both the world and his opponents. He wants to prevail by having his language game prevail. In "The Possibility of Ethical Action" Marais characterizes all thinking, following Levinas, as follows: it is "a mastery exercised by the thinker upon what is thought in which the object's resistance as an exterior being vanishes" (59). Once Lurie controls his thoughts, he practices what Marais calls, in "The Possibility of Ethical Action," "the violence of representation" (59), which means that "Through language, the subject negates the being or presence of things" (60). But he fails, leaving his opponents in control of definition and of reality.

[11] Poyner (2000) and Sanders (2007) argue persuasively that the committee is modeled on the Commission on Truth and Reconciliation, and that Coetzee is not-so-subtly critiquing the practices of that post-apartheid body.

[12] Attridge argues in "Age of Bronze" that what Coetzee is really objecting to is not the Commissions but the modern globalized world, and the bureaucratic forces that shape it. The way in which Attridge characterizes these forces resembles my argument about the world view of the university committee.

[13] This analysis suggests that language operates, with respect to power, as Levinas and Blanchot say it does (see note 10), but more particularly in the ways Michel Foucault suggested in *Discipline and Punish* and *Power/Knowledge*. When he travels to the country, the same linguistic hegemony obtains: Lucy identifies, in the way she talks, with the way those now in control talk, and Lurie's language games, once more, fail to compute.

[14] Rita Barnard (2007) makes the point that in "these times" the idea that the country represents any sort of refuge does not make much sense, a claim that is thoroughly seconded by the home invasion and rape. Lurie *is* a fugitive, whether he likes it or not.

[15] Nyman, Poyner (2000), Tremaine, and Marais (2000) are some of the critics who raise the questions of truth and knowledge in *Disgrace*. Nyman and Poyner see the work as a deconstructive critique of the hegemonic Western subject position.

[16] It is at this point that Lurie enters, or begins to enter, that state of grace so central to Attridge's concern, that place beyond definitions and outside of history that Marais (2000) discusses, that land of fables to which Wright alludes. Blanchot's *Literature*, cited in Marais (2000), talks about "what things and beings would be if there were no world . . . prior to the day" (333, 329). By this Blanchot is referring to a world before or outside of history, a world with no determinative forces shaping it, a world that comments on, rather than being a part of, historical process. Marais also cites Levinas's *Meaning* as it talks about the importance of "the subject's failure to reduce the other to an object," which "means that he or she is surprised by the other" (95–100). Beyond all language games and beyond all attempts to impose meaning, Lurie is now available to what Jolly, in "Going to the Dogs," calls "the corporeality of the other" (153). As Tremaine writes (2003):

"The ironic, skeptical tautly cerebral voice in which Coetzee treats textuality, rationality and ideology grows silent and we hear emerging instead a voice that insists, with a more visceral urgency, on the direct, factual and compelling reality of bodily suffering and death" (588).

[17] Others have noted the ubiquity of animal references in Coetzee's work in general (Nyman, Mason, Tremaine) and there is a complex critical discussion of what roles animals play in that work. Are they allegorical? synechdochal?, as Barnard (2002) suggests, or are they, as the character Dostoevsky avers in the *Master of Petersburg*, not signs at all, but just dogs? He "is waiting for a sign, and he is betting . . . that the dog is not a sign at all, just a dog among many dogs howling in the night" (83). Wherever one stands in that debate, there is no question that both dogs and other animals play a range of figurative roles in Coetzee's work from similes to metaphors to allegories. And there is even less question that, in *Disgrace*, as Herron says, the animals "emerge from under the shadows cast by the more obviously weighty ethical and political matters invoked by the text" (477).

[18] Tremaine suggests that Poyner (2000) and Seidel believe that Lurie's involvement with the animals *is* a form of retribution for past crimes against women and is also a form of redemption (604–5). Attridge (2000) explicitly rejects this claim (115–16).

[19] See Heidegger, 307–9.

[20] We cannot help but be reminded of the character Dostoevsky's warning in *The Master of Peterburg* about the importance of being able to tell signs from things that are not. In Lurie's case the animals do not seem to be signs of anything other than themselves, but that also seems to be enough.

[21] This is one of the key sentences that makes me disagree with the Levinasian critics. When Coetzee writes that Bev Shaw "enters into" the dog's life he cannot mean, as both Marais (2000) and Wright argue, that in *Disgrace* the sympathetic imagination fails. Wright mitigates her belief in the failure of what Elizabeth Costello advances as the nub of her position on animals by admitting that "Coetzee's writing reveals the often humorous, transparent beauty of the imagination at work, forever trying to place itself within the consciousness of the other" (124–25).

[22] Here, again, is an indicator that the animals are *not* other at all, but *know* in the same ways as Lurie knows. And, Lurie seems to know that they know. Even Marais (2000), the major Levinas/Blanchot proponent, shows what appears to be a slight inconsistency in arguing that Lurie comes to love the animals, something he would have a hard time doing if had really immolated his selfhood in their service. Furthermore, Marais does allow, in "Imagination," that "the questioning of the imagination and articulation of its aporetic nature paradoxically establish its ethical necessity," which means that because Lurie *cannot* really imagine how the dogs' minds work, his awareness that they have minds, and *might* have foreknowledge, leads to a deeper ethical appreciation (80). I think the passage just cited militates against this Levinasian reading.

[23] Herron and Tremaine make similar claims when they assert that Lurie has become a dog, or dog-like, by the novel's end.

II. Reading *Disgrace* with Others

11: Community Reading: Teaching *Disgrace* in an Alternative College Classroom

Matthew Gray

> I think the humanities classroom is the best model of the formation of collectivities.
> — Gayatri Spivak (2008)

Introduction

OVER ITS FORTY-YEAR HISTORY, the Johnston Center for Integrative Studies has developed a program based on the principles of collaborative learning. These principles have their roots in the alternative college movement of the 1960s and 1970s, and also strongly resemble those found in the literature on democratic classrooms (e.g., Brookfield & Preskill 2005), socially just pedagogies (Freire 1998 and hooks 2003), and student success-centered learning (Kuh et al. 2005). Methods inspired by this history and these thinkers have been put in practice on campuses around the world, and I take the Johnston Center version to be representative of the practices instituted by committed teachers and students at those schools. I also believe that these practices can be tailored to more traditional institutions, and I write in the hope that teachers in liberal arts colleges, and even Research I institutions, will find methods here that are both useful and inspiring.

I focus on the student-centered pedagogy of the democratic literature classroom as formed by what at Johnston is called "Community Reading" or "unsolitary reading." Community Reading motivates readers to journey self-consciously through the reading process together, regardless of class year, reading experience, or even their official role as professor or student. It begins with several simple assumptions: the unique identity of each participant, and the value of each person's intellectual inquiries, emotional responses, and personal history.[1] Next, it presumes that facilitators must be intentional about organizing the process; it doesn't happen automatically. Third, the classroom is not the only, and sometimes not even the most important, location where encounters about shared reading should happen. Community Reading deliberately extends the literary experience *out from* the classroom. Fourth, it naturally presumes solitary reading by each participant, and a return to that solitary reading at the end of the process. Lastly, creating a Community Reading process requires a "rigorous methodology" (Freire, 36) that, if followed, enables a class to explore more fully the depths of literary ideas, the intricacies of philosophical concepts, the scope of the novel, the nuances of a poem, a truth of humanity. This process for literary explorations can enrich reading environments outside the academy, certainly including book clubs. My essay explores the implementation and benefits of approaching literature through this method, with *Disgrace* and five other works by J. M. Coetzee serving as my case in point. While I anchor my presentation in the workings of a single Coetzee seminar, the methods can easily be exported to classrooms at significantly different institutions, and even to lecture-based courses. Finally, I hope to achieve more than the standard "Here's what we do at our school" presentation familiar to education and interdisciplinary conference attendees.

I. The Start of a Community: Building the Class

The teaching of *Disgrace* in the fall of 2006 began well before the start of that term. The main motivation for the seminar arose from the project that created this volume of essays. Since Bill McDonald, fifteen Johnston alumni, and five Redlands faculty planned on writing a collection of essays on narrative ethics, pedagogy, and "unsolitary reading" in Coetzee's 1999 novel, implementing Community Reading pedagogy into the course became an obvious complement to our project. Bill invited me to be the co-teacher.

Unlike most institutions where a faculty member, a department, or even a curriculum committee design courses, we invited the pre-registered students to meet with us in the spring of 2006 to plan the seminar. We came with just two "non-negotiable" items. We wanted to read *Disgrace* at the beginning and again at the end of the seminar, the second reading to be framed by the other Coetzee novels we chose to read, and we wanted to use Community Reading methods to learn together.

It took our fledgling group about two hours to develop the outline of our syllabus. We decided to read five of Coetzee's other novels in chronological order: *In the Heart of the Country, Waiting for the Barbarians, The Life & Times of Michael K, The Master of Petersburg,* and *Elizabeth Costello.* The participants also wanted to read articles about recent South African history, some pieces on narrative ethics, and selections from interviews with Coetzee published in *Doubling the Point.* So from the beginning, students felt shared ownership of "our" course: a crucial foundation block of Community Reading. And this wasn't the end of the negotiations: After the fall term began, the full class voted to substitute *Foe* for *The Master of Petersburg*, largely because several students wanted to explore the novel's intertextual connections with *Robinson Crusoe* as their seminar project. It proved to be a valuable change.

These plans drew several more students into the seminar, as well as three professors — Kathy Ogren and Julie Townsend from Johnston and alumna Nancy Best from California State University, San Bernardino — who joined the seminar as "students" and who participated actively along with our fifteen undergraduates (see Ogren and Best, below). With a collectively negotiated syllabus in hand, with students who felt full ownership of the course, and with the unusual bonus of three additional professionally trained readers, we felt confident about our foundation.

II. Agenda Building

The first part of our "rigorous methodology" consisted of committing to a "discussion agenda" developed anew at each meeting by the entire class, a method promoting "anti-racist, democratic diversity" (Kivel 2004). The shared agenda directly supports each student's autonomy and interconnectedness. To launch Community Reading for our seminar, we asked the students to read the first half of *Disgrace* prior to our initial class and to prepare two or three items from the reading to talk through with the seminar. Taken together, these embody the interests and passions of every class member; they are in effect condensed stories of how everyone experienced a particular novel. These items typically include standard subjects for literature seminars — literary motifs, character development and comparisons, ethical questions provoked by the text, close readings of specific passages, and so forth. That gets us started. Then, in these early meetings, we elaborate the qualities that make successful agenda building central to Community Reading.

Guidelines

Here are the main points, points that should be adapted easily to courses in other fields:

- Agenda building is a community activity, a chorus with individual parts not a sequence of solos. First, thoughtful preparation is central. Occasionally an "off the top" item will help everyone, but typically only after the ground has been well prepared. This means detailing for students what constitutes "thoughtful preparation," and relying on upper division students — and, in our lucky situation, five faculty members — to model that behavior for their less experienced classmates.
- "Thoughtful preparation" includes several things beyond just thinking carefully about the reading.

- Framing as specific a question as possible about a subject. "Time, Nature, and Destiny in Archaic Greece" probably won't help. Students quickly realized that such Big Topics actually made it harder for them to actively participate.
- Not just giving a character's name, but offering a few sentences that clarify a student's idea or difficulty with this character.
- Having specific passages, with their page numbers, at the ready.
- Framing a topic in a way that's likely to interest peers, and if at all possible, connecting new topics to ones discussed in earlier class periods. We urge everyone, certainly including ourselves, to think about the kinds of questions and ideas that have sparked discussion in the past, and to use them as models.
- Next, we ask students to distinguish between their "information items" — factual questions about references, for example — and their more substantive questions and ideas. We usually devote the first few minutes of our discussions to answering information questions, drawing on the knowledge of class members as well as our own.
- The next step may seem obvious, but it usually takes new students a while to take it seriously: we ask participants to raise only issues/questions that they care about, at least to some degree (anything from "I was just curious" to "really intriguing" to "this question may change my life"). We explicitly tell students — and remind ourselves — not to pose a clever question that doesn't really interest them. Rightly used, agenda building fosters honesty and full personal presence in the classroom, and helps to break down any lingering cynical student attitudes about playing roles to please, tricking teachers, "beating the system," and other holdovers from adolescence. This is one way that Community Reading breaks down the traditional difficulties of the boring, the detached, or the competitive classroom.
- An important corollary: we urge students, especially beginners, not to be afraid to appear "dumb," guaranteeing them that several of their classmates have the same "obvious" question in mind. This helps shift the emphasis from "What do you know?" to "What do you think?"
- Argumentative and/or persuasive items are welcome. An item may entail a more detailed statement from its proponent after the entire agenda has been built. But students should also feel free and confident enough to pose intuitions and hunches. We also encourage "process items," students reflecting on how their ways of reading have changed over the course as a way into a particular issue in a novel.
- Agenda building, like the discussion that follows from it, is not a scene of show-off performances or competitive one-upmanship.
- We write shorthand versions of each item on the board, and urge students to look for connections with ideas they have yet to pose, and also for fresh connections between items already posted. We may, with the

speaker's permission, shape the item a little to include subjects important to us about the reading. In other words, we ask students to cut us a little slack in formulating the agenda, and we honor their trust by not converting their ideas into simulacra of our own. Faculty members always have agenda items of their own, but their value and status are earned, not assumed.
- We urge classmates to learn from previous agendas: what worked and what didn't.
- We urge them to keep a record of each day's agenda: it's great for review, and for keeping the course current.
- We ask that each person bring at least two discussion items to each class, with the understanding that they may not all be discussed. An agenda offers a set of opportunities, not obligations; students whose topics we can't take up in one class often recast them for later discussions. As co-learners, willingly postponing, and even sometimes abandoning, topics, helps avoid purely personal interests from dominating a class discussion. One day a student's passions may linger on the fringe of a classroom, and focus a full discussion on the next. A powerful educational empathy grows out of the agenda-building process, when rightly done; humility, or its more social cousin, modesty, blossoms when students learn to put aside their own topics and devote themselves to those of others. Following this path, students learn to read through the eyes of their peers, to imagine other ways of encountering texts, and to complement their solitary preparation with communal interpretation.
- Finally, we urge students to develop discussion items together before class (more on this below). Agenda building prompts students to prepare for a class more thoughtfully than they otherwise might. As students feel the need for honesty and clarity so that others will take them seriously as Community Reading teachers and participants, they usually start listening more intently to the reading stories of others.

It's instructive to compare this kind of classroom organization to David Lurie's practice in *Disgrace*. In Lurie's "Romantic Poets" course, his students play "guess what teacher's thinking" or avoid responding to him at all. In the novel David Lurie had to bring what little remained of his passion for Byron and Wordsworth into the center of the classroom, already convinced that none of his students would bring anything to the discussion or share his feelings. At best he hoped to teach them what to admire; more likely, he taught them not to care much for poetry.

Facilitation

What have faculty who use agenda building given up? Control — or rather the kind of control that comes with knowing just what will be said in each class, and in what order. Faculty must be adaptable, alert, empathetic, tuned to hear the question behind the question, and ready to help students build connections between their ideas. It's hard, unpredictable, humbling, and inexhaustibly stimulating. Faculty authority resides in the quality of their ideas and the cooperative effort they help bring about among all the participants, not in their official position or in a well-scripted presentation of their own way of reading. Reading becomes a common project, not a virtuoso aria.

Can you build a lecture around an agenda? Of course, as long as you're willing to give up a canned talk for offering responses to the subjects of the day. Community Reading classes often contain "mini-lectures," presentations of background or elaboration that everyone, not just the faculty members, agrees would help things along. Most of these are given by the faculty, but sometimes students have invaluable background that the teacher can, gratefully, turn to. In these ways Community Reading works the pedagogical space between formal lecture and uncensored discussion. These intermediate spaces of mini-lectures, riffs from a student on their agenda topic, breakout-group discussions, free writes, or outside knowledge and experience presented by any seminar participant, enrich the central Community Reading commitment to discussion.

Now for a few examples from the Coetzee seminar. During our reading of *The Life & Times of Michael K*, a student brought in her first-hand knowledge of the human rights struggles in many countries in Southern Africa. Her honesty and her well-anchored accounts made it easier for other students to discuss charged issues of race, human rights, and social justice in the context of Michael K's escape and isolation. During our reading of *Foe* the *Robinson Crusoe* sub-group brought in a set of agenda items concerning intertextuality, and educated their peers in a way that also enriched our understanding of the intertextual play between Coetzee's fictions themselves. These led the class to pursue ideas of narrative authority, control of storytelling, theoretical issues concerning intertexts, and oppression of under-represented characters. A highlight of the semester came during our second reading of *Disgrace*, with one student's richly prepared close reading of the passage in which David Lurie loads the corpses of the dogs into the truck for delivery to the incinerator. This launched an energetic and lengthy conversation about "disgrace" as an ethical concept, animal rights, and the plight of David's search for meaning that was conducted almost entirely among the students themselves.

We also insist that we finish building our agenda before launching into any of its topics, and an event from our first meeting dramatizes the reason. A student briefly described his perspective on the violent but off-stage rape scene in the middle of *Disgrace*. He observed that, in his reading, the three men who came to rob and rape the Luries did so out of hatred for the white people still living on the frontier. This student saw the rural eastern Cape as a frontier, a place where racial contention was likely to be more open and violent. After students shared a few more agenda items, one of our other quieter students offered the provocative idea that the fate of South Africa was being decided on the bodies of women. She then developed a parallel to David and Melanie's relationship, observing that Melanie's body served as another decisive location of rape. Predictably, a tense debate then erupted over whether or not David raped Melanie, and if these scenes were a pertinent example for this topic about South Africa's fate. We quickly suspended the conversation, asking to finish the agenda building before jumping into discussion. Intuitively, this seems unnatural, since facilitators always want to encourage such passionate discussion. Yet by waiting until all students share their agenda items, new connections might appear (as this one had), helping to build a better framework for the forthcoming conversation. Had we begun conversation after the first person's agenda item, the quieter student's idea might not have worked in so nicely. Such mini-conversations do make ideal fodder for later dialogue. In this instance, when we returned to the topic a few minutes later, the passions remained high while the group's grasp of these tough issues seemed more assured: conscious and half-conscious reflection had deepened our perspectives. We helped this along by reorganizing the two topics into one agenda item — "Rape in the New S.A. Frontier," delineating the specific instances of power, dominance, and women's rights — something we had not immediately thought of; the small delay helped us as well.

So the facilitator must remain alert to new connections and possibilities suggested by agenda items while drawing the more obvious and necessary connections on the agenda. This always entails honoring (not manipulating) what each student says. We commonly asked, as we did on this particular night, "Is that rephrasing okay?" If the answer is no, then we ask the student to rephrase our rephrasing until we're both satisfied.

Preparation

The traditional classroom can lose many students in the space before the actual class begins. If students first need to understand their role as an active citizen during *and* before class sessions, then Community Reading facilitators initially need to motivate them. We must help students see the need for — and the delights of — preparation time prior to the classroom interactions; this seems obvious to faculty, but not always to students, especially those fresh from high school "busywork." Professors and experienced students must dramatize that solitary reading has two goals: the enrichment of the individual and also of the community.

If a particular agenda-building session goes poorly, facilitators should draw attention to the difficulty of carrying on a class conversation when students bring very few well-thought-out topics. Occasionally we encounter a further misstep in preparation: some students so value their interactions with their peers and, yes, even their professors, that they slight pre-class preparation. They unself-consciously believe that the feelings the class generates in them are the main thing, and that their enthusiasm and talkativeness are enough. Here the facilitators must help students interweave their feelings and ideas, things that they too frequently keep well separated.

Community Reading does not let facilitators off the hook; they too must prepare their own topics for the agenda. Devoting a good deal of time to developing sharper, more discussion-stimulating topics makes it easier for faculty to help students with their own topics. (As team teachers, we had the extra advantage of polishing our items together in our pre-class planning meeting.) For example, a student might have a glimmer of an idea quite like one we had prepared, and we could help him or her strengthen their idea without simply usurping their material.

III. Class Discussions

In the traditional literature classroom, students may well arrive with anxiety about *performing* their ideas in class (see the essay by Nancy Best). While some students thrive in a competitive environment, other students shy away. Courses founded on the principles of Community Reading encourage students to "practice" their ideas as they might a tennis stroke or dance step, not "perform" them in order to impress an audience of faculty or peers. This does not mean that "anything goes." Community Reading does not allow an immediate, uncritical accepting of any random impression — solitary preparation has been serious and thoughtful — nor does it dish out unmerited compliments, making students "feel good" about whatever idea may cross their mind. Rather the weight falls on working out the implications of a student's idea in concert, and being open to the fresh directions that such work frequently produces. Of course community members disagree, and of course students speak with conviction, but the goal remains to enrich everyone's learning, not to applaud the "winner." This practice furthers students' abilities to become co-learners and, eventually, co-teachers.

As the discussion unfolds the faculty member may point out connections between student ideas, draw attention to slighted topics or previous class conversations, bring in observations from critics and other secondary material, or share reading experiences of her own. When it happens, I openly confess that, like many students, I too struggled with a particular concept. For instance, consider these topics that we returned to several times: "What are the ethical implications of our narrative absence from Lucy's rape? Why does Coetzee keep that event from us, while detailing David's assault on Melanie?" Again, "does a male, whether her father, the author, the instructor of a course on the novel, or the reader, have a diminished authority in discussing Lucy's responses to her rape story?" When a facilitator humbly shares his own struggles, students feel more ready to share their reading insecurities. That openness encourages communal work, which often results in a quicker breakthrough to new levels of understanding.

Another common problem in seminar learning: a participant puts forward an idea that slights that of a fellow learner, or unintentionally offends another's feelings. In one class, for example, students disagreed sharply about the narrator of *Disgrace*. One saw the narrator as manipulative, and condemned an earlier speaker for "buying in" to the narrator's "deception" during David Lurie's hearing. As opposed to turning this difference of opinion into a debate between the two students to see who could better defend their point while others just watched, we inaugurated a conversation with the entire class. Everyone dived into the text for a closer read of the narrator in that section. Communally, we exposed intricate layers of characterization, narrative distance, and ethical discourse that affected our take on the narrator.

Further, co-learners in a reading community can speak directly and immediately with each other about those missteps; they know that seminars are for practice, and understand the pedagogy as well as the official facilitators. Our purpose is not to silence controversy but to make the controversy part of everyone's thinking. So potential rough spots such as these, if approached with modesty rather than impatience or a silencing authority, may be turned to advantage by illuminating the complexities of reading and our reading experiences. By reframing these encounters, students can more easily come to the aid of one another, enabling class participants to reach new levels of meaning collectively and individually. Such well-facilitated rough spots will assist the Community Reading later in the semester as even tougher textual ideas appear, and as reading conversations grow increasingly complex as our knowledge of the course material, here Coetzee's dense fictions, deepen.

Despite the ongoing, successful work of collective agenda building, discussions that promote communal struggle, active facilitation, and solid pre-class preparation, we have not done enough for our students' learning. For Community Reading to reach its full potential, we need to add another layer to this already dynamic pedagogy. Community Reading needs to disrupt the standard story that students' education resides entirely in their preparation and class participation.

IV. Building Community Reading Outside of the Classroom

Even though facilitators necessarily focus on classroom discussion, faculty should not miss the pedagogical opportunities outside of the classroom. In this regard, we see the classroom conversation as an apex: the point to *expand toward,* and therefore the point to *expand from* as well. Encounter outside of the classroom will occur in an array of venues and at varying times of day: during walks to and from a class, the porches of dorms, planned reading groups, passionate late-night discussions. These events do not occur without asking students intentionally to co-create such encounters with faculty. Just as students must become active citizens in their preparation, students ideally also become active citizens of the reading community by carrying the topics from the course beyond the confines of the classroom.

Understanding One Another

When something happens in the daily lives of participants, or students engage with one another's lives outside of the class, it affects the dynamics of a course. Walking to class, office-hour conversations with one or a small group of students, and other in-between spaces, provide crucial moments for co-learners to fall into sync with one another. Sometimes informal conversations — a student might express how a difficulty in another part of her life shaped her encounter with Martha *In the Heart of the Country* — gives invaluable context for the next class meeting. Like the intimacy of a close read, participants in Community Reading are more likely to recognize, and value, the emotions and nuanced reading circumstances each member bring into the class.

Practice in Passing

Casual encounters do the same, at least on a smaller campus; any effort to interweave class time with the rest of a student's life contributes to Community Reading's goals. As I encounter one of our students reading on the lawn or in the dorm lobby, I might ask to see his copy of *Disgrace* that he's re-reading. Flipping to one of my favorite paragraphs in the novel, I might read it out loud and praise it, pointing out a favorite detail or two, actively exciting him about posing the passage for a full seminar close reading in the next class. And of course the opposite exchange happens just as regularly. I'll be hurrying to a meeting, and a student will stop me to ask, "What motivates the magistrate's feelings for the "barbarian" woman in *Waiting for the Barbarians?*"

As the semester moves along, and as the overall seminar agenda becomes all-too-grand to finish during one period, *passing conversations* gain momentum in the reading community. In 2006 I was the Johnston Center Area Director and lived in one of the dormitories. Community readers, often late at night, feel less inhibited, and share more open conversation concerning the most difficult parts of the Coetzee novel before them. The torture of the magistrate in *Waiting for the Barbarians*, which reminds us of the violent events common to several of our novels, stands as a good example for those topics that can stall students in the regular classroom. Despite the concerted effort to encourage the practicing of ideas, students still sometimes restrain themselves or overcompensate for the inevitable silences in class; some topics seem too wrenching, or old habits of showing off for everyone die hard. So, in these meandering and enthusiastic informal conversations, uninhibited by the norms of even the most student-centered classroom, readers feel freer to tackle dark subjects or experiment with half-formed intuitions. Students sometimes knowingly throw initially incoherent topics and thoughts into the late-night conversation. One student who was simultaneously enrolled in a course on Nietzsche hesitantly compared the protagonists of *In the Heart of the Country* to the philosophical character of Zarathustra. Such topics get worked out over time. Ultimately, this reinforces the commitment to practice, the necessity of trying out even scary or far-out ideas publicly. As these sessions continue over a term, students fall into sharper step with one another. The ethos of the classroom thus stretches beyond the pale of the traditional learning environment, flowing into the hallways, into other academic inquiries, into conversations over dinner, even into weekend parties. The more students grow aware of the ways in which Community Reading assists their reading and their peers' reading, the more inclination they have to promote out-of-class encounters. Students in our seminar on Coetzee seemed particularly consumed by the benefits of Community Reading. This captivation identified these students to other members of the greater Johnston Center Community; our students became known as those "taking that monster course." They were participating in something bigger than themselves, and it showed; the ideas before them were not theirs alone, but part of a communal act arising from the communal read.

    As the semester unfolded, students stopped us more regularly, full of questions or ideas. They reexamined examples brought up by teachers and fellow students during class, while refining their own insights. More frequently, students gathered on their dorm's porch, or in one student's room, or in the library, not just to carry on the "banter" of informal reading groups but to work collaboratively through a knotty passage, or often just to read. I regularly saw people choosing sections to read aloud from one of our novels while relaxing on a couch in the dorm lobby. Each member in this partnership had a pen in hand so that they might stop reading out loud to write margin notes and underline passages together; even moments of solitary reading became communal by the end of the semester. And this pre-class preparation in community always spurred stronger, more coherent class conversations. Students soon gained the ability to push their ideas in class to new levels, and sometimes these students would even take over the facilitation of the discussion. Community Reading pushes a return to the classroom, not allowing ideas to just settle or fade into the hallways late at night. Knowing that agendas await the readers in the classroom, out-of-class encounters intentionally return to more formal class discussions.

Even Beyond Our Seminar

When students recognize their ability to co-create Community Reading, such interactions, questions, and responses happen not just between faculty and students, and between students and their peers in the reading community, but even between students and their friends *not* in the seminar. One evening, I witnessed three students talking about *Disgrace* as if all three were enrolled in the course, when only one was actually in our seminar. An inter-course dialogue about death and narrative ethics (prompted by David Lurie's attempted composition) unfolded, resulting in oral readings and comparisons to several seemingly unrelated novels. Nor was this confined to students; two faculty colleagues who decided to read *Disgrace* on the strength of our recommendation stopped us one afternoon with plenty of things to say about the novel. In this way the Coetzee seminar seeded conversations that touched people who never took the course.

Organized Reading Groups

Along with these informal gatherings, banter sessions, and partnerships are those reading groups officially facilitated by a student, or a teacher, of the course. These reading groups function as a hybrid between the more structured environment of the classroom, and the literary playfulness of dorm life. Much more like a book club, the Coetzee seminar students — though rarely all of them at once — gathered for a voluntary but scheduled weekly time in which they took up topics left over from the previous class agenda. Students also used these gatherings to rehearse ideas about the reading assigned for the next class period, developing an ad hoc agenda mingling old and new topics. Here it was easier to pose half-formed questions, or publicly struggle with an idea. Organized reading groups remove a level of anxiety that seems all but impossible to eliminate in the classroom. The most exciting moment arrives when the Community Reading cycle completes itself: members of the *Disgrace* Reading Group brought ideas into the following class period that they partially worked out in that week's session. Buoyed by the small group's thoughtful enthusiasm for the subject, the entire class could more readily invest in the topic. Everyone could then work out the question, idea, or puzzling passage together. In effect, these ideas came to the agenda communally.

Clearly, we enjoy these benefits of Community Reading partly because the physical space and the small size of the Johnston Center allow for such interactions. Without this physical space and set of traditions, we do not see Community Reading as doomed, but we recognize it to be an even greater challenge. Students and professors need that much more intentionality about creating encounters outside of the classroom, even at the risk of these encounters becoming more formal in nature (more frequently planned reading groups, weekly lunches in the cafeteria, an additional close-reading session in the student union, or an institutional push for more living-learning communities and co-curricular residential life structures). By building off the Community Reading ideas and values presented for classroom pedagogies, faculty can creatively adjust out-of-class encounters for individual institutions.

V. Limitations

This introductory look at Community Reading does not claim that such a pedagogical approach automatically produces utopian classrooms. Silences still ensue; people feel overmatched by some ideas or literary experiences, and fall into cognitive struggles that nearly shut them down. The community discourse can move so rapidly that younger readers may feel unable to synthesize all the ideas and new knowledge. A few students who don't, can't, or won't engage in the process get left out of the communal exploration and end up losing the opportunity to learn.

The Community Reading pedagogy clearly works best with certain types of learning styles. For those who resist, it pushes them in academic and intellectual ways that they may not eagerly embrace. The method can also leave some students feeling abandoned, lonely, and distraught when the course finishes. Students feel haunted when forced to return to solitary reading; they dearly miss their classmates and the reading community that motivated their intellectual growth. One woman missed our camaraderie enough to organize an afternoon "Coetzee reunion" three months later, an event that many other class members enthusiastically attended. That healed our loneliness for a short while, but it could only interrupt our ongoing struggle against reading in solitude.

Most disturbing for me as a facilitator of Community Reading in our seminar was the realization of the gaps that our agenda-building, class conversations, and out-of-class encounters allowed. One in particular sticks with me, and I will forever question why such a hole refused to be filled. Over the course of the semester, we found it very hard to dive deep into discussions of apartheid, and the ensuing consequences of living in a world where such brutality was possible. Though some conversations on these issues became easier as we read *Foe* and *Waiting for the Barbarians*, the class simply did not reach the levels of understanding and meaning that I had hoped for. Even students in the course who had studied in Africa, and who actively engaged with these issues in their co-curricular studies, could not turn their experiences into a sustained discussion. I believe that we have an ethical responsibility as educators, especially in self-proclaimed anti-racist, democratically diverse classrooms, to push these topics to their limits. Why did it not happen? Was it poor facilitation on our part? Should we have been more dictatorial in carrying out some agendas? Did we not set high enough standards about completing all of the reading of secondary assignments? Do Coetzee novels, especially *Disgrace*, push us away from these topics, or make us fight harder to get into them? Did we fail to build a context for our millennium-generation students that would promote a richer understanding about these issues? All of these factors played a part, and yet none of them excuses us from not meeting our portion of the responsibility. Simultaneously, I know that sometimes facilitators cannot control the entire outcome of a class. On our second night on *Disgrace*, I shared the following passage from *Crime and Policing in Post-Apartheid South Africa: Transforming under Fire*:

> On Saturday night 13 June 1998 four young African men from Alexandra township broke into a house in a neighboring suburb. The young men, who had been drinking heavily, found a white suburban family, the parents and two young children, sitting down to dinner. Armed with handguns, they shot both parents dead, and raped the daughter while the son cowered in the bathroom. The attackers left in the family car and were arrested later that night when the vehicle was spotted outside a nightclub in central Johannesburg. The accused have been linked through fingerprint records to a number of other serious cases in the same area over a five-year period.
> The incident had an immediate and sharp response. (Shaw, 42)

Though the class listened to the passage and responded with a collective sigh, the reading and the questions I posed after the reading did not generate any conversation of significance. How can a non-fiction passage this similar to the violent scene in the middle of *Disgrace* not produce a response? We asked that question openly, not blaming the students, but instead recognizing the complexities of teaching and the unforeseen outcomes of class dynamics. Just by the nature of Community Reading, continuing to pursue this inquiry shall remain at the forefront of my thinking about that course.

VI. Conclusion: The Haunting

As we have seen, the Community Reading cycle necessarily, and obviously, begins with the reader's individual contemplation of the text. That reader then enters the public world and reading relationships, which provide arenas of dialogue and interactive contemplation. The early stages of these interactions take place informally, outside of the classroom, where the reader feels less inhibited than in the more formal setting of the classroom. To gain even more value from classroom conversations, these informal moments should happen as frequently as possible, both before and after class. The reading community that forms behind a literary seminar gives a course and its students valuable depth and excitement.

From there the reader travels into the classroom: the breathing, living space with almost endless possibility kept organized by a savvy and experienced facilitator. Over an entire semester of Community Reading, class dynamics evolve so that by the last session, if not before, the class reaches an almost meditative ability to interact with one another. Of course the process is not perfect, or even near it; there remain awkward moments of silence, strange disconnects in conversations, and agenda items which never fully come to life. But it offers the best opportunities that we know for honoring the voices of each member, and for making class discussion both rigorous and exciting.

When the seminar comes to a close, and this particular Community Reading reaches its conclusion, we are cast back to the haunting experience of solitary reading. Haunting, in this context, is not a fit of fear, but a memory that triggers an emotion. This emotion reminds us of the Community Reading experience: visions of classroom conversations, the humble attempts to grasp complex concepts, the dedication needed to build a literary community, the completion of tough books, tragic moments and crisp prose from texts, and innumerable other intellectually and emotionally beneficial memories. This haunting evokes the influential, affecting experiences that permeate into our future academic pursuits. We need this haunting to sustain our journey beyond the Community Reading experience, into new courses and finally, into the world beyond college. The haunting meaningfully shadows our contemplations and readings in solitude, our integrative intellectual inquiries, and our struggles to understand the collective humanity in which we all participate.

Notes

[1] In this essay, the terms "citizen," "member," and "participant" interchangeably signify a particular type of student involvement that Community Reading invokes.

12. Out of the Father's House into a Community of Readers

Kathy Ogren

> He has long ceased to be surprised at the range of ignorance of his students. Post-Christian, posthistorical, postliterate, they might as well have been hatched from eggs yesterday. So he does not expect them to know about fallen angels or where Byron might have read of them. What he does expect is a round of goodnatured guesses which, with luck, he can guide toward the mark.
> — Professor David Lurie, *Disgrace*

WHEN I JOINED THE FALL 2006 COETZEE SEMINAR taught by recent Johnston Center graduate Matthew Gray and our editor, Bill McDonald, I was self-conscious about my status as a historian with over twenty years of experience in the classroom. I feared that students would expect me to read as an "expert," yet like them I was a newcomer to J. M. Coetzee, his work, and South African fiction generally. At first I planned to compensate by relying on my disciplinary expertise, including some knowledge of comparative South African and North American history, and by developing an essay on a long-contemplated theme — "fathers and daughters" — for this collection. But when the seminar started, I found little inspiration to be a "visiting expert" because I felt as newly hatched as the students. So I decided to follow that feeling, viewing the course largely as a beginner as well as a veteran. It proved to be an eye-opening choice in several ways. For example, when I expressed my ignorance or ambivalence or frustration with Coetzee, it seemed to make it easier for my younger classmates to do the same. It allowed me to empathize with the fears that most undergraduates bring to a challenging class. In discussions, I listened to my fellow students even more attentively, and easily learned as much from the students as (I hope) I offered to them. At the same time I used my veteran reader's eye and ear to track the shifting dynamics of our discussions, timing my contributions accordingly: a little pedagogy from the back row, as it were. I hold an endowed chair in teaching at Redlands, and found that this experience enriched my understanding of our craft in many useful ways. It's an experience I strongly recommend to every faculty member, especially full professors. I urge all readers, as you follow this senior faculty member's eye-opening return to the classroom, to also keep your eyes peeled for useful teaching ideas that this seminar's process conveys.

We students considered our class a "reading community" from the beginning, thus distinguishing it from a typical class led by a single faculty member. In addition to our official mentors, two other professors, Julie Townsend from the Johnston Center and Nancy Best from Cal State San Bernardino, joined the group. We three women student-faculty members sat at one end of interlinked tables, with some fifteen enrolled students seated to our right and left. Physically we were at the farthest distance from the front of the room, and this helped us to play less obvious, though very important, roles in the formation of this academic community.

The Johnston Center's egalitarian living-learning community also made it easier for me to see the course through undergraduate eyes. It features faculty offices in the residence halls, collective development of curriculum, and joint participation in many activities and programs. We are likely to know our students as multi-dimensional younger colleagues rather than as hatchlings wobbling around in our shadows. We knew many of our students well; we advised some on a regular basis, while others took classes with us at the same time as we all studied *Disgrace* together. Benefiting from the interpersonal relationships that our intimacy engenders, we assume common academic pursuits will develop every year, and we can more easily see a course's dynamics as they do. As our community gathered each week, the boundaries between faculty and students, excited and perplexed readers, younger and older people blurred. At the same time we also read apart from one another. The students met outside of class in informal subgroups. We five "teachers" met every Monday night after class, cooking for each other as we reflected on the evening's class. It was certainly far different from David Lurie's fictional classroom, in which he expressed little personal or intellectual connection with his pupils (apart from Melanie, of course).

I faced yet another problem: not only did I not know much about Coetzee's work, the most important text — *Disgrace* — didn't much appeal to me after the first read. My initial ambivalence about *Disgrace* — a reaction shared by at least some of the students and many members of our "unsolitary readers" alumni group — ultimately signaled possibilities. Critic Regina Janes's judgment also resonated with my reading: "One does not, of course 'like' Coetzee. Oily smooth, prickly, repellant, the prose presses, probes, and lets drop the conditions it touches."[1] Yet, as we read other Coetzee novels together, *Disgrace* rebounded in my estimation. Connections to the pastoral emerged. *In the Heart of the Country* proved particularly compelling because of its unusual narration by a daughter located on an earlier South African frontier. In that discussion, we considered how Magda's telling of her father's story could be juxtaposed with

Lurie's attempts to tell Lucy's story in *Disgrace*. Our unusual classroom configuration, certainly an attempt to reject the patriarchal model of authoritarian education, provided an analogy to Madga and Lucy's stories; we had all left the father's house. We could be viewed as pioneers on a frontier, boundary crossers who entered a liminal zone between the known world of conventional pedagogy and the unknown destination of our unusual seminar.

Our pedagogic practices aimed to honor all voices and resist any singular authority, which made it easier for me to participate without worrying about my expertise. None of us longed for the kind of hierarchical power that Davie Lurie lost; we did not seek to be "in charge" of this class, merely guiding students to hit "the mark" (and since Johnston Center students receive narrative evaluations, not grades, the "mark" is especially out of place.) We collectively generated questions, observations, themes, and close readings for each class session. I still looked for opportunities to analyze fathers, daughters, and frontiers — my original mission — but I also learned new material, just like an eager student reading Coetzee for the first time. On a number of occasions I was able to help a regular student sharpen her question or idea because I, too, had struggled with the same "beginner's" issue. I gained even more sympathy for the difficulties students face in a fast-moving course, and for the assumptions that faculty too easily make about what their charges know, or have understood. I put these insights to use in virtually every class, and discussed student anxieties and faculty blind spots with my colleagues at our after-class suppers.

Disgrace also made my growth as a student-faculty member possible in another way, since it prompted a reconsideration of the pastoral as genre that has long been important to my scholarly work. As Rita Barnard notes, in her analysis of Coetzee's critical appropriation of the South African *plaasroman*, *Disgrace* is "half academic novel and half anti-pastoral."[2] These two worlds need not be read as static opposites. As Raymond Williams points out, in the idealized "classical pastoral . . . there is almost invariably a tension with other kinds of experience; summer with winter; pleasure with loss; harvest with labour; singing with a journey; past or future with the present."[3] David Lurie embodies this tension as he transits back and forth between the city (with its universities) and the country (with its presumed refuge from the shame of the city). Alternating settings in *Disgrace* led me to imagine a future reading community focused on *Disgrace* and Wallace Stegner's *Angle of Repose*. In both novels, pastoral or anti-pastoral representations are gendered, as fathers, daughters, grandsons, wives, and mothers narrate an unstable historical and personal legacy of the once-alluring frontier of opportunity. Perhaps, I speculated, I could teach "Mothers and Daughters: Re-visioning the Post-Colonial Frontier."

Not a Nest of Vipers

> We put our children in the hands of you people because we think we can trust you. If we can't trust the university, who can we trust? We never thought we were sending our daughter into a nest of vipers.
> — Mr. Isaacs, Melanie's Father in *Disgrace*

> From class we can see how a few lines can be interpreted one way by David Lurie, another by a literature professor, another by a first year student . . . Coetzee has a talent for simplicity so complex it drives you crazy . . . Maybe that is the point, making the reader aware of the process of reading.
> — Junior Monica Barra, Coetzee Seminar, Johnston Center, Fall 2006

Should Johnston students negotiate "Mothers and Daughters" with me in the future, we would build on thematic and pedagogic successes of the Coetzee class. Chief among these, for me, was our achievement as a community of equal readers described by Monica Barra in my epigraph. Agendas created at the beginning of class document our process (see Matt Gray's essay for a detailed account of this method). On the surface, an agenda appears merely as a list of topics to discuss, close reads to consider. But it is much more than that. When students suggest topics, the agenda builder can point to connections between ideas and encourage elaboration. She can explicitly ask for cross-textual themes, which brings the previous seminar work into the discussion. Asking for page references helps us all learn to ground our ideas in the text at hand. Everyone can contribute, taking away from the class a set of questions and ideas that we've agreed to consider, even if we cannot get to all of them. The professor is not the sole expert who knows the important things to "read for"; instead we collectively learn from each other's readings. Since any seminar member can propose a starting point, we also see which readings are most relevant for everyone.

We read *Disgrace* at the beginning of the course and reread it at the end. It served as a bookend to the rest of the Coetzee fiction we studied: *In the Heart of the Country, Waiting for the Barbarians, The Life & Times of Michael K, Foe,* and *Elizabeth Costello*. Several seminar preoccupations emerged from these texts. We struggled with how the author's voice related to narrative authority — a problem closely related to my meditation on continuing to teach "outside the father's house." Students honed in on Coetzee's project through their repeated queries about the ethics of "speaking and telling stories for others," the authority of narrators, the role of memory and remembering in the novels, and "absences, gaps, and silences." Classmates put topics related to women, gender, sex, and the body on every agenda. The possibilities of reading as a "bricoleur" appealed to us, and violence, including sexual violence, torture, and spectacle, turned up on agendas for all the novels.

We repeatedly came back to problematic aspects of narrative authority: who can tell another's story; how do language, gender, social and cultural positioning mediate narration; how does free indirect discourse, or allegory, or the other structural and linguistic aspects of Coetzee's craft create a distance or, as several of my peers preferred to put it, a "gap" in the text? When students articulated this "gap," I thought about a different but related distance — the divide between faculty and student knowledge. The divide is real, of course, but it does not automatically show us the royal road to right pedagogy. Many students and teachers assume the instructor unilaterally closes the gap, delivers the material; the students "learn" it and, at the end, are assessed through tests and papers that validate what they've mastered. What gaps did we experience and how well did we challenge the academic hierarchy?

Comparison with David Lurie's sense of displacement gives us one answer to this question. In *Disgrace*'s classroom settings, for example, Melanie's boyfriend Ryan attends class following the end of Melanie's sexual relationship with Lurie and the vandalizing of Lurie's car. The "shamed" professor decides he must "grit his teeth and pay, what else." Lurie says, "'We continue with Byron,' . . . plunging into his notes" (31). He realizes that teaching Byron's poem "Lara" will prove awkward for both himself and Melanie; she sits in class "looking thin and exhausted . . . huddled over her book." Still, Lurie soldiers on, asks the class to "gloss the lines"; he apparently cannot or will not depart from his lessons or his requirements for Melanie or himself. The narrator reflects, "Scandal. A pity that must be his theme, but he is in no state to improvise" (31–32).

Lurie cannot improvise because he cannot let go of what is left of his professorial (and male) authority. He recognizes that the attack on his car "was evidently not enough." He continues: "Evidently there are more instalments to come. What can he do?" (31) This resignation anticipates his daughter Lucy's sense of a debt to be paid through violence later in the novel. But in the educational system he is not yet defeated; he still has power over Melanie. Indeed, he will insist that she "give more time" to her work, and "attend to class more regularly." He speculates about her state of mind: "*You have cut me off from everyone,* she seems to want to say. *You have made me bear your secret. I am no longer just a student*" (34). Although the notion of possession is complicated by their sexual trysts, Lurie embodies a patriarchal norm here, one in which students "belong" to the professor. Learning is not a collaborative enterprise. For me, as reader-student-professor in the Coetzee seminar, the real scandal is that Lurie was "never in a state" to reshape his lesson plan in the face of extraordinary personal and pedagogical circumstances.

Our Johnston seminar ideals differ from Lurie's, and the Coetzee seminar helped us refine those differences. We destabilized the binary authority suggested by a gap between teachers with all the knowledge that "counts" and students who must absorb professorial wisdom, a model that dictates much college instruction. Instead we created common readings together that encouraged students to become authorities, and, as is our practice in the Johnston Center, each negotiated a contract detailing individualized goals and specific plans for achieving them.

Johnston contracts may sound idiosyncratic, but our work with students to create collaborative learning can be used in a wide range of teaching environments. Indeed, our anthology itself provides a storehouse of useful information for teaching, and can be put to use in any classroom. The first section models many valuable skills: theoretical and thematic insights and argument; close reading; literature searches; appropriately contextualized references; even correctly formatted footnotes. Just as important, they also model academic criticism written with passion as well as ideas, a counterforce to many students' claim that criticism is "all in the head" and without feeling. Both undergraduate and graduate students seek examples like these to help them see how to participate in this broader community — a crucial yet difficult skill to learn. In this essay specifically, I offer examples of writing prompts that helped students integrate and synthesize readings of *Disgrace* with theoretical concepts about intertext and ethics. Their varied responses demonstrate that our learning goals for developing confident and competent literary analysis proved successful; additionally, we can see exciting new directions through which the text might be taught and learned.

We could not use this anthology in the Coetzee seminar of course, but the written and oral work that students brought to the conclusion of the semester at our end-of-term soirée can help us understand the cumulative synthesis of student learning. Professor Julie Townsend and I resumed our positions as faculty leaders that evening, facilitating a final discussion based on answers to several written questions distributed prior to class. Admittedly, we exercised some matriarchal authority — we did not negotiate the questions with students ahead of time — but both questions had frequently shaped our conversations, and thus honored collective knowledge. First, we asked, "What is a major preoccupation or theme for the author Coetzee and how many ways was it figured in the texts?" For the second: "After reviewing *Disgrace* and all the Coetzee novels we've read, which character offers the most engaging ethics? Which one the most disturbing?"

Students presented few pat plot summaries or simplistic answers. Instead, they offered sophisticated questions about the ethics of narration, practiced intertextual reading, and gave every indication that these hermeneutic practices would be carried into future classes. Classmates continued to think out loud on paper, searching to understand connections between the other novels and *Disgrace*. We did not put *Disgrace* down; we read on.

Our fellow classmates struggled with the ethics of representation and the complexities of authority in academic, narrative, social, and political terms. Gendered representation clearly emerged as a constant theme in the writing and discussion for that evening. We had the last of many heated discussions about David Lurie's pursuit of Melanie. The class divided between those who determined that Lurie was predatory in his sexual relationships and those who defended him. Professor Nancy Best nicely complicated the discussion by relating some "real life" incidences of conduct review inquiries at her college.

In student writing — a writing too frequently absent from essays on teaching and learning — the rereading of *Disgrace* was clearly influenced by gendered representations from Coetzee's other novels. The seminar had made us more sophisticated readers of Coetzee's remarkable narrative range and skill. One reader noted, "Many of the women in Coetzee are so strong, for example, Susan in *Foe*, yet there is still this air in the writing of Coetzee that explains the woman as something quite secretive, such as Lucy in *Disgrace*." Another writer commented on the synergy between David's authority as a professor and as a father: "David often finds himself examining Lucy's life in the context of his role as a parent. After that perspective has been addressed, he constantly switches to what her role is in history — what it all means on a bigger scale. . . . [He has a] respect for literature and for older and finer things [that] is usually trampled on by his students and gets in the way of seductive pursuits. It is as if his whole world is rejecting not only his age, but all that is wrapped within it — his mind, heart and humanity."[4]

On that final night our classmates ably articulated the value of intertextual reading. In particular, they noted the impact of reading and rereading *Disgrace* with other Coetzee novels as context. Consider this analysis of binaries and disruption:

> The presence of rape and sexual transgression in nearly all of the books we've read has disrupted what I originally thought about Coetzee's understanding of what it means for a male author to depict the rape of women. . . . One of my main problems with the trope was that women were not given a space to articulate themselves, which in my opinion diminished their authority. I've come to understand those absences as presences though; I see them, and interpret Coetzee's way of seeing them, as singularly substantive and [I] view Coetzee's habit of eschewing the narration of those spaces as a kind of reverence, as understanding that narrating them would be narrating over, and after a manner, displacing them."[5]

Another student found Coetzee's books "fragmented from each other." With further reflection, she asked, "Is Coetzee trying to educate us on the ethics of reading?"[6] Judging by this response, we succeeded in sustaining a dialogue about reading itself.

And finally, one classmate spoke to the intertextual importance of South African places in the novels, how rereading the "farm" after seeing "the setting of Michael K's journey, the isolated house and farm in Magda's story, and the trip of Susan Barton and Friday to Foe's home," all possess a bit of nostalgia along with the whimsical airs of country life." She was now able to see how the anti-pastoral is also at play in Coetzee. She explicitly credited Magda's "spooky, almost Hitchcock-*Psycho*-esque lens" for a better understanding of *Disgrace.*" Thanks to Magda, this reader, who experienced "blankness" when she initially read Lucy's rape scene, now has a "vision of the day that the three criminals arrived" that carries "tone and meaning." This reflection measures her growth as a reader who can take in the emotionally difficult power of Coetzee's narrations. Interestingly, she is also the only classmate to write about the politics of contemporary South Africa in her thematic summary: "As a reader, am I permitted to even attempt an assertion of Coetzee's views of South Africa[?] . . . I can look at the dialogue and silence between characters or the construction of narratives . . . and still be unsure."[7] This student spoke for many of us as we concluded the seminar; we realized that one reading would not satisfy us as the singular or final "truth" of the novel. The seminar ended but the "readings" are never finished.

Student answers to the second question further underscored the success of our reading community pedagogy. Our inquiry in this case related directly to one of the theoretical frameworks for the class. When we started *Disgrace*, we also read a selection from Geoffrey Galt Harpham's *Shadows of Ethics: Criticism and the Just Society* on the problem of narrative ethics. Harpham takes contemporary critics and theorists to task because they "try to preserve their self-righteousness intact by remaining on the margins, in the uncritiquable position of critique, avoiding the disorder and equivocality that attend worldly agency." He also challenges us to effectively engage as readers of Coetzee's embattled characters: "Genuinely responsible thought entails more than mounting an effective and rigorous critique of something; it means 'imagining the center,' placing oneself in the position, both powerful and vulnerable, of the lawgiver, the policy maker, the judge, the executive."[8] All of the textual choices our students selected as illustrations of "engaging" or "disturbing" ethics addressed this quality of responsibility. Taking those comments together and grouping the novels, we can also see how much our students found an "imagined center" in Coetzee's fiction.

My classmates identified varied examples of complex ethical behavior in Coetzee's characters. *Waiting for the Barbarians* provided obvious examples of moral choices. Colonel Joll "stands out" for one student as an example of the ethics of torture, because "he can't be appeased until the truth he has in mind emerges." The Magistrate proved more challenging to interpret; as one student wrote, he's a "man with a difficult job in a very difficult period of time in Africa, and yet he is still interested in finding the truth — the truth about his life, the truth about the girl, the truth about his job."[9]

Reading several of Coetzee's novels together taught all of us how to appreciate his varied, and masterful, understanding of narrative ethics. *Foe* engaged several writers in the dilemmas of speaking for "the other." One critic, a young woman who aspires to be a writer, found Susan Barton disturbing because "she knows the story she wants to be told is not hers alone, but in her efforts she is only able to tell her version." Another is more generous, seeing in Barton the character who "grants me as a reader the best opportunity to explore the ethics of a character's thoughts, experiences, and encounters . . ."[10] Magda from *In the Heart of the Country* fascinated and repelled students. One woman observed that the "ethics of storytelling" in Coetzee "create a situation in which readers, like the characters in the novels, are fighting with the world around them trying to articulate their voice." Magda offers the "most nuanced ethical standpoint," argued another, because "she is concerned with the substance of other utterances and their significance to her situation as a storyteller and trace-leaver, which is both an admirable and a promising starting point for other questions about narrative responsibility."[11]

One student described the figure of Sultan, the monkey in *Elizabeth Costello*, and then continued: "It is the allegorical burden of each of Coetzee's texts to teach the readers . . . how 'we' have found ourselves in our current state of torture, pain and disarray."[12] Coetzee's complicated and varied narratives helped students imagine not only how a powerful person like the Magistrate might take responsibility for his deeds, but also how they might *themselves* contribute to systems of exploitation and oppression. "How has 'our' thinking contributed to Empire and the rape of young Lucy," another writer asks, "held up in *Disgrace* as the image of the new post-apartheid nation?" We students, in reading Coetzee, also read ourselves.

Julie and I brought some of these ethical concerns to the forefront of our *Disgrace* discussion in the final class. David Lurie stood out for several students as the most ethically troubling character "because he slept with a student and showed no remorse." Another found "little moral conviction in his heart." One claimed sympathy for Lurie, yet "he seemed to want to do whatever he wanted to do and could always justify his actions, even if he agreed that he was immoral or wrong, but he could never [accept] the actions or justifications of others."[13] Students understood how Lurie, as well as other characters that represented the dual "powerful and vulnerable" position that Harpham described, challenges readers to wrestle with the question of how one can responsibly speak for and/or represent someone else.

My own struggle with ethics in the Coetzee seminar was directly related to the question of what constitutes responsible reading. As a historian and feminist I hoped that we would all be more interested in the political and material circumstances that took place in South Africa as Coetzee wrote the novels we read. For me, the fall of apartheid marked a centrally important global political victory of the twentieth century; I had expected Coetzee, *Age of Iron* aside, to more directly represent the transition from pre- to post-apartheid South Africa.

Yet, as a student, I read *Disgrace* with no knowledge about how specifically Coetzee's works had been received in the larger partisan political discourse about South Africa. My fellow students didn't know much about apartheid and post-apartheid struggles in the "new" South Africa. We consulted articles about the Truth and Reconciliation Commission hearings and the increase of violence and rape in post-apartheid South Africa, but we did not consistently incorporate that information into our discussions. Our lack of connection surprised me, given that two of our most politically aware activists in the class focused on African issues. One is a national leader of the "Invisible Children" movement seeking to improve the quality of life for African children affected by war; another is active with Amnesty International and seeks to address the humanitarian crisis in Darfur. South African politics provided few connections to this admirable activist work. I never made a strong case for the validity of the historical context that is so important to me because my shifting identity as student-faculty member worked against my desire to see greater discussion of historical content. When I raised these issues, I also felt responsible to provide answers — which I felt only marginally prepared to do. But we could have addressed this topic as a problem to solve collectively — not a pre-determined answer that any of us needed to know. I misjudged the difficult balance between exploration and authority that can be a valuable direction in seminar discussions.

By contrast, when we discussed *Waiting for the Barbarians*, Bill McDonald narrated a story from his own life about how he witnessed progress in the international sanctions against torture negotiated in documents beginning with the 1949 Geneva Convention. We listened, riveted, as he shared his anger that state-sanctioned torture is still widespread and now part of contemporary American foreign and military policy in places like Guantanamo Bay and Abu Ghraib. That testimony brought personal and cultural history into stimulating play with the novel. I wish I had done the same.

An Imagined Future Reading Community

> Like other Berkeley radicals, [my son] is convinced that the post-industrial post-Christian world is worn out, corrupt in its inheritance, helpless to create by evolution the social and political institutions, the forms of personal relations, the conventions, moralities, and systems of ethics (insofar as these are indeed necessary) appropriate to the future.
> — Another professor, Lyman Ward, in *Angle of Repose*

Although I was an unschooled reader of Coetzee when I started the seminar, our work on pastoral tropes, which distinguish between the city and country, inspired stronger confidence in my "expertise." Thanks to the structure of this course, I enjoyed a further, and surprising, benefit; I re-experienced the excitement I once felt as a college student learning new material with friends. I found fresh connections to my own work on the pastoral in cowboy poetry, or more generally in the literature of the North American West. A companion for David Lurie appeared — Lyman Ward, the cynical, disabled, aging college professor who narrates Wallace Stegner's *Angle of Repose*. Stegner's novel engages many of the same concerns that shape *Disgrace*; a comparison of the two quickly deepened the ethical questions we first engaged in the Coetzee seminar.[14]

I first taught *Angle of Repose* with Matt Gray as a student co-teacher in a seminar called "Rites of Passage in the American West." Threads from one reading community to another wove an intertextual web for our interdisciplinary curriculum that paralleled the more formal ones designed in course and graduation contracts. Matt and I discussed the Coetzee classroom as a liminal zone, an analogy to recent American historical scholarship that re-contextualizes the frontier as a site of cultural conquest and exchange rather than a nineteenth-century version of triumphal progress. Contemporary discussions of this concept are indebted to theorist Victor Turner, who argued that the physical and ritual spaces of liminal zones are always places of possibility. In fact, we've appropriated the term to describe the Johnston Center and its reading communities.[15]

If I were to bring Lyman Ward and David Lurie together in this unpredictable pedagogical space, what might happen? We could start by asking how the pastoral has been represented in the United States and South Africa, with *Disgrace* and *Angle of Repose* as central texts. Coetzee scholar David Attwell asserts that Coetzee "seriously addresses the ethical and political stresses of living in, and with, a particular historical locale, that of contemporary South Africa,"[16] and I would argue that Stegner did the same, with a particular emphasis on the environmental legacy of westward expansion. Stegner and Coetzee's narrations both reject an idealized pastoral history; they write with narrative forms that provide alternatives to dominant national discourses.[17]

Discussions could consider how similarities and differences in frontier histories for North America and Southern Africa specifically inform these novels as "postcolonial narratives." In the United States, where anti-colonial wars settled some questions by the beginning of the nineteenth century, the frontier came to be mythologized as a geographical feature that supposedly made the United States exceptional, ensuring economic opportunity, democratic political institutions, and social egalitarianism.[18] Much of the time, the North American frontier narrative was limited, written with the confidence of the victors, but since the Second World War, alternative and de-mythologizing points of view have shifted this paradigm. Stegner re-examined frontier mythology; his critical voice and his role as a mentor to other western writers challenged the earlier and more monolithic view. Similarly, Coetzee has written about the limits of the colonial pastoral in South Africa, both as a form that silenced the experiences of "the other," and as a particularly English genre that cannot speak to the multiple languages of Africa.[19]

In "Mothers and Daughters," we'd examine Stegner and Coetzee's stature as prominent writers and literary prizewinners. Wallace Stegner, lauded as the "Dean of Western American Writing" until his death in 1993, compares favorably with Coetzee, certainly now a writer of both national and international acclaim. Stegner received a Pulitzer in 1971 for *Angle of Repose* and a National Book Award in 1977 for *The Spectator Bird*. Coetzee has won two Booker Prizes for *Life & Times of Michael K* and *Disgrace*, and most notably the Nobel Prize in Literature in 2003. Both have also been at the center of debates about the social responsibilities expected of influential authors, debates echoing Harpham's questions about critical ethics generally. Our Coetzee seminar discussed Coetzee's gnomic Nobel Prize acceptance speech, "He and his Man," which our classmates found perplexing, even disturbing. Coetzee's narration of his writing of *Foe* seemed apolitical, clearly different from their expectation that Coetzee might use this international authority to speak directly about his ethical position as a writer. Instead, they puzzled through the speech, working to connect it to the novelist's craft. By contrast, Stegner rarely shied away from an opportunity to use his authority directly to speak "on behalf of the environment," particularly through Sierra Club activism.

When we turn to the writing itself, both writers have proved controversial in their representation of race, gender, and the "other." Critics question Coetzee's choice to write metafiction instead of realist fiction about South Africa, and he is careful not to "speak for the other." Instead, as critic Laura Wright asserts, Coetzee chooses to narrate "displacements" that "serve to shed light on subject positions that the author does not occupy."[20] By contrast Stegner writes through the subject positions of both Lyman and Lyman's grandmother, Susan Ward. *Angle of Repose* offers a "realist practice" through Stegner's appropriation of the letters of Mary Hallock Foote. Critics have accused Stegner of either silencing Foote or reclaiming her work, and *Angle of Repose* draws our attention to the unreliability of "authentic" voices through the character of Lyman Ward. He fabricates his grandmother's life from her letters while he copes with the trauma of becoming a "lying man," literally forced into a sedentary state by paralysis. Both texts provide students with examples of "displacement."

Each novel narrates a story centered on the lives of an aging male college professor who has lost prestige and/or status. Demoted from a professorship in Classics and Modern Languages to an adjunct professorship, David Lurie's story is narrated primarily through free indirect discourse.[21] Lurie's ill-advised sexual conquest of student Melanie Isaacs and subsequent refusal to "confess" to a university committee of inquiry ensures his dismissal. Lyman Ward suffers no specific disgrace like Lurie's, but a serious injury has forced him to leave a celebrated career at Stanford; he now must cope with confinement to a wheelchair. Like the divorcee Lurie, Ward is separated from his wife. Furthermore, he views with disdain the radical changes that the 1960s have brought to the orderly university he once knew. Ward depends on the services of his neighbors for food, bathing, household help, and his research. Although he is not a seducer — his grandmother and his wife are the alleged adulteresses here — he is nonetheless entangled in difficult relationships with women. Two women in particular "service" him, and although Lyman seeks no sexual gratification, uncontrollable sexual urges overtake him anyway, culminating in a tragic-comic dream sequence with the young woman Shelly Rasmussen. The story of Lyman's grandmother's marriage — ostensibly the focus of his work — mirrors his own battles with declining faculties and broken relationships.

These male narrators hope to give voice to the experiences of female family members. Lucy and Susan Ward negotiate a contested life on the frontier and in the country in which the illusion of a pastoral stability is ultimately shattered. Lyman's expansive tale about his grandmother's journey from the east coast through California, Mexico, Leadville, Idaho, and back to California with her engineer husband does not conform to an idealized past; the boom-and-bust economic fortunes endured by his grandparents weigh him down, and he must face his grandmother's complicity in the death of her daughter. Lurie, seeking some kind of escape from Cape Town and his disgrace at the University, will also "arrive at a house from the past." It "dates from the time of large families," the old, idealized pastoral age, perhaps. Lucy arrived there by way of a commune, and now finds herself attempting to manage the farm and kennel alone: "Now here she is, flowered dress, bare feet and all, in a house full of the smell of baking, no longer a child playing at farming but a solid countrywoman, a *boervrou*" (60).

Lurie has little affection for Lucy's pastoral life; indeed he finds it "curious that he and her mother, city folk, intellectuals, should have produced this throwback, this sturdy young settler" (61). But Lucy is not living in the past — far from it. She is living in unsettled country, a site of shifting power relationships in the new South Africa, as the attack on Lucy and David makes clear. This generational difference is most obvious in Lucy's refusal to leave the farm after the brutal attack and rape. She argues against her father's insistence that she move away, claiming that such a disgrace, for her, is "the price one has to pay for staying on" (158).

Lyman's recreation of the past is located on the former frontier — literally and figuratively — because he writes his history of his pioneer grandparents in the home they shared at New Almaden, California. He, too, will explore a "disgrace" endured by his grandmother and grandfather following infidelities and the death of a child. For Lyman, contemporary life and politics also intrude upon his relationship with his "sociologist" son. Lyman resents his son's visits and values, asserting, "Rodman, like most sociologists . . . was born without a sense of history. To him it is only an aborted social science. The world has changed, Pop, he tells me. The past isn't going to teach us anything about what we've got ahead of us. Maybe it did once, or seemed to. It doesn't anymore" (16). Both novels effectively represent paternal resistance to change through fathers, daughters, *and* sons.

Stuck between a known past and unknown future, both Lurie and Lyman are located somewhere between youth and old age. As the titles to the novels suggest, these personal circumstances provide analogies to the surrounding societies. The mining term "angle of repose" serves as a descriptor for "both human as well as detrital rest," according to Lyman Ward (24). He meditates throughout the novel about his own "rest," and that of his grandparents. We as readers must decide what his vantage point can provide. *Disgrace*, too, suggests a provocative position from which to survey a life. Like Lyman, who has only his writing as a solace in his old age, Lurie has his opera. Neither text is finished as the novels conclude; each turns to relationships at the end — Lyman with his family and Lurie with his daughter and his dogs. Our class debated Lurie's possible "state of grace" at the conclusion of the novel; I would ask "Mothers and Daughters" how it compares to an "angle of repose."

I finished the Coetzee seminar focused on *Disgrace* deeply impressed by the sophistication of our students' attention to reading as a process of learning texts and exploring the world around them. I also felt unsettled, concerned that I had not found sufficient answers to the questions about how daughters leave their fathers' houses on the frontier. But now, after several months, I read the seminar differently. Quite like David Lurie and Lyman Ward, I wanted some greater respect for the history and politics I find important. As a feminist, I wanted to see Lucy leave the farm where she was raped. But readers don't dictate the outcomes of novels, and teachers do well to see how a seminar moves rather than imposing a unilateral direction. Because we remained open to the future that our students might envision in the week-to-week experience of the seminar, I see how much their responses to Coetzee held up a mirror to my own authority as a professor in the academy. I benefited from the room we made for the richness of many Coetzee readings. I see now that I did not need to provide the authoritative reading about how daughters leave their fathers' houses. That question awaits a future semester, should anyone want to read and re-read *Disgrace* with *Angle of Repose*.[22]

Notes

[1] Regina Janes, "Writing With Authority," as cited in Wright, 1.
[2] Barnard (2002), 393.
[3] Williams, 18; Coetzee, *White Writing*, ch. 3.
[4] Classmates Jacque Materne and Emily Sernacker.
[5] Classmates Morgan Proctor and Monica Barra.
[6] Classmate Barra.
[7] Classmate Michelle Deyden.
[8] Geoffrey Galt Harpham, *Shadows of Ethics*, xiii.
[9] Classmates Richard Burton, Callie Spradley, and Morgan Proctor.
[10] Classmates Sara Joern and Emily Sernacker.
[11] Classmates Jacque Materne and Michelle Deyden.
[12] Classmates Monica Barra and Morgan Proctor.
[13] Classmates Brigid King and Ernest Hayes.
[14] Wallace Stegner, *Angle of Repose*.
[15] See Ashley.
[16] David Attwell, *J. M. Coetzee: South Africa and the Politics of Writing*.
[17] On the frontier thesis, see Turner. Leonard Thompson and Howard Lamar (14–16) offer a detailed historical comparison of North America and Southern Africa frontier history.
[18] "New Western historians" challenge Turner's seminal 1893 thesis "The Significance of the Frontier in America History," which is most often cited as the exemplary triumphalist text. See, for example, Limerick, 1987.
[19] J. M. Coetzee, *White Writing*, 63–81.
[20] Wright, 99.
[21] This is another example of Wright's understanding about displacement: "The displacements that characterize Coetzee's narratives — including the free indirect discourse of *Disgrace* — serve to shed light on subject positions that the author does not occupy by presenting the interaction of multiple subjectivities as performed dialogue between not only the characters within the novel, but also

between the inquisitive third-person narrative voice and the reader, who must attempt to pose some answers. Coetzee, therefore, as I have claimed earlier, writes dialogically, in the Bahktinian sense. . . ." (99).

[22] We thank Dr. Dorothy Clark, Professor of English, California State University, Northridge, for her insights about the usefulness of the anthology.

13: Sympathy for the Devil: On the Perversity of Teaching *Disgrace*

Daniel Kiefer

> On my saying, What have I to do with the sacredness of traditions, if I live wholly from within? my friend suggested, — "But these impulses may be from below, not from above." And I replied, "They do not seem to me to be such; but if I am the Devil's child, I will then live from the Devil."
>
> —Emerson, "Self-Reliance"

TEACHING J. M. COETZEE'S NOVEL *Disgrace* has revealed new complexities in the book and in my teaching, and not just because my students' reactions were different from what I expected. When I'm teaching fiction I usually ask students to reflect on the sympathy they feel with the protagonist of the narrative, and how that sympathy is established. But this novel exposes the tenuous dangers of sympathetic reading, challenging readers to examine our judgments in the light of eloquent expression.

These were fifteen willing students from various disciplines, taking an introductory literature course to fulfill a general education requirement at the University of Redlands. Though I had warned them about the violence in the novel, they weren't really disturbed by that. In fact, they were very willing to confront the difficult sexual and racial questions raised by the narrative. But they were outraged at the protagonist David Lurie for his transgressions. The more strongly I defended David's reflections on his own failings, the more determined were my students to find him guilty, and so the opposition between their reading and mine, quite a natural occurrence in teaching, became more pronounced. What divided us was the narrator's endorsement of David in the literary indirection of his self-reflection. I asked my students to take his part because the novel does, and to give themselves more willingly to the narrative on his terms. In my view, the spare eloquence of his self-revelation and self-concealment invites readers to follow him closely as he goes.

My students rejected David as someone too removed from ordinary human feeling, as these responses, written after we had discussed the book for two class meetings, show: "At the age of 52 David Lurie seems to be confused both sexually and intellectually." "The irony of David's state in life, this idea that he is a teacher who doesn't teach, a father who doesn't see his daughter, and a man who doesn't attract the opposite sex, is portrayed throughout the text. He is essentially devoid of emotion and love." "The protagonist's disgrace lies in his flippant attitude to his rape of Melanie and the fact that he doesn't seem to care enough about his career in order to save it." "The compassionate reader may view David as the protagonist of the narrative, but the uncompassionate reader may view him as the antagonist." "Does David ever lift himself from disgrace? Can the reader find any redeeming qualities in him? He is bound to his grandiose thoughts about literature and the scholarly life, and he cannot shed them. He lacks tact in his real life." These accusations have real incisiveness, for they center on David's aridity as a refusal of connection with anyone, even the reader. But they treat him as a real person, defective in his actual life, rather than as a literary construct within the design of the novel.

In fact, other accusations focused on David's escape into literature as the source of his troubles: "His lack of emotion is the reason for his seeming obsession with poetry. Without knowing so much poetry, and knowing so much about it, he would not be able to represent himself at all." "Despite all the emotional scenes in this novel involving love, David often drifts into his story of the life of Byron in order to escape from his emotions." "The main character does not appear to have feelings for anything. He uses the poetry of others to reveal what he feels, but instead of asking his class to discuss the emotions brought out by Wordsworth's lines in *The Prelude*, he discusses vocabulary." These reactions were no more strident than the others, but they saw David's literary analysis as a selfish refusal to hear what students feel, a retreat into mere "vocabulary." They seemed to attack the literary profession, and in turn I became very careful in my response, in order to separate my teaching and my conduct from David's.

His teaching has been pretty half-hearted, as he admits (4), but in the scenes where instruction is portrayed, as he turns Wordsworth and Byron to his own purposes, mixing literary passion with sexual, he becomes a more effective instructor. In talking alone with Melanie Isaacs, the student he has seduced, he describes his own passions by means of literary allusions: "From fairest creatures we desire increase," as he reflects to himself on the pentameter in Shakespeare's line and its estranging cadence (16). My students thought his efforts to speak with Melanie publicly by means of Wordsworth's *Prelude* and Byron's "Lara" were inept, or even treacherous. But his method takes figurative language and deploys it figuratively, in the way professors often do. Literal readers will charge a text with their own sensibility, while figurative readers attend more to the language, making the complexities of representation even more complex. If I bring my own experience into my teaching, I do it only indirectly because I value the literary experience over plain self-disclosure. Teaching Coetzee's novel puts my professorial tricks on display: turning from what's in the novel to how it's constructed, taking its literary design as a representation of feeling, and exploring the texture of language rather than content. When students see David performing those tricks for his own sake, they distrust him thoroughly as a professor.

My students were justifiably hard on him for taking Melanie against her will, and they refused to accept his complicated understanding of what she might be feeling afterward. They found his assigning of a stop-gap examination grade even more reprehensible than his taking up with Melanie in the first place. In that regard they responded as if they were fellow students in his course, treated unfairly by his dishonest grading. Perhaps the grade-change hit closer to their own experience than rape, or perhaps they were reluctant to enter a discussion of sexual violence at all. Nor could I convince them to see the later violent gang-rape of Lucy as much starker and more terrifying. The way that event is revealed to us makes it something we have to imagine, as David himself does. Because we don't witness it first-hand we join in David's reconstruction of it, and it seeps into our minds gradually, with greater and greater force as Lucy refuses to disclose it. Our deepening involvement in David's mind and heart is crucial to the novel's effect on us, as the narrator involves us subtly, but my students refused to get involved with David's self-reflections.

"For a man of his age, fifty-two, divorced, he has, to his mind, solved the problem of sex rather well" (1). The opening sentence of the novel offers the phrase "to his mind" as a kind of conversational aside, but the muttering emphasizes David's reliance on his own self-reflection, a reliance the narrative endorses. His habit of expressing himself to himself in spare suggestions matches the narrative's representation of consciousnesses in free indirect discourse, a technique ascribed to Flaubert's *Madame Bovary*. David's response to Flaubert's novel exemplifies the technique: "Well, if poor ghostly Emma were ever to find her way to Cape Town, he would bring her along one Thursday afternoon to show her what bliss can be: a moderate bliss, a moderated bliss" (6). As the narrator records David's strange boast of his power to engender both bliss and moderation in Emma, the narrator's alliance with the protagonist becomes secure. But the sentence expresses a weird intermingling of reality and fiction. Does David want Emma to watch, to watch and learn, or even to join in, under his supervision? The overlaying of "moderated" upon "moderate" shows David's scholarly habit of choosing the best word and then choosing again, as if precision were more important than feeling, as if diction could fashion event. Throughout the narrative he utters his thoughts in language that's full of remarkable twists and turns, poetical in their swervings.

David's indirection gives strength to his emotional expression, against my students' conventional wish for the frank admission of feeling. It comports with Wordsworth's praise of the imagination as the sublime human faculty that surpasses nature and obliterates it. As I enter David's mind I affirm the way he reveals himself through indications and interpretations, analogies and images, rather than direct speech. If students condemn his closed heart, I commend the poetical ways he has of investigating himself. I endorse his fidelity to the usurping imagination, his role as satanic angel, intent on his own dark designs. His ruthless honesty in careful nuances of speech comes upon new feelings, more human and complex.

Disgrace is terrifying because it depicts acts committed under the impress of fierce drives, while the writing is tensile, lyrical, apt, and revelatory. I asked my students to let that brutal eloquence soften their judgment of David, and of us, and of themselves too. I asked them to accept the difficulties, indeterminacies, and misdirections of the narrative as the kind of wayward movement that's so valuable in literary expression. Defense of this tragic hero became a defense of evasiveness in language — an attribute essential to the literary enterprise, which relies on figuration for its work of mimesis.

The novel tells the wrong story for students who expect redemption. Instead of showing David's return to grace, it makes acceptance of disgrace the only thing possible and exerts pressure on its readers to concur. But in the context of a literature course his seduction of his student Melanie, along with his falsification of her examination grade, feels to students like an assault they cannot forgive. The professor who takes David's side in the conflict between social expectations and the individual narrative consciousness becomes an assailant as well. I prepare David's defense, as the novel follows his inward explanations to himself, in place of the defense he refuses to give the academic committee of inquiry. By assigning the book in the first place, by affirming its strategies of narration, and by opening a fair-minded discussion of its merits, I am necessarily drawn into the ethical questions that he dodges and then confronts. If no one else in the classroom will take his side, I will, as I would with other tragic figures, in Shakespeare, say, or Milton, Dostoevsky, or Nabokov. In his interpretation of Byron's poem "Lara" David points out "that we are not asked to condemn this being with the mad heart, this being with whom there is something constitutionally wrong. On the contrary, we are invited to understand and sympathize. But there is a limit to sympathy" (33). I want to take students right to that limit and beyond, with David as our mad-hearted Lucifer. His self-reflective teaching imbues my own teaching with more self-reflection than I may like, because he represents my own darker drives, both erotic and violent. I feel exposed to my students as a Lucifer-David who advocates lust, contempt, dessication, self-castration, and revenge.

As an openly gay professor who has taught seminars on queer theory, culture, and politics and has served as advisor to the lesbian, gay, bisexual, transsexual student group on campus, I feel especially vulnerable to students' impressions of my sexual life. I understand that students may have many different responses to homosexual desire, from acceptance or endorsement to indifference or contempt. My immersion in David's sexual transgressions may strike them as an admission of my own perversion and further evidence that literature professors are interested in talking only about desire and violence, sex and death. This novel interrogates my teaching practice, examining my presentation of self as a passionate reader. And the tone of my teaching is often provocative, antithetical, even perverse.

In response to the scene in chapter 3 where David goes to Melanie's flat, embraces her, and takes her sexually, my students were certain that he rapes her. They became more adamant against him the more I kept referring them to the passage: "She does not resist. All she does is avert herself: avert her lips, avert her eyes," and "Not rape, not quite that, but undesired nevertheless, undesired to the core" (25). Here is the heart of David's reflective expression, caught in reiterative appositions, "avert, avert, avert" and "undesired, undesired," that move the sentence along in the rhythm of Tennyson's great line at the opening of "Tithonus": "The woods decay, the woods decay and fall." The reiterative movement adds more in order to confirm what's already known and thereby reaffirms what must be, persuading the hesitant observer. The soft subtlety of such an understanding will win the assent of a reflective reader, especially a professor who revisits a literary passage again and again to discern its melody. A literal-minded young reader will stick with the facts and side with Melanie, especially when David admits that what he does is undesired to the core: "As though she had decided to go slack, die within herself for the duration, like a rabbit when the jaws of the fox close on its neck. So that everything done to her might be done, as it were, far away" (25). The simile of the rabbit in the jaws of its predator marks David's recognition of his own blame, although in fanciful literary terms. The phrase "as it were" indicates his abstraction from his own action. The fiction-minded professor is inclined to take his side for providing evidence against himself, especially when his spirits falter: "He obeys, but then, when he reaches his car, is overtaken with such dejection, such dullness, that he sits slumped at the wheel unable to move" (25). For students that dullness is evidence against him, while for a teacher of Romantic poetry it signifies his reversion into the imagination. "What do others know of the voluptuous pleasure of sadness or despair?" writes Jens Peter Jacobsen in *Marie Grubbe*.[1] The delectable self-concern that melancholy brings on is very like the sweet self-reflection that literature engages in. And I found that the gulf between innocent student and voluptuously despairing professor opened ever wider as our discussion of the interchanges between Melanie and David continued.

Dejection as a Romantic topos and trope, most eloquently expressed in poems like Coleridge's "Limbo," "Dejection: An Ode," and even "Self-Knowledge" ("dark fluxion, all unfixable by thought") shows how the faltering mind seeks refuge in itself as all of nature falters. Melancholy obliterates the outer world, which can offer no recompense for inner darkness, according to "Dejection: An Ode": "I may not hope from outward forms to win / The passion and the life, whose fountains are within." The Romantic poets, especially Wordsworth, Coleridge, and Byron, make poems that find solace for that faltering of the imagination in their very making. Until now David has forced his erotic conquests to serve as his solace, and the failure of that force plunges him into even deeper loss.

In taking Melanie against her will he has violated the sacred code of Eros, a crime, according to his rationale, greater than rape. In chapter 11, when Lucy asks him to defend his actions, he reasserts his steadfast claim: "My case rests on the rights of desire." But the reassertion leads him to return to the scene in his mind and acknowledge Melanie's refusal in starker terms, though still expressed in simile: "while her arms flop like the arms of a dead person" (89). And immediately he reacts against his own proclamation: "*I was a servant of Eros*: that is what he wants to say, but does he have the effrontery?" (89). His mind reverts upon its own constructions as he gives justifications for his violation and then takes them away to give them again in new form. Wordsworth claims in the 1802 Preface to *Lyrical Ballads* that his poems have this purpose, "to follow the fluxes and refluxes of the mind when agitated by the great and simple affections of our nature" (598). David's affections are not as great and simple as he would make them seem.

With the narrator's guidance we see what David cannot see, that his teaching of Wordsworth's *Prelude* VI leads directly to his assault on Melanie. "Where is the flash of revelation in this room?" he wonders (21), referring to his earlier private instruction of her alone: "A flash of revelation and a flash of response. Like lightning. Like falling in love" (13), and looking ahead to the moment of her full recognition: "Her eyes meet his and in a flash see all. Confused, she drops her glance" (23). Already she is refusing him, but David reveals his own flash of love as if it were Wordsworth's flash of inspiration. Here the novel becomes an allegory of teaching as violation, with David standing in our place to address our students as they accuse him of wrongdoing. I want to enter the spirit of his Wordsworthian self-reflection, by which he moves back into memory in order to move forward into imagination. I hope to take my students along, to help them experience the flash of self or love that comes brilliantly into the 1850 *Prelude* in lines that David parses without quoting:

> in such strength
> Of usurpation when the light of sense
> Goes out, but with a flash that has revealed
> The invisible world. (*Prelude* VI.599–602)

In figurative form, the flash obliterates nature in strengthening the imagination, while David holds out for imagination and nature together. He claims that "Wordsworth seems to be feeling his way toward a balance" between the pure idea and the sense-image. He then makes his appeal to Melanie ("How to bring them to him? How to bring her?" [22]) so nakedly that she must drop her glance, as later on she must avert her eyes and herself from him. Once she does that, students want to avert their eyes from David as well, and my insistence that they keep looking becomes a kind of assault on them. Likewise, I endorse David's teaching of Byron's "Lara" (32–34) as a vindication of his own error and errancy, knowing that he will give up that vindication by the time he says, "The end of roving. Though the heart be still as loving and the moon be still as bright" (120), quoted from Byron's late poem "So We'll Go No More A-Roving" and echoed in "The end of roaming" (175). When the novel brings in the ghost of Byron ("the voice of a ghost" [183] and "pale as a ghost" [185]), it shows that David in his opera has moved beyond the Byronic self to embrace another in the character of Teresa Guiccioli.

The terrible assault on Lucy in chapter 11, not witnessed but rather imagined by David, is recognized by her as a story that must not be told. As he survives his own ordeal, "The scrape of a match, and at once he is bathed in cool blue flame" (96), he understands, "Everything is tender, everything is burned. Burned, burnt. 'Lucy!' he shouts. 'Are you here?' A vision comes to him of Lucy struggling with the two in the blue overalls, struggling against them" (97). His vision here has three parts, actually — the facing of his own mortality, the recognition that all is burned, and the knowledge of Lucy's violation. The three parts are summed up in the progress from "burned" to "burnt," not a reiteration, but a movement to the end, the perfective. Later in the novel, as he goes to visit Melanie's father, David flashes back to the phrase and extends it: "Burned — burnt — burned up" (166). Out of that fire he will be resurrected, but not by getting the story right, for Lucy keeps the rights to her own suffering: "I have told the whole story. The whole story is what I have told" (110) and "Stop it, David! I don't need to defend myself before you. *You don't know what happened*" (134).

Lucy's name recalls the innocent beloved in Wordsworth's Lucy poems, and David comes to participate in the mourning that those lyrics express. His acceptance of not knowing and of Lucy's inexpressible suffering deepens our sympathy for him, while his identification with the rapists threatens our sympathy considerably. "He does understand; he can, if he concentrates, if he loses himself, be there, be the men, inhabit them, fill them with the ghost of himself" (160). Here he assumes the character of the violators so vividly that we must avert our gaze, even though it's the ghost of himself he supplies, not the spirit but the pale shadow, the vestige of potency. Immediately afterwards he writes to Lucy in an attempt to be the woman instead of the men. In place of a face-to-face conversation, father and daughter exchange letters, though they're living in the same house. The text of those letters (160–61) becomes a kind of poem in dialogue, subject to the sort of literary interpretation that Romantic poems evoke from him. The documents speak more fully than David's and Lucy's spoken words to each other allow, achieving a nearly silent rapprochement between them.

David also expresses his distrust of the power of language, specifically in response to the political and racial disturbances in his native land: "More and more he is convinced that English is an unfit medium for the truth of South Africa" (117) and "Yet can Petrus be blamed? The language he draws on with such aplomb is, if he only knew it, tired, friable, eaten from inside as if by termites" (129). David's determination to go ahead with the articulation of his own inner life, despite the terrible inadequacies of the language, shows a Romantic devotion to the powers of the imagination. It's also a strong point of connection between a professor of literature and this character. Yet I separate from my students here again, on the question of reliance on the linguistic, the literary, as all there is, despite its frailty.

As a teacher I hope to embody more possibilities than my students have considered. I sometimes take up outlandish readings in hopes of challenging their received judgments. On the question of applying ethical standards to aesthetic questions, David stands for transgression in the service of divine Eros. He's a defender of the lack of faith. As a mad heart he exerts his power to think more deeply about Eros and death, a power teachers may claim for ourselves as well. We may ally ourselves with Nietzsche, quoted at the opening of Michael Ondaatje's novel *Divisadero*: "We have art so that we shall not be destroyed by truth" (1). Stern ethical judgment is even more destructive than truth. We may ally ourselves with Emerson, who in the essay "Self-Reliance" praises faithfulness to our own impulses: "Nothing is at last sacred but the integrity of your own mind" (261); "Nothing can bring you peace but yourself" (282). And we may ally ourselves with Freud, who imagines the super-ego as constructed of all our abandoned objects of desire. Actually it's the students who react to Melanie's plight with defensiveness, protecting the ego from instinctual demands, as Freud describes that process in the 1926 essay "Inhibitions, Symptoms and Anxiety."[2] Repression replaces defense in Freud's theory and assumes essential power in the unconscious: "And indeed the super-ego, originating as it does from the id, cannot dissociate itself from the regression and defusion of instinct which have taken place there."[3] Students react to David's transgression punitively, and I move to protect him against their attack. They want vengeance, and I hope to lead them to sympathy, or at least to an understanding of the sympathy that the narrator maintains for him. My classroom becomes a place for relieving moral constraint with aesthetic fervor.

Freud's thought helps us interpret the melancholy that ensues when the possibilities of desire are quelled, but he's most valuable in validating Eros as a driving force. David's fanciful version of that compulsion is rejected by his former wife, Rosalind, who allows him "no sympathy, no mercy, not in this day and age" (44). Of his predicament she says, "The whole thing is disgraceful from beginning to end. Disgraceful and vulgar, too" (45). David pleads "the rights of desire" to Lucy (89), as he does to the committee of inquiry (52), and I underscore the insistence of Eros. Whether or not we professors are guilty of "meddling with other people's children" sexually, as Rosalind puts it, we're always interfering with them, meddling with them intellectually and emotionally. In his latest novel, *Diary of a Bad Year*, Coetzee entitles a substantial part of the book "Strong Opinions" on a range of topics, including representations of pedophilia in section 12, which ends this way: "As for sex between teachers and students, so strong is the tide of disapproval nowadays that uttering even the mildest word in its defence becomes (exactly) like battling that tide, feeling your puny stroke quite overwhelmed by a great heft of water bearing you backward. What you face when you open your lips to speak is not the silencing stroke of the censor but an edict of exile" (57). The erotic imagery of the passage, describing utterance as frail stroke and opening lips, makes speaking itself a sexual act that will be decried as perverse. The edict of exile confronting the speaker may be a version of our students' submission to conventional moral principles. With bitter irony in the word "exile" Coetzee upholds the necessary, though ineffective, even dangerous act of defending sexual desire, no matter how universally it is reproved.

Although *Disgrace* holds Eros as a force to be obeyed, beyond morality, decency, or social convention, our students won't accept that force as determinant. Eros is itself a literary construction, especially in David's elaborately figurative descriptions of it as "a fire" (166), "a quick shudder" (35), and "a ripple" (65), as urged on by "the god who makes even the small birds quiver" (89). "Suffice it to say that Eros entered" (52), he announces, as if quoting Homer, although saying that is far from sufficient. He lectures Lucy out of Blake: "Sooner murder an infant in its cradle than nurse unacted desires" (69), and yet by nursing acted desires he does in a sense murder the infant Melanie. Lucy's acceptance of an infant conceived in violence helps transform David's fire from lust to compassion, a transformation that depends as well on his sexual affair with the plain and unsubtle Bev and his handling and dispatch of dying animals. As the compassionate force enters, Eros no longer reigns supreme in his psychic universe. He comes to terms with his impotence. As the novel progresses we are invited to read David's struggle more and more sympathetically. The narrative conducts us into his conflicted world of meddling, taking, violating, arrogating, and eventually submitting.

In this novel we are asked to identify with a character who is quite repellent in his selfishness. Because the narrative subscribes to his desire, or at least his defense of desire, it invites students to do the same, and to shift into middle-aged lechery, as they do in reading Nabokov's *Lolita*. Women students, especially, find it difficult to follow David's or Humbert Humbert's impulses towards erotic objects so like themselves without going through real contortions of feeling. But those contortions are supremely literary in their strange representations of strange feeling. Michael Holland argues in his essay on *Disgrace* that the reader of the novel is "powerfully gendered as male, and as such powerfully divided; we're constructed as 'the man of the book' . . . in both a repugnant and a seductive manner, bringing the moral and the aesthetic into stark conflict in a way that fundamentally affects [the book's] readability" (397). The starkness of that conflict forces us to accede to the demands of the narrative ever more closely. David's courage in following the commands of Eros may eventually inspire something like admiration, as he goes wherever he is taken and accepts his fate as bravely as any tragic hero of Aeschylus or Shakespeare.

Now I'm teaching *Disgrace* again, in a first-year seminar devoted to Nobel Prize-winning authors. Reactions from these students to David's transgressions and refusals are divided roughly along gender lines. The men in the class are more willing to see David as expressing their desire for sexual pleasure that women will not surrender to them. The women, while recognizing that Melanie neither accepts nor rejects him, are more dismissive of David's reasons for taking her without her consent. Both men and women want a deeper understanding of Melanie's inner life than the novel allows. The peer advisor for the seminar, Rachel Schy, a bright and genially contentious junior, has suggested that the narrative is not specifically masculine in its representation of David's mind. Rather, this scene "forces us to examine what constitutes rape and how power relations play into every sexual encounter," as she wrote on the first day of our class discussion. She sees in David's assault the dominance of a man used to exerting his power, a dominance that reflects the larger command that rulers of any kind exert upon those ruled. I see the narrative method of the book, in its reliance only on David's perceptions and reflections, as continually exerting its domination over us as readers. We may avert our gaze, but to keep reading we must endure the violation that the narrator inflicts on us. In some sense, if we want to absorb the novel's impact we must give in to David's mind.

The reactions of these first-year seminar students may be milder than the earlier class because they've just finished reading Elfriede Jelinek's *The Piano Teacher*. The sexual violence in that novel is far more disturbing than David's vanquishing of Melanie, because we're plunged into a volatile mixture of fantasy and fact, masculine and feminine, pornography and romance, aesthetics and civics, all heightened, subverted, and exchanged. The tightly coiled protagonist of Jelinek's novel, Erica Kohut, turns the leap into sex by her student Walter into a scene humiliating to his masculine prowess. Then she proposes by letter a thorough submission to his sexual command, and his response becomes terrifically destructive. These and other scenes of self-degradation and bloody lust-attack are narrated in a kind of free indirect discourse that's most unsettling. We feel Erica's compulsion to violence against herself, her mother, and her student as something inevitable and strange. By comparison David Lurie's actions and rationalizations seem quite ordinary.

My first-year students are pretty stunned by the bleakness of what we've read in this course: the sweet melancholy of Orhan Pamuk's *Istanbul*, the bitter banality of sexual commerce in Harold Pinter's *The Homecoming*, the desperate heroics in José Saramago's *Blindness*. Are all Nobel laureates bent on tragedy, they wonder, or is depression just this professor's delight? I reply that they'll come to depression of their own eventually, and while great writing can be comic as well as tragic, it must confront desires and violations we all struggle to repress. We seek consolation in the intercessory power of literature, as it intervenes between us and the ambitions, sorrows, desiccations, and brutalities that threaten to overwhelm us if faced directly. As intermediary between teacher and students, *Disgrace* challenges our deliberations about our own involvement in teaching. What is it that we're seeking so passionately? What do we hope to gain by overcoming our students' resistance to coldness, disappointment, and fury?

Sam Durrant describes Coetzee's fiction as "acts of sympathetic imagination that continually encounter their own bounds" (119). That encounter extends to the reader's confrontation with the limits of sympathy, as refuted by Elizabeth Costello: "There is no limit to the extent to which we can think ourselves into the being of another. There are no bounds to the sympathetic imagination" (80). Are there limits to sympathy? Where? How do we determine them? Surely this novel, like Milton's *Paradise Lost* and Dante's *Commedia*, expects us to surpass those limits and enter the hearts of the fallen. It directs us to follow the story of David's coming to accept limits on his actions when he surpasses the limits he has imposed on his own sympathy. The act of reading comes under the scrutiny of a narrative authority that is cast under suspicion by the novel, as the free indirect discourse lets David's self-explanations float off on their own. David may defend his right to violate Melanie and to conduct his own disciplinary hearing, without submitting himself to the judgment of his peers, but the narrator's detachment keeps him under examination. In the violent attack by assailants who nearly burn him up as they rape his daughter, he comes to accept himself as frail human rather than powerful demon. The ravisher becomes the ravished, and his child becomes his mother, as David comprehends his daughter's quiet suffering and his own tenderness for the dogs whom Bev conducts to a peaceful death.

With David Lurie standing in for literature professors, we are moved to defend him just as we defend indirection, subterfuge, and feigning as the aim of literary work and literary interpretation. The novel makes David's autobiographical account reprehensible because it is so self-interested, and instructs us to discern in the literary text not a single replica but multitudinous reflections of ourselves and others. We reaffirm the mediating power of literature to move us away from our literal selves to more evocative constructions. No matter how fully they want to follow our lead with us, our students will necessarily oppose our strange ways of reading, as they add in other, more conventional ways. But even that opening into old possibilities is something enacted by this novel, because its spare rendering of event and refraction, always from David's point of view, forces many a reading to become confused. We may encourage that confusion as a refusal of predetermined interpretation, as the text keeps exerting itself upon our minds over and over again in new ways. What transpires is reciprocal engagement. Students and professors enter an economy of mutual interference with each other's expectations, where rise and fall are interchangeable at times, "increasing store with loss and loss with store," as Shakespeare's sonnet no. 64 imagines it. In defense of dark and fateful feeling, our teaching of literature ventures deeply into the erotic and the deathly, the tender and the violent, and their fusion together.

Notes

[1] Quoted as epigraph to Jacques Hassoun's *The Cruelty of Depression*.
[2] *S.E.* 20:164.
[3] *S.E.* 20:115–16.

14: Teaching *Disgrace* in the Large Lecture Classroom

Nancy Best

I. Taking the Hun

I JUST LOVE A GOOD LECTURE! I love the buzz in the air as crowds file into theatre-style seats. I love pull-down chalkboards and electric podiums that rise and lower at the press of a button. I love the projection booths and electronic screens. I love the hushed whispers of early comers consulting each other about assigned readings and Scantron tests. I even love the hollow, amplified banging of the double doors at the top of the lecture hall; after all, something weird and wonderful might walk through them at any time.

Most of all, I love the distance between the lecturer and audience, the lecturer structuring her daily dose of truth and putting it up for grabs. That daily nugget may be terrible or terrific but it's out there, the whole of it, to be poked and prodded, affirmed or challenged, without much risk to the audience. This lack of risk can be as much of a gift as a curse to students, especially when it comes to reading literature, and *especially* when it comes to first reads of a work of literature.

In academia, we usually assume that small seminar-style classes offer more opportunity for building empathy and encouraging students to widen their perspectives. Seminar teachers may find that, if called to the podium, quite a few of their pedagogical devices can, with just a little imagination, prove useful in the lecture hall. The pedagogical scene of the larger classroom also offers opportunity to build a different kind of empathy, an empathy rooted in the act of reading. The large-lecture scene or environment, with its dim lights and theatre seating, mimics the anonymity of the reading experience, and this anonymity gives students a certain freedom in their reading.

Although some small-seminar students may totally forget themselves when they are engaged in reading assigned passages, I doubt that many do. In the back of their minds, they know they will be called upon to speak. What effect might this have on them? At the very least it will be an awareness of themselves as readers and interpreters of texts — indeed, this is usually considered a felicitous proposition by teachers — even as the story may ask for an abandonment of that self-awareness, for an empathy wholly engaged with the story rather than an awareness that talks back to it.

The abandonment of self is a crucial element of storytelling: readers forget the contingencies of their own lives, replacing them with the contingencies of made-up characters in made-up stories, and this is where great reading begins. No doubt the scene of a small-seminar classroom will honor multiple readings of a text and foster community in that struggle to make meaning. What is less clear is whether it fosters a fundamental empathy with the characters in the story.

One of the pleasures of a large lecture is that students are not immediately required to generate different readings. They will not be required to expose their inadequacy nor to parade their superior critical reading skills. They must only pay attention to the performance — the instructor's reading of the text. Because of the rhetorical scene, students and the teacher enter into a different relationship with each other. The teacher is not assessing each individual student's "read" of the text, but rather trying to woo the student, imparting her enthusiasm for a story, the context for the story, and the tools for a later close, critical read. The student's mission, should s/he choose to accept it, is to enter the world of someone else's story.

This love affair with the large lecture is more than a little unorthodox considering my alternative college education. My undergraduate classes were small and there was little lecturing. If there were truths to be delivered, they were usually delivered via consensus. This is not to say that consensus is or ever was the primary goal of the small seminar, but rather that the more people agree with any given reading, the more weighty and important it seems to the group as a whole. As opinions solidify and heads nod in unison around the seminar table, it can make it all the harder for an unconvinced individual to dissent.

It is a learning process that terrifies me, both as a student and as a teacher. There are other problems, problems familiar to any seminar teacher. What if no one in the seminar has anything to say? Or what if what is said is ultimately inconsequential? What if the class gets stuck on some arcane point that means a lot to one or two of the more eloquent members of the group, but not so much to the others? What if meaning is defined by junta — group rule by highly verbal students who can swing the content of a discussion, but who never truly have to define the terms of their own ideas? What if it's a mean group? I've had mean groups and I know they can tear a learning community to pieces. If it's a choice between a mean group and an Atilla-the-Hun professor spewing forth a narrow-minded read of some seldom-read story, I'd take the Hun every time. Of course these are only *my* fears, but I imagine everyone who has sat through a seminar faces some version of the same fears herself.

Although the opposite is usually assumed, it may well be that the authoritarian presentation of a lecture in itself is actually more egalitarian than the seminar. This is because class members, once the lecture has been delivered, can freely affirm or reject its arguments on the spot, or during after-class informal discussions. By contrast, in a small seminar, various readings of a narrative are put forth in bits and pieces. As a result, the most astute readers may be silenced and the most astute points glossed over in an effort to achieve maximum participation. In addition, a lecture may motivate student readings in ways that small classes do not; a good lecture performance might encourage students in their private readings and rereadings of the work, as they read without the pressures and expectations of addressing the class.

These are ideas I had in mind when I structured my own course's reading of *Disgrace*.

II. Teaching Disgrace at CSUSB

I have taught *Disgrace* four times, all four as a component of a course entitled "English 170: Studies in Literature," one of four classes that can be used to fulfill a General Education requirement in Humanities at California State University at San Bernardino (CSUSB). Three out of the four times I have taught the class, it has been in a large lecture format (average enrollment 90 students). At CSUSB, the English Department offers many more seminar-style courses than large lectures. But there are a number of lecture courses, and these are sometimes defended as a budget necessity, enabling the department to offer these smaller classes. The average enrollment in an undergraduate class is 22 students, so in the conventional view my 90-student course goes a long way toward covering the cost of the lower enrollments. But, as stated, I think there are real *learning* advantages for many students in the larger classes.

The third time I taught the class was Winter Quarter, 2007, immediately after auditing the Bill McDonald and Matt Gray Coetzee seminar at the University of Redlands. Auditing the class at the University of Redlands before beginning another stint teaching Coetzee at CSUSB was an illuminating experience. The student population at the University of Redlands is different to that at CSUSB. CSUSB, besides being much larger than Redlands, is a commuter campus. Although there are students who live in the dormitories, most drive to class. Most of them come from working-class families and continue to work while attending school. Often my students are the first of their family to attend college. They tend to be very pragmatic and regard a college education as a stepping stone to a better career rather than as something that might be pursued for its own sake. I imagine they are a lot like the students who attended Coetzee's fictionalized Cape Technical University, sons and daughters of a society in transition, ethnically diverse, often from impoverished backgrounds with a real stake in the idea that life can get better and that an education is a step in that direction.

The student population at the University of Redlands is more economically privileged and less ethnically diverse, and the Redlands faculty has deliberately chosen a pedagogical philosophy dedicated to establishing communities of learners in individual classes and in disciplines. The emphasis is on community and the communal making of meaning. Rather than large lecture classes where the faculty assumes a traditional professorial role, classes are usually seminars dedicated to a close reading of a shared text and to the dialogue that issues forth from that reading. In the Coetzee class I audited in the fall of 2006, fifteen students, the three faculty members who audited the class, and the two who taught it, sat around a seminar table and sweated out our readings of the six Coetzee novels on the syllabus. In that communal sweating out of meanings, this class was very similar to many of the best literature courses I took at Johnston and in graduate school.

My large lecture literature class requires a different and, I believe, equally valuable approach to reading texts like *Disgrace*. It is one of four courses offered through the English Department that fulfills a general education literature requirement. According to the CSUSB Bulletin, the official general education objectives of the course are to

> (a) Provide a basic typology of forms and genres within the particular field of study; (b) Introduce students to the elements and compound parts of the forms and genres as well as the standard critical terminologies for analyzing and describing them; and (c) Analyze the works within an appropriate context of cultural ideas and values, giving particular attention to the development of that cultural context and its influence on those works over an extended period of time.

I would add to these the following objectives, which I embrace as central to introductory studies of literature: (1) to experience a "connected knowing" [see below] of the texts' stories, and in so doing (2) to understand truths about human experience that the texts illuminate. The large lecture is a good medium for achieving these aims.

Though the class is just ten weeks long, we cover five genres — short fiction, long fiction, creative non-fiction, drama, and poetry — two weeks each, and in this order: seventeen short stories, a novel, a memoir, two full-length plays, nine one-act plays of varying lengths, and thirty to forty poems.

Rather than structuring the course historically or thematically, with characters and situations that might be familiar to the students, I structure it with genres and styles that are accessible to the students in the class. I begin with short stories because it seems to me students are most comfortable and familiar with them. I move on to the novel (*Disgrace*) because, by then, the class has a common vocabulary with which to discuss the longer work of fiction, having spent two weeks developing it in relationship to shorter works. From there the class moves on to drama, and finally poetry.

Considering the amount of material the course covers, there is little time to do close critical analysis of every piece we read. However, the variety does allow the students to experience a diversity of genres and ways that different authors handle those genres. It also allows them to develop a vocabulary of critical terms with which to discuss the texts they read, both aforementioned objectives of the course. The students see how exposition works in short stories, longer stories, and in dramatic pieces. They can identify the climax and dénouement in narratives and the turnings in the poems they read. They see metaphors at work in various genres. But perhaps the most important thing they learn is how to empathize with characters and voices and situations that differ from their own — they learn about the range of conditions that constitute the human experience, not abstractly as they might in other types of courses, but concretely experiencing conditions for themselves through the events of the story, the images of the poem, the scenes of a play, worlds that are both completely different and yet quite similar to their own.

Disgrace is a great laboratory for allowing them to do this. It is set not only in a different country, but in a different hemisphere. David Lurie is not a student, he is a teacher, and he is not young, but middle aged and obsessed with growing older. To compose an opera is an aspiration incomprehensible to most of them. And besides all of this, the politics and history of South Africa are completely unfamiliar. They have heard of apartheid, but usually assume it ended decades earlier than it did. Most of them are unaware of the colonial history and the geography of the country, the distribution of wealth and power in pre-apartheid South Africa, and many of the other elements of *Disgrace*'s historical, geographical, and physical setting. In the first lecture, I am able to present background about this complex setting.

To me the relationship between setting and character seems as integral as between plot and character, even when (or maybe especially when) the setting is undeveloped. Because of this, and because it is hard for students who live here to understand what it is like living in a colonized country, I spend a lot of time on the setting Coetzee uses for *Disgrace*.

To familiarize the students with the historical setting of *Disgrace*, two of the short stories we read are by South African writers: "A Bedtime Story" by Nadine Gordimer, and "Looking for a Rain God" by Bessie Head. Both stories deal with the ambiguities of making moral choices in a colonized country. We also read Divakaruni's "The Disappearance," and

Lahiri's "The Third and Final Continent," both of which examine what happens to citizens of colonized countries who move to the United States.

Bessie Head is a native South African writer, and her story, "Looking for a Rain God," is based on an actual event. It deals with native South African subsistence farmers who sacrifice their children and who then must deal with a colonial justice system as well as with their own guilt and grief. In presenting Head's story in lecture, I aim to introduce how complex the notions of ethics and justice can be in a colonial society, as well as to illustrate the complexities of point of view in narrative. Unlike with *Disgrace*, the reader is not given a focalizing character like David Lurie. It is a story that, finally, leaves me cold, with its objective third-person account of parents who become so desperate that they murder their own children. It seems more like a case study. The reader is offered little chance to empathize with any member of the family. We are the colonizers examining a perfectly good rationale of what colonialism might have to offer the native population, and it is as if Head, who was the illegitimate offspring of a white mother and a black South African father, had to give up her voice to tell it. Still, the point of view and the voice provide a different cultural perspective, a perspective not offered in Coetzee's narrative.

Nadine Gordimer's "A Bedtime Story," also nicely complements *Disgrace* in that it provides a more pointed political critique than Coetzee's narrative. Gordimer's short story opens with the first-person narrator waking in the middle of the night. The narrator is white and privileged. She has been asked to write a story for children and has declined. Then she hears something and fears that there is a burglar in the house, but realizes that it must really be the collapse of a shaft hundreds of feet below her house, where native South Africans often die mining gold. In order to sleep, she tells herself a bedtime story about a white family who build more and more defenses around their home until finally their child gets caught in the concertina wire surrounding their back wall in an attempt to rescue an imaginary princess.

To get a sense of the physical and geographical setting, the class views the opening sequences of Sir Richard Attenborough's *Cry Freedom*, the true story of South African journalist Donald Woods, who is forced to flee the country after attempting to investigate the death of his friend, the black activist Steven Biko. The opening shots of a township being leveled and its residents being terrorized by South African police and their dogs graphically illustrate the reality of being black in South Africa in the late 1970s and early 1980s, a time when David Lurie was teaching not as an adjunct professor of communications at Cape Technical University but as a professor of modern languages at Cape Town University College. A subsequent sequence depicts life in the wealthy white suburbs served by the citizens of those townships, as well as life in the rural frontier of a South African homeland.

In addition to giving a sense of setting, these texts sensitize the class to the silent underbellies of the stories we read. In lecture, I argue that the Steven Biko story gets cannibalized by Donald Woods in *Cry Freedom* much as the wife's story is cannibalized by the husband's in "The Disappearance," and that Lucy's story is consumed by David's in *Disgrace*. These intentional silences give as much shape to the narratives as the articulated stories of Donald Woods, Divakaruni's unnamed husband, and David Lurie himself.

One day in class, a student (a sixty-year-old white male) asked why we did not read more works about the suffering and injustice in our own country. "Aren't there enough situations to read about in our own back yard?" he asked. I explained how I sought reading selections that present diversity in gender, age, ethnicity, and historical perspective. A few weeks later, when another older student who chose to write on *Disgrace* turned in her essay, I was rewarded with this wonderful beginning paragraph, one that voiced a connected knowing of the text and implicitly answered her classmate's query:

> I was introduced to David Lurie a few weeks ago and feel as if I have known him all my life. . . . Not that I am like David Lurie, but I have seen him in many friends and family over the years. In fact, I would go so far as saying that every man has a little bit of David Lurie in him.

It's easily assumed that in a large lecture format, the teacher's "read" of the story will be passed on to the students. I asked one of the other contributors to this anthology what he thought best differentiated seminars and large lectures. There was, he thought, a consumerist element to the lecture absent from the seminar. I took this to mean that the lecturer, in presenting his or her own reading of the text, may offer students a sort of product which they are likely to "buy" uncritically. I can understand that assessment. However, it doesn't match my experience, either in taking or teaching a large lecture class. I never suggested to my students that "every man has a little bit of David Lurie in him." As a woman, I'd be embarrassed to promote this idea to a mixed-gender audience, even as a woman I'm embarrassed to admit that there's a little bit of David Lurie in me. However, I do share with my students some of my "read" on the story. I emphasize, for example, that I believe Lurie is transformed by the end of the story and that this transformation is especially evidenced by his ability to see his daughter differently. I invite my students to write on the subject of Lurie's transformation, and though it is only one of many essay options, many students choose it. In my last batch of *Disgrace* essays, twelve students wrote on Lurie. Seven felt he had changed; five felt he had not. Clearly, my students did not passively accept my interpretation of the text.

Finally, for those students who initially find *Disgrace* too spare or distant, there are several ways to make it more accessible and appealing in the context of a large lecture hall. Besides providing historical background on South Africa and apartheid, I use two strategies to engage students in the conflicts and tensions unique to *Disgrace*. The first of these is a "turn-to-your-neighbor" time. I develop a series of questions that ask students to extrapolate situations from the novel into stories they know from their own lives. In these moments students are given frequent opportunities to link the issues inherent in David Lurie's situation to their own experience. To take a provocative example, I might say to a class: "Certainly there are other men besides David Lurie who think they've 'solved the problem of sex rather well.'" Then I will ask the students to describe to their neighbor one or two men they know who seem smug about their relationships with their partners. I'll usually pair that question with its opposite: have they known men who have learned from a difficult situation? This list changes with the tenor of each class.

The second strategy I use is a variation on the first: written responses on note cards — or, as my teaching assistant calls them, the postcards. I pose questions such as, "Do you think David Lurie raped Melanie Isaacs?" or, "Do you think Lucy is doing the right thing by refusing to report her rape?" just before I'm ready to speak to those issues. Each student then writes a paragraph on a note card. I may ask a few students to read what they've written, and I may also have them exchange cards with a neighbor and give each pair a few minutes to read and discuss. Twosomes like this, a common strategy in small classes, can break up the potential monotony of a lecture, and keep students actively engaged with the novel's central issues. I collect all the cards afterwards. Reading through them gives me a better gauge of how well the class is grappling with *Disgrace*. They get credit for their replies as long as it is obvious that they have done the reading. Neither strategy calls for grading, yet both engage the students in conflicts and tensions within the plot and ask them to connect those conflicts and tensions to similar situations in their own experience.

III. Writing, Reading, and Abandonment to Story

There is a growing body of research in feminist studies, philosophy, and psychology that subscribes to a different type of "*non*-critical" thinking or connected knowing. For example, Blythe Clinchy, a developmental psychologist, equates critical thinking with "separate knowing" which she defines as

> detachment. The separate knower holds herself aloof from the object she is trying to analyze. She takes an impersonal stance. She follows certain rules and procedures to ensure that her judgments are unbiased. All dis-

ciplines and vocations have these impersonal procedures for analyzing things. (36)

Separate knowing is opposed to what researchers call "connected knowing." In one study Clinchy and her fellow researchers describe a more embracing way of "connected knowing".

> the knowers attempted to "get into the heads" of people they wanted to understand, trying to see through the other eyes — a position diametrically opposed to the separate knowing/devil's advocate role of traditional critical thought (78)

Dana Goia, poet and chair of the National Endowment for the Arts, discusses how in our educational institutions we tend to privilege science and philosophy rather than art and narrative. But art is distinct because it simultaneously engages memory, body, intellect, and emotion, an experience that cannot be duplicated by science or logic. Yet in the study of literature, particularly in the small classroom, we are asked, and in turn ask our students, to apply rational thought to their experience of narrative art, often before they/we have had a chance to let the experience sink in.

When writers give an account of their writing process, most of them describe the same phenomenon: Some writers write in the morning, some at night; some use computers, some write longhand on yellow legal tablets, some sharpen twenty pencils before they begin. Most need caffeine. Nearly all of them, though, describe a state of mind where they leave the intentional mind behind and enter into the world of the story. Nearly all writers of literary fiction, including Coetzee, describe a process where they become scribes — the story tells itself to them. The act of writing becomes more like dreaming — or perhaps more like reading. The writer gets lost in it. The magic is doubled when the reader enters that same world of the story, abandoning the confines of her personally circumscribed world. To literature professors, trained in theory and criticism, this might seem like an overstated claim, yet in artistic circles — amongst working writers — it is a widely recognized element of the practice of writing poetry and fiction.

In both writing and reading fiction, there is anonymity in which the self is, for a while, forgotten, and this seems important for encouraging deep and empathetic knowing of the text. The ability to read closely also seems to be a good thing, but sometimes those two things seem at odds. This may be because close, critical reading brings the self back into the narrative, and to bring the self back in before the self has ever been forgotten, and entered into a connected knowing with the characters and conditions of the story, seems to defeat what I see as the primary purpose of narrative.

Although teaching students to read closely and critically, to engage in analysis, to infer meaning, to synthesize and evaluate texts is undoubtedly important, these are all ways of knowing that are not unique to the study of literature. What literature, as well as other narrative arts, offers is a visceral experience of people and places beyond those that the reader might otherwise know. It seems to me that the primary purpose of literature is to move students to love stories and to be able to move beyond themselves. I can read Barbara Ehrenreich's *Nickel-and-Dimed: On (Not) Getting By in America* in sociology and I can read the "Income and Wealth Distribution of U.S. Families" in statistics. In a literature course I can read Toni Cade Bombara's "The Lesson" and feel what it's like to be poor.

Just as some composition teachers advocate teaching their student writers to put aside their critical faculties when they are generating material, I suspect that student readers might benefit from putting aside their critical faculties on their first reads to just experience the world of the story. In a small classroom, this is difficult because there is no anonymity in this type of learning community. The student reads, not with the idea of losing him or herself in the narrative, but with the idea that he or she must say something about the narrative in the next class session.

Disgrace is a particularly ironic narrative to examine through the lens of critical analysis because to a large extent, *Disgrace* can be read as the account of a man who has so rationalized all modes of knowing that he is incapable of the simultaneous engagement of which Goia speaks. David Lurie, at least in the opening of *Disgrace*, is a master of close reading, the mode of discourse most often used in the small classroom. We get his take on everything from Wordsworth and Byron to Soraya, Melanie, and his colleagues. We even get a close reading of Lurie on Lurie. And yet his mastery of the close read seems to have solved few of his problems. The close, self-conscious read simply isn't enough for Lurie. Perhaps Lurie's salvation is that at the end of *Disgrace* he seems more capable of connected knowing.

IV. Bible Studies and Sermons

Recently I discovered the root of my distrust in the close, critical read as the best approach to a narrative. A person I intellectually respect invited me to attend a Bible study he was leading on the book of Ephesians. As with thousands of such studies I had attended as a youth, the group was asked to closely read each chapter of St. Paul's epistle. We were provided with colored pencils so we could individually annotate the text. We were given a variety of translations, including Greek and Hebrew word derivatives. I read the passage several times. I listened to the various group members' analysis of what Paul's words meant in the context of their lives.

My ennui regarding such spiritual study is not a result of my lack of interest in the subject matter. A few years before I had been sent a taped lecture on the same Bible passage delivered by a dynamic preacher named

Earl Palmer. I put the tape in my tape deck, leaving Southern California for the drive back to Tucson where I was living at the time. Six hours later I ran out of gas. I had become so engaged in the lecture that I forgot to fill the tank. I can't remember agreeing with everything Palmer said; I was just so taken by the presentation, by his enthusiasm — by the performance.

The biggest difference between the small seminar and the large lecture is that the students spend less time listening in a small seminar. They spend more time struggling with their own interpretations of the narrative. I come to such classes with a bifurcated perspective — a perspective shaped not only by my academic experience, but also by my religious upbringing. On the one hand, that experience of closely reading a text fosters both a community of readers and a number of interesting interpretations of the text. On the other, the readings and interpretations often seem idiosyncratic. With a close critical reading, there tends to be straying away from the overarching structure and cultural context of the story meaning being deferred to both a denial of and obsession with the author's intention in constructing various parts of the text. Minor passages — say on Lurie's teaching of Byron — become hugely important vehicles for establishing meaning in *Disgrace*, whereas the larger story is lost.

Of course the same thing can happen in a large lecture, but in it the students begin by listening. And that's a good place to begin. It provides the lecturer opportunity to guide students into a holistic, connected sense of the story. Teaching students to read closely and critically for themselves is an invaluable skill. But what seems as important is that they learn to apply close and critical reading to stories they love or at least know in some empathetic sense: To love a story *and* then read it closely.

V. "Just as I am, I come": Altar Calls in Large Lecture Classes

In many ways my undergraduate training always reminded me of church. In the classroom, a small community is engaged in the admirable task of reading, analyzing, and interpreting texts with the belief that each person's reading had value. But what power did I have in shaping the vision?

In my old church we also had altar calls. On Sunday mornings and especially on Sunday nights, the minister would give as rousing a performance as he could muster (in the church I grew up in, it *was* always a "he"). Then "with every head bowed and every eye closed," and with the organist playing "Just as I am, without one plea," — thundering, crying, pleading — he would call the sinners to repentance. And who knew? If the performance was good enough — if the lights were low, if the congregation got lost in it — perhaps the crowd would come forward, though few of us trained in close reading ever did. I believe there was a good reason for those of us who learned the art of the close read always to hang back. We were asked to do close reads before we did open-hearted reads, allowing the story to speak for itself. We learned to be critical of the story *before* we learned to enjoy it.

What surprises and pleases me most about teaching a large lecture class is this: I have faith that most of the students sitting in that cavernous hall with its electronically controlled lectern, projection booths, and theatre seating will at one time or another take the leap. If I can get them to read the book and connect with the story, they will speak up. And in front of every person sitting in the room, eyes open and heads unbowed, they will say what David Lurie's story meant to them and tell a story of their own.

15: Discussing *Disgrace* in a Critical Theory Class

Bradley Butterfield

WHENEVER I TEACH "ENG 355: CRITICAL THEORY" here at the University of Wisconsin-La Crosse, there are at least a few students who dare to ask what "all this" has to do with literature, or even English. My usual reply is that while their question is perfectly understandable, while what we are reading is technically called twentieth-century philosophy, not literature, not literary criticism even, its relevance is nonetheless manifold. Theory is transportable, I tell them; you can take it anywhere and use it to contextualize an inquiry or a debate about anything, and for literature majors, that thing is literature. This year, for the first time, I decided to put literature to the test by assigning J. M. Coetzee's *Disgrace* for our last class and using it as a sort of case study, something to compare our theorists to. I told my students on the first day that a group of "unsolitary readers" from my alma mater had asked me to teach the book and then write about the experience. I told them that on our last class meeting (we met once a week for three hours), the following questions would be at issue: "What would *Disgrace* and its characters have to say to these theorists, and how would the theorists reply? What would Coetzee say if he were a theorist? What would *you* say?" Little did I know at that time that such questions — "What would (blank) say?" — would be problematized in a way that might have served as the beginning for a whole new course called "Critical Theory and The Novel." To wit: what is at stake when one person attempts to speak for another? As I say, we did not begin with this quintessential question, but arrived at it naturally, as it were, at the end of a long discussion.

Out of eighteen students, a dedicated crew of thirteen made it to the finish line that semester. After gulping hard theory straight from the fire hose all semester, *Disgrace* was a welcome reward for all of us. For upper-division literature courses, I usually have the students generate their own discussion questions and then play spin-the-bottle in class (to see whose questions get discussed), but for Critical Theory, because of the level of difficulty, I always hand out my own discussion questions the week before and tell them to bring their own if they have them. Since this is what we were used to, and since I wanted to make the most of our time for this special class on *Disgrace*, I chose to stay with the program and give them my own set of questions. A good class discussion depends first on good discussion questions, and while it is necessary that students practice posing questions on their own, teacher-generated questions have the advantage of adding focus to a discussion, as the students have spent their prep-time thinking of their individual answers to a short list of questions, instead of generating a long and unruly list of individual questions themselves.

Handing out discussion questions is something none of my professors ever did, and I don't see why. The "decentered classroom" sometimes worked in miraculous ways when I was in college at the Johnston Center, but by graduate school I began to tire of unfocused, student-generated discussions. My favorite classes were classes in which the professor would spend part of the time lecturing in a way that helped clarify the reading, and part of the time directing a spirited and pertinent discussion. The worst were the ones where the professor would just show up and say, "So, what do you guys want to talk about?" I wanted to come out of each class feeling like I had taken part in a learning event. Now I try to teach those kinds of classes, in preparation for which I spend a good deal of time on discussion questions, whether I'm having students generate their own or not.

A good discussion question must call for complex and varied responses. Yes/No and single-right-answer questions get you nowhere, unless you are lecturing. I tell students, however, that the discussion questions are just a springboard, and that they are free to take the discussion in different directions if they feel inspired.

As a discussion moderator, I often paraphrase what a student says so that everyone knows what's on the table; or I call on another student to do the same: "Stacy, how do you understand John's remark?" I explain that by asking them to be ready to play the "teacher" role, I hope to make them more responsible to each other as participants. These explicit expectations foster this behavior, I feel.

Some of my colleagues might object that routinely restating students' comments assumes that students aren't clear to begin with, or that it's a way of co-opting what they say and making it one's own. To the first charge, I can only say yes, students are frequently unclear and sometimes are not even sure what they want to say. Some also tend to mumble. I think it's my job to make sure students' messages are heard. Too often teachers simply nod their heads and say "right, right" when they have no idea what a student is getting at. When this happens, the other students will likely be too shy to demand clarification, and some will conclude that their duty to the class is to simply sit quietly and wait for the bell to ring. As to the second charge, that such clarifications appropriate the words of the other, I can only say yes again, with the caveat that this is not such a bad thing. As Gadamer suggests in *Wahrheit und Methode*, good communication requires one to put oneself in the shoes of the other, to translate the other's statements into one's own terms. Anyone can repeat what someone else says, but translation requires understanding.

Once I am sure that a student's idea has been understood, I pose another question, one that will problematize or clarify the issue, or take us further. I prefer to weave my own opinions into the discussion in this way, rather than challenge students. Sometimes I may present my opinions as ironic ("Don't trust me, I might be the devil, but . . .") or as "the view that *some* might take." But sometimes I give them what I always appreciated getting from my professors: I give them myself, my honest feelings and opinions. When my professors did this, I came away feeling inspired or changed by what they had said.

I usually begin worksheets or class discussions with identification questions, which require students to sort out and articulate the explicit level of meaning in a text. "What is going on in this story? What is being said here? What does it mean?" I often ask them to paraphrase important passages. Translating like this, again, implies a hermeneutics of trust, in which I ask them to step into the character's or implied author's shoes. This practice makes our understanding more concrete and more personal.

However, I did not begin this discussion of *Disgrace* with questions of identification or explicit meaning. For *Disgrace*, my instincts told me to begin *in medias res*, that is, with the question, "How do you judge David Lurie?" I felt that the energy would be high coming off all that theory, and that the students were advanced enough that explication/identification questions would be superfluous. The best class is the class that resembles a party, where everybody dances (together!) and the DJ keeps picking good tunes. Having spent most of the semester on the explicit level of theoretical texts, I suspected the students were eager to make it more personal. So we went straight to their interpretations and opinions.

We make a theorist out of a novelist by using our understanding of him to "speak for him" and then argue for or against what we understand. And to get at this personal understanding of the author, students need to explore who *they* are in relation to this text, to this character, to this moral dilemma or this implied meaning or interpretation. Such questions often generate the best discussion as they implicitly confront students with issues of their own identity and choices. They must ask themselves, "Who am I, and how should I live?"

Finally, beneath the implicit meaning of the text, we explore symptomatic and relational meaning: "What caused Huxley to think this way? What does this have to do with our own society? How does this relate to what we talked about yesterday?" My class discussions often move from the text to the real world, and I welcome political and ethical debates about current matters that the text brings closer to us. I want students (ideally) to move from an understanding of the text, to an understanding of themselves, to an understanding of the world they live in, each class session offering a microcosm of the liberal arts education they have embarked on.

This is the general framework of my approach to teaching a novel, but I don't follow it slavishly. I try to let the text and its context in my class determine my line of questioning. With that said, here are three of the questions I handed out the week before reading *Disgrace* at the end of my "Critical Theory" class. (One need not be conversant with all the theorists listed here to follow my description of our discussion below.) They are by no means the perfect questions for the perfect class, but as part of the ongoing experiment that is teaching, particularly the teaching of Coetzee's *Disgrace* in relation to the question of ethics in a Critical Theory class, I hope they are instructional.

* * *

Sample Discussion Questions for Disgrace

1. Let's start with David's affair with Melanie. If you were to take Geoffrey Harpham's advice and try "imagining the center, placing yourself in the position, both powerful and vulnerable, of the lawgiver, the judge," what would your verdict be? In what way is David guilty of being unethical, if you think he has been; or what would you say on his behalf if you were to try to defend him? What are the ethics of inter-generational sexual relationships, and of such relations between teachers and students, or employers and employees (President Clinton and Monica Lewinsky, for example)?

2. Related to question #1, what do you think the Foucault of *Discipline and Punish* would say about the situation? What should David's punishment be? Or what about the later Foucault? What would the Stoics, for instance, say regarding the ethics of the situation? How would you judge in terms of an "aesthetics of existence"?

3. Next, let's consider the rape of Lucy. What is the effect of juxtaposing this crime against David's daughter with David's lesser infraction against Melanie? What are the similarities and differences? What do you think the book means to say about rape in general, and the specific rape of a white woman by black men in South Africa? How do you explain David's and Lucy's differing reactions to the crime? Whose point of view do you sympathize with more, and why?

Succeeding questions took up the theme of "disgrace" itself; race and the politics/history of South Africa as a context for assessing the novel's alleged racism; our sympathy with and judgment of David Lurie; and the ways in which the ideas of our theorists engaged *Disgrace*.

* * *

In our class discussion, questions #1 and #2 dovetailed quickly, as the students were eager to weigh in on the meaning of David Lurie's disgrace and the question of what Foucault would say about it. We discussed some of the other questions too, but these first two got the most time. I was careful to stress that we mustn't simply bend the text to Foucault's terms, or to any theorist's terms, but that we should consult the theorists as "expert witnesses," as people who would (if they were present) have opinions about the characters and their dilemmas. Coetzee too, I suggested, must be brought to testify against his characters. "Would Coetzee consider David guilty? Why or why not?" Thus, we brought a whole constellation of perspectives into the discussion, including the theorists', the novelist's, the characters', and the students' own opinions. I reminded them of Adorno's conception in *Aesthetic Theory* of the truth content of a work being comprised of just such a constellation, or force field, of differing perspectives.

Some might object that speaking for a novelist is impossible, that we can only speak for ourselves, but one of the differences between critical theory and a novel is that in most novels, the author's explicit opinion seems to be absent. We are invited to make the implicit explicit, and to do that is to speak for the text and its author, or to perform what Mark Edmundson in *Why Read?* calls "inspired ventriloquism" (53). Though Edmundson rails against "Foucaultian readings" (38–42) and the reduction of literature to theory (and I tend to agree), as long as one is turning Coetzee into a theorist by explicating his ethical philosophy, one might as well bring him into dialogue with other ethical philosophers. Comparison is not the same as reduction.

One faction of the class quickly developed on behalf of the early Foucault (from *Discipline and Punish*). They argued that Lurie's soul was on trial, and that the committee had no right to discipline his soul for a crime his body *may* have committed. "And did it? Did Lurie's body break the law?" I asked. One student recalled that the letter the committee sent to David contained the university's conduct code regarding the victimization or harassment of a student, so we pursued the nature of the code. Did Lurie break it? Is it ethical? Was Lurie's behavior unethical? And if so, what, if anything, should be his punishment?

Coetzee doesn't tell us what the code is, an obvious and characteristic omission, so we deduced that this meant we had to decide for ourselves what it was, and also what it should be.

Harassment, some students claimed, is a matter of consent. If someone consents without coercion or threat, she cannot claim to have been harassed. "So, did David harass Melanie?" I asked. Some in the early Foucault faction argued that Melanie was not forced, that she could have gotten out of it any time, that she came to him willingly. I noted that Foucault said little about the actual guilt of the prisoner or about how to judge guilt, that he was more concerned with noting the different ways guilt has been determined and punished. This gave a new faction a way to argue against the young Foucaultians. They believed that Melanie was harassed because the sex was undesired and because he was in a position of power over her. I told them what the harassment code is at our university — professors cannot have sexual relationships with their current students, and in any other relationship between a student and a teacher, the University will take the student's side if the student decides to file harassment charges. They all agreed that if that were the code, then Lurie was guilty of breaking it.

"But does he deserve that guilt?" I asked. I then got them to talk about their feelings while reading about the affair. We consulted the most disturbing moments of the text, "not rape, not quite that, but undesired . . ." (25), and here the Foucaultians were quieter. Others spoke of feeling queasy or downright disgusted while reading those passages, so I tried to get them to follow that feeling. It came from imagining how she felt, they said. I added that perhaps we also are sickened by feeling what he felt, since the narrative represents his point of view, or by the uncanny sense that Lurie is both conscious and unconscious of his own queasy feelings.

Putting themselves in the "powerful but vulnerable position" of being the judge, as Geoffrey Harpham had recommended to us the week before in his *Shadows of Ethics*, most of them felt that Lurie had done something wrong, law or no law. The young Foulcaultians did, however, stick with their view that Lurie's crimes were private, not public, matters, and that David should therefore not be punished in any public sense, that he should not be punished for his inner feelings but rather only if his *body* could be proven to have transgressed the law.

A male student observed that all the men were taking Lurie's side and the women were taking Melanie's. "And what conclusions do we draw from this?" I asked. Silence, of course. Students are often paralyzed when the obvious is pretty much all there is to say. I pushed on: "Perhaps that we are more likely to sympathize with those who are the same than we are with those who are different in a patriarchal society. This results in the oppression of women, no?" A few heads nodded.

I asked what they thought the later Foucault would say about Lurie's guilt. Foucault's Stoics, someone said, would have seen Lurie as guilty of failing to discipline his own desires. I pointed out that the Stoics would nevertheless see his guilt in *aesthetic*, not *moral* terms. For the Stoics, a lack of self-control was an *ugly* way to live, unbecoming of a philosopher. Someone suggested that the "ugliness" of the scene may have had something to do with why it was uncomfortable to read about, beyond our moral queasiness.

In one three-hour seminar, we of course were not able to do justice to such a complex text, nor were we able to address all the discussion questions. I would especially have liked to have spent more time on Lurie's opera and on the historical/political aspects of the novel, but the ethical was the main focus of our Critical Theory class. I believe we emerged with a better understanding of David as a character and of the ethical questions surrounding his case. More importantly, perhaps, I think we came out with new self-understanding, having put ourselves in David's and Melanie's shoes and walked through the moral dilemmas of the story. The theorists we had studied were also illuminated by the discussion. Using Foucault, and later Butler and Derrida, as lenses for analyzing *Disgrace* helped clarify their theories by providing examples of how they might be applied. With these examples to recall, students will be better able to utilize these theories in other contexts; they will know better how to live according to them, if they should so choose.

We had a good debate, everyone got in on it, but when it came to drawing final wisdom from the text itself, there was a lot of thoughtful silence. Final questions about the author's intent often leave students mute in my classes, and I too sometimes find it awkward posing them: "What is the *moral* of this story, as long as we're talking about ethics in the novel? What is the implicit message here? What does Coetzee's story teach us about this character and about life?" However clichéd or old-fashioned such questions may sound, they are essential if we are to give the (implied) author his or her due and not just use the novel as a testing ground for theory. Students are often reluctant to draw moral conclusions in front of each other. Most of our time as academics we spend questioning and problematizing issues that on the surface may seem simple, but I believe that, at the risk of seeming reductive or too simplistic ourselves, there comes a time when we must seek clarity and pose answers to our questions, however out of vogue that may be. So, not knowing that my attempts would again be problematized before we left, I did my best to impress upon them the following points:

1.) That though they seem to represent opposite viewpoints, both David and his daughter Lucy, the conservative and the liberal (we had not talked as much about their relationship as we had about David and Melanie's) feel in their own ways superior to the blacks of South Africa (Lucy's desire to humble herself before history presumes that blacks cannot be held to the same standards as whites). Moral: forgive if you want, but hold people to the same moral standards as you hold yourself.

2.) David is guilty of a most basic breach of ethics: not attempting to see things from the other's point of view, and using his power over others to his own benefit. Moral: put yourself in the other's shoes and treat that person as you would if there were no power differential.

3.) David, like Emma Bovary, perhaps demonstrates the danger of living one's life through literature (Emma with her romances, David in imitation of his literary hero) while ignoring one's real ethical relationships. However, one might also argue that David's moral development in the end depends upon his own literary endeavor, which leads him to abandon his hero, Byron, the seducer of younger women, and to see the world through the eyes of Byron's abandoned lover, Teresa. Teresa's real-life equivalent is Bev Shaw, and I would add that Driepoot, "a young male with the withered left hindquarter which it drags behind" (215), is the darkly playful counterpart of Byron with his club foot. David sacrifices the favored old dog in both cases, and learns to see things from the point of view of his long detested "other," an older, unattractive woman. By the end of the book, then, David has expanded what Richard Rorty would call his "final vocabulary" (see Richard Rorty, *Contingency, Irony and Solidarity*, 73); he has widened his understanding of himself by sympathizing with another. Moral: art can help us to imagine the other's perspective, but we must remember to apply this to our lives. There are people all around us who need our consideration, who need us to see their point of view, and who need and deserve our compassion. Old dogs can learn new tricks.

There were a few minutes left, so I pushed the question back to them. "What do *you* think? Has this book *changed* you in any way?" They were thoughtful, quiet, and just when I thought it was over, a very shy but studious student came through with a question that could easily have been the central question of our next discussion. Having read more about Coetzee on the internet, she had determined that one of his primary themes was that "in light of South African politics, we should be careful about speaking for other people, or presuming that we understand what it's like to walk in their shoes. Isn't this at odds with your way of trying to get us to speak for the characters and for the author?" We were unfortunately out of time, so I was forced to leave the question unanswered, but it followed me home, and though I will incorporate it in the next class I teach on *Disgrace*, there is no way to end this essay without attempting to address it.

Though I agree with Gadamer that communication and understanding are possible where there exists the "good will" to imagine the world from the other's perspective and to, in effect, speak for him or her, I am reminded of Derrida's refusal to understand Gadamer at a conference dedicated to the latter on his ninetieth birthday (see *Dialogue and Deconstruction: The Gadamer-Derrida Encounter*). Derrida's response to Gadamer's paper on the necessity of a "good will to understand" for hermeneutics and human communication to be possible was a *will*ful misreading, a deconstruction, of the paper that left Gadamer perplexed and left me reservedly on Gadamer's side. Whereas Gadamer trusts in the possibility of a shared context for understanding when both parties act in good faith, Derrida's Nietzschean response is to expose such faith as metaphysical and such "good will to understand" as nothing but "will to power," thus casting a dubious light on any "truth" arrived at through our imagined abilities to think with or for each other.

Since *Disgrace*'s David Lurie, and it would seem Coetzee himself, come across as decidedly in the Derridean camp, my student's comment forced me to confront my reservations. The "handbook" explanation for the discipline David finds himself reduced to teaching sums up, rather unflatteringly, the type of communication theory my pedagogy presupposes: "Human society has created language in order that we may communicate our thoughts, feelings and intentions to each other" (3–4). David, on the other hand, believes that "the origins of speech lie in song, and the origins of song in the need to fill out with sound the overlarge and rather empty human soul" (4). Indeed, the book seems to make a strong case for the impossibility of speaking for anyone else (the committee for David, David for Lucy, Melanie's father or boyfriend for Melanie, and so forth).

We did not read any communication theory in our class, so I did not press this issue, but for myself, I found an uneasy resolution: both notions about the origins of language have an element of truth, if one has the good will to understand them. Likewise, one cannot deny a certain complicity with violence when, say, the white minority attempts to speak for the black majority in South Africa, or when men attempt to speak for women. Coetzee would likely say (if I may be so bold as to speak for him here) that such violence is inevitable. And yet his writing also suggests that we must try anyway, that without such attempts to "read" the other, communication is impossible, and the potential for violence only becomes worse. Much of the vital tension at the heart of Coetzee's work results from, I suspect, his living in and writing from this purgatorial dilemma. *Disgrace* cautions us about our assumptions when we try to represent the other, but it should not dissuade us from trying. If we can never understand and therefore speak for/from another's perspective, then the point of literature is lost, except for those who feel the need to fill out their empty souls with songs sung only for themselves.

Whether my students and I understood the implied ethics, the "theory," of *Disgrace* any better than we understood the theories of Foucault et al., I cannot say. Coetzee's own intentions aside, our identification with his characters, our attempts to speak for them, and ultimately for him, did help us to better understand some of the theories we had studied — the main goal for our Critical Theory class.

16: *Disgrace* in the Classroom: A Tale of Two Teaching Strategies

Raymond Obstfeld

> Timms: Sir. I don't always understand poetry.
> Hector: You don't always understand it? Timms, I never understand it. But learn it now, know it now and you'll understand it whenever.
> Timms: I don't see how we can understand it. Most of the stuff poetry's about hasn't happened to us yet.
> Hector: But it will, Timms. It will. And then you will have the antidote ready! Grief. Happiness. Even when you're dying. We're making your deathbeds here, boys.
> — from Alan Bennett's play, *The History Boys*

THIS EXCHANGE BETWEEN A PERPLEXED STUDENT (Timms) and his earnest but eccentric teacher (Hector) captures the dilemma every English teacher faces when choosing what works to use in a literature course. The teacher wants to select works of Enduring Value, meaning ones that display the craft of writing at its highest level while also presenting themes that offer useable insights into the complexities of our daily lives. On the other hand, those "enduring values" will be totally lost if the works selected are irredeemably boring to the student. Plus, you run the risk of forever alienating them from the joys of reading. What English teacher wants to be responsible for causing students to *not* want to read a book ever again?

Selecting appropriate reading material in a community college English class is generally not the same process as it would be for an English class at a four-year university. The audience is significantly different. Most community college English literature classes are introductory in nature. For some of our students, this is the first time they will be reading a novel. For most of the others, this is the first time they will read a novel as anything more than entertainment. Many will be disappointed at the lack of deadly lasers or heaving breasts. This makes teaching a novel like J. M. Coetzee's *Disgrace* especially challenging. The novel already comes with a lot of strikes against it: the author won the Nobel Prize in Literature (translation: a bunch of old dudes with dust in their veins liked it cuz nothing happens);

a 2006 poll of "literary luminaries" by *The Observer* concluded that this was the "Greatest Novel of the Last 25 Years" (translation: that's because these snobs never read *The Da Vinci Code*); it's about a guy in his fifties (translation: nerds who like these kinds of books are all old farts who don't remember what it's like to be young). Of course, you can make the case that the book is about universal themes that affect each of their lives. But the response is usually a less articulate version of the above exchange from *The History Boys*: "What do I care what some guy in his fifties, who's royally screwed up his life, thinks or feels?"

Don't bother coming to the book's defense. Those students are right. Most of them aren't ready for the book yet and teaching it to them would benefit two or three students who, let's face it, would benefit from pretty much any selection you make. They are the transfer students who will probably major in English and they love the kind of deep-massage analysis the book demands. But the community college teacher has to be mindful that most students aren't in the class because they elected to be, they are there because *they need the class to transfer*. The challenge then is to introduce them to literature through works they would more likely identify with (translation: novels featuring protagonists near their own age). That's why I teach those classes novels such as Martin Amis's *The Rachel Papers* or Nick Hornby's *High Fidelity*. The protagonists are young enough for the students to relate to and the superficial accounts of love and sex are interesting to them. Yet, both deal with the usual suspects of literary themes, allowing me to launch into various lectures about everything from Joseph Campbell's Quest of the Hero to existential bad faith. All painlessly inserted like a literary suppository.

However, there are exceptions, even at the community college level. I teach a novel-writing workshop every semester. Because of the demands of the course, as well as the fact that it's offered at night, the students are a very different mix than in my other classes. First, the students run a broader spectrum of ages. Of the thirty-five students, only four or five will be under twenty; half will be over forty. Second, while many students in two- or four-year programs must also work, ninety percent of these students will have full careers, not just temporary jobs. My current class has a surgeon, two attorneys, two advertising company executives, a journalist, and several business owners. Many have children; some have grandchildren. Two of my students have masters degrees in English, one from UC Berkeley, the other from Stanford University. None of the others has any serious literature background, meaning they have never done any close readings, or if they have, it was twenty years ago. But they are all united in a passion to write a novel. To tell their story. Or at least *a* story.

The class regimen is grueling: each week they must read five excerpts of student novels (twenty-five pages each!) while working diligently on their own novels. During the four-hour weekly meetings, I lecture for about an hour on various writing techniques or the use of theme or the approaches to structure, after which we discuss each of the five student manuscripts, line by line, praising what works and offering suggestions to improve what doesn't work. At the end of each class, we discuss whatever literary work I've assigned. Sometimes I use short stories, other times novels. The novels I've assigned in the past include A. L. Kennedy's *So I Am Glad*, Larry McMurtry's *The Last Picture Show*, Budd Schulberg's *What Makes Sammy Run*, and Ellen Currie's *Available Light*. I especially like to use first novels or story collections when they are initially published because the students find them particularly motivating ("If they can do it, so can I!"). I find these first works to be especially inspiring to the students because they are often filled with the kinds of flaws that are typical of beginning writers, yet they are also powered by a passion and sincerity that overcomes those minor flaws. That's an important lesson for many of my students: it doesn't have to be perfect. So, over the years I've taught Brett Easton Ellis's *Less Than Zero*, Jay McInerney's *Bright Lights, Big City*, Zadie Smith's *White Teeth*, Tama Janowitz's *Slaves of New York*, Laurie Moore's *Self-Help*, and many others.

I approached teaching *Disgrace* with a lot of trepidation. The style is subtle, without some of the overwrought metaphors and similes that so many renowned literary writers employ (I admire Don DeLillo and E. Annie Proulx, but, man, they can overwrite like nobody else). The protagonist is passive-aggressive in a way that makes him unsympathetic and unlikable in the first third. While that may have thematic necessity, I didn't want students to grudgingly read the book, dutifully marking pages while longing for the sweet release of *Heroes*. Although I teach a lot of techniques about how to make an unlikable protagonist compelling enough that the readers are still involved, Coetzee is more subtle in this technique as well. If he's too subtle, will students merely resent the crafty bastard rather than learn from him?

First, Do No Harm: What Does the Student Need?

Like stand-up comedy and juggling chainsaws, teaching is all about timing. I don't assign the novel until at least six weeks into the semester for two reasons. First, by then those cocky students who are there merely to show off their genius will have dropped out. I use an opening-day exercise that, though not designed for this reason, identifies those students who see themselves as superior to all the others and will therefore be especially nasty in their critiques and completely resistant to suggestions about their own writing. (Sometimes they identify themselves directly, like the student who approached me before the first class to announce, "I went to Yale and don't care what any of these people have to say about my writing.") The exercise is simple: I pass out a packet consisting of the first two pages of seven novels, without identifying the titles and authors. I select novels from various genres, but always what I consider to be excellent writing. I then ask the students to read each sample and give it a grade from A to F, and to jot down a few notes supporting that grade. After they've finished reading, we discuss each selection. Invariably, each selection has loyalists who give it an A or B, and detractors who give it a C or worse. The discussions are lively and enjoyable. Students get to a chance to talk about writing, I get to see what each student's taste is so I can guide that individual better, and, most important, they get to see that they must give up the notion that, when they submit their manuscripts for discussion, everyone in the class will weep openly over their brilliance. Look how many people gave John Updike a C or D; how many hated Pagan Kennedy. When they see that, they all breathe a collective sigh of relief. The pressure is off.

But beware: the students who don't like any of the selections are the ones who are there to be praised, not taught. The pattern is familiar: their criticism of others will be vague yet harsh; but when their work is discussed, every time they receive a suggestion they will launch into a staunch defense (which is why I don't permit students whose manuscripts are being discussed to explain or defend until everyone else has spoken). More important, once you've critiqued these students, they will probably not return again. Therefore, it is best to assign them to submit early in the semester so they can quit before they do any damage. Those who do not quit usually turn out to be pretty good students. They overcome their ego-attachment to the manuscript and start looking at it for what it is: an arrangement of words that can be rearranged over and over at no cost to one's soul or destiny.

The second reason I wait six weeks to assign the outside novel is that I need that time to teach them about the psychological model, world visions, Joseph Campbell's model, the three-act model, and other lectures that explain the general thematic structure of a novel. These lectures are designed to help them make plot decisions about what happens next based on a deeper understanding of character conflict and motivation rather than their usual panicky, "Quick, make something happen! Anything!" that often results in inappropriate melodrama.

Be aware that I have nothing against melodrama. Sometimes melodrama can be fun and entertaining and highly satisfying. But I don't want my students limited to making melodramatic choices just because they don't think they have any other options. In the beginning of the semester, I make it very clear that I am not here to teach them to write the novel *I* want them to write; I'm here to help them write the novel *they* want to write. Sounds very noble and teacherly, a poster to hang in the classroom with the photo of a joyful student holding up her first published novel.

Of course, it's a partial lie. I *am* here to help them to write the novel they want to write; but I'm also here to help them see the greater potential in their novel that they might not yet see. At least half of the thirty students will be writing genre works: mystery, sci-fi, fantasy, suspense, romance, young adult, and so forth. Assigning them to read mainstream literary fiction like *Disgrace* is designed to teach them how to see their novels outside the confines of the genre. Most students writing within a genre feel the necessity to mimic the books within the genre. And, because most of them aren't trained readers, they worry more about plotting and describing setting than they do about the nuances of characterization or subtleties of style. The result is often a pale imitation of other books in the genre. Exposing them to mainstream fiction is meant to expose them to different writing techniques that they can then choose to use or to ignore. But at least they now have a choice.

As for the other half of the class who claim they are writing mainstream literary novels — many of them really aren't. They are writing some variation of *Sex and the City*, a thinly disguised memoir, or a sex-drugs-and-punk-rock romp designed to shock and awe the older students by frequent use of the word "fuck" and riffs on the joys of anal sex. A few of their classmates are indeed startled, but most have seen it all before, especially if they're veterans of my workshops.

It is important to note that students at Orange Coast College may take the same novel workshop class three times, after which many return to audit. Some students have been in my class for four or five years; some have published novels and returned because they were stuck on their second novels; some have little hope of publishing their novels but are as dedicated to their writing as Olympic athletes are to their sports. We are a community within the community college; a place for them to go to be taken seriously as writers. Because most have other careers, families, children, responsibilities, the student in my class faces two obstacles that the typical four-year university student doesn't face: guilt and scorn. My students worry that their passion to write is frivolous self-indulgence that takes time away from their family and other duties. They also face the mild-to-spicy-hot scorn of others, who dismiss this "hobby" as the result some sort of mid-life crisis. The hardest part of teaching this class is to keep convincing the students that what they're doing is worthwhile and not to abandon it because they feel guilty wasting time on something that doesn't earn them any money. The funny thing is that they don't care at all about making money from their work; they mostly want the money to justify the time spent writing. Basically, earning a few bucks would keep their naysaying family and friends off their backs.

Some taxpaying citizens might quibble about the fact that students can repeat my class so often. Those citizens aren't writers. Writing a novel is often a long and arduous task, the course of which brings out every self-doubt you've ever had about your talent, your intelligence, and your character. I've written about thirty novels and during each and every one I reached a point in which I decided to quit, not just that novel, but writing altogether. Our class is designed to teach the student the craft and art of writing novels, but it's also a support system: we cheer on the marathon runner as she passes by, handing her a water cup, a towel, a hearty "Don't give up!"

The last group of writers consists of those who actually are writing literary mainstream novels. These people are generally well read and articulate. They often have an impressively professional style, with clever metaphors and multi-layered characters. The problem many of them face is that they get stuck around page fifty. They don't know where to go next, so they keep polishing their prose, expanding descriptions, fussing over the same pages — afraid to move on. The first fifty pages of a novel are relatively easy because you're introducing new characters, creating suspenseful plot conflicts, and building a setting from scratch. Those first fifty pages are referred to as "the Promise," in which you make promises about all the exciting things that are going to happen in your novel. The rest of the novel is "the Pay-off," in which you have to make good on some of those promises. That's when some of the best writers get scared that what comes next won't live up to the promises they made. Reading works like *Disgrace* can help nudge them forward because we don't focus on the whole novel, just the small steps taken to make each sentence, each paragraph, and each page successful.

Plan A: The Close-Reading Approach

The first time I taught the novel, I decided we would do a modified close reading. Although we would certainly examine the literary and thematic nuances, my focus would be on writing techniques that the students might employ in their own novel writing. I assigned the students to read only the first three chapters. As always, I insisted that they resist the temptation to read ahead because that would interfere with our discussions about creating suspense and our speculations about choices the writer might make regarding plot. *This restriction is a crucial element in teaching the novel to writing students.* Those who read ahead start to focus on the bigger picture of structure and pay-off scenes and lose sight of the details of the writing techniques. In other words, they end up reviewing the novel rather than learning how to use the devices.

Here's how I thought this would go: I'd ask a few general questions, then go through the first chapter or two almost line by line. Then, after my students were exhausted by this approach, I'd pull back to more general questions for the rest of the novel. That's not what happened. One of the joys of teaching is to experience an unforeseen classroom adventure. For that to happen, you have to relinquish The Plan and give yourself over to the exhilaration of freefalling, like blindly diving into the mosh pit only to be buoyed back up by the unexpected passion of your students.

My first question was an easy one, designed to allow any student to answer, even those who may feel a bit shy about discussing "literary matters." "Is David Lurie a reliable narrator?" I ask. The use of the reliable and unreliable narrator is an ongoing discussion in the novel workshop because it is such a crucial tool for the writer. With the unreliable narrator, I lecture (probably waving my reading glasses in an all-knowing manner), suspense is created in the same way a movie creates suspense by showing us a romantically spurned teenager driving too fast through blinding rain, then cutting to show us the oil tanker truck approaching around a blind curve, the driver distracted by the cigarette that's fallen in his lap and the busted wiper scraping uselessly against the windshield. The unreliable narrator tells us the truth — as far as he sees it. But the audience has superior knowledge that the way he sees his life is wrong and is leading to a crisis. We root for him to come to his senses. This is especially true when one has an unreliable narrator who is also unlikable. Then we need the addition of a "redeemable quality" that makes us have some hope that he will come to his senses and be redeemed. It doesn't matter whether or not he's actually redeemed, but without that hope, the suspense is drastically reduced. Alex in *A Clockwork Orange* is a murdering rapist, but his wit and love of Beethoven (and the fact that everyone else is somehow worse) are redeemable qualities that allow us to hope for his redemption.

That question is the perfect ice-breaker because the students feel comfortable contributing to a subject they've been discussing for weeks. I thought the discussion would last three or four minutes, with everyone agreeing that Lurie is indeed an unreliable narrator. Well, they did agree he was an unreliable narrator, but the discussion went on for twenty minutes, with a lot of side discussions regarding his likeability and whether or not he had redeemable qualities and if the novel generated enough suspense to overlook his character defects. The consensus was a resounding, "Yes, he's a schmuck, but I feel compelled to keep reading." "Really?" I said. "Why?" In essence, the students felt that his misguided romanticism made him, if not likable, at least vulnerable. And his obvious intelligence, as conveyed though the prose style, was invigorating. Also, they were intrigued by a narrative style that seemed to fluctuate between a distant omniscient voice and a limited omniscience that is intimately his own voice.

After that discussion, we started in on the text. I'll provide a few selected sentences as examples of the nature of the discussions:

- "For a man of his age, fifty-two, divorced, he has, to his mind, solved the problem of sex rather well."
  Q: Is this a good opening sentence?

  Summary of the discussion: Five commas in the first sentence can make for a very choppy style. It's as if Coetzee is deliberately keeping the reader at arm's length from the protagonist. Perhaps the staccato style reflects a certain fussiness and need for order on Lurie's part. This need for ritualized order is reflected in the next sentences when we discover he goes to the same place every Thursday and that he is extremely punctual. Also, the clauses that are separated by commas are now highlighted because of the forced pauses, making the reader stop to absorb the information.

  "For a man of his age . . ." has two meanings, his chronological age and the historic Age, suggesting that he represents a certain faction of this Age.

  ". . . fifty-two, divorced . . ." announces that he's in what seems to be a somewhat helpless and hopeless stage of being alone.

  ". . . to his mind . . ." tells us that we can't trust his perception, that he is an unreliable narrator.

  ". . . solved the problem of sex rather well." This phrase is universally acclaimed by the students as being the part of the sentence that most intrigues them about the narrator. That he considers sex to be a problem makes them curious about what kind of man he is. Finding out what his solution is creates suspense, making them want to read on.

- "He strokes her honey-brown body, unmarked by the sun; he stretches her out, kisses her breasts; they make love."
  Q: What does this sentence tell us about his attitude toward Soraya?

  Summary of discussion: The opening phrase ("He strokes her honey-brown body") is deceptive in that it seems the sentence will be about his passion for her. Surprisingly, the sentence reveals just the opposite, that his relationship with her is routine and manipulative. In fact, that's why he derives such satisfaction from it. By the time we read the end of the sentence ("they make love"), we realize that this act is anything but "love" — more like a re-enactment of making love.

  ". . . strokes . . ." suggests how one might approach a pet more than a lover. There are many other, more passionate word choices, he might have used.

  ". . . unmarked by the sun . . ." Why include this phrase at all? Yes, it tells us her skin color, and that it's not the result of a tan, but there are many other ways to do that, other sentences where this information could have appeared. The fact that it appears in a sentence about him stroking her reveals that her skin color is part of the sexual attraction. We don't know yet whether her skin color is arousing because he's defying social norms, or because it's a continuation of white dominance over people of color. In addition, the word "unmarked" suggests a kind of virginal quality. But since she's a prostitute, we know he doesn't mean that literally. Instead, he means that she's something of a blank page that he can manipulate to be whoever he wishes her to be. This relationship is less about sex than about art. He's the artist creating a woman character he wants to be with. This introduces the continuing theme of David as an artist.

". . . he stretches her out . . ." The phrase is active, in that David is the one doing the action. This emphasizes that he is arranging her body the way he wants it; indeed, he is stretching her out the way an artist would stretch out a blank canvas.

". . . kisses her breast . . ." The phrase is deliberately unerotic because David's trying to convey his romantic touch. However, it reveals just the opposite. The way the phrase is stacked among the list in that sentence makes it seem like a routine — just another thing to check off his to-do list. This attitude is emphasized by the use of semi-colons after each task, giving each action more of a mechanical, habitual feel. The fact that he kisses just one breast rather than both also tells us that it is a routine more than a passion.

Well, you get the point. We actually go through the entire novel like this. Because of time restraints, I kept trying to hurry along the discussions, skip some sentences so that we could focus only on the most important ones. My students would have none of it. They looked at me like I was David, running through my perfunctory list of foreplay. "What about this sentence?" they'd ask. "Why this phrase?"

As a teacher, I am not afraid to wield my absolute power over all things mortal. If I want to move on, we will move the hell on and you will tremble at my wrath. However, teaching is a liquid, not a solid. It flows according to the terrain. And if I'm fortunate enough to have a bunch of students who want to learn more, then we will change the lesson plan. Originally, my lesson plan called for four chapters a week for six weeks. Instead, we spent all of the remaining ten weeks on the book. During our last two meetings, we had no choice but to skip around a bit or we wouldn't have finished the book.

So, How'd Plan A Work Out for You?

Anytime you get a group of diverse, non-lit majors to not only appreciate a novel, but also feel passionate about it, that's a success. However, inspiring their passion was only a part of the goal; the major goal was to use the novel to illustrate various writing techniques that they might then try in their own novels. The problem the creative writing teacher faces when using texts that are so well written is that they can then intimidate the student writers. They'll be too afraid to try a technique because they know it won't be as good. I could force them to try new techniques by assigning them to do exercises that incorporate those techniques. But over the years I've come to the conclusion that writing exercises are mostly an end in themselves, and don't really make writers any better. They end up competing against each other to do the most impressive exercise and don't think about how to apply that to their novel.

So, I don't push them to use anything from the novel. Yet, I notice over the long haul of reading their new chapters that I will see a line, a paragraph, an exchange of dialogue, or perhaps even a whole character will appear in their manuscripts that will indeed reflect what they learned from a close reading of *Disgrace*. Be patient. Novel writers only listen to that part of the instruction that affects what they are doing at the time. I used to worry that my repeat students would grow bored with hearing the same lectures over and over each semester. But over and over again, students would approach me in the third or fourth semester and say, "Now I get what you mean about . . ." (fill in the blank: characterization, setting, plot, etc.) That's because they were focused on some other aspect of their novel the other times they heard the lecture and so they didn't really pay attention.

The same is true with using fiction in the classroom. All the students will come away with a clearer idea of all the possibilities of what can be accomplished in a novel, and they will all come away with a new appreciation of the subtleties of technique a master writer employs. But only a handful will try what they observed. However, next semester, when I bring in a new novel, some of those same students who were afraid to try a new technique, or who just didn't see how it applied to their novels, will be ready to try something new. Not because of the novel. Not because of the author. Not because of the teaching. Just because they are ready.

Plan B: The Shotgun Approach

After teaching *Disgrace* through the close-reading approach, I decided that the following semester I would use a broader approach. Plan A was pretty much precision sniper shooting, picking off each word, each phrase, each line. And, while that was an enormously rewarding approach, it was also remarkably time-consuming. My class meets once a week for four hours. Yup, four hours. Add to that the fact that we meet from 6:00 P.M. to 10:00 P.M., and that most of the students are coming straight from work. Many enter the classroom with a caffeinated drink and a snack (despite the giant red sign glaring at them over the whiteboard that says: NO FOOD OR DRINK). But they've just raced from work, circled the packed student parking lot, jogged to the snack machines, and raced to my classroom, breathless and exhausted. I'm not mentioning this information to provide amusing texture; this is important information for a teacher.

I need to construct my classes keeping in mind the energy levels of my students. Their energy level is highest at the beginning of class, so I use the first hour to lecture. This cuts down on the number of students who fall asleep or count the number of holes in the ceiling paneling. After a fifteen-minute break, we resume class. If the break is any longer, they start to get tired again and wonder if they shouldn't just slip on out to the parking lot and drive home to their families. Once we're back in the classroom, I divide the students up into five groups. Each group is responsible for critiquing a specific student manuscript. All the students have already read all the manuscripts, which were distributed the week before. Each manuscript has a cover sheet with categories that they should specifically address (effectiveness of dialogue, development of plot suspense, etc.). These critique groups are there for them to compare notes, to argue amongst themselves, to promote or defend their opinions in an articulate manner, then to make a specific list of "what works" and "suggestions for improvement."

After each group has come to some consensus, we sit in one big circle. For each manuscript, a spokesperson from the appropriate group tells us what the group concluded. Other students may add their comments, either agreeing or disagreeing or offering additional observations. When they have finished, I offer my general opinions and suggestions. Then we do a page-by-page analysis, focusing on every aspect of that novel that we can. Sometimes we'll spend five minutes discussing a word choice on one page. Sometimes we'll dissect a narrative paragraph to see if it includes too much description. Sometimes we'll linger over the construction of dialogue to show how rearranging the sentence or changing the identifiers (the tags that say who's speaking) could be more effective.

Critiquing five manuscripts takes about two hours. Which puts us at 9:00 P.M. For many students, this is the highlight of the class, especially if it's their manuscript we're discussing. Yet, we still have an hour left! This is the time I use for discussing the outside fiction. Like *Disgrace*.

Because of the time restraints, Plan B would allow me to use that one hour more efficiently than Plan A. Instead of a close reading, I would hand out discussion questions each meeting that they would be expected to be able to answer the following meeting. This approach would give me the best of both worlds: I could still do a close reading whenever I thought it appropriate in terms of illustrating a writing technique, but I could also better control how much time we spent discussing the book, guaranteeing we would finish in the six weeks I allotted. My plan was so brilliant that I gave myself a high-five. (Okay, I followed it with a low-five and an awkward chest-bump against the wall.)

Don't Ask, Don't Tell

The novel has twenty-four chapters, so there were six discussion-question sheets, each covering four chapters. Here's a sample from the first set of discussion questions (remember that this is a novel *writing* class, so the questions mixed literary analysis and writing techniques).

Questions for Chapters 1–4

- What is David's attitude toward Soraya?
- What specific lines or word choices reveal that attitude?
- What does that attitude reveal about David's character?
- List the main plot conflicts that are introduced in the first four chapters.
- Identify passages in which Coetzee uses misdirection to give us plot and character information.
- How is David's job important to the overall themes being developed?
- How is David's job important to the internal and the external plot conflicts being presented?
- Coetzee uses the technique of introducing a phrase, then following it with an explanatory phrase (for example, "Cape Town: a city prodigal of beauty, of beauties." "Women are sensitive to it, to the weight of the desiring gaze.") Identify this technique as often as you can in the first four chapters. What is the effect of using this technique?

There's no need to present more questions. Every teacher will create questions to elicit the responses she needs to illustrate whatever lessons she's presenting. All that we need to know is that this "Plan B approach" (patent pending) worked beautifully.

For about ten minutes.

As we discussed each question, we were forced to go back to the text to examine word choices, sentence structures, dialogue exchanges. When the class ended, we had worked our way through only half the questions. Either I would have to ask fewer questions, cut short the discussions by focusing more on the big thematic questions, or extend the number of weeks we would take to finish the book. But, after considering all these options, I applied a cost-benefit analysis and realized the benefits of abandoning my plan far exceeded the cost. This was clearly a case in which the lessons to be derived from the novel required a certain amount of time and that time couldn't be hurried along. Some dishes had to be slow-cooked in an oven, not zapped in a microwave.

Once I submitted myself to this notion, I was able to incorporate some specialized classroom discussions. For example, on pages 88 and 89, David discusses the nature of desire with his daughter, Lucy. He tells the story of the male dog who was beaten every time he got aroused by a female dog. This discussion is a key thematic passage, dealing with the conflicts between id and superego, male and female notions of civilized behavior, David's rationalization and romanticizing of his own behavior, and more. Below is an excerpt, which begins with David as the speaker:

> "But desire is another story. No animal will accept the justice of being punished for following its instincts."
>
> "So males must be allowed to follow their instincts unchecked? Is that moral?"
>
> "No, that is not moral. What was ignoble about the Kenilworth spectacle was that the poor dog had begun to hate its own nature. It no longer needed to be beaten. It was ready to punish itself."

When the class met to discuss these pages, I handed out this poem by Stephen Dobyns called "Desire." Here are the opening four stanzas:

Desire

> A woman in my class wrote that she is sick
> of men wanting her body and when she reads
> her poem out loud the other women all nod
> and even some of the men lower their eyes
>
> and look abashed as if ready to unscrew
> their cocks and pound down their own dumb heads
> with these innocent sausages of flesh, and none
> would think of confessing his hunger
>
> or admit how desire can ring like a constant
> low note in the brain or grant how the sight
> of a beautiful woman can make him groan
> on those first spring days when parkas
>
> have been packed away and the bodies are staring
> at the bodies and the eyes stare at the ground;
> and there was a man I knew who even at ninety
> swore that his desire had never diminished.

After reading the poem, we discussed the similarities of the themes in both works. The discussion was very lively and animated, encompassing everything from gender stereotypes to the various uses of sex in a relationship to the meaning of pornography in society. More important than the details of the discussion was the intense emotional and intellectual commitment the students expressed about the topics as it related to the novel. We brought every discussion back to the novel (sometimes I brought it back, but most of the time the students did it themselves). Their focus on how to express themes in literature impressed me.

Another specialized classroom discussion involved the uses and abuses of teachers as protagonists. After some general discussion of various examples of teachers as portrayed in film and literature, I narrowed the topic down to "How to Write a Classroom Scene." Classroom scenes are very difficult to write because we have seen them so often that we are immune to their charm. That's because they almost all have the same function: to prove how witty and smart and dedicated the teacher is. Examples include *Dead Poets Society, The Mirror Has Two Faces, Marathon Man, Getting Straight, Paper Chase, Goodbye, Mr. Chips, Dangerous Minds, Freedom Writers, Fame*, and a billion others. But the classroom scene in *Disgrace* has more in common with *The History Boys, Educating Rita*, and *The Prime of Miss Jean Brody*. Coetzee's demonstrates David's flaws as well as his strengths, as do the three examples mentioned above. To illustrate this point, I showed the classroom scenes from several films from both lists and we compared the writers' techniques. This turned out to be one of our best classroom experiences out of both semesters.

Please, Not the Old Apples-and-Oranges Bit

So, which plan worked better? Both. Neither. Each worked fine. The students loved reading and discussing the novel, even the ones who didn't like the novel. Everyone felt as though they were "real writers" discussing weighty literary matters. Many students incorporated writing techniques in their own novels. The students emerged from class with more confidence in their ability to read as writers, and in their ability to write like Writers.

Disgrace now goes on my special shelf to be rotated into the Novel Workshop line-up every two or three years. While awaiting the novel's next turn, I will be busily formulating Plan C, in which I will revise the questions I used in Plan B and select more passages that will allow me to incorporate additional specialized classroom discussions involving teaching both thematics and techniques.

Meanwhile, one of the students from that class — the one who actually refined much of his writing as a result of reading the novel — has sold his novel to MacMillan. Any correlation? Probably not. He was a damn good writer before he ever read the book, before he ever met me. (See how I used a Coetzee-style technique there?) He would have published that novel without my class. But the important thing — and this is the most important lesson every teacher must learn — is this: He never has to know that fact.

He sure won't hear it from me.

Addendum: If Coetzee Were My Student

Disgrace was indeed a classroom success. Students learned novel-writing techniques. Discussions were lively and insightful. The workshop members felt more like writers. Many were inspired to work harder on their own novels. [Cue music, throw up a crawl about how the students all went on to become successful writers and gathered at my grave (many, *many* years later) to pay homage to their mentor. A woman in a short black dress, fighting back tears, gently places a copy of *Disgrace* on my grave. Roll credits.]

Not so fast. After weeks of accolades and unseemly fawning like swooning Coetzee groupies, we finally had one brief discussion about the novel's shortcomings. It was brief, not because there wasn't a lot to discuss, but because those shortcomings mostly involved plot structure problems in the third act, and the students aren't yet ready for too much detail in that area. Now, I'm perfectly aware that when I suggest the novel has shortcomings, I'm saying so from the safety of my classroom cornerhole. Who the hell am I to point the finger? Coetzee's got a Nobel Prize, among other prizes, cluttering up his fireplace mantel. My mantel is piled high with DVDs of *SpongeBob SquarePants* and *The Fairly OddParents*. When does the waiter ever have the right to criticize the master chef?

In *my* classroom, that's where.

There's an odd change in the students when we shift gears to criticize a work of such obvious renown. Everyone speaks in lowered voices, as if we were all smoking cigarettes and reading porn under the bleachers and mean ole Mrs. Bladder, the Latin teacher, could catch us at any moment. Everyone feels just a little naughty. That's good, because students need to feel free to challenge Great Literature. They need to be able to ask whether there's actually enough thematic depth to justify what they consider to be writing flaws. That's really the main question whenever we discuss literary fiction: yes, the work contains Big Themes that we could discuss for days and maybe all write essays about with footnotes and Works Cited pages. But does the work hold together on a simple storytelling level? Does the novel make you want to hurry home from work to read the next chapter?

For many students, it did not.

While all were in awe of his style, characterization, and the pacing of the first two acts, most agreed that the third act (the final seventy pages) had problems. Many passages seemed repetitious, covering the same thematic ground but without offering any new depth. David Lurie wasn't as compelling because he, too, seemed stuck on the same thematic merry-go-round. His internal monologue repeated the same concerns. The plot — Lurie returning to visit the places and characters from the first act — seemed predictable, a Joseph Campbell template. Some students argued that this return, though predictable, was inevitable, a thematic necessity. Others disagreed, saying that they had no problem with the concept of the

Return; they just expected the actual scenes to pay off more, both intellectually and emotionally. Many students complained that there was very little suspense in the final act. They had lost hope that anything surprising would happen or that what did happen would take them to a place they hadn't already been thematically. In other words, they stopped caring. However, everyone adored the ending scene, finding the final paragraph very powerful and moving.

Although I did my best to remain the removed facilitator during the discussion, when the students had finished their shootout and the smoke cleared, it was my job as the writing teacher to actually take a stance. In this case, I agreed with the criticisms. A devotee for the first two acts, I lost interest in the third as the author seemed more intent on his thematic master plan than maintaining a consistent style and pace. Had Coetzee been in my class, I would have advised him to rethink those last seventy pages. "Johnny," I would have said, "brilliant opening act and middle act. But the characters in the third act are stiffer, more obviously symbolic. Their dialogue is a bit too studied, too purposeful — not nearly as subtle and realistic as before. Sure, that could be part of your plan, but if so, you're doing that author intrusion thing, making the reader conscious of the writing rather than allowing them to experience the story on their own. C'mon, John, don't walk out. Yeah, right, you're going to be famous someday and come back here and rub it in my face. You know how many times I've heard that? We'll see, loser!"

17: The Bodies of Others: A Meditation on the Environs of Reading J. M. Coetzee's *Disgrace* and Caryl Phillips's *The Nature of Blood*

Jane Creighton

I

I BEGIN AT AN OPEN WINDOW, leaning on the sill to feel the air outside, a cold breeze on my skin. I'm looking out across a fenced zone, barbed wire and concrete wall, beyond that a road I can't see but for the tops of vans, small trucks going by, the sound of tires, and beyond that a field fringed by trees in the middle of February, gray and misting, near freezing, but not quite. Beyond those trees, maybe a river. I don't know.

I'm finding likeness, looking at a scene that, but for the wall and wire, could come from the late February landscape of central Pennsylvania, let's say in the early sixties when I was ten or so and out roaming the woods, so often confidently by myself or with the family dog following trails and bushwhacking, climbing, sliding, tramping across the stream that ran through our property, warmed by my exertions but feeling also the marvelous edge of cold. This memory returns often enough to be emblematic of a self I understand to be the girl I carry with me as I'm aging. There she is — agile, cheerful, thoughtful, a spring in her step, excited by the heat she can build inside her against the cold, but delighted also by what the cold gives her, the sense of living in her own skin. Her body creates itself, is its own weather system pushing into the bank of frigid air. She knows this to be her independence, and she also knows she can be, inside ten minutes, back in the kitchen with her mother, liberated of boots and wet mittens and socks, stretching her toes as she sits on the kitchen stool waiting for hot chocolate, perhaps, the sound of mother and daughter talking now a murmur of daily life. Without thinking about it, not for a moment (the subject doesn't come up), she believes she's going to live forever.

I begin at an open window looking out and away from bolts of cloth in the display case to my back on the far side of a long room. The air inside is musty, the room dark lit by its starboard bank of windows. To the left behind me is the other long case I think I have known about most of my life, without giving much thought to whether I would ever be in its presence. The great mass of hair fills the case, its contents rising high against its back wall, and I have just walked its terrible length, unwilling to stop just yet, heading for the window to look out and breathe the outside air because I don't know how to be here, how to meet the visage of the crime.

Captions are applied. No one should be confused in the first instance about the content. The bolts of cloth woven from human hair remind us, in case we should forget or might never have known, how the Nazis thought of economies during mass murder, how hair was shorn from corpses to be woven into industrial cloth. The removal of gold fillings, the harvesting of skeletons for use in medical education, experimentation on the newly dead in the dissecting room contiguous to the gas chambers, all of it known, one way or another, across a good portion of the contemporary world.

In truth there is little here in Auschwitz that I did not, in a surface sense, already know by the time I was an American teenager. The revelations must have come by way of the large picture magazines during Eichmann's trial in 1961. Maybe I saw the hair then, maybe later. I must have seen photographs of survivors, a first view of what starvation does to a body clothed in institutional stripes, the kind of clothing I had only seen before on Saturday morning cartoon miscreants, usually plump. And then there were those photographs of the pits, the tumble of bodies caught at a middle distance in impossible, bone-breaking positions. What might have been a girl's reluctant fascination with the first, I think now the very first, sighting of the full nakedness of others beyond fleeting glimpses of her own family turned to profound dismay. This is how I remember it: I looked at the pictures by myself in a house with its own complications, but nonetheless amidst a loving family for the time being intact, in no way fearing that anyone would come for us because we were white Anglo-Saxon Protestant, American, albeit secularized, and no, the subject wouldn't have come up. Not us, not then, not now. But I perhaps felt in my bones the impossibility nevertheless possible, that bodies could be broken like this by other human beings, and that my own growing, lively, unpredictable and intensely private, young body could be so rendered, made to mirror that emaciated extremity, exposed to the raw air and then later viewed by someone else like me whose horror and pity would be useless by the time it was called into play. There would be no *me* any longer, no self, no family left to tell the story. And that other looking at me might weigh likeness and difference, as I did then, as I do now, wondering what it would be to take someone else's place in a killing field, at the same time knowing, as if the knowledge were somehow palpable, that I am myself and not the other, that what happened here happens to others, not to me.

A young girl looking at photographs of Holocaust victims might simultaneously engage and reject the metaphor of the mirror. She might see herself in the other, then might as quickly turn away from that fate, understanding in whatever way she understands it that the forces of history have not planted themselves in her hometown or on her body in such a way. Different choices are possible, then. She could put the thought of it down, never to pick it up again as part of her American life. She could, if it is the early 1960s in America, watch the movie version of Leon Uris's *Exodus*, fall in love with Paul Newman's character, and think of Israel as the shining answer to the horror of the photographs. She might recognize later, at least as far as movies are concerned, that her romance with *Exodus* does not begin to measure the persistent consequences of the European Holocaust on the Middle East. She might also recognize that in all this looking at pictures that came to her out of the culture of her times, she responded more thoroughly to what came first and to what was familiar — the greater semblances to herself that she found in European culture — than to anything that came from wars and famine elsewhere in the world. But not long after *Exodus* came *To Kill a Mockingbird*. And after Eichmann, reports made their way to her house about the Mississippi freedom rides, along with certain details of the violent, racist history surrounding them. She, among others, would need to find different ways of thinking about the world she was growing into.

It is difficult to reconcile one thing to another, to make ends meet over the problem of recognizing what constitutes one person's knowledge of another, a process that so often starts with identifying likeness and difference in the other as rendered through the self's gaze, her way of seeing. Heavily theorized in our time across gender, across race, across class, across culture, the problem continues to raise certain square-one questions. Does claiming likeness make invisible or less important those qualities of the other that are different? Conversely, is empathy for another really possible when there are irremediable differences, or do we simply project some version of ourselves onto another in order to understand what has happened to them? And if we don't do that, how is it possible, really, to respond to the evidence all around us of what Adam Zagajewski has called "the mutilated world"?[1] What violence do we wreak upon others (or ourselves) when we assume their desires are the same as ours, and what violence is wrought when we think, if we think about them at all, that their desires are different, unknown, unknowable? And when these others that I am imagining now are actually gone from this world, carried away by murder and by fire, by monstrous events commemorated in the fields of Europe, in synagogues that have become museums, in crumbling or restored houses of interrogation used both by Nazi and Soviet secret police, in plantations, slave cabins, courthouses, and churches across the American South (among any number of other places and historical crimes that might be referenced), how are we to remember them? And to what end?

So that we can say — never again? How notoriously difficult it is to use apparent lessons from history to prevent mass crimes. As if any and every element of the specific and exceptional horrors ranging, for instance, from the cold calculations of the Final Solution through the cold calculations of King Leopold in Africa could be catalogued and boxed, those demons contained as petrified relics of a past that cannot, will not be given room to move again. I raise these questions in part because as a teacher, I wonder what it means for students to read literature that, among its possibilities, so often delivers through their reading of it performances of the past. How do they find ways within their discoveries of a text (an often complicated combination of aesthetic pleasure and disturbing content) to contend with histories that seem distant — even if only by a generation — when they have no memory of them, when those events are past, and, additionally, when they might be tired of hearing about the obsessions of their elders? A Polish student in 2007 reading Faulkner will wonder whether the conditions in the American South could be at all as they were when Faulkner was writing. Having grown up almost entirely surrounded by Polish Catholics, he will wonder if he has any grounds upon which to write about race in America. Another student reading Morrison will shake her head, moved beyond speech by the evocation of resistance to slavery. But as much as the text may render into life a woman's anguished, heroic crossing of the Ohio River as she escapes the overseer, the image memorializes a time other than this one. Comparable images of people fleeing across borders all over the world — among them some of the parents and grandparents of the students in Krakow with whom I spent an academic year — arise according to their own circumstances, as the shifting, twentieth-century maps of Poland suggest. To compare them too easily is to diminish the specificity of those circumstances. For so many students, for so many of us, it's all so far away, unless we have lived it.

What time, what place, what circumstances draw us far enough into a text that we might look back out? I use, in Auschwitz, what avails itself, a wave of feeling from my own life that washes across the border between self and other, present and past, and across which I am compelled to make some connection, however partial and impaired, however subject to confusion and cultural misreading. Oświęcim, also Oshpitzin, the names in Polish and Yiddish of the town that existed before and still exists within walking range of the mutilated crematoria, the fire and ash of Auschwitz-Birkenau, has few if any Jews and a difficult project ahead for those Poles undertaking the rehabilitation of sites commemorating hundreds of years of Polish-Jewish cultural life. That life, rich and variegated, marked at least as much by real measures of tolerance as it was by periodic repression, all but disappeared in 1939 — banished from the memory of several generations of Poles through genocide and the subsequent forty-plus years of Soviet-backed national policy. Looking out across barbed wire into the Polish countryside and thinking of Pennsylvanian fields does not equate the two, does not make parallel their histories. But it does open one corridor into the problem of how to look into a past about which I can only surmise. I cannot bear witness, not in any immediate sense, and yet it seems urgent that something must be learned, something not yet learned. I am here, reckoning with the expected, but also reading the ground as a text filled with unexpected passages into a continuous present where it is, so often, alarmingly easy to misrepresent the past. Layered into the problem of reading are the ethics concerning what one does with the knowledge one has drawn and shaped out of this text, defined and conditioned as that knowledge is by all that has gone into the creation of the one who reads, her family, class status, education and experience, the condition of her own body and even, perhaps, her mood at the moment when she looks into the display case of human hair shaved from the heads of hundreds of thousands of women, while they were alive, or when they were dead, before burning. The weight of the mass pitched against individual life, the terrible silence of the room alive with the voices I might imagine for them, the women who cannot turn to me and speak. What could they say?

II

> How much of the concentration camp world is dead and will not return, like slavery and the dueling code? How much is back or is coming back? What can each of us do so that in this world pregnant with threats at least this threat will be nullified?[2]
> — Primo Levi

I don't always know what risks to take, what connections are possible, why someone who thinks in as roundabout a way as I do has the nerve to go into a classroom week after week armed with the authority a doctorate and a certain number of years on this earth apparently give her. This, at any rate, is the 2:00 A.M. thought that wakes me into a gnashing of teeth and curses. Nevertheless.

    I first read J. M. Coetzee's *Disgrace* while I was teaching Caryl Phillips's *The Nature of Blood* in a "Studies in Fiction" course, both about a year before I spent two semesters in Poland teaching mostly American literature to university students. Contiguous in my reading, they began to tail each other in my mind. It's hard to pinpoint the intuition with which I hold these two, as it were, in one hand while the other flips the pages of diverse texts chasing more solid thematic links. But when I sight these novels, when I imagine them together before words, the image just under my eyelid is a globe mapped in permeable continents, themselves composed of shivering, penetrable layers of historical time. Within those layers, highlighted at different moments, the lives of characters illuminate the complex, treacherous landscapes to which they are immediately subject. Postcolonial theory, in a perverse match-up with the god's-eye view of Google Earth, makes possible this way of looking in one sweep across continents and into locales, leveraging the ongoing "post-" legacies of metropolitan causes against colonial effects. The globe brought to some kind of life by my reading flares up in post-apartheid South Africa, southern and central Europe in the fifteenth and twentieth centuries, Cyprus, Palestine, and Israel of the 1940s and 1980s. A predatory literature professor, an African general, a Holocaust survivor, among others, stand immersed in these geographies, looking into the thicket of their predicaments — all distinct, all connected by the question, how am I to live? Add to these figures the weight of other readings and my globe is lit by electric threads spanning the Atlantic triangle — the Middle Passage to Sethe pregnant, bleeding, and in flight from the master's narrative, Joe Christmas running circles in the Mississippi brush, back to Marlow on the African coast staring eastward, the *éminence grise* of European opacity and detachment blanketing the African interior with his narrative gaze, corrupt and longing.

The places of reading, the Polish and Texas classrooms where I have taught and am teaching Phillips and Coetzee, also flicker on this globe, although the globe itself is not a fully realized concept. Or is it rather too much of one (like the luminous, fragile balloon butted into the air by Chaplin's *Fuehrer* in *The Great Dictator*), too crisp and convenient an image to hand to students as a model for the web of connections we might make? Instead we read, the students and I, each from a sense of our own present locale. If I can hazard one generalization about all of them, it might be that their presence in these classrooms is a testament to their futures, to their desires and abilities to enter ongoing and elevated conversations about a world they can lay hold of, creating their place in it according to those desires and abilities and against darker aspects of pasts that are, in any case, impossible to really know. Thus, the return to sites of collective trauma through fiction presents us with the challenge of moving through an exasperating somberness, as in the moment I find difficult to maneuver when a student shakes her head and says, "But this is so depressing." The student wants, perhaps, an acknowledgment of the demarcation that separates those past sorrows from how much better we are now. How does any of this, really, apply to us anymore? To what end do we dwell on it? And yet the questions Levi raised near the end of his life require a reckoning not simply with the past but with "how much is back or is coming back," in a world whose progress in human affairs we can neither clearly dictate nor control.

Wrenchingly focused on the unique legacy of the Nazi *Lager*, Levi understood the importance of articulating "the gray zone" — the terrain of coerced collaboration where victims are inexorably molded by their relation to their persecutors, becoming bound in every sense by a web of complicity and guilt to the forces that constrain, enslave, even murder them.[3] The perpetrators likewise are transformed by the power they have and the circumstances in which they wield it, fundamentally guilty in ways that their victims are not, but nevertheless within the range, many of them, of common people we might know, the common people we might be. Intent on the dynamics of the *Lager*, Levi nevertheless recognizes degrees of applicability across the breadth of human experience, suggesting that the totalizing horrors of the Final Solution cannot be fully consigned to a rare shelf of history. What he terms "our essential fragility" subjects humankind to the enticements of power, the full implications of which we often cannot, or will not, see (69). That fragility, as well as the inevitable impaired vision that is a consequence of the position from which we view the world and our ranking in it, challenges our capacity for ethical judgment. In the long aftermath of great crimes, Levi argues, we risk too much if we simplify the story, if we cleanly separate good from evil and detach ourselves through long, narrow sight lines into the past that leave us doubtless about the moral clarity of our escape from those times (36–37). What remains with us? In distinct and subtle ways, both Phillips and Coetzee provoke inquiry into this world, "pregnant with threats," and into what coming to terms with such a world might be.

One could say that *The Nature of Blood* and *Disgrace* both navigate, to various explicit and implicit degrees, the ongoing consequences of intersecting nationalism and racism as played out on the bodies of central characters. But they are largely disparate, except for the depth, and perhaps the bleakness, of their inquiries. In different ways, both novels have provoked unease: *The Nature of Blood* for posing correspondences among European anti-Semitism, the Holocaust, European racism in Africa, and racism in the state of Israel, thus risking the accusation of oversimplification and the reduction of one to another;[4] *Disgrace* for, well, any number of things surrounding the descent of its difficult-to-like white male protagonist into the agonies of, and complicity with, sexual coercion, rape, and racial thinking whether crude or discreet. It is a novel whose references to post-apartheid times, as Derek Attridge deftly points out, are so bleak as to raise questions among South African critics over whether wide reading of the novel will "impede the difficult enterprise of rebuilding the country" (164).

Neither *The Nature of Blood* nor *Disgrace* tidies up the disturbing connections suggested between, for instance, the devastated concentration camp survivor and the African general Othello who abandoned his African wife and child in order to establish himself as an uncomfortable outsider in Venice, or the rape of a white woman by three black men and the "tax" owed to Africans in the new South Africa. These novels take up nothing less than the sometimes brutal, sometimes subtle, and certainly pervasive effects of coercive cultural practices wielded by one set of human beings against another.

I find myself stumbling over this last statement, variations of which I have uttered time and again in classroom discussions of texts related to the long histories of social injustice across cultures in American literature. The need to summarize, to make clear what might be learned, to come to a point, remains central, doesn't it, to the purpose of teaching? "We are compelled," Levi wrote, "to reduce the knowable to a schema: with this purpose in view we have built ourselves admirable tools in the course of evolution, tools which are the specific property of the human species — language and conceptual thought" (36). But his ultimate argument against the simplified story, a simplified history constructed in answer to the human need for clear distinctions between us and them, between enemy and friend, tells me something about what I do in the classroom facing students.

I have, after all, subjected them to deadlines they must hold to for papers they must write in an academic discourse that demands logic, clarity, and focus. They must absorb, synthesize, and produce accessible lines of thought deviating only on tangents that promise, and produce, a return to the thesis. They must try to avoid becoming lost. To different degrees all of us, students and professor, must negotiate a fear of becoming lost in the texts we read and in the discussion that follows. We are learning something about the violence we do in the shaping of our ideas, cutting this or that in a text from consideration because the idea produced is too vague, too large, too difficult, there is not enough time for it, etc. And yet, the way I have been reading these two books amid the contexts thus far referenced teaches me a kind of pedagogical resistance to certainty and to central, fully realized claims. I have been offered, instead, an open-ended reckoning with the world and its discourses, the meanings of which shift even as we use them.

I might say that both novels inhabit territories undergoing various stages of an aftermath. *The Nature of Blood* is composed of four major narrative perspectives threaded across each other in a loose coexistence. They include Eva Stern in 1945, the twenty-one-year-old sole survivor of her family who enters the novel watching British trucks pouring in to liberate the camp where she has lingered for four months, having survived in reverse order the forced march, the previous camp, the ghetto, and the early street assaults marking the deep trench between before and after, but whose chances of surviving the corridors of her memory seem doubtful. They include Othello in the sixteenth century, tentative and awkward, narrowly respected and largely despised by the Venetians who have hired him to fight their war with the Turks, as he makes his way toward the center of

Venetian culture. They include a fifteenth-century Jewish community just outside of Venice undergoing deadly persecution consequent to a blood libel. The novel opens and closes with Stephan Stern, Eva's uncle, who left Germany for Palestine in the 1930s and who frames the novel — beginning just after the war in Cyprus in a displaced persons camp where he guides young refugees toward the hope of an Israeli future even as he finds himself in a kind of hopeless longing for his German past — and ending in a 1990s encounter with Malka, a young Ethiopian immigrant Jew suffering "the problem of the color line" in modern Israel.[5] The central aftermath of the Holocaust, both immediately after it and toward the end of the time when anyone with living memory of it could still be alive, is edged in this novel by the deeper historical time in which stories about otherness are shaped — the ancient accusation that Jews during Passover murder Christian children for their blood, and the appearance, just at the dawn of the European slave trade, of an African general who dares marriage to a white woman in the heart of the European empire.

The Nature of Blood both compels and resists the focus a central character provides. The terrific horror of Eva Stern's story, told mostly in riveting first-person voice, lives in uneasy proximity to Othello's strained syntax and his mournfully undramatic night-time wanderings across Venice, ignored rather than persecuted. Their themes echo across the other narratives amid a further proliferation of discursive perspectives (a 1940s psychiatrist, encyclopedic entries, a disembodied Black Power voice from the American sixties), voices that are, as Stephen Clingman says, "handed over tightlipped to the reader who has to work hard to interpret them" ("Forms" 159).

The reader has to work just as hard with *Disgrace*, but from a different angle. Coetzee's third-person narrative closely follows the devolution of the tight-lipped control David Lurie imagines he has over the management of his pleasures. The near claustrophobic perspective holds fast to the multiplying complications of Lurie's body (and what he does with it, and what is done to it) as if that body were the sole earth, the island from which the reader must learn to interpret the physics of the world. Lodged firmly in South Africa's first decade after the end of apartheid, *Disgrace*'s major sites are Cape Town and a rural district of the Eastern Cape, both places where the profound changes being wrought out of a violent history surface and submerge within an ostensibly smaller story: the sexual transgression of a middle-aged professor of English Romanticism whose intellectual passions are passé in the new South Africa. The transgression is common enough, an old story — the middle-aged professor coerces his student into sex, netting her in his discursive web with references to what her feminine beauty owes the world, and to himself, it seems, as its representative. He thus regards himself as worldly, a man who knows his way around the subjects of romanticism, of eroticism and desire. He imagines he can command the terms framing such ambiguities as the presence or absence of his young student's desire for him, manipulating them in ways that serve his inexorable moves toward possession of her, even as he sees that his terms for what is happening are not quite right. The person he thinks himself to be — an intellectual, a lover of women, an independent, self-contained, self-managing, contentedly divorced man who remains, in some version of the term, a devoted father — appears to collapse within the shifting forces of the new era that continually re-draw the lines of his story. To others, he is variously a perpetrator, rapist, the leftover, decaying wreckage of an old order, white, irrelevant, tedious, expendable. Or worse — in the realm of the sophomoric, he is the errant dunce caught in a student newspaper photograph reaching for the camera as a (presumably virile) young man holds a wastebasket over his head. To himself, a skeptical, aging man given nearly as much to weighing his desires in the troubled aftermath of their flash appearances as he is to acting upon and defending them, he is, in the end, "not a bad man but not good either. Not cold but not hot, even at his hottest" (195). Caught in a dangerous intersection between wavering self-perception and the demands of desire, he might also be a man common enough to represent lines of transgression that, given the right circumstances, any of us could cross.

III

> We don't have any choice in the twenty-first century but to understand that we are not limited by what we see when we look in the mirror.[6]
>
> — Caryl Phillips

If a young Caryl Phillips did not immediately see a young Jewish girl when he looked in the mirror, he saw something of himself in the story of Anne Frank. Born in 1958 in the West Indies, an infant when he arrived in Great Britain, as an adolescent growing up in Leeds he well knew of the persecution of Jews during the Holocaust and subsequently under Soviet rule, because the fate of the European Jews was by his time a part of public memory and education. The study of European anti-Semitism gave him ways to think about, and it might be accurate to say, rage against the consequences of racial thinking that, in regards to Africa and the long history of slavery and colonialism shadowing his own entry into Europe, remained untaught, and thus unknown to him. The first piece of fiction he wrote involved a Jewish boy from Amsterdam forced to wear a Star of David. When the inevitable transport comes, he jumps from the cattle car carrying his family toward the death camps, in the process knocking himself unconscious. As he lies bleeding near the tracks, the star gleams in the sunlight, drawing the attention of a farmer who squirrels him away to safety

(*European Tribe*), an irony that ought not be lost. The symbol that marks the Jewish body for extermination becomes something else in the hands of the young writer, who shunts aside the meaning the Nazis assigned to both star and boy, replacing that meaning with an alternate, restorative reading of the value of a Jewish life in northern Europe. "The Dutch boy was, of course, me,"[7] the mature writer will say, and perhaps this may be the last moment of direct, if only slightly altered, mirroring.

Over the course of a number of novels and works of non-fiction, he'll pursue what lives within and beyond the reflected image, giving voice to a range of figures rising out of colonialism in Africa, the Atlantic slave trade, and European anti-Semitism without necessarily tying them together, without equating one to another, often without the kind of narrative persuasiveness that allows the teacher to say with a compelling flourish, yes, this way, this is how these novels, so intent on a kind of reconnaissance of historical catastrophe, this is how they link one legacy to another. This is how they teach us the meaning of our complex, multiply figured inheritance of this one world.

My desire as a teacher may be for that flourish, but my desire as a reader seems looser, more complicated, more willing to persist in uncertainty, less willing to hammer things down as I sometimes wish we could do in the last five minutes of a class, as if, somehow, my students would benefit from carrying away the package of a final point, whether theirs or mine. I extend, in a sense, Phillips's method in *The Nature of Blood* to an ongoing reading across these novels, weighing disparities within the reverberations that link them. The disparities both within and across the novels are markedly apparent in the classroom. For students in the first reading, Othello remains an enigma, difficult to place and largely unsympathetic, a character who has betrayed his roots and whose tragic end is left unstaged. Eva Stern far outpaces him as the riveting subject — the emotional center whose tragic survival is most immediately, if by no means thoroughly, understood. To them she is the clear victim and therefore, along with the persecuted Jews of fifteenth-century Venice, occupies the martyr's place, the heart of sympathetic identification, for all the good it does her.[8] David Lurie, on the other hand, provokes discomfort as an arrogant predator, but also anger and contempt for the presumptive nature of his desires — a man of fifty two, after all, and so *vividly* aging, whose perspective we cannot escape. This is likely the most irritating thing, that the reading student must remain with Lurie looking out at his students, persons rather like herself — or himself — and, according to gender, either exploited or ignored. What reverberations can there be?[9]

A mirror. An open window. As a fifty-something professor engaged in the push and pull of interpretation, I have myself followed this trajectory I describe as belonging to my students, a path qualified by a particularly virulent early resistance to Lurie borne out of my reluctant recognition of and partial identification with him as an aging proponent of discourses that he senses hold a dwindling purchase on the world before which he stands and speaks. He regards the current state of his profession as a kind of instructive penance: "it teaches him humility, brings it home to him who he is in the world. The irony does not escape him: that the one who comes to teach learns the keenest of lessons, while those who come to learn learn nothing" (5). The fallacy that pecks away at the truth of this observation, made early in the novel, lies in its world-weary tone. Whatever humility Lurie finds in his classroom is marred by his sense of himself as the beleaguered subject whose leaden students never avail themselves of the "the flash of revelation" he restlessly intones as he teaches a passage of Wordsworth, the subtext of which ultimately is his idea of love played out on the body, if not the mind, of his student, Melanie Isaacs (21–22).

His own flash of revelation resists fronting the probability that Melanie is of mixed race — although her darkness is a feature of his desire, as is Soraya's "honey-brown body, unmarked by the sun" (1). The narrative does not, either here or in most other places in the novel, speak directly of race, suggesting Lurie's resistance to a discourse that will inevitably fling him into the hard outlines identifying the perpetrator. With "his good bones, his olive skin" (7), he is himself marked by the suggestion of indeterminacy — attaching, perhaps, the idea of racial status to the fragility of identity, particularly in regards to his awareness of the ways his body is changing. Never to know what the women he pursues actually think of him (that knowledge seems available only from his ex-wife Rosalind, whose ridicule of his aging body conjured *in flagrante* is matched only by his own [44]), he must find his way to knowledge by other routes. So much of what happens in *Disgrace* happens in the boundaries of identity privately held against the demands of public discourse — David Lurie's identity certainly, and to a real extent his daughter Lucy's, although we are not privy to what she thinks beyond what she says to her father. The profound change Lurie undergoes in his sense of himself is initiated by the crucible of the academic hearing regarding his alleged abuse of a student, but is by no means finished there. Lurie's resistance to the terms proposed by members of the committee — that his actions toward Melanie Isaacs constituted "abuse" rather than his considered impulse to be a "servant of Eros" — illustrates what a difficult project humility is. Unwilling to have the terms of his guilt dictated to him, he genuinely accedes to Melanie's version of the facts, whatever it is, but refuses to publicly state his remorse, particularly as framed in a "package" presented by committee. Cut loose from his profession as a result of this refusal to adopt the terms — funneled through the voice of Farodia Rassool — of redress for "the long history of exploitation of which this [abuse? harassment? rape?] is part," Lurie heads for the Eastern Cape, taking up his identity as the aging father to an adult daughter who has chosen a country life far different from his (53).

But because that country is South Africa, in a world, Levi reminds us, "pregnant with threats," negotiating one's own terms for one's actions is no easy business. In his effort to explain to Lucy his version of the events in Cape Town, he presents the case he could not make in the contemporary public discourse of his profession. In one of many parallels to the life of dogs, he makes his claim for the "rights of desire," likening his complicated pursuit of Melanie to the instinct of a male dog pursuing a bitch in heat. That dog, when punished for the same, falls into the terrible position of being taught to "hate its own nature." No defense, he knows, of the rationalizations that allow him to justify "kneeling over" Melanie, "peeling off her clothes, while her arms flop like the arms of a dead person." But he cannot, perhaps should not suppress his tenuous yet persistent sense that "in the whole wretched business there was something generous that was doing its best to flower" (89–90). That he puts on this defense for Lucy just prior to her rape by three men who may or may not be exacting a "tax" in redress for the history of apartheid while he is locked in the bathroom and set afire, unable to know what is happening to her beyond what his imagination will provide him either then or later, has the punch of irony missing from his earlier observation about teaching. A mirror, perhaps, with more in the reflected image than is immediately available to the eye. In this mirror, Melanie's body becomes Lucy's, here suffering an assault fueled in great part by a history of racial discourse that she, in its aftermath, will refuse to engage as a claimant. His efforts to understand his daughter, to help her in what has happened to her become, instead, his understanding that "he can, if he concentrates, if he loses himself, be there, be the men, inhabit them, fill them with the ghost of himself. The question is, does he have it in him to be the woman?" (160). A perpetrator, a predatory professor in Cape Town caught in the ambiguities between what he wants and what he does, victimized (and unmanned) in the Eastern Cape by men whose discourse, not being based in white Europe or in the terms of English Romanticism, he cannot hear, becomes in his own mind as he tries to help his daughter both victim and perpetrator, a tangle of guilt and remorse that prevents him, for an excruciating period, from being a person who can help her. Lurie's crucible, here, seems to be his own body.

The humility he learns, finally, he learns through the proliferating meanings of "fire" in the Eastern Cape, an image I invoke here, along with Phillips's mirror, as a way to think across the territories both these novels occupy, returning as well to the layered globe and the sense of individual lives shaped and flaring within cultural landscapes rendered by the legacies that shape them. There are a number of correspondences that might be discussed, a bevy of connections that might arise, for instance, in any given classroom discussion or that might surface in the arguments of student papers. But I think of these three now, Othello, Eva Stern, David Lurie, as the bodies of others subject to versions of a crucible, their senses of self under duress, subject to extremity, to the process of being burned away.

Fire is not the immediate element that attends the Othello Phillips conjures, a figure who lives in a decaying, once upscale house near the heart of the Venetian empire, darkly pacing the edges of its society in pursuit of ways to accommodate himself beyond the narrow corridors of military service offered him. A former slave, former king, a student of manners, immigrant, general, husband and father in another country, on another continent, as well as a suitor both earnest and courtly, he wrestles with the problem of inventing himself within and against what Europe expects of him — the successful performance of a job no one else wants. A man's man, mocked, envied, out of his element, successful in love but uncertain, he speaks in a stilted voice, tensely imagining that he might not be limited by what he sees when he looks in the mirror. He stands on the lip of Europe, really, gazing into it, a kind of mirrored inversion of Marlow gazing into an African heart of darkness created out of English syntax. But the European heart of darkness hangs in the air surrounding him, noticed, certainly, but brushed aside as he gazes at his new wife "among twists of white linen sheeting" in the brief period of time imagined before Shakespeare's Othello succumbs to murder and suicide. In his effort to recreate himself, he has chosen to leave behind native language, home, and family, following his desire into a marriage that we last see in the languorous aftermath of lovemaking in Cyprus, awaiting his return with her to Venice, where they will live a "new life of peace in the remarkable city-state" (173). What remains unsaid, the connection he cannot see, is perhaps best imagined not only in the smoky darkness of his skin, but in the smoke and ash that haunt the text arising out of the fifteenth-century burning of the Jews in Venice and reaching into the twentieth century.

Eva Stern, her identity obliterated and reconstituted in the crucible of the *Lager's* gray zone, may not be limited by what she sees in the mirror, but whatever sense of possibility that might attach to the idea of limitlessness belongs to the world of deadly force. The lone survivor of her family to be transported out of a German death camp, what Eva might see in any mirror held up to her tends to defy the starving, sometimes naked, always haunted body of a barely recognizable young woman confronted with painfully inarticulate liberators. It's the kind of starving that goes beyond hunger, a woman whose substance frays in the bureaucratized survival of a displaced persons camp, while memory swamps her mirror with the far more articulate details of all she's lost: mother, father, sister, the pained but once possible history of her parents' difficult journey toward the professional center of a world gone out of existence for German Jews, and the yearning self she once was as a daughter and sister. For a time she becomes mother to the ghostly woman who haunts her, the mother she couldn't save. And then, finally, one begins to see another figure behind the screen of that haunting: a gray, twenty-year-old Eva turned *Sonderkommando*, whose job it becomes to burn the bodies of others — a horrible subversion of her mother's ritual lighting of the Shabbat candles. "And does the weight of the dead add itself to the earth?" she asks of no one, of everyone, sitting alone and fretting in her camp hut just days into the liberation. "And if so, will the earth stop moving?" (32).

The profound lack of choice she faces in being able to own the terms of her existence suggests both contrast with and connection to the far different dilemma David Lurie faces. Eva remembers a life where she imagined her future happiness to be a marriage with two children, parents who loved her, a sister who didn't leave her behind. She perhaps remembers a time when she lived in anticipation of as yet unnamed desires. An innocent, she is broken down by losses that culminate in her becoming what Levi calls a "crematorium raven." The intention of the Nazis in creating and coercing collaborators, he argues, is "to bind them . . . to burden them with guilt, cover them with blood, compromise them as much as possible, thus establishing a bond of complicity so that they can no longer turn back" (43). Bound she is, haunted by ghosts that in the course of the narrative inexorably bring her to the self she has become, a being forged out of the concentrated shattering of a family for whom "the hinge of generation will not move" (198). For her, there will be no future, because she has been made over, made sexless, a skeletal figure who, once a burner of bodies, can no longer imagine such a place as the future.

Moving toward David Lurie after Eva Stern presents a challenge in the sequence of classroom reading. My Texas students, although they had basic knowledge of the Holocaust, had more catching up to do on its scale. Most did not know about the blood libel legends plaguing European Jews, and for some, Phillips's narrative constituted their first close description of life on the ground in the *Lagers*. Polish students knew more, but it was knowledge rising out of efforts to reconstitute a history officially banished for generations in a country where Jewish culture was almost eradicated. Thus, Eva's story, so complexly narrated, tended toward the unspeakable for students trying to shape the terms they might use. If David Lurie after Eva Stern seemed in some ways puny and contemptible in his concerns, he also suggested possibility, creating a certain open-endedness in discussions about the problem (and nature) of desire. In the Polish classroom, one student — an American man, as it happened — jumped in on the idea that desire, though it might be suppressed, cannot be altered at will. Women students challenged him on Lurie's actions, but worried the question of the appropriateness of his desire, and whether that could be addressed. In the far more ethnically diverse Texas classroom, students gave readier, and interestingly more sympathetic, responses to their sense of Lurie as a white man subject to the consequences of racial discourse. For all of them, Lucy's silence about her rape proved the most disturbing, particularly as measured against Lurie's efforts to frame the assault in a public discourse that he — in regards to his relations with Melanie — refused. Yet in Lurie, students could discern what it might mean to discover one's self and one's integrity in new circumstances, under new terms.

Living through his transformation from a self-determined manager of his own sexual prowess to a skinny-shanked, mildly disfigured instrument of desires upon which he cannot, or is it, will no longer act, Lurie's trial by fire is nevertheless marked by choices that Eva, his virginal opposite, never had under the terms of the Final Solution. He can to some degree determine how he will suffer the consequences of what he has done. The fire that Lurie harbors for Melanie is, at least as he confesses it to Mr. Isaacs, "a flame-god . . . that kind of flame your daughter kindled in me. Not hot enough to burn me up, but real: real fire" (166). This is one version of a number of ways that the language of desire intersects or overlaps the language of force. He chooses this language, but its meanings are not entirely within his control. It isn't out of bounds to remember that as Lurie struggles with the words to make his case to Mr. Isaacs on a path toward contrition, he has already suffered being locked in the bathroom "helpless, an Aunt Sally," and "bathed in cool blue flame" (95, 96). Real fire, in other words, his hair turned to soot, his flesh blistering, while the dogs are killed and while Lucy suffers the gang rape that she will keep private, not allowing what has happened to her to enter the language of public discourse, mirroring, yet altering, Lurie's unwillingness to do the same when faced with the crime of being "on fire" for his student. Assault, attack, rape, the marking of territory, "the price one has to pay," she finally says, "for staying on" (158). This is the array of terms dissolving into what Lucy comes to, the price she pays — avoiding the abstractions Lurie favors — in order to find the horizon of her harshly narrowed, but still viable sense of place.

But it is how Lurie moves through the meaning of *Lösung* that both links him to and marks his departure from a world that makes Eva's future impossible. If *Lösung* for Eva meant a coerced and total dissolution of self in the service of burning the bodies of others into white ash, Lurie's (and Coetzee's) appropriation of the term for the handling of animals suggests the incremental saving grace available to Lurie as he fashions a daily life out of the ruins of his disgrace. If he is unable to put to rest the terms of transgressive sexual desire forged in particular ways by the collision between himself and his times, and if he is unable to save his daughter from a world that marks her body as a target of redress, he can find a different way to live, both in relation to her and in relation to a future that remains as close as the moment where he and Bev Shaw preside over the passage of "the animal they are killing, giving it what he no longer has difficulty in calling by its proper name: love" (219). He shifts the freighted meaning of *Lösung* to an abstraction of his own making, in practical terms, a useless, but nevertheless palpable "idea of the world . . . in which men do not use shovels to beat corpses into a more convenient shape for processing" (142, 146). That is what is left him, no mean thing. He is the figure with burnt ear who spends his time between ushering dogs into death and refashioning his Byronic opera into a song for a middle-aged woman who sings her "immortal longings" without shame and in the company of the sweet, mournful sound of a howling dog. His is an answer — albeit small, incrementally realized, bleak, perhaps, in its horizons — to the question of what it means to live in this world, and take responsibility for it. It is, I think, a question students share, looking into these texts and then away from them into the promises of a dangerous world, looking, as it were, through an open window, leaning on the sill to feel the air outside.

Notes

[1] The phrase comes from Zagajewski's poem, "Try to Praise the Mutilated World," published in the aftermath of the attacks on the World Trade Center on September 11, 2001. The poem pleads for love of a world whose beauties dwell and survive across the visible consequences of war, exile, and execution.

[2] Primo Levi, 20–21.

[3] See "The Gray Zone," in Levi, 36–69.

[4] For example, Stephen Clingman cites Hilary Mantel's contention that Phillips's correlation of racism against Africans with anti-Semitism is "a colonial impulse, dressed up as altruism" (qtd. in Clingman, "Forms of History" 147).

[5] Malka's predicament as an Ethiopian-Jewish outsider with "primitive" cultural roots in a thoroughly modern Israel is one of myriad variations extending the long reach of W. E. B. Du Bois's assertion that "the problem of the Twentieth Century is the problem of the color-line" (from "The Forethought" to *The Souls of Black Folk*). The ironies attending Malka's treatment as a subaltern in Israel eclipses Jewish solidarity in a standoff between the European Israeli center and African Israeli otherness.

[6] Clingman. "Other Voices: An Interview with Caryl Phillips," 135–36.

[7] Quoted in Clingman, "Forms of History," 144, the original statement appears in Phillips, "On 'The Nature of Blood' and the Ghost of Anne Frank," 6.

[8] Levi is persuasive in arguing against the idea of sanctification of victims that martyrdom here implies. "On the contrary," he writes, National Socialism "degrades them, it makes them resemble itself, and this all the more when they are available, blank, and lacking a political or moral armature" (40). His argument, clarifying in itself, allows no simple clarification of what it means to be a victim.

[9] See Daniel Kiefer's essay in this volume, for a vivid discussion of responses to Lurie from both student and professorial perspectives.

18: *Disgrace* as a Teacher

Rabbi Patricia Karlin-Neumann

IN HIS BOOK, *The Genesis of Ethics: How the Tormented Family of Genesis Leads us to Moral Development*, Rabbi Burton Visotzky makes a surprising assertion. We do not learn how to live ethically from the rosy, pristine, and immutable portraits of Biblical exemplars perpetually taught in Sunday School. Rather, Visotzky claims, our education begins by reading the Genesis text carefully in community and unearthing the failings of the much-vaunted patriarchs and matriarchs. Only by studying how deeply flawed and fractured are the figures of Genesis, only by grappling with their limitations and mistakes and considering the contrast between the contrived and the described do we discover "the genesis of ethics" (9–13, 15–16).

As a rabbi and teacher, examining texts for moral wisdom in community is a familiar enterprise. But it is not only in canonized texts that one can discern the genesis of ethics. Indeed, readers of *Disgrace* are familiar with a deeply flawed and unappealing protagonist, a welter of ethical challenge, limitations, and mistakes. Whether as a teacher, a student, a father, a friend, a man, a protector of dogs, or a chaperone of the dead, David Lurie confronts his own unexpected education. For Coetzee's readers, too, *Disgrace* is a teacher, a text that awakens controversy, troubles complacency, and like Lurie himself, raises questions about how to live a life.

> Rabbi Hanina said, "I have learned much from my teachers, and from my colleagues more than from my teachers, but from my students I have learned more than from them all."
> — *Babylonian* Talmud, Tractate Taanit 7a

For David Lurie, there was a time before disgrace: before disillusionment, before disconnection, before making do in both love and work. But by the age of fifty-two, he is diminished and alone. He asks little of life, and offers less.

"He is in good health, his mind is clear. By profession he is, or has been, a scholar, and scholarship still engages, intermittently, the core of him" (*Disgrace*, 2). This stammering, tentative description glimpses a man resistant to embracing a vigorous scholarly self. In scholarship, like in love, Lurie renounces obligation. Working in prose, the medium of his previous books, he declares to be tedious. He muses instead about writing an opera on Byron, and plays with this idea while he is in front of his classroom. "Through his mind, while he faces his Communications classes, flit phrases, tunes, fragments of song from the unwritten work" (4). Even in a room full of students, David Lurie is cloaked in isolation, hearing different music, inside his own imagination, his current scholarship inchoate, his work undone.

If "scholar" is an identity that Lurie ambivalently dons, "professor" is an ill-fitting job title: "Once a professor of modern languages, he has been, since Classics and Modern Languages were closed down as part of the great rationalization, adjunct professor of communications" (3). Stripped of authority and status, perhaps understandably David Lurie designates his teaching as merely a job, a living to earn, rather than a calling to pursue. A demotion to adjunct status and the relegation of his college to a technical school have drained all color from an already anemic enthusiasm for teaching. Classics and Modern Languages have been "closed down"; he is academically homeless. Replaced by Communications, a discipline whose premise he declares "preposterous," Lurie earns his livelihood in an "emasculated institution" to which he precariously and almost unwillingly belongs (3). Detached from his own aspirations, he is simultaneously detached from both his subject and his students. "Because he has no respect for the material he teaches, he makes no impression on his students. They look through him when he speaks, forget his name" (4).

His teaching and research interests flicker only in one Romantics course. "Like all rationalized personnel, he is allowed to offer one special-field course a year, irrespective of enrolment, because that is good for morale" (3). Lurie does not understand himself as a teacher, lavishing care upon students, or as a member of the faculty, sustained by colleagues and conversation, but as "personnel," a cog in the wheel, part of an anonymous collective. The special dispensation permitting this class only highlights the insult of his diminishment. There is more than a touch of impotence in how he views his professional situation.

In *The Courage to Teach: Exploring the Inner Landscape of a Teacher's Life,* Parker J. Palmer asserts that, "Good teachers join self and subject and students in the fabric of life. Good teachers possess a capacity for connectedness. They are able to weave a complex web of connections among themselves, their subjects and their students so that students can learn to weave a world for themselves. . . . The connections made by good teachers are held not in their methods but in their hearts — meaning *heart* in its ancient sense, as the place where intellect and emotion and spirit and will converge in the human self" (11).

Sadly, there is little emotion, spirit, or heart conveyed in David Lurie's classroom. He has no academic progeny, no students eager to learn from him. His faith in the students has faltered; in his smallness, he anticipates precious little from them and they willingly comply with his expectations.

In Lurie's estimation, the only learner is himself; the fruit of teaching is bitter — humility and self-defeat. "The irony does not escape him: that the one who comes to teach learns the keenest of lessons, while those who come to learn learn nothing" (5). In the classroom, even surrounded by others, learning is disconnected, solitary. He learns "the keenest of lessons," but they are for his edification only. While he dutifully "fulfils to the letter his obligations" (4), his classroom is bloodless, lacking heart, lacking grace.

The only student exempt from Lurie's torpor and resignation is Melanie — after his intentions toward her depart from the pedagogical. Paradoxically, only when she becomes an object of his sexual desire does he pay attention to the prerogatives and pitfalls of being a teacher: "she is a student, his student, under his tutelage. No matter what passes between them now, they will have to meet again as teacher and pupil. Is he prepared for that?" (12). Unprepared, even heedless, Lurie confuses teaching and wooing; he takes the raw materials of passion, pedagogy, and power found in healthy, enthusiastic, and engaged classrooms and shapes them into a makeshift vessel to achieve his own ends. In Lurie's classroom, subject, self, and student are rearranged in service to personal ambition. The subject acquires a hidden intimate commentary, intended only for Melanie. Lurie misrepresents first Shakespeare, then Wordsworth; his extracurricular intentions take precedence over his scholarship. Both professor and scholar are subsumed by desire. Lurie compares the flash of revelation he experienced at his home with Melanie to its absence in the classroom. There are no epiphanies, none of Wordsworth's "spots of time" in this lesson. "Silence again. The very air into which he speaks hangs listless as a sheet" (21). He picks out the phrase, "usurp upon" — to take over entirely — and, unable to draw out his students, Lurie takes over the classroom entirely. He commands attention like a leading man on stage. The listlessness in the air may be a result of Lurie's authoritative and educated voice; although he asks questions, he does not seem to wait for answers. He reads complaints at the complexity of Wordsworth's imagery on the faces of his students, presuming they want simplicity. He is stymied about how to animate his students, how to lure them into his passions. But Lurie's passions are not unadulterated; they are a conflation of the classroom and the woman. "How to bring them to him? How to bring her?" (22). This time, not fragments of song, but memories of her body, his desires absorb his attention. Melanie is no longer pupil, but prey. The other students are uncomprehending bystanders, unintentionally implicated in Lurie's romantic aspirations. The heart aroused in this classroom is scarcely what Parker Palmer hopes for in a learning community.

Palmer conceives of the possibilities inherent in a community of learners. But Lee Shulman, in the title essay in his book *Teaching as Community Property: Essays on Higher Education*, sounds a note of caution. We usually think of the scholar as a "solitary individual, laboring quietly, perhaps even obscurely somewhere in the library stacks, or in a laboratory, or at an archaeological site; someone who pursues his or her scholarship in splendid solitude" (140). In contrast, we regard the teacher as a member of a community, interacting with others, in the classroom. Shulman's insight is that we have it backwards. "We experience isolation not in the stacks, but in the classroom. We close the classroom door and experience pedagogical solitude, whereas in our lives as scholars, we are members of active communities; communities of conversation, communities of evaluation, communities in which we gather with others . . . It is not that universities diminish the importance of teaching because they devalue the act itself; it is not that research is seen as having more intrinsic value than teaching. Rather, we celebrate those aspects of our lives and work that can become, as we say in California, 'community property'" (140–41).

For David Lurie, teaching is arguably the most solitary experience he has. His is the only voice in his classroom. His students display ignorance, blank stares, and persistent silence. These are exacerbated when, following an earlier confrontation with Lurie, Melanie's boyfriend Ryan attends class: "But today, he is met with silence, a dogged silence that organizes itself palpably around the stranger in their midst" (32). Lurie interprets a hush, in place of the more usual buzz of his students, as judgment, perhaps reflecting his concerns about how he is regarded. But Lurie readily judges his students. He dismisses them as ignorant, "Post-Christian, posthistorical, postliterate, they might as well have been hatched from eggs yesterday" (32). Uninterested in what they do know, or how they might find their own path into Byron, Lurie at best considers their "goodnatured guesses" feeble attempts at understanding, a bit of momentum he uses to direct them on his already developed, well-trod path. Curiosity or appreciation of their experience — perhaps their disappointment that their education is technical rather than liberal, perhaps their hope that matriculation will yield an escape from a bleak future, perhaps their fear that education will cause them to become foreigners in their own families — is absent in his classroom. For Lurie, *tabula rasa* is not an opportunity but an absence. The students are defined by what they have missed — Christianity, history, and literacy — and these are the touchstones that Lurie values. David Lurie does not believe that, beyond self-referential humility, there is anything to be learned from his students.

Lurie may have projected the judgment of his students, but the judgment of the stranger, Melanie's boyfriend, is not imagined. In the hapless confluence of subject — Byron's Lara — and self, evasion is impossible. Randy both issues and accepts a challenge. For a change, the air is charged. The superficially academic conversation has an intimate undertone, a double meaning, as if the two were dueling in the presence of spectators. The leading man flickers in and out, alternating places with a defendant on trial.

With each word of Byron, the text for the day, Lurie sinks deeper into an allegory of his own state — "He doesn't act on principle, but on impulse, and the source of his impulses is dark to him . . . a mad heart" (33). Perhaps seeking consideration for his own predicament, Lurie says to his challenger and to the class, "Note that we are not asked to condemn this being with the mad heart . . . we are invited to understand and sympathize" (33). But, naming his own reality, Lurie adds, "He will be condemned to solitude" (34).

The Talmud teaches, "From my students, I have learned."[1] Ryan menaces Lurie, unmasks him, penetrates his pedagogical solitude, and lays bare to Lurie — the primary student in this classroom — the subtext of his life. He is unnerved by what he sees in Ryan's defiant stare. After this class, in his office, alone with Melanie, Lurie summons a professorial demeanor, for the first time speaking to her coldly, without flirtation and intimacy, indeed, without any intimation that they share a history of any kind. He insists that she keep her friend out of the classroom. He lectures her on his duty to the other students as well as her academic obligations to attend class and make up an exam.

These apparently disinterested words of a concerned teacher are not for her benefit but for his — he seeks her compliance to paper over his misconduct. He has seduced, even forced her. He has provisionally recorded a fraudulent grade on an exam she missed; he has contaminated the learning environment of his classroom; he has betrayed his scholarship; he is attempting to intimate, even with that professorial voice, that he is prepared to compromise his ethics still further, when she does take the examination. In the privacy of his classroom and his office, Lurie wields power, but he does so primarily to protect himself. "Melanie, I have responsibilities. At least go through the motions" (35). The classroom, and all that transpires in it, is his fiefdom. Through the prism of his relationship with Melanie, juxtaposed with his understanding of Byron's Lara, Lurie is presented with a portrait of his own moral inadequacies as a man, as a scholar, and as a teacher. Along with his isolation, his selfishness and carelessness are revealed. Turning the ideal presented by Parker Palmer on its head, Lurie has succeeded in compromising his students, his subject, and finally, himself.

When Melanie files a complaint of harassment against him, David Lurie has the potential to learn still more from his student, but he does not yet relinquish the self-justification that prevents learning. In the disciplinary process that ensues, Lurie experiences pedagogical solitude, even pedagogical humiliation, but the community of scholars envisioned by Shulman does not mitigate his isolation. At the hearing, some of his colleagues recognize an implicit fellowship, or at least sympathize with his predicament. But Lurie's absence of remorse, coupled with his ironic insistence upon truth — an insistence absent both in the classroom and in his interactions with Melanie — ensure that whatever empathy they attempt to extend remains unreciprocated. He does not try to save himself, freely acknowledging his culpability both for the affair and for academic fraud. Laid bare in the hearing is not only Lurie's misconduct but also the inadequacy of such a forum for addressing ethical lapses. Lurie refuses to play his part in this flawed, self-interested, and imprecise attempt at justice. His lack of heart for teaching is matched by an unwillingness to constrict himself even more with another pretense. Lurie no longer has to play at being a teacher amid students who are invisible to him and colleagues to whom he is indifferent. David Lurie resigns in disgrace. Not unhappily, he chooses exile.

In leaving academia, Lurie has chosen both a physical and an existential exile. Clearly, he leaves his teaching post, but concomitantly, he also leaves scholarship, a place where his heart once was. He reveals to Bev, "Teaching was never a vocation for me. Certainly I never aspired to teach people how to live. I was what used to be called a scholar. I wrote books about dead people. That was where my heart was. I taught only to make a living" (162). Yet Lurie willingly forsakes that place. He abandons his library, his office, his academic identity, and, after his books are stolen in the robbery and rape, he is separated not only from secondary but also even from primary texts. The building blocks of scholarship are no longer in his possession. What might have once been a source of connection to colleagues, to his discipline, is irrevocably severed. Lurie has moved from the promised, if unrealized, camaraderie of the scholarly world to the isolation of the country recluse.

Lurie's tools for his one act of scholarship or creativity in the book — his opera — highlight this separation. The instrument upon which he composes his score symbolizes his isolation. Rather than composing for an orchestra whose lush music embodies community, he writes for a solo instrument, a child's toy, an "odd little seven-stringed banjo" (184) played not by a musician, but by an amateur. It conjures images of kindergarten or grammar school, a tool for beginners. But beginner is an accurate assessment of Lurie's status as a learner. He cobbles together the tools and toys available to him to fashion a beginning arising out of his disgrace.

In the classroom, standing before his pupils, Lurie felt himself to be the student only through humiliation. Once in exile, he unabashedly becomes the learner. His subject is disgrace and grace, guilt and repentance, isolation and identification. In this curriculum, Lurie goes from being a "servant of Eros" (52) to becoming a student of life.

In exile, stripped of students, subject, and colleagues, recalcitrant and disinclined to learn from others, Lurie has to forge a new path to recover grace. Neither post-Christian nor postliterate, Lurie himself echoes the isolation and exile of the Biblical prophet Jonah. Rather than advocate for or trust in flawed people to learn and grow, Jonah retreats from prophecy into exile. In an attempt to inculcate the value of repentance and compassion, God becomes the educator, providing a castor bean plant to shade Jonah, and then causing it to wither. Jonah, distressed at its loss, begs for death rather than life without it. God patiently teaches an almost comical object lesson — if Jonah can care for a short-lived plant, he has the wherewithal to be compassionate and generous toward human beings.[2]

For Lurie, who is not "a believer" (172), the lessons are less direct and didactic; his teachers emerge from his own creativity, seclusion, and ritual innovation. His human teachers are variously Lucy, the rapists/robbers, Bev, Mr. Isaacs. But surprisingly, Lurie's most faithful teachers are the dying and dead dogs. Through his teachers, both human and especially canine, Lurie begins to learn about compassion and repentance in his exiled life.[3] Like Jonah reacting to the castor bean plant, Lurie's isolation and armor are pierced not by being protected but by protecting. His attention turns to the dogs — which, even in life, are oblivious to his disgrace. But it is in death that he serves them. After Bev euthanizes the sick and unwanted dogs, Lurie carefully, ritually disposes of their remains. While he describes Bev as a "priestess" (84), he likewise appropriates for himself the role of priest, treating the corpses of the dead dogs with respect, even reverence (146). Lurie thus creates his own innovative penance. He willingly accepts upon himself an obligation — one that nobody assigned to him and for which he receives no passing grade. The dead dogs and he become a community. For one whose heart was once in studying dead people, learning from dead dogs brings with it familiarity, continuity, and shelter. Neither dead dogs nor dead writers can protest, disappoint, or dispute. Lurie manages to identify with the dead dogs, as he once identified with dead writers. But unlike the writers, whose words he once twisted and invoked for his own purposes, Lurie does not try to interpret or translate the howls of the dogs. To them, he offers simple respect and reverential witness. While not yet accompanied by people, not even accompanied by the living, nonetheless he is breaking through his isolation, practicing how not to be completely alone. His students are the dead dogs. He takes care of the dogs; he opens his heart to them in a way that had been absent in his classroom. The "servant of Eros" (52) has transformed himself into a respectful escort for the unloved, the unwanted, and the forgotten. When he returns briefly to Cape Town, his thoughts remain with the dogs. He fears that his absence is a betrayal. "From Monday onward the dogs released from life within the walls of the clinic will be tossed into the fire unmarked, unmourned. For that betrayal, will he ever be forgiven?" (178) Disgrace no longer eclipses all else. Loyalty and an idiosyncratic honor slowly insinuate themselves. "From my students, I have learned."

Taught by the dogs, Lurie reconsiders his past. Some lessons beg for practical applications. Having suffered as a father incapable of protecting a daughter, Lurie appreciates what Melanie's father endured, and he seeks forgiveness. Lurie understands his transgression not only intellectually, but also viscerally, having absorbed the trauma of his own daughter's predation. He comes as a penitent to Melanie's father, Mr. Isaacs, a simple champion of his daughter and a man he once regarded with disdain, equipped with the wisdom he learned from caring for the dogs. Both Melanie and her father trusted him to take care of her with the respect due a student, and he failed them; he violated their trust. The only students he did not fail were the dogs. Mr. Isaacs listens to his apology and probes deeper, asking what God wants of him.

> Normally I would say, that after a certain age one is too old to learn lessons. One can only be punished and punished. But perhaps that is not true, not always. I wait to see. . . . I am being punished for what happened between myself and your daughter. I am sunk into a state of disgrace from which it will not be easy to lift myself. It is not a punishment I have refused. I do not murmur against it. On the contrary, I am living it out from day to day, trying to accept disgrace as my state of being. Is it enough for God, do you think, that I live in disgrace without term? (172)

Prostrating himself before Melanie's sister and mother, as if he were answering the Muslim call to prayer as Soraya might have done, bowing down before women, whose needs had been always secondary to his own, Lurie, the master of words, invokes silence and gesture. In so doing, Lurie communicates with the women as he communicates with the dogs. It was with his body that he violated her body, her trust, her innocence; so too it is with his body that he tries to make amends to these surrogates for Melanie and by extension, to all women.

Coetzee suggests that, for Lurie, even amid disgrace and punishment, there is learning. The lessons precipitated by Lurie's role as a teacher continue beyond his tenure in the classroom. Indeed, once he is no longer cast as the one from whom others learn, he becomes freer to learn himself. He continues to learn from his students, both human and canine. He finds a small measure of grace within disgrace. He moves from total isolation and exile to the beginnings of identification, accepting a modicum of responsibility for causing another's pain. Lurie has learned to be careful with those entrusted in his care. He becomes a listener, rather than always the one who recites, lectures, and imposes. He learns a language of connection that is not solely dependent upon words, a language composed of gesture, silence, music, and presence. Honoring the dogs in death, he grows with Lucy to accept the uncertainty and promise of new life. The book ends with Lurie promising a sacrifice — he "is giving up" the crippled, unwanted dog (220). This dog, the sole witness to his scholarly forays with the toy banjo, is the one creature in which Lurie finds some solace and even takes some joy. He has allowed himself to acknowledge the satisfaction of attachment, to have a companion; he allows himself to love. He is slowly learning to ask more of life. He feels for this creature. Learning first from dead dogs and then from a loving, living dog, he is coming to realize that the humility of being a student does not necessarily entail self-defeat; it can also open a heart. Without fraud, though without distinction, David Lurie manages to pass his course.

> I have learned much from my teachers, and from my colleagues more than from my teachers, but from my students I have learned more than from them all.

Finally a real, if recalcitrant learner, David Lurie can now imagine for himself a makeshift and unconventional community in the Eastern Cape: serving the dispossessed dogs; being a grandfather; "giving up" the demand that others act according to his desire. He has become a student of the dogs, and of his times. Simply imagining such a future may seem a paltry achievement, but that is all that any of the characters — Lucy, the Shaws, even Petrus — living in their country's interregnum can do. Lurie's provisional community suggests that traditional definitions of kinship and neighborhood will be stretched and recalibrated in hopes of a new future. The novel insists on the unknowability of that future in many ways, from its silence about Petrus's motives — critics anxious for conclusion have judged him as everything from a tolerant, self-actualizing man to a Machiavellian plotter of Lucy's rape — to the suspension in its final sentence ("I am giving him up": see Sanders, 2002b). It contravenes those who imagined that the abolishing of apartheid and the work of the Truth and Reconciliation Commission would decisively weaken old divisions, lessen violence, and stifle revenge. Still, we can glimpse a future in which a disgraced and divested David Lurie, with his banjo, canine carcasses, mixed-race grandchild, and stripped-down self-understanding, provides some incentive to his fellow dwellers to build tentative alliances into a new world.

Creating makeshift communities need not be the projected experience only of the novel's protagonist; it can also be the experience of J. M. Coetzee's readers. Indeed, the community formed by unsolitary readers who honor the novel's ending is one quite like the community David may imagine; open-ended, uncertain, determined not to impose its desire on the action or the future — and to do these things together. This may provide a direction for those readers who initially found only isolation and hopelessness in Coetzee's canvas. So joining together as a community of readers, whether in the classroom, the library, or the living room, moving from a solitary absorption of this challenging novel to the welcome and animated exchange of the questions and issues raised by it can complicate an initial read and even redeem *Disgrace* for skeptical readers. *Disgrace* is a novel about the perils of isolation. By breaking through isolation, by discussion and dialogue, the ethical and critical questions inherent in the novel come alive — from rape to pedagogy, from relationships to penitence — encouraging readers to reflect on both the world Coetzee created and the one his readers inhabit. Through chronicling Lurie's unique education in *Disgrace*, J. M. Coetzee has created the opportunity to encounter another distinctive community, a community of unsolitary readers, who have shadowed Lurie in his classroom, followed him into exile, and witnessed both his mistakes and his hard-won insights. Even after the book is finished, his community of readers endures.

Notes

[1] Babylonian Talmud, Tractate Taanit 7a. *Rabbi Hanina said, "I have learned much from my teachers, and from my colleagues more than from my teachers, but from my students I have learned more than from them all."*

[2] Jonah 4:10–11: "You cared about the plant, which you did not work for and which you did not grow, which appeared overnight and perished overnight. And should I not care about Nineveh, that great city, in which there are more than a hundred and twenty thousand persons who do not yet know their right hand from their left, and many beasts as well?"

[3] For a thoughtful treatment of Bev as Lurie's teacher, see Michael McDunnah's essay in this volume.

Works Cited

Abrams, M. H. *Natural Supernaturalism: Tradition and Revolution in Romantic Literature*. New York: W. W. Norton Co., 1971.

Achebe, Chinua. "An Image of Africa." *The Massachusetts Review* 18.4 (Winter 1977): 782–94.

Alcoff, Linda, and Laura Gray. "Survivor Discourse: Transgression or Recuperation?" *Signs* 18.2 (Winter 1993): 260–90.

Alter, Stephen G. *William Dwight Whitney and the Science of Language*. Baltimore: Johns Hopkins UP, 2005.

Altieri, Charles. "Lyrical Ethics and Literary Experience." Home page: "Manuscripts." http://socrates.berkeley.edu/%7Ealtieri/manuscripts/LITETH.html.

Amsterdamska, Olga. *Schools of Thought: The Development of Linguistics from Bopp to Saussure*. Dordrecht: Reidel, 1987.

Arens, Hans. *Sprachwissenschaft: Der Gang ihrer Entwicklung von der Antike bis zur Gegenwart*. 2nd ed. Freiburg/Munich: Karl Alber, 1969.

Ashley, Kathleen M. *Victor Turner and the Construction of Cultural Criticism: Between Literature and Anthropology*. Bloomington: U of Indiana P, 1990.

Attridge, Derek. "Age of Bronze, State of Grace: Music and Dogs in Coetzee's *Disgrace*. *Novel* 34.1 (2000): 98–121.

———. "Expecting the Unexpected in Coetzee's *Master of Petersburg* and Derrida's Recent Writings." In *Applying to Derrida*, ed. John Brannigan, Ruth Robbins and Julian Wolfreys, 21–40. London: Macmillan, 1996.

———. *J. M. Coetzee & the Ethics of Reading; Literature in the Event*. Chicago: U of Chicago P, 2004.

———. "J. M. Coetzee's *Disgrace*: Introduction." *Interventions: The International Journal of Postcolonial Studies* 4.3 (2002): 315–20.

Attwell, David. *J. M. Coetzee: South Africa and the Politics of Writing*. Berkeley: U of California P, 1993.

———. "Race in Disgrace." *Interventions: The International Journal of Postcolonial Studies* 4.3 (2002): 331–41.

Augustine. *On Christian Doctrine*. Trans. D. W. Robertson, Jr. Prentice Hall: Upper Saddle River, NJ, 1958.

Bailey, Cathryn. "On the Backs of Animals: The Valorization of Reason in Contemporary Animal Ethics." *Ethics and the Environment* 10.1 (2005): 1–17.

Bakhtin, Mikhail. *The Dialogic Imagination*. Ed. Michael Holquist, trans. Michael Holquist and Caryl Emerson. Austin. U of Texas P, 1998.

———. *Problems of Dostoevsky's Poetics*. Ed. and trans. by Caryl Emerson. Minneapolis: U of Minnesota P, 1988.

Barnard, Rita. *Apartheid and Beyond: South African Writers and the Politics of Place*. Oxford: Oxford UP, 2007.

———. "Coetzee's Country Ways." *Interventions: International Journal of Postcolonial Studies* 4.3 (2002) 384–94.

———. "*Disgrace* and the South African Pastoral." *Contemporary Literature* 44 (Summer, 2003): 199–224.

Bennett, Alan. *The History Boys*. New York: Faber, 2004.

Blanchot, Maurice. "Literature and the Right to Death." In *The Work of Fire*. Trans. Charlotte Mandell, 300–343. Stanford: Stanford UP, 1995.

Boehmer, Elleke. "Not Saying Sorry, Not Speaking Pain: Gender Implications in *Disgrace*." *Interventions: The International Journal of Postcolonial Studies* 4.3 (Nov 2002): 342–51.

Boito, Arrigo. *Mefistofele*. Libretto translation supervised by Gwyn Morris. Angel recording SCLX-380-6, 1974.

Brookfield, Stephen D., and Stephen Preskill. *Discussion as a Way of Teaching: Tools and Techniques for Democratic Classrooms*. San Francisco: Jossey-Bass, 2005.

Brown, Bill. "The Dark Wood of Postmodernity (Space, Faith, Allegory)." *PMLA* 120.3 (May 2005): 734–50.

Brown, C.F. Wemyss. "St. Hubert." *The Catholic Encyclopedia*. Vol. 7. New York: Robert Appleton Company, 1910. 27 Dec. 2007. http://www.newadvent.org/cathen/07507a.htm.

Brown, Wendy. *States of Injury*. Princeton: Princeton UP, 1995.

Brownmiller, Susan. *Against Our Will: Men, Women, and Rape*. New York: Ballantine Books, 1993.

Buchwald, Emilie, Pamela Fletcher, and Martha Roth, eds. *Trasforming a Rape Culture*. Minneapolis: Milkweed Editions, 1993.

Burrus, Virginia, and Catherine Keller, eds. *Toward a Theology of Eros: Transfiguring Passion at the Limits of Discipline*. New York: Fordham UP, 2006.

Burt, Martha R. "Cultural Myths and Supports of Rape." *Journal of Personality and Social Psychology* 38.2 (1980): 217–30.

Butler, Judith. *Giving an Account of Oneself*. New York: Fordham UP, 2005.

Byron, George Gordon. *A Critical Edition of the Major Works*. Ed. Jerome J. McGann. Oxford: Oxford UP, 1986.

Calasso, Roberto. *The Marriage of Cadmus and Harmony*. New York: Vintage, 1993.

Cavarero, Adriana. *Relating Narratives: Storytelling and Selfhood*. Warwick Studies in European Philosophy Series, trans. Paul A. Kottman. London: Routledge, 2000.

Chirimuuta, Mazviita. "Letter to Elena From Joanna S." *State of Nature: An Online Journal of Radical Ideas*. Autumn 2005. www.stateofnature.org/contentsOne.html#top.

Clinchy, B. McV. "On Critical Thinking and Connected Knowing." In *Re-thinking Reason: New Perspectives on Critical Thinking*, ed. K. S. Walters, 33–42. Albany, NY: SUNY Press, 1994.

Clinchy, B. McV., and C. Zimmerman. "Connected and Separate Knowing." Paper presented at the Eighth Biennial Meeting of the International Society for the Study of Behavior Development, Tours, France, 1985.

Clingman, Stephen. "Forms of History and Identity in *The Nature of Blood*." *Salmagundi* 143 (2004): 141–66.

———. "Other Voices: An Interview with Caryl Phillips." *Salmagundi* 143 (2004): 113–40.

Coetzee, J. M. *Age of Iron*. New York: Random House, 1990.

———. *Boyhood: Scenes from Provincial Life*. New York: Penguin Books, 1998.

———. *Diary of a Bad Year*. New York: Viking, 2007.

———. *Diary of a Bad Year* (excerpt). *The New York Times Review of Books* 54.12 (2007).

———. *Disgrace*. New York: Viking, 1999.

———. *Doubling the Point: Essays and Interviews*. Edited by David Attwell. Cambridge: Harvard UP, 1992.

———. *Dusklands*. New York: Penguin Books, 1974.

———. *Elizabeth Costello*. New York: Viking, 2003.

———. "Erasmus' *Praise of Folly*: Rivalry and Madness." *Neophilologus* 76.1 (1992): 1–18.

———. *Foe*. New York: Viking, 1987.

———. *Giving Offense: Essays on Censorship*. Chicago: U of Chicago P, 1997.

———. "He and His Man." *Nobelprize.org*. 22 March 2007. http://nobelprize.org/nobelprizes/literature/laureates/2003/coetzee-lecture-e.html.

———. "Interview with Djurens Rätt." *Satya* (May 2004). http://www.satyamag.com/may04/coetzee.html.

———. *In the Heart of the Country*. New York: Penguin Books, 1977.

———. *Life & Times of Michael K*. New York: Viking, 1983.

———. *The Lives of Animals*. Princeton: Princeton UP, 1999.

———. *The Master of Petersburg*. New York: Viking, 1994.

———. "On the Edge of Revelation." *New York Times Review of Books* 33.20 (December 18, 1986). http://www.xs4all.nl/~jikje/Essay/coetzee.html.

———. *Slow Man*. New York: Penguin Books, 2005.

———. *Waiting for the Barbarians*. New York: Penguin Books, 1980.

———. *White Writing: On the Culture of Letters in South Africa*. New Haven: Yale UP, 1988.

———. *Youth: Scenes from Provincial Life II*. New York: Viking, 2002.

Coleridge, Samuel Taylor. *Selected Poetry*. Ed. H. J. Jackson. Oxford: Oxford UP, 1997.

Cooper, Pamela. "Metamorphosis and Sexuality: Reading the Strange Passions of *Disgrace*." *Research in African Literatures* 36.4 (2005): 22–39.

Cornwell, Gareth. "Disgraceland: History and Humanities in Frontier Country." *English in Africa* 30.2 (2003): 43–68.

Cottingham, John. "'A Brute to the Brutes?': Descartes' Treatment of Animals." *Philosophy* 53 (Oct. 1978): 551–59.

Dante. *The Paradiso*. Trans. John Ciardi. New York: New American Library, 1970.

De Graef, Ortwin. "Suffering, Sympathy, Circulation: Smith, Wordsworth, Coetzee (But there's a dog)." *European Journal of English Studies* 7.3 (2003): 311–31.

Derrida, Jacques. *The Gift of Death*. Trans. David Wills. Chicago: U of Chicago P, 1995.

———. *The Work of Mourning*. Ed and trans. Pascale-Anne Brault, ed. Michael Naas. Chicago: U of Chicago P, 2003.

Dickens, Charles. *A Tale of Two Cities* (1859). New York: Bantam Books, 1989.

Dienstag, Joshua Foa. *Pessimism: Philosophy, Ethic, Spirit*. Princeton: Princeton UP, 2006.

Dobyns, Stephen. "Desire." *New American Poets of the '90s*. Ed. Jack Myers and Roger Weingarten. Boston: D. R. Godine, 1991.

Doctorow, E. L. *Creationists: Selected Essays, 1993–2006*. New York: Random House, 2006.

Dostoevsky, Fyodor. *The Brothers Karamazov*. Trans. Richard Pevear and Larissa Volokhonsky. New York: Vintage, 1991.

———. *Crime and Punishment*. Trans. Richard Pevear and Larissa Volokhonsky. New York: Vintage, 1992.

Du Bois. W. E. B. *The Souls of Black Folk*. New York: Barnes and Noble Classics, 2005.

Dumeige, Gervais. *Richard de Saint-Victor et l'idée chrétienne de l'amour*. Paris: Presses Universitaires de France, 1952.

Durrant, Sam. "J. M. Coetzee, Elizabeth Costello, and the Limits of the Sympathetic Imagination." In *J. M. Coetzee and the Idea of the Public Intellectual*, ed. Jane Poyner, 118–34.

———. *Postcolonial Narrative and the Work of Mourning: J. M. Coetzee, Wilson Harris, and Toni Morrison*. Albany: State U of New York P, 2004.

Edmundson, Mark. *Why Read?* New York: Bloomsbury Publishing, 2004.

Emerson, Caryl. *The First Hundred Years of Mikhail Bakhtin*. Princeton: Princeton UP, 1997.

Emerson, Ralph Waldo. *Essays and Lectures*. Ed. Joel Porte. New York: Library of America, 1983.

Farred, Grant. "Back to the Borderlines: Thinking Race *Disgrace*fully." *Scrutiny2* 7.1 (2002): 16–19.

———. "The Mundanacity of Violence: Living in a State of *Disgrace*." *Interventions: The International Journal of Postcolonial Studies* 4.3 (Nov. 2002): 352–62.

Fisher, Philip. *The Vehement Passions*. Princeton: Princeton UP, 2002.

Foucault, Michel. *Discipline and Punish*. Trans. Alan Sheridan. New York: Vintage Books, 1995.

———. *Power/Knowledge: Selected Interviews and Other Writings, 1972–1977*. Trans. Colin Gordon. New York: Pantheon, 1980.

Freire, Paulo. *Pedagogy of Freedom*. Lanham, MD: Rowman & Littlefield, 1998.

Freud, Sigmund. *The Standard Edition of the Complete Psychological Works*. Ed. James Strachey. Vol. 20. London: Hogarth, 1959.

Gane, Gillian. "Unspeakable Injuries in *Disgrace* and *David's Story*." *Kunapipi* 24.1–2 (2002): 101–13.

Gantz, Timothy. *Early Greek Myth: A Guide to Literary and Artistic Sources*. Baltimore: Johns Hopkins UP, 1993.

Gaylard, Gerald. "Disgraceful Metafiction: Intertextuality in the Postcolony." *Journal of Literary Studies* (Dec. 2005). http://www.thefreelibrary.com/Disgraceful+metafiction%3a+intertextuality+in+the+postcolony.a0153049540.

Goethe, Johann Wolfgang von. *Faust I and II*. Trans. and ed. Stuart Atkins. Princeton: Princeton UP, 1984.

Gordimer, Nadine. "Once Upon a Time." In *Jump and Other Stories*. New York: Farrar, Straus, Giroux, 1991, 3–22.

———. "Six Feet of the Country." In *Selected Stories*. New York: Viking Press, 1976.

Graham, Lucy Valerie. "Reading the Unspeakable: Rape in J. M Coetzee's Disgrace." *Journal of Southern African Studies* 29.2 (2003): 433–44.

———. "'Yes, I am giving him up': Sacrificial Responsibility and Likeness with Dogs in Coetzee's Recent Fiction." *Scrutiny2* 10.1 (2002): 4–15.

Griffin, Susan. *Woman and Nature: The Roaring Inside Her*. San Francisco: Sierra Club Books, 2000.

Hacking, Ian M. "Our Fellow Animals." *New York Review of Books* 47.11 (2000): 20–26.

Harpham, Geoffrey. *Shadows of Ethics: Criticism and the Just Society*. Durham: Duke UP, 1999.

Harrison, Peter. "Descartes on Animals." *The Philosophical Quarterly* 42.167 (April 1992): 219–27.

Hassoun, Jacques. *The Cruelty of Depression: On Melancholy*. Trans. David Jacobson. Reading, MA: Addison-Wesley, 1997.

Head, Bessie. "Looking for a Rain God." In *The Collector of Treasures and Other Botswana Tales*. London: Heinemann, 1992, 57–60.

Head, Dominic. *J. M. Coetzee*. Cambridge: Cambridge UP, 1997.

Heidegger, Martin. *Being and Time*. Ed. John Macquarrie and Edward Robinson. London: Blackwell, 1962.

———. *The Question Concerning Technology and Other Essays*. New York: Harper Torchbooks, 1977.

Herron, Tom. "The Dog Man: Becoming Animal in Coetzee's *Disgrace*." *Twentieth Century Literature* 51.4 (2005): 467–90.

Hesford, Wendy. "Reading Rape Stories: Material Rhetoric and the Trauma of Representation." *College English* 62.2 (1999): 192–221.

Holland, Michael. "'Plink-Plunk' Unforgetting the Present in Coetzee's *Disgrace*." *Interventions: The International Journal of Postcolonial Studies* 4.3 (Nov 2002): 395–404.

Holquist, Michael. *Dialogism*. New York: Routledge, 1990.

hooks, bell. *Teaching Community: A Pedagogy of Hope*. New York: Routledge, 2003.

Huggan, Graham, and Stephen Watson, eds. *Critical Perspectives on J. M. Coetzee*. London: Macmillan, 1996.

Humboldt, Wilhelm von. *Schriften zur Sprachphilosophie*, Werke in fünf Bänden, vol. 3. Darmstadt: Wissenschaftliche Buchgesellschaft, 1963.

———. *On Language: On the Diversity of Human Language Construction and its Influence on the Mental Development of the Human Species*. Cambridge Texts in the History of Philosophy. Trans. Peter Heath, ed. Michael Losonsky. Cambridge: Cambridge UP, 1999.

Interventions: The International Journal of Postcolonial Studies. Ed. Derek Attridge, 4.3 (2002). J. M. Coetzee's *Disgrace*. Includes essays by David Attwell, Derek Attridge, Ruth Barnard, Elleke Boehmer, Eric Cheyfitz, Arif Dirlik, Grant Farred, Michael Holland, Peter McDonald, Graham Peachey, and Mark Sanders.

Jacoby, Günther. *Herder als Faust: Eine Untersuchung.* Leipzig: Felix Meiner, 1911.

Jameson, Fredric. *Postmodernism, or, the Cultural Logic of Late Capitalism.* London: Verso, 1991.

Jelinek, Elfriede. *The Piano Teacher.* Trans. Joachim Neugroschel. London: Serpent's Tail, 1999.

Jolly, Rosemary. "Going to the Dogs: Humanity in J. M. Coetzee's *Disgrace, The Lives of Animals,* and South Africa's Truth and Reconciliation Commission." In *J. M. Coetzee and the Idea of the Public Intellectual,* ed. Jane Poyner, 148–71.

Kant, Immanuel. *Groundwork of the Metaphysics of Morals.* Ed. Mary Gregor. New York: Cambridge UP, 1978.

Kessow, Sue, ed. *Critical Essays on J. M. Coetzee.* New York: G. H. Hall, 1998.

Kirsch, Adam. "Criticism From a Winner" (Review of Clive James's *Cultural Amnesia*). *New York Sun* (March 14, 2007). http://www.nysun.com/article/50441.

Kivel, Paul. *Uprooting Racism: How White People Can Work for Racial Justice.* Gabriola Island, BC, Canada: New Society Publishers, 2002.

Kuh, G. D., J. Kinzie, J. H. Schuh, and E. J. Whitt. *Student Success in College: Creating Conditions That Matter.* Washington, DC: Jossey-Bass, 2005.

Lacan, Jacques *Le Séminaire, livre VII: L'éthique de la psychanalyse.* Text established by Jacques-Alain Miller. Paris: Seuil, 1986. Trans. Dennis Porter as *The Seminar of Jacques Lacan, Book VII: The Ethics of Psychoanalysis.* New York: W. W. Norton, 1992.

Lamar, Howard, and Leonard Thompson, eds. *The Frontier in History: North America and Southern Africa Compared.* New Haven: Yale UP, 1981.

Lanchester, John. "A Will of His Own." Review of *Slow Man* by J. M. Coetzee. *New York Review of Books,* 17 November 2005, 4–6.

Lenta, Margaret. "Autrebiography: J. M. Coetzee's *Boyhood* and *Youth.*" *English in Africa* 30.1 (2003): 157–69.

Levi, Primo. *The Drowned and the Saved.* New York: Vintage International, 1989.

Levinas, Emmanuel. "Meaning and Sense." (1957). In *Collected Philosophical Papers.* Ed. and trans. Alphonso Lingis, 75–107. Dordrecht: Martinus Nijhoff, 1987.

Lewis, C. S. *The Allegory of Love.* London: Oxford UP, 1938.

Lilje, Hanns. "Herder, Theologie im Weimarer Kreis." In *Goethe und seine grossen Zeitgenossen: Sieben Essays,* ed. Albert Schaefer, 115–39. Munich: Beck, 1968.

Limerick, Patricia Nelson. *Legacy of Conquest: The Unbroken Past of the American West.* New York: Norton, 1987.

Littleton, Heather L., Danny Axsom, and Matthew Yoder. "Priming of Consensual and Nonconsensual Sexual Scripts: An Experimental Test of the Role of Scripts in Rape Attributions." *Sex Roles* 54.7/8 (2006): 557–63. 20 Aug 2008. http://search.ebscohost.com/login.aspx?direct=true&db=aph&AN=23037658&site=ehost-live.

Lonsway, Kimberly A., and Louise F. Fitzgerald. "Rape Myths." *Psychology of Women Quarterly* 18 (1994): 133–64.

Lopez, Barry. *Apologia*. Athens: U of Georgia P, 1998.

Lowry, Elizabeth. "Like A Dog." *London Review of Books* 21.20 (1999): 12–14.

Magona, Sindiwe. *Mother to Mother*. Boston: Beacon Press, 2000.

Makhaya, Gertrude B. "The Trouble with J. M. Coetzee." *The Oxonian Review of Books* 4.2 (2005). 22 March 2007. http://www.oxonianreview.org/issues/3-2/3-2-5.htm.

Marais, Mike. "J. M. Coetzee's *Disgrace* and the Task of the Imagination." *Journal of Modern Literature* 29.2 (2006): 75–93.

———. "'Little Enough, Less Than Nothing': Ethics, Engagement and Change in the Fiction of J. M. Coetzee." *Modern Fiction Studies* 46.1 (2000): 159–82.

———. "The Possibility of Ethical Action: J. M. Coetzee's *Disgrace*." *Scrutiny2* 5.1 (2000): 52–63.

Marcus, Sharon. "Fighting Bodies, Fighting Words: A Theory and Politics of Rape Prevention." *Feminists Theorize the Political* (1992): 385–403.

Mardorossian, Carine M. "Toward a New Feminist Theory of Rape." *Signs* 27.3 (2002): 743–75.

Mason, Travis V. "Dog Gambit: Shifting the Species Boundary in J. M. Coetzee's Recent Fiction." *Mosaic: A Journal for the Interdisciplinary Study of Literature* 39.4 (2006): 129–44.

McDonald, Peter D. "Disgrace Effects." *Interventions: The International Journal of Postcolonial Studies* 4.3 (2002): 321–30.

McMullin, Darcy, and Jacquelyn W. White. "Long-term Effects of Labeling a Rape Experience." *Psychology of Women Quarterly* 30 (2006): 96–105.

Mda, Zakes. *The Madonna of Excelsior*. New York: Picador, 2004.

Meffan, James, and Kim L. Worthington. "Ethics before Politics: J. M. Coetzee's *Disgrace*." In *Mapping the Ethical Turn: A Reader in Ethics, Culture and Literary Theory*, ed. Todd F. Davis and Kenneth Womack, 131–50. Charlottesville, VA: U of Virginia P, 2001.

Meis, Morgan. "*Malo immaginario*: Why J. M. Coetzee and James Wood Are Both Right and Wrong." *The Smart Set*. October 3, 2007. www.thesmartset.com/article/article10030701.aspx.

Michelfelder, Diane, and Richard Palmer, eds. *Dialogue and Deconstruction: The Gadamer-Derrida Encounter*. New York: SUNY Press, 1989.

Moran, John H., and Alexander Gode, eds. and trans. *Two Essays on the Origin of Language*. Chicago: U of Chicago P, 1986.

Morphet, Tony. "Two Interviews with J. M. Coetzee, 1983 and 1987." *TriQuarterly* 69 (Spring–Summer 1987): 454–64.

Morson, Gary Saul, and Caryl Emerson. *Mikhail Bakhtin: Creation of Prosaics*. Stanford: Stanford UP, 1990.

Nagel, Thomas. "What Is It Like to Be a Bat?" *Philosophical Review* 83 (1974): 435–50.

Neiman, Susan. *Moral Clarity: A Guide for Grown-Up Idealists*. Orlando: Harcourt, 2008.

Nussbaum, Martha C. "Animal Rights: The Need for a Theoretical Basis." *Harvard Law Review* 114.5 (2001): 1506–49.

Nyman, Jopi. *Postcolonial Animal Tales from Kipling to Coetzee*. New Delhi: Atlantic Publishers and Distributors, 2003.

Ondaatje, Michael. *Divisadero*. New York: Knopf, 2007.

Page, Tim. Review of "Lord Byron's Love Letter," by Tennessee Williams and Raffaello de Banfield. *New York Times*, "Arts," May 26, 1986.

Palmer, Earl. "Roots & Wings." Sermon Series. Audio Archives, 2004. http://audio.upc.org/audioarchives2004.asp.

Palmer, Parker L. *The Courage to Teach: Exploring the Inner Landscape of a Teacher's Life*. San Francisco: Jossey-Bass, 1998.

Peterson, Zoe D. "Was it Rape? The Function of Women's Rape Myth Acceptance and Definitions of Sex in Labeling Their Own Experiences." *Sex Roles* 51.3/4: 129–44.

Phillips, Caryl. *The European Tribe*. New York: Vintage, 1987.

———. *The Nature of Blood*. New York: Vintage International, 1998.

———. "On *The Nature of Blood* and the Ghost of Anne Frank." *CommonQuest* (Summer, 1998): 6.

Plato. "Republic." In *Complete Works*. Ed. with introduction and notes by John M. Cooper. Trans. G. M. A. Grube, 971–1224. Indianapolis: Hackett Publ. Co., 1997.

———. "Phaedo." *Plato I: Euthyphro Apology Crito Phaedo Phaedrus*. Trans. Harold John Fowler. Cambridge: Harvard UP, 2001.

Poyner, Jane, ed. *J. M. Coetzee and the Idea of the Public Intellectual*. Athens, Ohio: Ohio UP, 2006.

———. "Truth and Reconciliation in J. M. Coetzee's *Disgrace*." *Scrutiny2: Issues in English Studies in Southern Africa* 5.2 (2000): 67–77.

Reef, Anne. "Representations of Rape in Apartheid and Post-Apartheid South African Literature." *Textual Studies or Locating Ethics* 26 (2005): 245–61.

Reinhard, Kenneth. "Freud, My Neighbor." *American Imago* 54.2 (Summer 1997): 165–95.

Richard of St. Victor. *The Twelve Patriarchs; The Mystical Ark; Book Three of The Trinity*. Trans. Gordon Zinn. New York: Paulist Press, 1979.

Rorty, Richard. *Contingency, Irony and Solidarity*. Cambridge: Cambridge UP, 1989.

Rose, Gillian. *Mourning Becomes the Law. Philosophy and Representation.* Cambridge: Cambridge UP, 1996.

Rubin, Gayle. "The Traffic in Women: Notes on the 'Political Economy' of Sex." In *Literary Theory: An Anthology*, ed. Julie Rivkin and Michael Ryan, 770–94. 2nd ed. Malden, MA: Blackwell Publishing, 2004.

Samuelson, Meg. *Remembering the Nation, Dismembering Women?: Stories of the South African Transition*. Durban: University of KwaZulu-Natal Press, 2007.

Sanders, Mark. *Ambiguities of Witnessing: Law and Literature in the Time of a Truth Commission*. Stanford: Stanford UP, 2007.

Sanders, Mark. *Complicities: The Intellectual and Apartheid*. Durban: University of KwaZulu-Natal Press. 2002.

———. "Disgrace." *Interventions: International Journal of Postcolonial Studies* 4.3 (2002): 363–73.

Saussure, Ferdinand de. *Cours de linguistique générale*. Ed. Charles Balley and Albert Sechehaye. Paris: Payout, 1973.

Schlegel, Friedrich Wilhelm von. *Über die Sprache und Weisheit der Inder*. Heidelberg, 1808.

Scrutiny2: Issues in English Studies in Southern Africa 7.1 (2002). Special issue, "Symposium on Disgrace," ed. Leon de Kock. Essays by Lucy Graham, Grant Farred, Louis Bethlehem, Georgina Horrell, Ariella Azoulay, Hannah Hever.

Segall, Kimberly Wedeven. "Pursuing Ghosts: The Traumatic Sublime in J. M. Coetzee's *Disgrace*." *Research in African Literatures* 36.4 (Winter 2005): 40–54.

Seidel, Linda. "Death and Transformation in J. M. Coetzee's *Disgrace*." *Journal of Colonialism and Colonial History* 2.3 (2001): 22.

Shaw, Mark. *Crime and Policing in Post-apartheid South Africa: Transforming under Fire*. Indianapolis: Indiana UP, 2002.

Shulman, Lee. *Teaching as Community Property: Essays on Higher Education*. San Francisco: Jossey-Bass, 2004.

Sikorska, Liliana, ed. *A Universe of (Hi)stories: Essays on J. M. Coetzee*. Polish Studies in English Language and Literature 15. Frankfurt am Main: Peter Lang, 2006.

Spivak, Gayatri Chakravorty. "Ethics and Politics in Tagore, Coetzee, and Certain Scenes of Teaching." *Diacritics* 32.3–4 (2002): 17–31.

———. "Reply" in "Conference Debates: Gayatri Chakravorty Spivak's Influences: Past, Present, Future." *PMLA* 123.1 (January 2008): 248.

Stanton, Katherine. *Cosmopolitan Fictions: Ethics, Politics and Global Change in the Works of Kazuo Ishiguro, Michael Ondaatje, Jamaica Kincaid and J. M. Coetzee.* New York and London: Routledge, 2006.

Stegner, Wallace. *Angle of Repose.* New York: Doubleday & Co., 1971.

Strode, Timothy Francis. *The Ethics of Exile: Colonialism in the Fictions of Charles Brockden Brown and J. M. Coetzee.* New York and London: Routledge, 2005.

Tremaine, Louis. "The Embodied Soul: Animal Being in the Work of J. M. Coetzee." *Contemporary Literature* 44.4 (2003): 587–612.

Turner, Frederick Jackson. *The Significance of the Frontier in American History.* New York: Holt, Rinehart, and Winston, 1920.

Visotzky, Burton L. *The Genesis of Ethics: How the Tormented Family of Genesis Leads us to Moral Development.* New York: Three Rivers Press, 1996.

Wachtel, Eleanor. "The Sympathetic Imagination: A Conversation with J. M. Coetzee." *Brick* 67 (2001): 37–47.

Weiss, Gail, ed. *Perspectives on Embodiment: The Body in Nature and Culture.* New York: Routledge, 1999.

Wicomb, Zoë. "Translations in the Yard of Africa." *Journal of Literary Studies* 18 (2002): 209–23.

Williams, Raymond. *The Country and the City.* London: Oxford UP, 1973.

Wittgenstein, Ludwig. *Philosophical Investigations.* Trans. G. E. M. Anscombe and Elizabeth Anscombe. London: Wiley and Blackwell, 2001.

Wood, James. "Coetzee's *Disgrace*: A Few Skeptical Thoughts." In *The Irresponsible Self: On Laughter and the Novel.* New York: Farrar, Straus, Giroux, 2004.

———."A Frog's Life" (Review of Coetzee's *Elizabeth Costello: Eight Lessons*). *London Review of Books* (October 23, 2003). http://www.lrb.co.uk/v25/n20/wood02_.html.

———. "Parables and Prizes." *The New Republic Online,* May 10, 2001. www.tnr.com/ currentissue/index.html or www.powells.com/review/2001_05_10.html.

Wordsworth, William. *The Major Works.* Ed. Stephen Gill. Oxford: Oxford UP, 2000.

———. *The Prelude (1799, 1805, 1850).* Ed. Jonathan Wordsworth, M. H. Abrams, and Stephen Gill. Norton Critical Edition. New York: W. W. Norton Co., 1979.

Wright, Laura. *Coetzee. Writing "Out of All the Camps": J. M. Coetzee's Narratives of Displacement.* New York: Routledge, 2006.

Zagajewski, Adam. "Try to Praise the Mutilated World." *Records of Academy (American Academy of Arts and Sciences).* Trans. Clare Cavanagh (2001): 9. JSTOR. University of Houston—Downtown, W. I. Dykes Library. 25 Oct. 2007. www.jstor.org.

Contributors

NANCY BEST (Johnston 1981) is a Lecturer in English at California State University, San Bernardino. She earned her MFA in creative writing from San Diego State. An accomplished diver and underwater photographer, she is completing a novel about deep sea diving.

JAMES BOOBAR (Johnston 2002) graduated from the Stonecoast Writing Program at the University of Southern Maine. He is a visiting alumni faculty member at the Johnston Center. For the last eight years, he has led a "seminar in the streets" on the life and writings of Fyodor Dostoevsky for the internationally recognized Summer Literary Seminar in St. Petersburg, Russia.

BRADLEY BUTTERFIELD (Johnston 1986) is an Associate Professor of English at the University of Wisconsin, La Crosse. He has published essays on twentieth-century critical theory and fiction.

JANE CREIGHTON (Johnston 1973) is a poet, writer, and Associate Professor of English at the University of Houston–Downtown, where she also serves as the Director of the Cultural Enrichment Center. Her work has been published in such journals as *Ploughshares*, *The American Voice*, and *Gulf Coast*, as well as in the anthologies *We Begin Here: Poems for Palestine and Lebanon* (Interlink Books); *Still Seeking an Attitude: Critical Reflections on the Work of June Jordan* (Lexington Books); *Unwinding the Vietnam War* (Real Comet Press); and *Close to the Bone: Memoirs of Hurt, Rage, and Desire* (Grove Press). In 2006/2007, she held a Fulbright Fellowship at Jagiellonian University in Kraków, Poland.

MATT GRAY (Johnston 2005) is a Civic Engagement Educator at Johnson and Wales University in Denver, Colorado. His pedagogy focuses on integrating issues of social justice, personal authenticity, and sustainable living. He was recognized as a young leader in his field when he and his colleague won a National Case Study Competition in 2007. He is currently working on a collaborative collection of poetry and wine ink drawings with his brother, Daniel Gray (Johnston 2001).

PATRICK HARRIGAN (Johnston 1994) is a Minneapolis-based writer and editor. He has worked on new media projects with Improv Technologies,

Weatherwood Company, and Wrecking Ball Productions, and as Marketing Director and Creative Developer for Fantasy Flight Games. He is the co-editor of *The Art of H.P. Lovecraft's Cthulhu Mythos* (2006, with Brian Wood), and the MIT Press volumes *Third Person: Authoring and Exploring Vast Narratives* (2009), *Second Person: Role-Playing and Story in Games and Playable Media* (2007), and *First Person: New Media as Story, Performance and Game* (2004), all with Noah Wardrip-Fruin (Johnston 1994). He has also written a novel, *Lost Clusters* (2005).

GARY HAWKINS (Johnston 1991) is a poet, essayist, and teacher. His work — poems, criticism, and pedagogy — collects around his concerns of beauty, identity, and democracy, and it has appeared in the *Virginia Quarterly Review*, the *Emily Dickinson Journal*, *American Book Review*, and the forthcoming *Teaching Creative Writing in Higher Education* (Palgrave Macmillan). Collaborator on *artefact*, a re-current letterpress anthology of poetry and beauty, he lives in Black Mountain, North Carolina and directs the Undergraduate Writing Program at Warren Wilson College.

RABBI PATRICIA KARLIN-NEUMANN (Johnston 1976) is the Senior Associate Dean for Religious Life at Stanford University. She was ordained at the Hebrew Union College-Jewish Institute of Religion in 1982. She teaches and lectures widely on the relationship between religion and education, student well-being, rabbinical ethics, Jewish feminism, and social justice. She works on campus with profound gratitude for those at Johnston who lavished blessings upon her as an undergraduate and helped her to imagine vistas beyond what she had previously known.

DANIEL KIEFER has taught at the University of Redlands since 1991, in the Department of English and the Johnston Center. He offers a wide range of courses in Romantic poetry, Shakespeare, Milton, Dante, critical reading and theory, and queer culture. He also directs the university's Proudian Interdisciplinary Honors Program. Before coming to Redlands he taught Romantic and Victorian poetry at Southern Illinois University at Carbondale, after taking his doctoral degree at Yale in 1985. He has written on W. B. Yeats and on Tony Kushner's *Angels in America*, and he's working on a book about Walt Whitman and the figural body, entitled *Whitman's Darkest Leaves*.

BILL MCDONALD is a Faculty Fellow Emeritus of the Johnston Center and a Professor of English and the Virginia C. Hunsaker Chair of Distinguished Teaching Emeritus of the University of Redlands (1969–2005). He has co-authored two volumes on the Johnston Center (1989, 2004) and published a book on Thomas Mann (1999). His other academic fields include international modernism, literary theory, ancient Greece, pedagogy, and interdisciplinary studies in the humanities.

MICHAEL MCDUNNAH (Johnston 1991), an independent scholar, has been a nonprofit fundraising and communications professional for ten years, and currently serves as the Communications Director for Project Vote, a national organization working on voting-rights and election administration issues. He lives in Washington, DC.

KIM MIDDLETON (Johnston 1994) is an Assistant Professor of English and an affiliated faculty member in the American Studies Program at The College of Saint Rose in Albany, New York. Her classes and previous publications concern the connections between popular culture and contemporary literature.

RAYMOND OBSTFELD (Johnston 1972) teaches creative writing at Orange Coast College. He is the author of over forty books, including poetry (*The Cat with Half a Face*), novels (*The Joker and the Thief*), and non-fiction (*On the Shoulders of Giants* with Kareem Abdul-Jabbar). He has also co-authored, with his wife Loretta, books on the Italian Renaissance, Napoleon Bonaparte, and *Moby Dick*. He has been nominated for an Edgar award and has a new novel in print: *Anatomy Lesson* (2007).

KATHY OGREN is the Virginia C. Hunsaker Chair of Distinguished Teaching at The University of Redlands, where she teaches in the Johnston Center as well as the History and Women's Studies Departments. Her scholarly interests include Jazz Studies and the history of cowboy poetry and music. She is the author of *The Jazz Revolution: Twenties America and the Meaning of Jazz* (Oxford, 1989), as well as essays, articles and book reviews in her field.

KEVIN O'NEILL is Professor of Philosophy at the University of Redlands and a founding faculty member of the Johnston Center. He has co-written a history of the Johnston program (with Bill McDonald) and has presented and published papers on representations of death, Greek philosophy, and interdisciplinary teaching and learning. He is currently working on a project involving representations of death in the work of J. M. Coetzee.

KENNETH REINHARD (Johnston 1976–78) is Associate Professor of English and Comparative Literature at UCLA. His fields of research and teaching include the History of Critical and Aesthetic Theory, Contemporary Critical Theory (Psychoanalysis, Philosophy, Political Theory), and Jewish Studies. He is the author, with Slavoj Zizek and Eric Santner of *The Neighbor: Three Inquiries in Political Theology* (U of Chicago P, 2005) and with Julia Reinhard Lupton, of *After Oedipus: Shakespeare in Psychoanalysis* (Cornell UP, 1993). Currently he is writing a book on the ethics of the neighbor in religion (Torah, Talmud, and Patristic writings), philosophy (Kant, Kierkegaard, Adorno, Rosenzweig, and Levinas), and psychoanalysis (Freud and Lacan) for Princeton University Press.

SANDRA D. SHATTUCK (Johnston 1977) is a Lecturer in the Department of English at the University of Alabama in Huntsville. An intrepid blogger, her research interests include the use of technology in writing pedagogy and reading/writing connections, as well as multicultural and international young adult literature.

PATRICIA CASEY SUTCLIFFE (Johnston 1990) is an editor for the German Historical Institute in Washington, DC. Her graduate work in Germanic Studies at the University of Texas at Austin focused on the history of linguistics, particularly in Germany in the nineteenth century. She held visiting assistant professorships at Colgate University and Montclair State University, and she continues to pursue research on nineteenth-century language scholars. Since 2000, she has published articles on Wilhelm von Humboldt, Friedrich Max Müller, Charles Lutwidge Dodgson, Benjamin Lee Whorf, and William Dwight Whitney among others.

JULIE TOWNSEND is an Associate Professor of Interdisciplinary Humanities in the Johnston Center at the University of Redlands. Her research focuses on representations of dancers in literature and the visual arts. Recent articles include "Staking Salomé: The Literary Forefathers and Choreographic Daughters of Wilde's 'hysterical and perverted creature'" in the forthcoming edition *Oscar Wilde and Modern Culture: The Making of a Legend* and "*Synaesthetics*: Symbolism, Dance, and the Failure of Metaphor," which appeared in the *Yale Journal of Criticism* in April 2005. Her forthcoming monograph, *The Choreography of Modernism: La Danseuse, 1830–1930*, will be published by Legenda Press in 2009. At the Johnston Center she teaches seminars in literature, aesthetics, dance theory, and French conversation.

Index

Abelson, R. P., 135n1
Achebe, Chinua, 139
ACORN, 2
Adorno, Theodor, 130, 292
Alcoff, Linda, 135n6
allegory, 71–72, 78–79, 80, 89, 108, 111, 252, 269, 334
Altieri, Charles, 87–88, 92n33
Amis, Martin, 298
Amsterdamska, Olga, 183
aporia, 59, 61, 122
Arens, Hans, 195, 201nn22–23
Argento, Dominick, 77
Ashley, Kathleen M., 262n15
Attenborough, Sir Richard, 281
Attridge, Derek, 9, 10, 11, 47nn2–3, 57, 59, 60, 62, 138, 140, 146–47n1, 170n3, 217, 218, 219, 223, 225–26n1, 227n6, 228nn12–16, 229n18, 319
Attwell, David, 9, 10, 147, 170n3, 217, 258, 262n16
Augustine, 66, 94, 104n1
Axsom, Danny, 135n1

Bakhtin, Mikhail, 48–52, 54, 55, 57, 58, 59, 61, 62
Banfield, Raffaelo de, 90n18
Barnard, Rita, 10, 92n31, 218, 224, 226n1, 227n6, 228n14, 229n17, 250, 262n2
Beckett, Samuel, 8, 76
Benedict, 52, 75, 151–52
Berlin Academy of Science, 183
Bernard of Clairvaux, 66
Biehl, Amy, 140
Biko, Steven, 281–82
Blake, William, 64, 65, 75, 84, 272
Blanchot, Maurice, 218, 227–28n10, 228n13, 228n16

Boehmer, Elleke, 10, 170nn3–4, 171n6
Boito, Arrigo, 65, 85, 92n27, 92n30, 93, 173–77, 181, 198, 199, 200n9
Bonaventure, 66
Booker Prize, 1, 259
Bopp, Franz, 183, 194
Breytenbach, Breyten, 146n1
Brookfield, Stephen D., 233
Brown, Bill, 89n33
Brown, C. F. W., 90
Brown, Wendy, 136n7
Brownmiller, Susan, 122, 135n3
Buchwald, Emilie, 118
Burrus, Virginia, 89n11
Burt, Martha R., 135n5
Butler, Judith, 117, 130–34, 137n15, 294
Byron, George Gordon, Lord, 3, 23, 35, 37, 41–42, 65, 75, 78, 85, 109, 115nn3–4, 127, 141, 174, 175, 182, 205, 209, 237, 248, 269, 285, 286; in David Lurie's opera, 10, 11, 42–45, 65, 76–79, 84, 90n18, 96, 110, 168, 171n9, 173, 193, 195, 270, 295, 329, 330–31
Byron, George Gordon, Lord, works by: "Lara," 15–16, 108, 175, 252, 265, 267, 270, 333–34

Calasso, Roberto, 91n24
Campbell, Joseph, 298, 300, 311
Cavarero, Adriana, 130, 132, 133, 134
Centre for the Study of Violence and Reconciliation, 117
Chaplin, Charlie, 318
Chernyshevsky, Nikolai, 50
Clinchy, B. McV., 283–84
Clingman, Stephen, 321, 329n4, 329nn6–7

Coetzee, J. M., 1, 17, 27, 49, 54–55, 73, 76, 88, 90n19, 102–3, 147n1, 171–72n13, 202–3, 216, 225n1, 226n2, 227n6, 228n12, 229n17, 229n20, 259; biography, 15, 46n1, 47n3, 65, 73, 140, 175; as South African writer, 5–9

Coetzee, J. M.: *Disgrace*:
animals in, 8–9, 21, 32–34, 48–50, 55–57, 59–63, 86–88, 95–97, 103–4, 106–7, 170n3, 184, 202–29, 329–30 (see also *Disgrace*, characters in: Driepoot; Katy)

characters in (for David Lurie, Lucy Lurie, Petrus, and Melanie Isaacs, main discussions only):

Driepoot, 46, 48–51, 55–56, 58–63, 78–79, 87, 176, 181, 188–89, 198, 295

Ettinger, 31–32, 130

Melanie Isaacs, 21–30, 35–37, 40–41, 52–53, 74–75, 80–81, 91n25, 104–5, 107–9, 118–27, 149–50, 155–71, 178–80, 188, 205–6, 239, 252, 265–70, 272–74, 292–94, 324–26, 328–30, 332–37

Mr. Isaacs, 39–40, 46, 141, 164–65, 215, 251, 328, 336–37

Katy, 32, 33, 79, 83, 98, 144, 215–16

David Lurie: and animals, 32–34, 48–51, 54–63, 78–79, 202–29, 336–38; and desire/Eros, 19–26, 34–35, 39–42, 46, 52–53, 74–76, 80–82, 107–10, 150–51, 155–63, 166–67, 208–10, 267–75, 291–93, 309–10, 321–25; ethical choices and dilemmas of (*see Disgrace*: ethical issues in); as father, 28–32, 36–38, 123–25, 210–15, 260–61; and relation to women (see *Disgrace*: rape in; women and feminism); as Romantic, 148–72, 175–201, 268–70; as scholar and teacher, 3, 64–65, 152–57, 173, 252–53, 264–66, 331–37;

as visionary, 64–88, 93–105, 151–56, 160–69, 174–81, 278

Lucy Lurie, 28–46, 53–54, 61–62, 67–69, 78–85, 97–104, 109–14, 123–36, 140–47, 177, 186, 189–91, 209–15, 219–21, 261–62, 270–72, 291, 324–28

Manas Mathabane, 164, 208

Petrus, 100–101, 109, 127–34, 136n12, 141–44, 186, 191, 338

Pollux, 38, 78, 141–46, 213

Farodia Rassool, 163, 196, 324

Rosalind, 64, 68, 78, 109, 167, 197, 200n7, 207–8, 209–11, 213, 227n6, 227n10, 272, 324

Ryan, 23, 41, 175, 186–87, 252, 333

Bev Shaw, 32–36, 38, 53, 61, 72, 77, 78, 79, 87, 96, 111, 130, 131, 138, 143, 170n3, 178, 188, 190, 191–92, 200n16, 212, 214, 216–21, 223, 225, 229n21, 272, 274, 295, 328

Bill Shaw, 31–32, 33, 36, 130, 186, 200n13

Soraya, 19–22, 24–25, 29, 36, 41, 42, 43, 45, 47n4, 52–53, 74, 78, 82, 84, 150–51, 156–58, 159, 161–62, 175, 178, 188, 207–8, 209, 210, 214, 227n6, 304, 324, 337

ending of, 44–46, 48–50, 55–63, 74, 83–88, 93, 106, 180–81, 261–62, 312, 338–39

ethical issues in, 3–6, 8–12, 15–16, 23–24, 27–29, 32–42, 44–47, 48–63, 65–91, 94–104, 106–14, 116–35, 140, 144–47, 157–63, 167–69, 202–28, 234–35, 238–41, 246, 251–62, 267–75, 281–84, 290–96, 317–20, 324–30, 330–39

language in, 10, 11, 23–25, 33, 43, 61, 107, 119, 152–54, 173–201, 208–11, 225–26n1, 227–28n10, 228n13, 228n16, 265–67, 271, 296, 328, 337

Lurie's opera in, 11, 21, 42–45, 50, 60, 65, 76–80, 84, 90n18, 96, 110, 156, 168, 173–74, 185, 195, 224, 270, 330, 335
narrative structure of, 7–8, 15–47, 52–53, 72, 75, 78, 84, 86, 106–7, 112–14, 120, 123–24, 149, 157, 165, 170n3, 171n7, 177, 181, 241, 251–52, 262–63n21, 266, 273–74, 311–12, 322, 324
race in, 6, 27, 46, 97, 99, 100–101, 109, 135n4, 136nn10–11, 138–47, 169n1, 170n3, 171n11, 177, 281, 291–92, 294, 296, 316, 317–29
rape in, 1, 11–12, 29, 37–39, 53, 67–69, 72, 100, 102, 104n2, 111–12, 115n5, 116–37, 138, 140, 141–44, 146n1, 147nn2–3, 150, 161, 170n3, 212–13, 238–39, 241, 254–55, 256–57, 265, 266, 273, 274, 291–93, 320–21, 323, 325, 326–29, 338
reception of, 5–6, 10, 139–40, 319
style of, 23–25, 28–29, 81, 106–8, 299, 311–12
teaching in, 32–35, 72, 78, 151–53, 155, 167–68, 197, 205–6, 237, 252–53, 265–70, 296, 331–40
visions and the visionary in, 64–88, 94–98, 103, 151–52, 161–62, 169, 175
Coetzee, J. M., other works by:
Age of Iron, 6, 7, 8, 15, 16, 42, 45, 73, 88, 92n29, 257
Boyhood: Scenes from Provincial Life, 7, 15, 46n1, 47n3
Diary of a Bad Year, 9, 17, 21, 102, 105n5, 137n13, 272
Doubling the Point: Essays and Interviews, 6, 7, 8, 9, 27, 49, 54, 55, 63, 76, 83, 89nn1–2, 89n9, 91n19, 140, 145, 234
Dusklands, 6, 17, 27, 73
Elizabeth Costello, 7, 9, 15, 26, 28, 32, 35–36, 42, 49, 73, 76, 107, 223, 226n2, 229, 234, 238, 246, 251, 254, 255, 256, 259

"Erasmus' *Praise of Folly*: Rivalry and Madness," 225
Foe, 8, 17, 235, 238, 246, 251, 254, 256, 259
Giving Offense: Essays on Censorship, 6, 9
"He and His Man," 138, 259
"Interview with Djurens Rätt," 32
In the Heart of the Country, 8, 17, 24, 73, 147, 234, 242–43, 249–50, 251, 256
Life & Times of Michael K, 7, 17, 18, 47n2, 234, 238, 251, 254, 255, 256, 259
The Lives of Animals, 9, 90n17, 226n2
The Master of Petersburg, 8, 49, 55–57, 86–87, 229n17, 229n20, 234, 235
"On the Edge of Revelation," 114
Slow Man, 9, 47, 106
Waiting for the Barbarians, 6, 7, 9, 15, 18, 19, 73, 90n15, 234, 242–43, 246, 251, 255, 257
White Writing: On the Culture of Letters in South Africa, 6, 9, 147, 202, 262n3, 262n19
Youth: Scenes from Provincial Life II, 7, 15, 46n1, 47n3, 73
Coleridge, Samuel Taylor, 171n13, 268, 269
Condillac, Étienne Bonnot de, 184
Conrad, Joseph, works by: *Heart of Darkness*, 139
Cooper, Pamela, 37–38
Cornwell, Gareth, 10, 137n16
Cottingham, John, 227n8
Critchley, Simon, 226n1

Dante Alighieri, 65, 66, 96, 274
De Graef, Ortwin, 169n2
Demorest, A. P., 135
Derrida, Jacques, 218, 222, 294, 295–96
Descartes, René, 204, 205, 206, 213, 226n2, 227nn7–8
Dickens, Charles, 112, 113
Dienstag, Joshua Foa, 92n32

Divakaruni, Chitra Banerjee, 280, 282
Dobyns, Stephen, 309
Doctorow, E. L., 73
Dostoevsky, Fyodor, 8, 48, 50, 58–59, 63, 76, 82–83, 229n17, 229n20, 267
Du Bois, W. E. B., 329n5
Dumeige, Gervais, 91n21
Durrant, Sam, 274

Edmundson, Mark, 292
Eichmann, Adolf, 314–15
Emerson, Caryl, 50, 54, 55
Emerson, Ralph Waldo, 264, 271
Ernisius, abbot, 89
Eros, 269, 271–72
Euripides, 147n3

Farred, Grant, 10, 47n5
Faust, 85, 92n27, 173–201
feminism. *See* women and feminism
Fisher, Philip, 30, 47n6
Fiske, S. T., 119, 135n1
Flaubert, Gustave, works by: *Madame Bovary*, 266, 295
Foucault, Michel, 136n6, 223, 228n10, 228n13, 291, 292–93, 294, 296
Foote, Mary Hallock, 260
Freire, Paulo, 233–34
Freud, Sigmund, 21, 78, 83, 95, 271
Fugard, Athol, 146n1

Gane, Gillian, 136n8
Gantz, Timothy, 147n3
gender roles. *See* women and feminism
Genesis, 66, 68, 126–27, 330
Gerard, H. B. 135n1
Gluck, C. W., 77, 96
Gode, Alexander, 183, 184
Goethe, Johann Wolfgang von, 183, 200n10
Goethe, Johann Wolfgang von, works by: *Faust*, 10, 65, 85, 92n, 173, 174–77, 181, 182, 184, 185, 187, 192, 194, 196, 198–99, 200n6, 200n8, 200n11
Goia, Dana, 284, 285

Gordimer, Nadine, 8, 79, 138, 139, 226n1, 280, 281
Graham, Lucy Valerie, 10, 11, 91n25, 117, 147n1, 170n4, 217, 227n6
Gramsci, Antonio, 226n1
Gray, Laura, 135
Griffin, Susan, 226n3
Grimm, Jacob, 183, 194
Guiccioli, Teresa, 11, 41, 43–45, 61, 65, 72, 77–80, 83–84, 90n18, 96, 110, 111, 168, 174, 191, 193, 195, 198, 224, 270, 295

Hacking, Ian, 215, 224
Hardy, Thomas, 219
harijan, 55, 58, 60, 79, 88, 191, 221
Harpham, Geoffrey, 68, 255, 256, 259, 262n8, 291, 293
Harrison, Peter, 227n8
Hassoun, Jacques, 275n1
Head, Bessie, 138, 280–81
Head, Dominic, 9, 89n13
Heidegger, Martin, 98, 104, 105n3, 217, 229n19
Herder, Johann Gottfried, 183–84, 194, 196, 198, 200nn10–12
Herron, Tom, 226n4, 229n17, 229n23
Hesford, Wendy, 135n6
Holland, Michael, 11, 171n10, 171n12, 273
Holocaust, 220, 313–23, 326–29
Holquist, Michael, 49, 51, 58
Homer, 92n27, 96, 272
hooks, bell, 233
Hornby, Nick, 298
St. Hubert, 75, 90n16, 217
Huggan, Graham, 227n6
Hugh of St. Victor, 66, 89n4
Humboldt, Wilhelm von, 183, 184, 186, 194–95, 201n22

intertextuality, 3, 8, 11, 72, 73, 77, 127, 129, 136, 147, 177, 235, 238, 253, 254–55, 258–62, 317–28

Jacobsen, Jens Peter, 268
Jacoby, Günter, 183, 198, 200n11

James, Henry, 77
Jameson, Fredric, 71–72, 89n13
Janes, Regina, 249, 262n1
Jelinek, Elfriede, 273
Jerusalem Prize, 27
Johnston Center, 1–3, 10–12, 116, 233–47, 248–53, 258, 279, 289
Jolly, Rosemary, 10, 90n17, 147, 212, 217, 218, 223, 228n16
Joyce, James, 82

Keller, Catherine, 89n11
Kirsch, Adam, 112
Kivel, Paul, 235
de Kock, Leon, 9

la Guma, Alex, 138
Lacan, Jacques, 91n19, 99–100, 105n4
Lamar, Howard, 262n17
Lanchester, John, 27, 47n3
Langland, William, works by: *Piers Plowman*, 65, 81–82, 96
Leibniz, Gottfried Wilhelm Freiherr von, 205
Lenta, Margaret, 46n1
Lessing, Doris, 138, 139
Levi, Primo, 317, 318–20, 325, 327, 328nn2–3, 328n8
Levinas, Emmanuel, 10, 130, 218, 223, 227–28n10, 228n13, 228n16, 229n21, 229n22
Lewis, C. S., 89n12
Lilje, Hanns, 200n10
Limerick, Patricia Nelson, 262n18
Lindfors, Bernth, 138
Littleton, Heather L., 119, 135n1
Livy, 127
Lopez, Barry, 91n22
Lucian, 147n3
Lucifer, 15, 24, 108, 175, 267
Lykophron, 147n3

Mahfouz, Naguib, 139
Makhaya, Gertrude B., 138, 139
Malkovich, John, 11
Marais, Michael, 10, 11, 18, 170n3, 171n5, 171n13, 203, 205, 217, 218, 221, 225–26n1, 226n5, 227–28n10, 228nn15–16, 229nn21–22
Marcus, Sharon, 121
Mardorossian, Carine M, 122, 125
Martin of Tours, 99–100
Mason, Travis, 222, 226n4, 229n17
McDonald, Peter D., 10, 147n1, 169n1, 170n3, 171n9
McMullin, Darcy, 120, 135n2
Mda, Zakea, 89n8
Mefistofele, 65, 85, 92n30, 93, 173–75, 177, 179, 181, 198, 199n1
Meis, Morgan, 12n1
Menotti, Jean Carlo, 90n18
Michaels, Anne, 86
Moran, John H., 183, 184
Morrison, Toni, works by: *Beloved*, 316, 318
Morson, Gary Saul, 57
Mphalele, Ezekiel, 138

Nabokov, Vladimir, works by: *Lolita*, 272–73
Nazis, 103, 220, 314, 323, 327
Neiman, Susan, 222, 223
Neoplatonism, 94
Nietzsche, Friedrich, 243, 271, 296
Nkosi, Lewis, 138
Nobel Prize, 1, 138–39, 259, 273–74, 297, 311
Nyman, Jopi, 223, 227n6, 228n15, 229n17

Ondaatje, Michael, works by: *Divisadero*, 271
Origen, 74, 75

Page, Tim, 90n18
Palmer, Earl, 286
Palmer, Parker, 331–32, 334
Pamuk, Orhan, works by: *Istanbul*, 274
Pastoralism, 224, 249, 250, 258–59, 260–61
Phillips, Caryl, works by: *Nature of Blood*, 317–27, 329n7
Pinter, Harold, works by: *The Homecoming*, 274

plaasroman, 9–10, 147n2, 250
Plato, 203, 204, 205, 206, 213, 227n7, 227n9
Plutarch, 127, 128
Poyner, Jane, 9, 90n17, 147n1, 210, 227n6, 228n11, 228n16, 229n1
pragmatism, 181–82, 185, 196–201
Preskill, Stephen, 233
Pseudo-Dionysus, 94
Puccini, Giacomo, 90n18

reading communities. *See* teaching *Disgrace*
Redlands, University of, vii, 1, 2, 234, 248, 264, 278–79
Reef, Anne, 117
Richard of St. Victor, 3, 10, 64–90, 93–95, 99, 100, 101, 173
Richard of St. Victor, works by: *Benjamin Major*, 66, 69–71, 79, 81–82, 86, 91–92n26; *Benjamin Minor*, 66–68, 70, 92n28; *On Contemplation*, 66, 81; *On the Four Degrees of Violent Charity*, 67; *On the Trinity*, 66, 71–72, 78
Rilke, Rainer Maria, 10, 65, 115n6, 145
Robertson, Mary, 117
Romantic language theory, 182–99
Romanticism, 3, 65, 69, 88, 148–71, 174, 175, 181–85, 190, 192–93, 197–99, 209, 268–69, 271, 321, 325
Rorty, Richard, 169, 295
Rose, Gillian, 222, 223
Rousseau, Jean-Jacques, 76, 184, 185, 200n12
Rushdie, Salman, 213

Samuelson, Meg, 10, 117–18, 135n4, 136n11, 221, 223, 227n6
Sanders, Mark, 10, 11, 92n34, 104n2, 171n7, 228n11, 338
Saramago, José, works by: *Blindness*, 274
Saussure, Ferdinand de, 185, 187, 201n24
Schank, R. C., 135n1

Schlegel, Friedrich Wilhelm von, 182–83
Schreiner, Olive, 138
Seidel, Linda, 211, 226n5, 229n18
Shakespeare, William, 109, 158, 265, 267, 273, 275, 326, 332
Shaw, George Bernard, 199
Shulman, Lee, 332–34
Seidel, Linda, 211, 226n5, 299n18
Sikorska, Liliana, 147n1
Socrates, 204, 206
South Africa, 3–4, 7–9, 27, 82, 91n20, 95, 97, 127, 152, 170n3, 177, 191, 226n1, 234, 239, 248, 249, 255, 258, 259, 291, 294, 295, 296; apartheid and post-apartheid, 1, 6, 10–11, 27, 60, 69, 80, 88, 93, 97–102, 106, 116–17, 133, 136n8, 137n13, 138–46, 147n1, 148, 169n1, 171n11, 197, 213, 227n5, 228n11, 245, 246, 256, 257, 261, 280, 283, 318, 319, 320, 321, 325, 338; South African literature, 4, 10, 11, 117, 139, 145, 248, 319; Truth and Reconciliation Commission, 6, 90n17, 117, 134, 145, 147n1, 228n11, 257; urban/rural, 22, 27, 43, 69, 79, 174, 189, 207–9, 239, 255, 321, 338
Spivak, Gayatri Chakravorty, 136n9, 233
Stegner, Wallace, 3, 250, 258–60, 262n14
Stoicism, 293–94
Strauss, Richard, 90n18
Strode, Timothy Francis, 10, 91n23
student learning and writing projects. *See* teaching *Disgrace*

Talmud, 330, 334, 339n1
Taylor, Jane, 205
Taylor, S. E., 119, 135n1
teaching *Disgrace*: and creative writing, 297–312; and critical theory, 288–96; lecturing, 276–87, 300; practical suggestions, 235–38, 239–40, 240–41, 279–80, 282–83, 289–92, 295, 300–301, 303–10; problems in,

241, 245–46, 249–50, 252–54, 264–75, 277–78, 296, 297–98, 305–6, 318–20; reading communities and "unsolitary reading," 2, 4, 233–47, 248–54, 258–62, 278–79, 331–32, 333–34, 337–39; student projects, 238–39, 251–57; student-centered teaching, 233–45, 251–57
Texas, University of, at Austin, 138, 199n3, 200n15
Thiong'o, Ngugi wa, 139
Thomas of Canterbury, 66
Thompson, Leonard, 262n17
Thompson, Virgil, 90n18
Tlali, Miriam, 138
Tremaine, Louis, 222, 227n6, 228n15, 228n16, 229n17, 229n18, 229n23
Truth and Reconciliation Commission, 6, 90n17, 117, 134, 145, 147n1, 228n11, 257, 339
Turner, Frederick Jackson, 262n17, 262n18
Turner, Victor, 258, 262

unsolitary reading. *See* teaching *Disgrace*
Uris, Leon, works by: *Exodus,* 315

Virgil, works by: *Aeneid,* 86
Visotzky, Burton, 330

Wachtel, Eleanor, 48, 49, 76
Watson, Stephen, 227n6
Wharton, Edith, 79
White, Jacquelyn W., 120, 135n2
Wicomb, Zoë, 10, 11, 117
Williams, Raymond, 250, 262n3
Williams, Tennessee, 90n18
Wittgenstein, Ludwig, language games, 207–9, 227n10, 228n16

women and feminism: David Lurie's relation to women, 37, 41, 43, 53, 64, 74, 75, 76, 81–82, 84, 90n15, 94, 95, 158, 166, 167, 178–80, 225, 229n18, 257, 260, 261–62, 295, 322, 324, 338; feminist readings, 36, 68, 116–34, 135n3, 162, 170n3, 239, 251, 254, 257, 261, 283, 293, 317; gender roles, gendered representations and responses, 159, 171n6, 188, 250, 251–52, 254, 272–73, 283–84, 293, 301, 304, 309, 323, 327; other representations of women, 37–38, 74, 81, 114, 117, 147n1, 254, 260
Wood, James, 9, 10, 12n1, 107
Woods, Donald, 281–82
Wordsworth, William, 3, 10, 65, 69, 76, 85, 93, 98, 149, 153–57, 159–62, 163, 166, 167–68, 169n2, 171n8, 178n13, 174, 182, 189–90, 193, 209, 216, 220, 237, 266, 269, 270, 285, 324, 332
Wordsworth, William, works by: *The Prelude,* 11, 151–53, 156–57, 167, 189, 205–6, 211, 265, 269
Wright, Laura, 10, 11, 55, 56, 213, 217, 218, 223, 227n5, 228n16, 229n21, 259, 262n1, 262nn20–21

Yeats, William Butler, 65, 80, 115n6

Zadney, J, 135
Zagajewski, Adam, 315, 329n1
Zinn, Gordon A., 66–67, 70, 89n3